Israel's Armor

The United States and Israel have long had a "special relationship." The USA became the first country in the world to recognize the state of Israel in 1948, and has been an important ally and benefactor ever since. A critical component of the special relationship is the pro-Israel lobby. Although the lobby has been a controversial topic in public affairs, it has been widely understudied. *Israel's Armor* fills a gap in the existing literature by examining the origins and early history of the Israel lobby, looking at its influence on American foreign policy and weaving its activities into the diplomatic history of the first generation of the Palestine conflict. Covering the period roughly from World War II to the pivotal June 1967 War, Walter L. Hixson demonstrates that from the outset the Israel lobby played a crucial role in mobilizing US support for the Zionist state.

Walter L. Hixson is Distinguished Professor of History at the University of Akron. He is the author of several books focused on the history of US foreign relations, including: *American Foreign Relations: A New Diplomatic History* (2016); *American Settler Colonialism: A History* (2013); *The Myth of American Diplomacy: National Identity and US Foreign Policy* (2008); *Parting the Curtain: Propaganda, Culture and the Cold War, 1945–1961* (1997); and *George F. Kennan: Cold War Iconoclast* (1989).

D1453626

JUN 0 6 2019

Cambridge Studies in US Foreign Relations

Edited by

Paul Thomas Chamberlin, *Columbia University*
Lien-Hang T. Nguyen, *Columbia University*

This series showcases cutting-edge scholarship in US foreign relations that employs dynamic new methodological approaches and archives from the colonial era to the present. The series will be guided by the ethos of transnationalism, focusing on the history of American foreign relations in a global context rather than privileging the US as the dominant actor on the world stage.

Also in the Series

Israel's Armor

The Israel Lobby and the First Generation of the Palestine Conflict

WALTER L. HIXSON

University of Akron, Ohio

327.7305 H

CAMBRIDGE
UNIVERSITY PRESS

379 4015

CAMBRIDGE
UNIVERSITY PRESS

University Printing House, Cambridge CB2 8BS, United Kingdom

One Liberty Plaza, 20th Floor, New York, NY 10006, USA

477 Williamstown Road, Port Melbourne, VIC 3207, Australia

314–321, 3rd Floor, Plot 3, Splendor Forum, Jasola District Centre,
New Delhi – 110025, India

79 Anson Road, #06–04/06, Singapore 079906

Cambridge University Press is part of the University of Cambridge.

It furthers the University's mission by disseminating knowledge in the pursuit of
education, learning, and research at the highest international levels of excellence.

www.cambridge.org
Information on this title: www.cambridge.org/9781108483902
DOI: 10.1017/9781108594424

© Walter L. Hixson 2019

First published 2019

Printed in the United Kingdom by TJ International Ltd. Padstow Cornwall

A catalogue record for this publication is available from the British Library.

Library of Congress Cataloging-in-Publication Data
NAMES: Hixson, Walter L., author.
TITLE: Israel's armor : the Israel lobby and the first generation of the Palestine conflict /
Walter L. Hixson.
DESCRIPTION: Cambridge, United Kingdom ; New York, NY : Cambridge University
Press, 2019. | Series: Cambridge studies in US foreign relations | Includes
bibliographical references and index.
IDENTIFIERS: LCCN 2018055108| ISBN 9781108483902 (hardback) | ISBN
9781108705325 (paperback)
SUBJECTS: LCSH: United States – Foreign relations – Israel. | Israel – Foreign relations –
United States. | Zionists – Political activity – United States. | Zionism – United States –
History. | American Zionist Emergency Council – History. | American Israel Public
Affairs Committee – History. | Lobbying – United States – History. | BISAC: HISTORY
/ United States / 20th Century.
CLASSIFICATION: LCC E183.8.I7 H58 2019 | DDC 327.7305694–dc23
LC record available at https://lccn.loc.gov/2018055108

ISBN 978-1-108-48390-2 Hardback
ISBN 978-1-108-70532-5 Paperback

Contents

Figures

Abbreviations

ACJ	American Council for Judaism
ACPC	American Christian Palestine Committee
ADL	Anti-Defamation League
AEC	Atomic Energy Commission
AFME	American Friends of the Middle East
AHC	Arab Higher Committee
AIPAC	American Israel Public Affairs Committee
AJA	American Jewish Archives
AJC	American Jewish Committee
APC	American Palestine Committee
APCs	Armored personnel carriers
AWF	Ann Whitman File
AZC	American Zionist Council
AZCPA	American Zionist Committee for Public Affairs
AZEC	American Zionist Emergency Council
BBIA	B'nai B'rith International Archives
CIA	Central Intelligence Agency
DDE	Dwight D. Eisenhower Presidential Library
DOS	Department of State
DMZ	Demilitarized zones
FARA	Foreign Agents Registration Act
FRG	Federal Republic of Germany
FRUS	*Foreign Relations Series of the United States*
HSTL	Harry S. Truman Library Institute
IAEA	International Atomic Energy Agency
IDF	Israel Defense Forces

IRMEP	Institute for Research: Middle East Policy
JA	Jewish Agency
JCS	Joint Chiefs of Staff
JFKL	John F. Kennedy Presidential Library
JNF	Jewish National Fund
KP	Kenen Papers
LBJL	Lyndon B. Johnson Presidential Library
LOC	Library of Congress
NATO	North Atlantic Treaty Organization
NER	*Near East Report*
NSF	National Security Files
NIE	National Intelligence Estimate
NSA	National Security Agency
NSC	National Security Council
OT	Occupied territories
PCC	Palestine Conciliation Commission
PLO	Palestine Liberation Organization
RG 59	Record Group 59 (General Records of Department of State)
SFRC	Senate Foreign Relations Committee
UAR	United Arab Republic
UN	United Nations
UNGA	United Nations General Assembly
UNSC	United Nations Security Council
UNSCOP	United Nations Special Committee on Palestine
UNRWA	United Nations Relief and Works Agency for Palestine
WRB	War Refugee Board
WRHS	Western Reserve Historical Society
WZC	World Zionist Congress
WZO	World Zionist Organization
ZOA	Zionist Organization of America

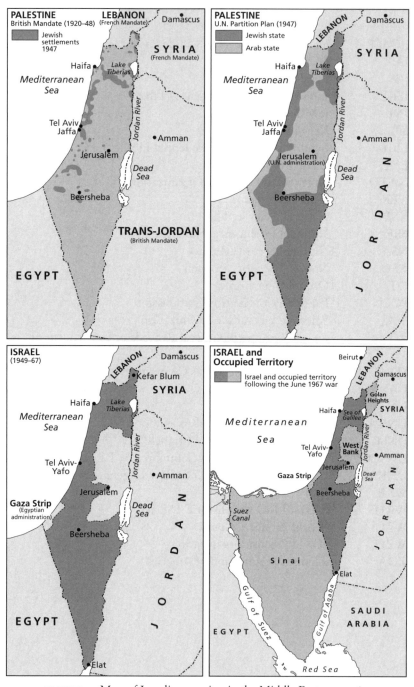

FIGURE 1 Map of Israeli expansion in the Middle East 1920–67

Introduction

The United States and Israel have long had a "special relationship." In May 1948 the United States became the first country in the world to recognize the Zionist state, and has been a critical ally and benefactor ever since. One measure of the special relationship is financial. The small state of Israel, with a population of about 8.5 million, is "the largest cumulative recipient of US foreign assistance since World War II."[1]

This book analyzes the foundations and early history of a critical component of the special relationship: the pro-Israel lobby. The lobby has proven to be a controversial topic, and perhaps for that reason it remains understudied. One result of the absence of historical analysis is the tendency to associate the Israel lobby with the more recent past. In fact, however, the extensive lobbying efforts of American Zionists predate the creation of Israel and flourished throughout the first generation of the special relationship. The Israel lobby today is broadly based, well funded, and more powerful than ever, but from the outset it has played a crucial role in mobilizing US support for the Zionist state.[2]

The "Israel lobby" can be defined as a continuous campaign of advocacy on the part of Israel and its American supporters to secure US foreign policies that are perceived as favorable to the Israeli national interest. The lobby is both highly structured – including well-organized and well-funded entities, notably the American Israel Public Affairs Committee (AIPAC) – but also decentralized, encompassing a broad array of individuals and groups, Christian as well as Jewish, which offer spontaneous support of Israel. AIPAC and its precursors, backed by local councils and advocates across the United States, have long lobbied the president, members of Congress, and ultimately the public in order to secure political support and financial and military assistance. The lobby stresses Israel's vulnerability to various neighboring regimes while emphasizing that Israel seeks to live in peace, shares common goals and values with the United States, helps anchor security, and is the "sole democracy" in the Middle East. Finally, the lobby condemns critics of Israel. When they perceive political threats to Israeli interests, lobby supporters strive energetically to limit or obstruct debate.

The Israel lobby is "widely viewed as the most powerful diasporic lobby seeking to shape US foreign policy."[3] Thus, no other country's partisans in the history of US foreign policy – including the venerable China Lobby, Irish-Americans, or the influential Miami-based Cuban-Americans – have had a commensurate impact on American diplomacy. As the most influential pressure group associated with another nation in the history of American foreign relations, the Israel lobby clearly merits sustained analysis.

This study offers a foundational history that illuminates the broad trajectory of pro-Israel influence throughout the course of the special relationship. Rooted in documentary evidence drawn from multiple US archives, this book weaves the activities of the Zionist lobby into the diplomatic history of the first generation of the Palestine conflict. Covering the period roughly from World War II through the pivotal June 1967 War and its aftermath, the work draws extensively on Department of State (DOS) records and the archives of four American presidents (Truman through Johnson) and their aides to assess the diplomatic history. It also exploits multiple sources on the Israel lobby, notably the papers of Isaiah Leo Kenen. From the time of Israel's creation to his death in 1988, "Si" Kenen was a tireless advocate for Israel and the workhorse of AIPAC and its precursors. By the 1970s, as he was introduced at speaking engagements, presenters noting that Kenen went by the initials I. L. became fond of declaring, "Everybody knows what I. L. stands for. It stands for 'Israel Lobby!'"[4]

During the formative years studied here, Kenen and his colleagues organized and campaigned in support of Israel to counter various US diplomatic initiatives in the Palestine conflict. On multiple occasions, American diplomats, advisers, and all four presidents became frustrated and angry at the pressures placed upon them by Israel and its domestic supporters. Yet whenever US leaders or diplomats appeared to challenge Israeli actions and policies, the lobby counterattacked and typically proved highly effective in achieving its aims.

The Zionist lobby glossed over Israel's aggressiveness in the Palestine conflict while depicting its own advocacy as purely defensive. Kenen

FIGURE 2 Israeli diplomat Abba Eban (left) and Isaiah L. Kenen (right) were primarily responsible for establishing the Israel lobby. By the time this photograph was taken at a dinner party in the 1970s, the Israel lobby had become by far the most powerful diaspora lobby in American history.
Center for Jewish History/New York

entitled his memoir *Israel's Defense Line*, and his mentor, Louis Lipsky, a founding father of the lobby, described it as "the armor Israel cannot get along without." The lobby insisted that its work was essential to counter the "pro-Arab bias" of American professional diplomats.[5]

The Israel lobby sharply opposed efforts led by US diplomats to forge an "impartial" or "balanced" approach to the Palestine conflict, which from the outset had tilted in favor of Israel. In opposing the tilt toward Israel, the professional diplomats argued that there were many Arab states and one small Zionist state; that the Arabs, if alienated by pro-Israeli US policies, might withhold oil supplies upon which the West was growing dependent; and that they might drift into the Soviet-led communist orbit or succumb to Muslim radicalism. The diplomats also argued that even after Israel had achieved essential security, the Zionist state pursued aggressive and unreasonable policies concerning borders, Palestinian refu-gees, nuclear proliferation, and a host of other issues. The diplomats thus focused overwhelmingly on security policy and their perception of national interests rather than being motivated by a "pro-Arab bias" or anti-Jewish prejudices.

The lobby, by contrast, persistently asserted that Israel was isolated, vulnerable, and under constant existential threat from the hostile Arab states. This was an exaggerated claim, but hardly a surprising one coming from people dreadfully traumatized by the Nazi genocide. There was no shortage of Arab hostility, to be sure, though on balance the evidence suggests that beginning in 1949 most of the Arab states were becoming grudgingly more amenable to a possible settlement than is generally acknowledged – and more amenable than Israel. Over the years of this study, the Zionist state, dominated by David Ben-Gurion and other hard-liners and militarists, notably Moshe Dayan, showed contempt for Palestinians and other Arabs, equated negotiations with appeasement, and frequently resorted to borderland aggression that typically proved disproportionate to the provocation. Israel was militarily superior to the Arab states, which lacked cohesion in any case, and thus the Zionist state faced no actual threat of being driven, as the cliché would have it, "into the sea." The fact of Israeli military superiority should come as no surprise, as it was repeatedly borne out by Israel's domination in the three wars that occurred during this period.

CULTURAL FOUNDATIONS

While the Israel lobby would indeed provide the "armor Israel cannot get along without," the forces of propaganda, persuasion, and political clout could not have been as successful as they were – and still are today – in the absence of a cultural foundation on which to build. In the United States, immigrants and lobbies with perceived foreign ties traditionally have been viewed with suspicion, "as a reflection of potential disloyalty and a threat to national security." Thus, diaspora lobbies are able to exert influence on American foreign policy only "when convergent interests and goals become recognized, whether these are preexisting or constructed."[6] The Israel lobby built on an existing cultural foundation of US affinity for Zionism while also constructing and reinforcing additional bonds.

Popular support for Israel in part reflected a sense of atonement for American inaction in the face of the Nazi genocide. This factor became increasingly significant, however, in the years after those with which this study is concerned. It was not until the 1970s that the Holocaust began to be framed as a distinctive phenomenon within the history of global genocide.[7]

American religiosity played a major role in establishing a foundation for the special relationship on which the lobby was able to build.[8] During the period of this study, the residence in the United States of the world's largest Jewish population was clearly a key factor. Concentrated in New York, accessible to Washington, and holding some influential positions in business and national politics, prominent American Jews were able to exert significant pro-Zionist influence. However, the American Jewish "community" was not monolithic in its support of Zionism. Many American Jews were disengaged, while others opposed the idea of a Jewish homeland and the conflation of Jewish identity with a theocratic state in the Middle East. Even among supporters of Zionism, there was considerable dissension and myriad organizations that often pursued conflicting goals or differed sharply on appropriate strategies and tactics. That said, over time the Israel lobby ultimately proved remarkably successful in linking American Jewish identity with the fate of Israel and marginalizing both Jews and Gentiles who felt otherwise.

American Jews alone could not steer the US ship of state into the welcoming Israeli port. Vastly greater numbers of American Protestants, both modernist and Christian fundamentalists, provided crucial support for Zionism. American religiosity, encompassing widespread and enduring faith in the biblical narrative[9] and biblical prophecy, undergirded growing US support for Israel and continues to serve as ballast for the special relationship to this day. For many Americans, support for Israel seemed to be the right thing to do, not only because of the legacy of the Nazi genocide, or because Israel was small and appeared vulnerable, but because the Jews belonged in the Promised Land. In this respect, Presidents Truman and especially Johnson, who held such views, proved representative of the broader American public.

Both the Americans and the Zionists viewed themselves as chosen peoples. Both were settler societies fired by perceptions of their "manifest destiny" to inherit a promised land.[10] Ultimately, the special relationship cannot be fully understood apart from the historical and cultural affinities – both "preexisting and constructed" – between the United States and Israel. Indeed, these forces are what made the relationship special – and enduring.[11]

PREVIOUS STUDIES OF THE "ISRAEL LOBBY"

This study is not the first on the Israel lobby, and it will not be the last, yet the subject is a difficult one and typically there is a price to pay for taking it on. Especially in the United States, critical studies of Israeli policy are certain to be targeted for condemnation. Studies of the lobby are even more susceptible to attack. Paradoxically, the condemnation of these works underscores both the intensity of the special relationship and the clout of the Israel lobby.

In the 1980s, critical studies of Israeli policy and substantive analysis of the role of the lobby began to emerge in the wake of Israel's turn to the right with the electoral triumph of the Likud Party. The Camp David Accords (1978) led to a separate peace with Egypt, but failed to lead to a broader resolution of the Palestine conflict. A longtime proponent of annexing the biblical Israel, Prime Minister Menachem Begin accelerated the development of already proliferating Jewish settlements in the Palestinian territories. In 1982, Israel also launched a punishing attack on Lebanon. By this time the lobby had grown powerful and multifaceted, with AIPAC as the spearhead. AIPAC boasted of ousting elected officials critical of Israel, a process book-ended by two chairmen of the influential Senate Foreign Relations Committee (SFRC), Sens. J. William Fulbright (D-AR), defeated in 1974, and Sen. Charles Percy (R-IL.), targeted by the lobby and defeated in 1984.[12]

In 1982, Seth Tillman, a former member of the SFRC staff, published a book arguing that "the powerful Israeli lobby" impeded efforts to pursue a Middle East diplomacy grounded in the national interest and dedicated to achieving settlement of the Palestine conflict. Fulbright wrote the foreword to the study. Another critic of US Middle East policy, Rep. Paul Findley (R-IL), who had been targeted by AIPAC and ousted in the 1982 congressional elections, condemned the lobby and lauded its critics in a book published in 1985, *They Dare to Speak Out: People and Institutions Confront Israel's Lobby*.[13]

More impactful than the early works on the lobby was the broadside delivered by the linguist turned foreign policy critic Noam Chomsky. In *The Fateful Triangle: The United States, Israel and the Palestinians*, published in 1983, Chomsky condemned the United States and Israel for the destruction in Lebanon and the ongoing repression in Palestine. The MIT professor acknowledged the clout of the organized lobby, but argued that it was "far from the whole story" and that an excessive focus on it, "underestimates the scope of the 'support for Israel' in American life." Chomsky explained that one-sided US policies backing Israel sprang from sources "far broader than the Jewish community," including Christians, liberals, labor unions, the oil and gas industries, and a power elite that benefited from constructing Israel as an American "strategic asset."[14]

Defenders of Israeli policy found Chomsky's incendiary account difficult to refute and the book became a classic (the latest edition was released in 2015). While Chomsky offered a broad indictment of US and Israeli policies, other works homed in on the Israel lobby. In 1986, political scientist Cheryl A. Rubenberg published a book with a nearly 50-page chapter arguing that pro-Israel advocacy had achieved "a virtual stranglehold" over US Middle East policy. As with Chomsky, critics condemned Rubenberg for her "polemical tone" and alleged animus toward Israel – a familiar refrain.[15]

In 1987, Edward Tivnan secured a major mainstream publisher for his journalistic assessment of the lobby and its influence. Whereas a capsule review in *Foreign Affairs* concluded that Tivnan's "research is sound and his tone temperate, but somber," a reviewer in *Commentary*, the magazine of the American Jewish Committee (AJC), declared Tivnan's account was "so fevered, so riddled with errors of both methodology and substance, so driven by animus, as to render his book useless except to those similarly tormented." In the *Los Angeles Times*, political scientist Steven Spiegel likewise condemned the book as a "snide, sometimes bitter, largely trivial and even boring account of the role of the American Jewish community's efforts on behalf of Israel." Two years previously Spiegel had published his own book on US relations with Israel, which had downplayed the role of the lobby.[16]

In a book coauthored with his son in 1992, veteran DOS diplomat George Ball invoked President George Washington, who had warned in his farewell address in 1796 about the pitfalls of developing a "passionate attachment" for any foreign nation. The first president was referring to revolutionary France, but the Balls were targeting Israel and the lobby in a substantive study published by a major mainstream press. They warned that the "passionate attachment" to Israel had produced a morally as well as financially irresponsible foreign policy divorced from the realities of the Middle East conflict. Despite George Ball's celebrated sagacity for having advised Johnson against escalation of the Indochina War in the mid-1960s, *The Passionate Attachment* was widely ignored.[17]

The same was not true, however, of another coauthored and now famous – or, to some, infamous – book: *The Israel Lobby and*

US Foreign Policy, by John J. Mearsheimer and Stephen M. Walt. Published by a mainstream popular press, *The Israel Lobby* ignited a vitriolic response from Israel's defenders. The book and its authors – two highly accomplished political science professors from distinguished institutions, the University of Chicago (Mearsheimer) and Harvard (Walt) – became a national if not international *cause célèbre*. Never before was the Israel lobby so widely discussed, nor chroniclers of its influence so bitterly condemned.

The Mearsheimer–Walt thesis was clearly stated, bolstered by evidence, and forcefully driven home in the book. "Today," they argued,

America's intimate embrace of Israel – and especially its willingness to subsidize it no matter what its policies are – is not making Americans safer or more prosperous. To the contrary: unconditional support for Israel is undermining relations with other US allies, casting doubt on America's wisdom and moral vision, helping inspire a generation of anti-American extremists, and complicating US efforts to deal with a volatile but vital region.

They added, "We believe the activities of the groups and individuals who make up the lobby are the main reason why the United States pursues policies in the Middle East that make little sense on either strategic or moral grounds."[18]

Pro-Israeli public officials, academics, journalists, and pundits tore into the book, setting the tone for a campaign of discrediting the study as simply an anti-Israel, if not anti-Jewish, diatribe, rather than an analysis of one of the most powerful lobbies in American politics. Writing in *The New Republic*, Jeffrey Goldberg equated Mearsheimer and Walt's views of Israel with those of September 11 terrorist Osama Bin Laden. Most Jewish organizations harshly condemned the book, including the Anti-Defamation League (ADL), which published its own book in rebuttal, entitled *The Deadliest Lies*. Former CIA Director James Woolsey discerned a "commitment to distorting the historical record," while Israeli historian Benny Morris, whose work had been quoted in the book, found it "riddled with shoddiness and defiled by mendacity."[19]

Writing in the wake of the public controversy over the book, diplomatic historian Andrew Preston observed, "Many reviews have been so extraordinarily passionate that future historians will undoubtedly study the book's reception as much as they will the book itself." Preston noted that the book had been "vilified on a deeply emotional level" replete with ad hominem attacks and "spurious charges of anti-Semitism" that ultimately amounted to nothing less than a campaign of "character assassination" against two scholars whose previous studies, centering on realist diplomacy, had been received with almost uniformly high praise.[20]

Both the timing of the book and the two authors' prestigious reputations – which required that they be smeared in order to discredit the work – account for the intensity of the campaign. Raising the stakes, the publication and debate over the book came in the wake of another punishing Israeli assault on Lebanon in 2006 with extensive civilian casualties. Moreover, Mearsheimer and Walt had charged that the pro-Israel lobby had played a critical role in the 2003 US decision to go to war in Iraq, a conflict that had become a quagmire by the time of the book's publication. Ultimately, the perfervid reaction to the book revealed, as Tony Smith pointed out, that even though the "lobby had always prided itself on its influence in Washington, its attitude changed dramatically when the sinews of power it possessed were clearly laid out by this study for all to see, and when responsibility was assigned to it for getting the American government to march in lockstep with Israeli foreign policy."[21]

The major weakness of the Mearsheimer–Walt book was not its argument that the lobby influenced US policy in a lopsided pro-Israeli direction, to the detriment of the national interest, but rather their inability to acknowledge the broader cultural and historical dimensions of support for Israel. As previously noted, without a cultural foundation rooted in American religious affinity and settler colonization, among other factors, the lobby could not have been as effective as it has been and remains today. Thus, to reiterate, while the Israel lobby plays a monumental role in shaping the pro-Israeli American foreign policy, it does so in dialectical relationship with deeply rooted American religious and cultural forces.

The brutal reaction to the Mearsheimer–Walt book doubtless exerted a chilling effect on scholarship on the lobby. The only major academic study produced since the controversy has been a richly detailed recent book on the origins and evolution of the lobby by Israeli scholar Natan Aridan. *Advocating for Israel: Diplomats and Lobbyists from Truman to Nixon* is especially useful for its exploitation of sources in Hebrew and its elucidation of disputes as well as cooperation between and among the Israeli government and the American lobby.[22]

A nationalistic assessment – indeed, virtually a court history – Aridan's book is the antidote to Mearsheimer and Walt, as it reflexively celebrates Israel and the lobby. Throughout the work Aridan castigates American diplomats and the Arab states for their alleged unprovoked hostility to Israel. The book thus reflects an orthodox school of interpretation of Israeli innocence in the Palestine conflict, thereby eliding two generations of post-Zionist scholarship. It also appears to aspire to deflect attention from the US lobby by emphasizing the primacy of Israeli *hasbara* (a Hebrew term for generating favorable propaganda for foreign audiences) in propelling Zionist advocacy.[23] As this study will show, Israeli hasbara played a crucial role, but key Israeli officials – notably the skilled diplomat Abba Eban – collaborated with the American lobby rather than creating or controlling it.

Originating in 2002, a growing counterlobby has emerged in Washington to challenge the Israel lobby. The Institute for Research: Middle East Policy (IRMEP) has amassed a substantial archive on the Israel lobby, offers polling data and policy analysis on the Middle East conflict, and hosts an annual conference in Washington that is televised by C-SPAN. The IRMEP conference features speakers critical of Israeli policies, and the lobby's role in bolstering them, and is held on the eve of AIPAC's signature annual conference in Washington. IRMEP's full-time director Grant F. Smith has published a series of books analyzing the history and current activities of the Israel lobby.[24]

OUTLINE OF THE STUDY

This book opens with a Prologue analyzing the roots of the Palestine conflict from the dissolution of the Ottoman Empire to World War II. The Prologue examines the growing conflict between Palestinian nationalism and the rising tide of Zionist migration to the British mandate. As the title "Erect a Jewish State at Once," a quote from David Ben-Gurion, suggests, the Prologue explores the intensity of the Zionist commitment to the colonization of Palestine. The Prologue concludes with analysis of the growing strength of American Zionism, which established the foundation of the Israel lobby.

Chapter 1 – "Friendship of the American People for the Zionist Idea," a quotation of Harry Truman – analyzes the growth of Zionist political influence amid World War II. The chapter explores the role of key figures in the budding Israel lobby, notably Abba Hillel Silver, Isaiah Kenen, Emanuel Celler, Abraham Feinberg, David Niles, and Edward Jacobson. The chapter explains how the lobby drove President Truman's support for settlement of increasing numbers of Jewish refugees in Palestine and ultimately for partition of the British mandate as well as de facto recognition of the new state of Israel.

The title of Chapter 2 employs a quotation – "New Forms of Propaganda had to be Found" – from Louis Lipsky, a longtime Zionist and a key organizer of the lobby. The chapter analyzes the highly success-ful effort of Lipsky, Kenen, and myriad other US Zionists, working closely with Israeli diplomat Abba Eban, to establish a more permanent and structured lobby. The effort helped fend off UN-sponsored peace efforts that were sharply opposed by Israel and the lobby, and culminated with growing political clout, as manifested in the 1944 and 1948 political campaigns. Homing in on the Congress as well as presidential candidates, the lobbying effort secured for Israel badly needed funding for refugee resettlement while beating back proposals for repatriation of Palestinian refugees and international status for Jerusalem.

Chapter 3, headlined by the quotation from President Eisenhower, "We Should Not Be Deterred by Political Pressures," analyzes the admin-istration's ultimately futile efforts to counter lobby influence. Eisenhower and Secretary of State John Foster Dulles sought to reassert the "impar-tial" Middle East policy, rein in Israeli border aggression, and forge a comprehensive peace plan, but failed on all counts. Eisenhower did force Israel to relinquish territory occupied through its aggression against Egypt in the Sinai War, but not before Israel received critical security guarantees and benefited from a strong defense of its interests in the United States.

"What Kind of Relationship Was This?" (Chapter 4) asked adviser Robert W. Komer in frustration over the inability of the Kennedy admin-istration to force compromise on critical issues, including the Palestinian refugees as well as Israel's secret nuclear weapons program, even as Israel achieved an arms supply breakthrough in 1962 by securing Hawk defen-sive missiles from the United States. This chapter chronicles a reorganization of the lobby as the AIPAC and the critical insider role played by adviser Myer Feldman as the US–Israel "special relationship" solidified during the Kennedy years.

The title of Chapter 5, "The Best Friend that Israel Could Have," was Israel diplomat Ephraim Evron's description of President Johnson. The chapter details Johnson's longtime support of Israel rooted in his personal religious views, as well as his deference to the Israel lobby on arms sales and nuclear proliferation. The chapter concludes with the administration's policies enabling Israel in the run-up to the 1967 "Six-Day War."

"Let the Israelis Do This Job Themselves" (Chapter 6), Middle East expert Harold Saunders advised on the eve of Israel's initiation of the June War. The chapter details US acquiescence to the Israeli aggression and the sweeping influence exerted by the Israel lobby throughout the conflict and in its immediate aftermath. The chapter covers the Israeli attack on the naval intelligence vessel the USS *Liberty* and the beginning of a momentous shift in US policy away from support for territorial integrity and toward enabling Israeli territorial expansion in the wake of the Six-Day War.

"Israel Will Remain Where She Is," a quotation from Ambassador Yitzhak Rabin, sums up the outcome of the June 1967 War. In defiance of the UN and the international community, Israel rejected offers to negotiate land for peace with Jordan, Egypt, or a Palestinian entity and chose instead to maintain an occupation and authorize illegal settlements in the newly annexed territory. Under intense pressure from the Israel lobby, the Johnson administration acquiesced to the Israeli occupation. The administration also dramatically increased US military assistance to Israel, establishing the framework of US Middle East policy for decades to come. The study ends with a Conclusion analyzing the impact and the implications of the Israel lobby on American foreign relations in the Israel–Palestine conflict.

This book would not have been possible without the help of many scholars and friends. They are too many to name them all individually, but they know who they are (that especially includes you, Maurice Labelle!) The final product was enhanced by the incisive criticism of two external reviewers secured by Cambridge University Press and by the tireless efforts of the editors and staff at the press.

PROLOGUE

"Erect a Jewish State at Once"

Centuries of anti-Jewish prejudice and pogroms laid the groundwork for the Zionist movement. In the late 1890s, the Austro-Hungarian-born Jewish journalist Theodore Herzl, greatly disturbed by the Dreyfus Affair in France,[1] launched the drive to establish a separate Jewish homeland. In 1896 Herzl published *The Jewish State*, and he founded the World Zionist Organization (WZO) the following year. In 1897, he convened the first Zionist Congress in Basel, Switzerland. In 1901, the fifth Zionist Congress created the Jewish National Fund (JNF) "to purchase land for the people with donations from the people."[2]

After considering but rejecting Argentina, Uganda, and Madagascar, the Zionist movement homed in on a Jewish return to the holy land and to Jerusalem, the biblical Zion. Although he was "a cultivated, dilettantish Viennese Jew, who knew neither Yiddish nor Hebrew and had little experience of Jewish religious customs," Herzl recognized that the selection of the holy land as the site of Jewish migration would add "potency" to the movement. Asserting that "Palestine is our ever-memorable historic home," Herzl simultaneously appealed for broader European support by invoking a popular imperialist argument, declaring that a Jewish homeland could serve as a "rampart against Asia" and "an outpost of civilization against barbarism."[3]

By the time of his death in 1904, Herzl and his followers had established two core principles that would thereafter characterize the history of the Zionist movement: one held that Zionism would require the support of powerful nations in the "civilized" world; the other held that the beliefs and aspirations of the indigenous residents of Palestine would not stand in the way of the colonization project. While European nationalists defined

13

themselves by excluding others, including the Jewish other, Zionism had become "the nationalist movement of the Jewish people." Unable to find peace in "civilized" Europe, the Zionists would transplant European civilization into a "primitive" land.[4]

In 1882, on the eve of the first *Aliyah* ("ascent" in Hebrew), about 24,000 Jews lived in Ottoman Palestine. Most were pilgrims who confined their activities to rabbinical sites of Jerusalem, Hebron, Tiberius, and Safad. By 1903, the migration had been transformed into the *Yishuv*, the Hebrew word for settlement, and had more than doubled to some 50,000 Jews. By the end of the Second Aliyah in 1914, an estimated 85,000 Jews lived in Palestine.[5]

Russian-Jewish socialist influence outweighed biblical motivations within the Yishuv. Zionist pioneers sought to create a new Jewish society in Palestine based on cooperative labor. Labor Zionism, "the colonizing movement of socialist pioneers," centered on the worker organization *Histadrut*, which "created an intricate countrywide network of social, economic, and political institutions." The labor movement increasingly dominated the work force and "determined much of the infrastructure of the Jewish state-in-the-making."[6]

The Zionist influx coincided with the end of the Ottoman Empire and the rise of European colonialism across the "Middle East." For generations, life for the Arab residents in the area of Palestine had centered on families and villages under the supervision of *hamulas*: patrilineal clans or lineages. While leading families dominated the hamulas, nomadic pastoralists known as Bedouin traversed the region. People tended to their olive groves, using the oil for cooking and soap making, while raising grains and gardens, and herding livestock. The people were overwhelmingly Sunni Muslim, with a minority of Christians and a smattering of Jews. An autonomous peasantry led by patrilineal clans thus dominated the region and proved resistant to outside authority.[7]

One of the keys to the long-term success of the Ottoman Empire, which spanned from the Balkans to the Middle East and lasted for centuries, was its decentralized style of imperial rule. Recognizing that Arab lands were highly diverse and far from the center of their power, the Ottomans strove to accommodate the preexisting political order while still establishing ultimate oversight. Pragmatic Ottoman administrators collected taxes but otherwise granted considerable autonomy to the Arab provinces in return for order and stability. Ottoman administrators ensured access for Islamic pilgrimages to Mecca and Medina.

From 1839 to 1876, the Ottomans carried out a series of reforms known as the *Tanzimat,* or "reordering," that enabled the Ottoman rulers to "strengthen the empire by adopting the successful techniques of the West."[8] Technological advancements, including roads, railroads, telephone and telegraph, water and sewer systems, parks, and electricity, "changed life in the region in numerous ways." Advances in educational, intellectual, legal, and political life were "numerous and far-reaching."[9]

Despite Ottoman efforts to reform and adapt, Europeans made inroads through diffusion of their culture and technology as well as direct intervention. In Egypt, British occupiers exported cotton, built a railroad linking Alexandria and Cairo, and collaborated with the French in construction of the Suez Canal, completed in 1869. In 1830, France ended three centuries of Ottoman rule with a forcible annexation of Algeria replete with indiscriminate violence. Algeria was thus the first European settler colony in the Middle East; the only other one would be Palestine. The French subsequently expanded into Tunisia and Morocco in North Africa and into Lebanon and Syria. Spain received an enclave on the Moroccan coast while Italy claimed authority over Libya.

As the Europeans expanded across North Africa and the Middle East, the Ottoman Empire unraveled. Defeated by Russia in war in 1877–78, the Ottomans simultaneously lapsed into indebtedness to European banks. By the time of the Congress of Berlin in 1878, which formalized the loss of territory in the Balkans, the Europeans viewed the Ottoman Empire as the "sick man of Europe."[10] Despite Orientalist depictions of the Islamic empire, the Ottomans persevered into the twentieth century and fought effectively in a World War I alliance with Germany, including a stiff resistance before surrendering Palestine in 1918. As the war ended, the Ottoman Empire collapsed altogether and modern Turkey was born.[11]

In the midst of the Great War (1914–18), the British made three critical decisions with far-reaching implications: establishment of an independent Arabian kingdom; partition of Mesopotamia and Syria between Britain and France; and endorsement of the Zionist homeland in Palestine. In 1915 the British, determined to establish control over the Persian Gulf, a vital link between the Mediterranean and British colonial India, concluded a treaty with the powerful ruling family led by Abdul Aziz Ibn Saud. The treaty enabled Saud to establish a kingship over most of the Arabian Peninsula. Like the Ottomans, the British had wisely concluded they would be unable to control the orthodox Wahabbi sect in central Arabia, site of the holy cities of Mecca and Medina.[12]

The collapse of the Ottoman Empire in World War I conjoined with rising anticolonial sentiment to fuel independence movements across the Middle East. The British and French in 1916 had entered into the Sykes-Picot Agreement, carving out their respective colonial spheres of influence in the region. The Bolsheviks publicized the theretofore-secret treaty, embarrassing the European powers and spurring widespread resentment of their colonial policies. In 1919 and 1920, the British brutally repressed uprisings in Egypt and Iraq, while the French subdued nationalists in North Africa, Lebanon, and Syria.[13]

The Treaty of Versailles brought an end to World War I and created the League of Nations, which sanctioned the "mandate" system for the perpetuation of postwar European colonialism. Under the mandate framework, the European powers assumed the "white man's burden" to shepherd the African and Muslim nations toward civilization and progress. Despite the resonance of the call for self-determination in President Woodrow Wilson's Fourteen Points, neither the American nor the European leaders meant for the "backward" nations of the world to receive independence any time soon. "The mandate system was essentially colonial rule in new guise, and was understood as such locally," Gudrun Kramer observes.[14]

Under the League-sponsored mandate system, formally put in place in 1923, the British popularized the term "Palestine," which had lacked defined boundaries and had not been an administrative unit under the Ottoman regime. During the centuries of Roman, Byzantine, and Ottoman rule, Muslims, Christians, and Jews at various times applied the term Palestine to the holy land around the city of Jerusalem (from Hebrew and Arabic roots meaning, ironically, "city of peace").[15]

The Balfour Resolution (1917) had the most enduring impact of all the British and Allied actions carving out colonial space in the final stages of the Great War. Supported by all the major powers, including Wilson and the Americans, the one-sentence declaration asserted that the British government would pursue "the establishment in Palestine of a national home for the Jewish people," without "prejudice [to] the civil and religious rights of existing non-Jewish communities in Palestine."[16] In order to facilitate the creation of a Jewish homeland west of the Jordan River, the British severed Palestine from Transjordan, both of which became British colonial possessions.

Inextricably linked with an increasingly discredited European colonialism, the Balfour Declaration was a "formula for communal conflict." Although Balfour insisted that the "adventure" would not come at the expense of Arabs, the Zionist declaration contradicted the purpose of the mandate system, which pledged to place subject peoples on a path toward independence and democracy. In view of Palestine's "very limited resources, there simply was no way to establish a national home for the Jewish people in Palestine without prejudice to the civil and religious rights of existing non-Jewish communities," Eugene Rogan points out. "Palestine would prove Britain's greatest imperial failure in the Middle East," one that condemned the region "to conflict and violence that persist to the present day."[17]

At the time, the Balfour Declaration was a pivotal triumph for the Zionists, who had effectively lobbied the British government. Chaim Weizmann, a Russian chemist who had moved to London in 1905 to promote the Zionist cause, was a driving force behind the Balfour Declaration. In 1918, the British government named Weizmann head of the Zionist Commission to travel to Palestine and make plans for the future state. In 1920, he became head of the WZO, later headed the Jewish Agency (JA), and in 1949 became the first president of Israel. "About the moral superiority of the Jewish claim over the Arab claim to a homeland in Palestine, he never entertained any doubt," Avi Shlaim points out.[18]

The Balfour Declaration provided the Zionist movement with instant legitimacy and fueled a spike in Jewish migration to the holy land. Of crucial importance, the Balfour Declaration became part of the mandate treaty and therefore achieved legal status under international law. Moreover, the knowledge that marrying their cause to the most powerful country in the world would advance Zionism established an enduring precedent.

From the outset, the Zionists had American as well as British backing. The synergy between Zionism and the supportive Western powers paved the way for Jewish settler colonialism at the expense of the indigenous population that had been living in Palestine for centuries. Zionists assigned such tropes as "barren, deserted, miserable land," but in fact Palestine was a settled territory, albeit not a densely populated one, and the proponents of Zionism knew it. As Balfour acknowledged, "The weak point of our position of course is that in the case of Palestine we deliberately and rightly decline to accept the principle of self-determination."[19]

While the carefully worded Balfour Declaration declared support for a Jewish home "in" rather than "of" Palestine, the Zionist settler movement ultimately sought to secure as much land as possible for the new Jewish state, with as few indigenous residents as possible living within it.

As Ze'ev Jabotinsky, the founder of so-called Revisionist Zionism acknowledged, the maximalist approach inevitably would generate conflict with the local Palestinian population. As "indigenous people will resist alien settlers as long as they see any hope," Jabotinsky advocated confronting the Arabs with an implacable "iron wall" of military force. In 1923, the Russian Zionist, whose views would become increasingly dominant during the mandate and after independence, laid out the militant approach in a famous essay, "On the Iron Wall."[20]

Jewish migrants and their sponsors thus understood that Zionism would stifle Palestinian nationalism and generate widespread opposition. Arab nationalism was a palpable force in the wake of the war and the Ottoman imperial collapse. Nationalist leader Amir Faysal proclaimed a government in Damascus and traveled to Paris to press for Allied support of a united Arab confederation, one that might incorporate Palestine. Britain and France stifled the effort to forge a unified Arab state, which would undermine their colonial empires. Wilson had spurred nationalist aspirations by promising the Arabs in the twelfth of his Fourteen Points "an absolutely unmolested opportunity of autonomous development," a vague pledge directly contravened in any case by his endorsement of the Balfour Declaration.[21]

Palestinian nationalism was only in a germinal state in the aftermath of World War I, yet the indigenous population held deep attachments to their homeland. The local population had long embraced "the idea of Palestine as a special place and sacred land with Jerusalem as its focus." Since the Crusades, indigenous people had viewed the area around Jerusalem as a holy land threatened by Western aggressors. This view readily transferred to resentment of the Zionist settlers. In addition to religious attachments, the commonalities of Arabic language, localized loyalties, and rising literacy and education created a foundation for Palestinian nationalism. While Palestinian nationalism was still in formation, it did not arise purely in response to Zionism, as is sometimes claimed.[22]

As with other emerging Arab states, Palestine was poised for takeoff after World War I. The term "Filastin" had been used sporadically as an indicator of a shared local Arab identity. The war, the collapse of the Ottoman Empire, and European colonialism fueled nationalist sentiment and spurred "a strong and growing national identification with Palestine." Absent the British–Zionist collaboration, "It seems almost certain ... that a separate sense of Palestinian identity, and ultimately territorially based nation state nationalism," would have evolved.[23]

Wilson staved off the conflict between Arab nationalists on one side and the Western powers on the other by authorizing a multinational commission to travel to the region to gauge Arab public opinion. Britain and France refused to participate in the King–Crane Commission, undermining the intended multinational thrust of the investigation. Viewing the region through an Orientalist/colonialist lens, the Western powers saw the Palestinian Arabs as a people but not as a nation. The historic region, and particularly the holy sites of Jerusalem, were deemed too important to be left in the hands of backward people. In 1919, the commission found clear evidence of Arab anticolonial sentiment, citing a large number of petitions against Zionism. The indigenous people clearly opposed Zionist immigration and condemned Britain and the international community for attempting to determine the future of Palestine without their consultation or consent.

The King–Crane Commission highlighted the fundamental contradiction inherent in the Balfour Declaration: that a Zionist homeland could be created without prejudice to the rights of Palestinians. "The fact came out repeatedly in the commission's conference with Jewish representatives that the Zionists look forward to a practically complete dispossession of the present non-Jewish inhabitants of Palestine, by various forms of purchase." The Jewish migrants thus meant to displace the Palestinians, not coexist with them. The King–Crane findings and recommendations were ignored.[24]

Local opposition to Zionism began to surface in the 1880s and 1890s, but did not constitute a major movement until after the Balfour Declaration. In the early decades of the Yishuv, Jews purchased mostly uncultivated, sparsely settled land, thus Arab losses were minimal. Nonetheless, in 1891 the first anti-Zionist petition was signed and circulated. From 1919 to 1921, Jewish immigration to Palestine spiked as 18,500 Zionist migrants arrived. The growing Jewish immigration was a threat to nationalist aspirations, while Zionist land purchases were displacing farmers from land they had been on for generations.

By this time, Jewish migration to Palestine had become a highly organized movement fueled by "systematic planning." The JNF was the principal Zionist agency securing land purchases and facilitating the colonization of Palestine.[25] Zealous and hardworking, the Jewish migrants, mostly from Eastern Europe, organized communal settlements (*kibbutzim*), labor units, and farms, consistent with Histadrut's socialist values of mutual aid and cooperation. They emphasized adoption of Hebrew as the lingua franca. The communal societies opened schools and libraries, and promoted music and the arts. "Israeli society was molded ... in the decisive years of the British mandate."[26]

ARAB RESISTANCE

Denied a political role in the construction of an independent nation state of Palestine, local Arabs responded with spontaneous violent resistance against the influx of Jewish migrants. In 1920 and 1921, respectively, major rioting erupted in Jerusalem and in Jaffa, with scores of Jewish and Arab deaths and injuries.[27] As tensions arose with local Arab residents, the Jewish migrants established local militias, the *Haganah* ("defense") to guard the settlements. From the outset, consistent with Jabotinsky's "iron wall" thesis, Zionism was "closely associated with militarism." In time, the Haganah paramilitary forces would train and work closely with the British in repressing Palestinian resistance. Ultimately, the Haganah, the precursor to the Israeli Defense Forces (IDF), would turn against the British as well as the Palestinians and lead the fight for an independent Zionist state.[28]

From 1922 to 1929, some 70,000 Zionist migrants reached Palestine. To accommodate them the JNF purchased 240,000 acres of land in northern Palestine. The more land and property the migrants assumed, the less empowered were the Palestinians in search of transition from colonial rule to self-determination. In August 1929, some 250 people were killed and hundreds injured in a clash in Jerusalem stemming from disputes over shrines around the Western Wall. Both religions viewed the area around the Wall as sacred: the Jews because it was the site of the last ancient temple, and the Arabs because Muhammad was said to have ascended to heaven from the adjacent Dome of the Rock after tethering his horse to the wall. Violence also erupted in the holy city of Hebron, as scores of people suffered injuries and died across Palestine.

British authorities understood that the rapidly changing facts on the ground flowing from Zionist migration and land purchases spurred the violent conflict. Officials in London drafted a series of studies and reports on Jewish land purchases exacerbating tensions, but Zionists lobbied the British government into repudiating a white paper that called for limitations on land acquisition. Violent communal conflict became chronic as Zionists increased their hold on the land while collaborating with the British to fend off Palestinian self-determination.[29]

The rise of Nazi Germany added urgency to the Zionist project, as the regime revivified centuries of demonizing discourse against Jews.

Beginning in the early 1900s, thousands of anti-Semitic pamphlets, books, and articles, many originating in Russia, trumpeted a Jewish plot to take over the world. At the root of the chimerical conspiracy were wealthy Jewish financial elites, notably the Rothschild family, which had originated in Germany and amassed great wealth through banking and finance. The Jewish conspiracy theory proliferated with the publication and distribution in multiple languages of *The Protocols of the Elders of Zion*, which originated in Russia but began to circulate widely in the West in the midst of the Dreyfus Affair.

Many Russians, among others, subsequently blamed the Bolshevik Revolution (1917) on the Jewish conspiracy. Karl Marx had been a Jew, as was the prominent Bolshevik internationalist Leon Trotsky, though both had rejected religion. Yet many Russian and European Jews were socialists, including the proponents of revolutionary uprisings in central Europe, Béla Kun and Rosa Luxemburg.[30] Atrocities against Russian Jews proliferated during World War I and the ensuing Russian Civil War. The worst occurred in the Ukrainian city of Proskurov in February 1919, as Ukrainian military forces slaughtered some 1,200 Jewish men, women, children, and babies in a three-hour paroxysm of violence. From 1917 to 1921, more than 2,000 pogroms were carried out in Eastern Europe, killing an estimated 75,000 Jews and leaving many more injured and homeless.[31]

Despite periodic outbursts of anti-Semitism, Jewish history up to this time had been "essentially a positive trajectory of emancipation, modernization, and integration." Jews had "coped with anti-Semitism and crafted many creative ways to be Jewish while also becoming part of the societies in which they lived."[32] The Nazis shattered perceptions of progress and replaced them with an ultimately genocidal regime. Hitler, an embittered foot soldier who blamed the "soulless Jews" for Germany's defeat and humiliation in World War I, took power and began to construct his fascist regime. Anti-Jewish propaganda and attacks produced the discriminatory Nuremburg Laws and violent attacks on Jewish people, homes, businesses, and synagogues, culminating in 1938 on *Kristallnacht*, "night of the broken glass." Ninety Jews were murdered, some 30,000 Jewish men sent to concentration camps, and more than 300 synagogues were burned.[33]

The rise of the Nazis spurred massive Jewish migration to Palestine, exacerbating the ethnic conflict. In 1933, the year Hitler came to power, more than 30,000 Jews poured into Palestine; more than 42,000 entered in 1934; and a peak of nearly 62,000 arrived in 1935. By 1936, in just five years the Jewish population had more than doubled from 175,000 to 370,000. Jews, comprising 9 percent of Palestine's population in 1922, comprised 27 percent by 1936.[34]

The skyrocketing Zionist immigration and accompanying land purchases ignited a massive three-year revolt, one of the most momentous events in the history of Palestine. The revolt of 1936–39 devastated cities, towns, and the countryside, where the overwhelming majority of Arabs and Muslims lived. The revolt ultimately crippled both British authority and the prospects of Palestinian self-determination. Though scores of Jews suffered and died in the conflict, Zionism emerged as the chief beneficiary of the violence.[35]

Beginning in 1936, a six-month general strike devolved into a mandate-wide anticolonial nationalist rebellion that required an emergency influx of thousands of British troops to suppress. By the time they had quelled the first stage of the rebellion, the British had come to the conclusion that the mandate was no longer tenable and that Palestine should be partitioned between Arabs and Jews. The 400-page Peel Commission Report released in 1937 declared an "irrepressible conflict" stemming from competing "nationalist aspirations." The Royal Commission recommended partition into two states, in which both could access holy sites from Jaffa to Jerusalem under a redefined mandate.[36]

The partition plan distinctly favored the Zionists whose leaders therefore embraced it. "This will give us something we never had," declared David Ben-Gurion, who had emerged as the leader of the Yishuv.[37] Uniting various factions within the Histadrut, Ben-Gurion established the dominance of *Mapai*, the Labor Party, with him at the helm. The Polish-born Zionist leader outmaneuvered Weizmann and fended off the right-wing Revisionist Zionists, though he shared with them the desire to colonize as much of Palestine as possible. All factions opposed accommodating Palestinian nationalism and worked with the British to keep the local population under control. All sharply opposed British efforts to limit Jewish migration into the emerging Zionist state.

When the Peel proposals were announced, Ben-Gurion seized the opportunity to establish a "really Jewish" state with a homogeneously Jewish population. Under the Peel Commission Plan, Jews would receive 20 percent of the land of Palestine, but that portion would include most of the coastland and the most fertile agricultural land. The majority Palestinians would get not only 80 percent of the mandate, but also the poorest lands such as the Negev Desert, the hill country of the West Bank, and the Gaza Strip. Moreover, the existing population in Palestine did not correspond to the geography of the partition, as major Arab towns and cities lay within the proposed Jewish state. The Peel Commission envisioned the possibility of "population transfers" of tens of thousands of Arabs, thus providing a foundation for subsequent Zionist removal campaigns.[38]

Even under these highly favorable terms, the Zionists viewed the partition plan as a first step. Although accepting the plan, Ben-Gurion would not be bound by the terms of partition. As head of the JA, Ben-Gurion explained the matter to the Zionist Congress in August 1937: "There could be no question ... of giving up *any part* of the Land of Israel" [emphasis added]. Gaining authorization from the Congress to pursue additional territory in the future, Ben-Gurion emphasized that the "ultimate goal" would "be achieved most quickly by accepting the Peel proposals ... Erect a Jewish state at once, even if it is not in the whole land," he advised. "The rest will come in the course of time. It must come." Refusing to rule out eventual Jewish colonization of Transjordan, Ben-Gurion flatly declared, "The boundaries of Zionist aspirations are the concern of the Jewish people and no external factor will be able to limit them."[39]

While the Zionists pressed for unlimited immigration and an expansive state, the Palestinians were to receive no state at all under the Peel Commission Plan. Not only did the Arabs receive the least favorable land under the partition plan, that land would be appended to British-dominated Transjordan under the Hashemite family leader Amir Abdullah rather than made into a Palestinian nation. Eager to expand the frontiers of Transjordan, Abdullah accepted the partition plan. "For the Palestinians," Rogan notes, "the Peel Commission's recommendations represented the worst possible outcome for their national struggle. Far from securing the rights to self rule, the population was to be dispersed and ruled by hostile foreigners – the Zionists and Amir Abdullah."[40]

Faced with the expanding Zionist state and ongoing British rejection of Palestinian nationalism, the local population ignited the second phase of the revolt: a violent resistance that lasted from the fall of 1937 to early 1939. Palestinians attacked the British police and army patrols as well as Jewish settlements. They carried out sabotage, assassinations, and hit-and-run assaults, but had neither sufficient weaponry nor a coordinated strategy to prevail over superior British and Jewish forces. Internal divisions also worked against the spontaneous uprising, as the Palestinians remained disunited and leaderless. With the spiritual leader, the Mufti, driven out of the country and Abdullah and other Arabs pursuing their own self-interests, the Palestinian resistance lacked coordination, and was also undermined by collaborators.

Dispatching thousands of troops in the largest deployment of forces since the Great War, the British put down the Arab revolt. The British instituted emergency decrees, press censorship, and other forms of political repression; conducted military tribunals and night raids; imprisoned and tortured hundreds of people; carried out deportations and summary executions; destroyed some 2,000 "rebel" homes; and engaged in other forms of collective punishment.[41]

Beginning in 1938, British authorities worked directly with the Haganah, which had by now evolved into a well-armed militia. A more militant irregular faction, *Irgun* (National Military Organization in the Land of Israel), conducted terror campaigns, including the bombing of Arab marketplaces. By the end of the revolt in 1939 an estimated 5,000 Palestinians had been killed, many more thousands wounded, and some 9,000 languished in make shift prisons. British authorities subsequently executed more than 100 prisoners. The revolt left the male population of Palestine depleted, but thousands of women and children suffered and died as well. The British suffered 69 deaths, while 292 Jews died in the revolt.[42]

Though often overshadowed by the first Arab–Israeli War in 1947–48, as well as the June 1967 War, the 1936–39 Revolt laid the foundation for creation of a Zionist state in Palestine. Indigenous forces suffered staggering losses, which left them vulnerable when war erupted again less than a decade later. "The crushing of the 1936–39 revolt largely determined the outcome of the 1948 war," Rashid Khaladi declares.[43]

The Arab revolt also marked the beginning of the end of the British in Palestine, though another world war would be required to finish off the mandate. In a dramatic reversal of policy two years after the Peel Commission Report, the British proposed a binational state with boundaries more proportionate to the population and with meaningful restrictions on Jewish immigration. Concerned about the vulnerability of their empire across the Middle East as World War II loomed, the British sought to bolster Arab support in the region to enable them to focus their military and other resources on the defense of Europe and the home isles.

Rejecting the Peel Commission partition plan as "impracticable," the [Malcolm] MacDonald White Paper, published in May 1939, explained, "The framers of the Mandate, in which the Balfour Declaration was embodied, could not have intended that Palestine should be converted into a Jewish State against the will of the Arab population of the country."[44] Accordingly, the new proposal called for restrictions on Jewish immigration, land purchases, and settlement. The Zionists summarily rejected these terms as they opposed any limits on immigration, land purchases, and occupation rights. Weizmann, Ben-Gurion, and other leaders of the Yishuv had no intention of accommodating the indigenous Palestinians or acquiescing to British restrictions that would render them a permanent minority in Palestine.

The Palestinians also rejected the MacDonald plan, which would have required them to wait ten years in hopes that an independent state would then be created. The British, seemingly the masters of the Middle East and Persian Gulf after World War I, had now alienated both the Jews and the Palestinians, thereby underscoring the ultimate irrationality of colonialism.

Zionist extremists turned against the British with a vengeance. The group *Lehi* (the Hebrew acronym for Freedom Fighters of Israel), robbed banks, attacked and assassinated mandate officials, and, astonishingly, in 1939 approached the Nazi regime about an alliance against the British. The Germans ignored the approach from Lehi, popularly known in the West as the Stern Gang for its leader Abraham Stern. In 1942, the British tracked down and killed Stern in his Tel Aviv apartment.[45]

World War II reinforced the growing Zionist drive to establish an expansive Jewish state *of* rather than merely *in* Palestine, as the Balfour Declaration had proposed. As the vicious Nazi regime stepped up its assault on European Jews and other minority groups, Zionists increasingly viewed a Jewish homeland as essential to their survival. Ironically, the majority of the Jewish migrants appeared to view the Palestinians as *untermenschen*, as they showed no regard for the nationalist aspirations of the indigenous Arabs.

Jews continued to flee Europe and pour into Palestine, establishing facts on the ground with the ultimate ambition of dispossessing the Arab residents. The Yishuv began construction of a massive JA Executive Building on St. George Street in Jerusalem, a symbol of permanence. Zionists expressed bitter frustration with British policies enforcing restrictions on the number of Jewish refugees entering the mandate. In 1942, outrage peaked amid the *Struma* disaster, as 769 Romanian Jews died with the sinking of their overloaded ship in the Black Sea after British authorities had detained it for two months.[46]

Zionist leaders opted to fight both for and against Great Britain during World War II. "We will fight with the British against Hitler as if there were no white paper," Ben-Gurion explained, and "we will fight the white

paper as if there were no war."[47] Ben-Gurion prevailed over Weizmann in
a decision to authorize the Haganah to collaborate with Lehi and Irgun in
waging a violent guerrilla campaign against the British. Following the
Allied victory over Nazi Germany in 1945, the British declared a state of
emergency and concentrated 100,000 troops in Palestine in an effort to
rein in the Zionist settler revolt. As an irreconcilable conflict unfolded
with the British, the Yishuv turned its attention to winning over the new
global superpower: the United States.

AMERICAN SUPPORT FOR ZIONISM

American connections with the "holy land" were deeply rooted.
Throughout the nation's history, religious narratives "helped forge the
connection that allowed many people in the United States to see themselves as intimately involved with the Middle East."[48] Identification with
the covenant of ancient Israel flourished from the seventeenth-century
Puritans through the era of Manifest Destiny and beyond. Americans
"defined their place in prophecy" in Israel's image. As "God's favored
nation," the United States would prosper "just as the Israelites had flourished when they walked in God's ways."[49]

While they identified with the ancient Israelites, many Americans nurtured Orientalist perceptions of the Muslim world, blending religiously
infused contempt with "exotic fascination." After clashing with the North
African "Barbary pirates" at the dawn of the nineteenth century, decades
later Americans came to the aid of Greek Christians against their
"Mohammedan" oppressors in the Ottoman Empire. At the turn of the
century, as the United States displaced Spain as the occupier of the
Philippines, US forces denigrated and slaughtered Islamic "Moro tribes-
men" in the southern part of the archipelago.[50]

As World War I ushered in sweeping changes in global politics, many
Americans backed Zionism. They followed the lead of Presidents
Theodore Roosevelt and Wilson, both of whom endorsed the Balfour
Declaration and condemned "Mohammedanism." A devout Christian,
Wilson received added encouragement from Supreme Court Justice Louis
Brandeis, the driving force behind the creation of the Zionist Organization
of America (ZOA) in 1918. A nonreligious Jew from Louisville who
nonetheless advocated converting *all* of Palestine into a Jewish state,
Brandeis played a decisive role in Wilson's decision to embrace the
Balfour Declaration. Wilson also received encouragement from funda-
mentalist Christians who called for the "restoration" of Jews in fulfillment

of biblical prophecy on the return of Christ ushering in the "end of times." During the World War I era, the US Congress overwhelmingly supported Zionism and passed resolutions to that effect.[51]

Wilson, who viewed himself on a mission to remake the war-torn world, told Rabbi Stephen S. Wise "two lands will never go back to the Mohammedan apache. One is Christian Armenia and the other is Jewish Palestine."[52] Through his allusion to the southwestern indigenous tribe, which had long resisted subjugation to the United States, Wilson invoked the shared history of settler colonization between the Zionists and the Americans.

Growing support for Zionism coincided with the persistence of American anti-Jewish prejudices, which had long existed but proliferated with the influx of nearly three million European Jews, more than two-thirds of them Russian, between 1880 and 1914.[53] Many of the Jewish immigrants encountered hostility and poverty in the ghettos of New York and other East Coast cities. Anti-Jewish prejudice materialized in the South as well, most sensationally in the case of Leo Frank, the manager of a pencil factory in Atlanta who was accused of murdering one of his employees, a 13-year-old girl. Tried and found guilty, though he very likely was not, in 1915 Frank was hauled from jail by a mob, shouting "Hang the Jew," which they proceeded to do.[54]

In 1924, in the wake of deep divisions over race and ethnicity exacerbated by US intervention in World War I, Congress passed the National Origins Act, cutting off immigration into the country by Asians and Eastern Europeans. The European restrictions effectively brought an end to immigration by Jews, who were defined under the law as a separate (non-white) "Hebrew race." Throughout the interwar period, purveyors of Jewish conspiracy theories and anti-Semitism, notably the automobile manufacturer Henry Ford, the evangelist Gerald L. K. Smith, and the Detroit Catholic "radio Priest" Father Charles Coughlin, resonated with many Americans.[55]

Preoccupied with business growth in the 1920s, followed by the shattering effects of the Great Depression in the ensuing decade, the United States had limited involvement in world affairs, including the Zionist movement. To be sure, American Zionists such as Democratic Party insider and future Supreme Court Justice Felix Frankfurter, an Austrian Jewish emigrant and a protégé of Brandeis, lobbied for the cause, yet relatively few Americans engaged with the issue. Frankfurter attempted to broaden support by emphasizing a staple Zionist argument: namely, that settlement would benefit not only Jews, but also the backward Arabs.

Zionist land purchases and economic activity would, as he put it, "ameliorate the Arab's lot through Jewish enterprise."[56]

While debate was muted in the interwar period, some experts, echoing the King–Crane Commission, warned of inevitable conflict between "the opposing forces of two distinct nationalisms" in Palestine. In an extensive study, Elizabeth MacCallum of the Foreign Policy Association explained in 1929, "The Arabic-speaking inhabitants, to whom it is known as Filistin ... do not acquiesce in a doctrine that a country which they are accustomed to think of as being their own should suddenly be called *Eretz Israel* without their consent, simply because it has pleased other nations to set up a Jewish national home."[57]

By the late 1930s, the Nazi regime and its virulent anti-Jewish pogroms discredited American anti-Semitism and built empathy for Jews and Zionism. President Franklin D. Roosevelt, a longtime Zionist, stepped up condemnation of the Nazis. In response to the 1938 *Kristallnacht* attacks, Roosevelt became the only world leader to withdraw his ambassador from Berlin in protest. While the United States maintained its restrictive immigration policies, Roosevelt advocated relocation of refugees and facilitated the settlement of some 40,000 European Jews, mostly in Latin America.[58]

Among American Jews as well as many Christians, support for Zionism accelerated in the progressive New Deal era and amid the Nazi pogroms. Building on "American Jewry's centuries-old fascination with the Holy Land" was growing support for the Labor Zionist movement in Palestine. American Zionists increasingly viewed Palestine as "a progressive Jewish society-in-the-making" and were "especially entranced with the Yishuv's pioneers, cooperative spirit, and renascent Hebrew language," Mark Raider points out.

As Labor Zionism became *the* American variant of Zionism, "the veneration of the pioneers in Palestine cemented relations between disparate Zionist and Jewish camps." The Nazi pogroms spurred a series of conferences, conventions, grassroots activism, and fundraising that "solidified American Jewry's profound sense of Jewish peoplehood and commitment to the Jewish national home." The combination of the "social democratic character" of the Yishuv along with spiking Nazi anti-Semitism built a groundswell of support for the Zionist cause. By the 1940s, what one scholar has called "the Americanization of Zionism" was on a trajectory to "contribute significantly in preparing American public opinion for the establishment of a Jewish state."[59]

American Jewish identity thus became increasingly linked with the success of the Zionist project in Palestine. Brandeis emphasized that US Jews could support Zionism, even though they had no intention of migrating to Palestine, thus without compromising their Americanism. A progressive Jewish state would promote acceptance of the Jewish Diaspora worldwide and enhance the vitality of American Jewry. American Zionists attempted "to mobilize popular support for the Yishuv without escalating public anti-Semitism or exacerbating American Jewish feelings of vulnerability and insecurity."[60] The effort to impose restrictions on Jewish immigration in the 1939 MacDonald White Paper "shocked and enraged American Zionists," heightening their support for the Yishuv.[61]

Galvanized by the Nazi pogroms as well as the white paper, American Zionists collaborated with the Christian Zionist members of the American Palestine Committee, which had been created in 1931 in support of a Jewish state in the holy land. By 1941 the APC had enlisted a bipartisan array of eminent politicians, including future President Truman (D-MO) and future Vice President Alben Barkley (D-KY), as well as Republican presidential candidate Wendell Willkie and Rep. Joseph Martin (R-MA).

The APC embraced "reunion of the Jewish people with the land of its ancient inheritance." The group adopted as "an essential part of APC propaganda efforts" the argument that a Jewish state would uplift the backward Arabs. A Zionist commonwealth would, declared Sen. Robert Wagner (D-NY), bring "agriculture, industry, and commerce" to the region. Sen. William King (D-UT) asserted that it was the duty of the United States in its "pre-destined role of arbiter of world affairs" to embrace the Zionist cause. In December 1942, 63 senators and 182 representatives issued a proclamation commemorating the twenty-fifth anniversary of the signing of the Balfour Declaration.[62]

The leaders of the Yishuv sought to tap into the rising tide of American Zionism, particularly as their relations with the British deteriorated. They recognized that the support of the United States – which possessed the largest Jewish population in the world – could facilitate realization of the Zionist dream of a Jewish state. In the wake of the Pearl Harbor attack, it was clear that the United States would fight the world war to the finish, and if victorious would be in position to enhance the prospects of Zionism.

The American Zionist movement spurred the evolution of a nascent Israel lobby. In 1939, the JA legally registered as a foreign lobbying agent with the US Department of Justice, as required under the Foreign Agents Registration Act (FARA), which had become law the previous year.[63] During the war, the Yishuv began to work systematically with leaders of the American Zionist movement in efforts to unite American Jewry to lobby for support of a Jewish "commonwealth" in Palestine. During World War II, the United States thus became the most important country in the world for the realization of Zionist ambitions.

I

"Friendship of the American People for the Zionist Ideal"

The pivotal moment crystallizing the American special relationship with Zionism came in May 1942 with the historic meeting at the Biltmore Hotel in New York City, the heartland of American Jewish life. Ben-Gurion and Weizmann collaborated in the meeting, attended by 586 American Zionists and 67 from other countries. The meeting culminated with passage of a resolution known as the Biltmore Program that centered on the pledge "that Palestine be constituted as a Jewish Commonwealth integrated into the structure of the new democratic world." Denouncing the "cruel and indefensible" British white paper, the Biltmore resolution also called for unrestricted Jewish immigration.[1]

The Biltmore meeting marked the birth of the Israel lobby – the collaboration of American Zionists and Yishuv leaders in support of an independent Jewish state in Palestine. The meeting also marked the ascendance of a more aggressive American Zionist leadership embodied by Rabbi Abba Hillel Silver, who presided over the nation's largest Jewish congregation in Cleveland. An immigrant from Lithuania, Silver, like leaders of the Yishuv, had migrated from the "pale of settlement," the vast area of east-central Europe where the tsars had exiled Jews before Hitler and Soviet leader Joseph Stalin converted the region into the "blood lands" of Europe.[2] Like the Yishuv leaders, Silver spoke Hebrew and promoted the creation of a Jewish settler state encompassing as much of Palestine as possible.

While the more moderate Zionists led by Wise had focused on a gradual approach of working through the Roosevelt administration, Silver brought a public urgency to the demand for Jewish statehood. An imposing figure and a gifted orator, Silver won over the delegates at

Biltmore when he declared, "The ultimate solution is the establishment of a Jewish nation in Palestine." Silver's advocacy played a key role in convincing many American adherents to Reform Judaism – a denomination that emphasized reason, ethics, and personal autonomy over religious law and ritual – to embrace Zionism.[3]

The mounting evidence of an unfolding Nazi genocide added immediacy to the Zionist movement, which came to embody not merely establishment of a state but a drive to preserve the lives of a people. As the Nazi armies lashed across east-central Europe they established forced labor and, ultimately, annihilation camps. Paramilitary groups followed the German army into previously held Soviet territory to carry out the Reich policy of removing and summarily executing Jews. In 1942, Hitler's regime formally adopted "the final solution of the Jewish question" and began systematically to exterminate Jews as well as Roma, communists, Jehovah's Witnesses, disabled people, and homosexuals. The genocide ultimately took the lives of some six million European Jews.[4]

Zionist leaders appealed to Roosevelt to support Jewish refugees and come out forcefully behind the creation of a Jewish state. The president declared his opposition to the British white paper restrictions on Jewish immigration to Palestine. In consultation with Henry Morgenthau, his Jewish secretary of the treasury, Roosevelt at one point averred that 90 percent of Palestine should be Jewish, with the Arabs being moved onto adjacent land. However, he rejected Zionist pressure for precipitous action that would provoke a war between the Arabs and Jews and result in "millions of people being killed in a *jihad*."[5]

Confronted with evidence of the Nazi genocide in 1942, Roosevelt refrained from publicizing the issue – a task that Jewish leaders assumed instead. As a latecomer to the European war, the United States was not in position to liberate the Nazi victims. The Allies did not launch a general assault in Western Europe until 1944, by which time most of the killing had already been accomplished, and most of that achieved through starvation and summary execution by gunshot rather than through the industrial-style slaughter of the death camps. The US military never drew up, and thus Roosevelt did not receive and reject, an option to bomb rail lines into Auschwitz, the most active death camp, located in Poland, but just one of many dispersed killing centers. In 1944, as Morgenthau and Zionist leaders pleaded with him to take action on behalf of Jewish refugees, Roosevelt created the War Refugee Board. Though underfunded and confronted with political opposition, the WRB "helped to save as many as 200,000 Jewish lives."[6] Ultimately, the United States did little to stop

FIGURE 3 Rabbi Abba Hillel Silver (left) and Rabbi Stephen Wise briefed the press following a meeting with Franklin Roosevelt on March 9, 1944, in which they urged the president to facilitate opening the doors of Britain's Palestine mandate to Jewish refugees. By this time Silver, a gifted orator from Cleveland, had outflanked Wise as the vocal leader of the American Zionist movement.
Bettmann/Getty Images

the genocide, which produced perceptions of guilt in subsequent years, especially as the full scope of the Nazi horrors emerged.[7]

Armed with a new sense of urgency, Henry Monsky, the president of B'nai B'rith, the oldest and largest US Jewish organization, convened the American Jewish Conference in an effort to unify Jews behind a program of rescue and lifting restrictions on Jewish immigration. At the meeting in New York from August 29 to September 2, 1943, with more than 500 delegates representing more than 2 million people from 64 national organizations, Silver again seized the spotlight. "There is but one solution for national homelessness," he declaimed. "That is a national home!" To "thunderous applause," Silver concluded by calling on the conference to "stand by those who have given their tears and their blood and their sweat to build for them and for us and the future generations, at long last, after the weary centuries, a home, a national Home, a Jewish Commonwealth, where the spirit of our entire people can finally be at rest." By all accounts Silver electrified the audience and won over the conference, a subcommittee of which voted 60–2 in favor of establishment of the "Jewish Commonwealth."[8]

THE LOBBY BORN

Having eclipsed Wise and others at the head of the American Zionist movement, Silver assumed chairmanship of the first iteration of the Israel lobby, the American Zionist Emergency Council (AZEC). Formed in the wake of the Conference, the organization's name underscored the life-or-death urgency of the struggle for Jewish survival and statehood. The creation of AZEC "heralded a new and forceful public relations campaign aimed at winning the American government's support for Jewish statehood in Palestine."[9] For the duration of the war, AZEC amassed funds and lobbied effectively for a Zionist state. In addition to uniting a majority of Jewish groups, AZEC secured declarations of support from thousands of non-Jewish organizations, state and local government, and ever-growing numbers of congressmen.[10]

While American Zionism was clearly ascendant after World War II, the Jewish "community" was far from monolithic, as substantial numbers of American Jews either opposed or were disengaged from the quest for a Jewish homeland. The American Council for Judaism (ACJ), founded in 1942, emphasized that Judaism was a religion and not a national movement, hence the group was "unalterably opposed to the establishment of an independent national Jewish State in Palestine or elsewhere." In addition to embracing Judaism as a religion and not a theocratic state, ACJ members expressed concern about perceptions of "dual loyalty" that would undermine the standing of Jews as patriotic Americans.[11]

Originating in 1906, the AJC promoted civil rights and economic, educational, and social equality for Jews worldwide, but it too was not a Zionist organization. The AJC advocated liberalization of immigration laws allowing more Jewish refugees in the United States while opposing formal affiliation between American Jews and a Zionist commonwealth. The AJC initially participated, but later pulled out of the American Jewish Congress proceedings, declaring that with Zionists attempting to monopolize American Jewish opinion, "there was no adequate opportunity for an exchange of views."[12]

Even within the Zionist movement, "endless discussions about organizational rivalry and prestige" impeded speaking with a unified voice.[13] Silver's ascendance "represented a sharp break" and thus rankled Wise, Frankfurter, and others who inherited the mantle of the movement from Brandeis (who died in 1941).[14] Zionists crisscrossed the country "from one large Jewish center to the other" in an effort to forge "a permanent democratic body" to mobilize public opinion and policy "for the good of the Jewish people," but in the end this protean effort failed.[15]

Impervious to opposition, Silver tapped a fellow Clevelander, Isaiah Leo Kenen, to anchor an extensive AZEC campaign of publicity and persuasion. More than any other single individual, Kenen came to personify the Israel lobby in the United States. Born in Canada to parents who had emigrated from east-central Europe, Kenen migrated from Toronto to Cleveland, where he became a journalist and president of a Zionist organization in the city. A tireless worker throughout his life, Kenen secured a law degree through an evening program but never practiced. His lifelong client, however, was the Zionist state. While Silver mesmerized audiences from the stage, Kenen quietly mobilized "a political and public relations offensive to capture the support of congressmen, clergy, editors, professors, business, and labor."[16]

Kenen and other activists wrote reams of bulletins and press releases, organized rallies, and established the budding Zionist lobby as a major force in national politics. On March 21, 1944, a "Rally for Palestine" at Madison Square Garden featured Wise, Silver, and Sens. Wagner, Barkley, and Robert Taft (R-OH), a close ally of Silver. Wise read from a statement he had secured from Roosevelt, pledging his opposition to the British White Paper, adding that "full justice will be done to those who seek a Jewish national home."[17]

The signature strategy of the Israel lobby – lining up support for the Zionist state in the US Congress – first materialized in the 1944 electoral campaign. In February of that year, Kenen reported that lobby activities promoting the establishment of the Jewish Commonwealth – "the unprecedented flood of telegrams, telephone calls, and letters" – had "profoundly impressed the Capitol, evoking many assurances of support from Congressmen." He called for a "similar and immediate approach to President Roosevelt."[18] The APC weighed in at its 1944 national convention, declaring that "The Christian world must rededicate itself to the heritage it has received from Judaism, the mother faith of Christianity" and support creation of a Jewish state as an "outpost of democracy" in the Middle East.[19]

Tapping into the growing American support for Zionism, AZEC secured the endorsement of both major political parties in the 1944 presidential campaign. The Democratic platform endorsed "unrestricted Jewish immigration and colonization" and establishment of a "democratic Jewish commonwealth." The Republican platform also called for unfettered immigration, and condemned Roosevelt for failing to do more to back the Balfour Declaration.[20] Silver worked with Benzion Netanyahu, a professor at Cornell University, supporter of the right-wing Revisionist Zionists, and father of the future Israeli prime minister Benjamin Netanyahu. Much as his son would do generations later, Netanyahu advised Silver, "We have made a special effort in our political work to gain the active support of all the influential Republican leaders."[21]

The 1944 campaign was a watershed event, demonstrating early on the potential political clout of what would become the full-blown Israel lobby. In 1964 Kenen reflected that major party political platforms "have actually changed the course of history. They certainly did in 1944. All party platforms since 1944 have evidenced a positive interest in Israel. There is a bipartisan national commitment, which has grown steadily stronger."[22]

While the Zionist lobby began to assert itself effectively in American political life, nothing comparable existed for Arabs or Palestinians in the United States. The Arabs were woefully less organized and united than the Zionists. The Arab League, founded near the end of World War II, failed to unite the "Arab world" as a coherent political entity. Divided into factions, Palestinians lacked leadership, as the Mufti, the Islamic religious leader, and others had been forced into exile since the Arab revolt of the late 1930s. Transjordan's King Abdullah opposed creation of a Palestinian state as he sought to gain control of the West Bank of the Jordan River. Pan-Arab resistance to the establishment of the Zionist state thus ultimately proved halting and futile.[23]

As Roosevelt's fourth presidential term began, the Arab governments, backed by the British as well as the DOS, began to push back against the growing clout of the American Zionist movement. In March 1945, all three protested when Wise announced that Roosevelt had confirmed during a meeting in the White House that he supported unrestricted Jewish immigration in Palestine. Warning of "serious repercussions," diplomat Wallace Murray pointed out that the policy contradicted previous pledges to Saudi Arabia, a wartime ally, that Washington would take no major action without "full consultation" with Arab world leaders.

World War II had underscored the importance of access to petroleum, which motivated US oil companies and investors to cultivate relations with Arab countries, especially the Saudi regime. The DOS also expressed growing anxieties about the spread of communism as a new "cold war" began to unfold. Murray offered a worst-case scenario: "The continued endorsement by the President of Zionist objectives may well result in throwing the entire Arab world into the arms of Soviet Russia."[24]

As with many other issues, Roosevelt "juggled" conflicting policies, often telling competing forces what they wanted to hear while deferring resolution of major issues until the end of the war, an approach that left crucial matters undecided at the time of his sudden death on April 12.[25] Before his death, Roosevelt had attempted to reassure Saud, who reminded him that Palestine was sacred Muslim territory and ought to be controlled exclusively by Arabs. Despite his public support for the Zionist agenda, Roosevelt informed Saud that no decision would be taken "with respect to the basic situation ... without full consultation with both Arabs and Jews." On the day he died in Warm Springs, Georgia, Roosevelt wrote the same message to the Syrian president, assuring him "no decision regarding the basic situation in Palestine" would come "without full consultation with both Arabs and Jews."[26]

ENTER TRUMAN

Little experienced in foreign affairs and largely kept in the dark by Roosevelt, Truman faced monumental challenges pertaining to postwar reconstruction, global decolonization, and the emerging Cold War. While Truman took the advice of the DOS and others to draw a hard line against communism, he ultimately rejected the advice of the professional diplomats on the Arab–Zionist conflict. Driven by pressure from the Zionist lobby, Truman grudgingly offered crucial backing for the cause. While the Zionists cultivated and ultimately celebrated Truman, the president's actions alienated professional diplomats, the Arabs, and the British.

Although he had joined the APC, Truman had no innate emotional attachment to Jews or to Zionism. Like many Protestant Americans of his generation, Truman had made a number of remarks reflecting "casual anti-Semitism" over the years.[27] However, he genuinely sympathized with the well-publicized plight of Jewish refugees, not least because they called to mind stories he had been told by his mother and grandmother about Missourians being driven out of their homes during the American Civil War.[28] At the same time, despite a reverence for the biblical narrative,

Truman did not initially subscribe to the view that the Jews should forge a religious state in the midst of the Arab world.

Faced with an increasingly assertive Zionist lobby, Truman came under strong pressure, first to open the gates of Jewish immigration, and ultimately to back the creation of Israel. Warning that the "Zionist leaders" would be "pressing" him on the issue, Secretary of State Edward Stettinius advised the new president to avoid making precipitous decisions, as the Palestine issue was "highly complex and involves questions which go far beyond the plight of the Jews of Europe."[29] Diplomat Loy Henderson advised Truman that "The United States should refrain from supporting a policy of large-scale immigration into Palestine" until a broader political solution could be effected.[30] As head of the DOS Near East division, Henderson became a lightning rod for Zionist charges of pro-Arab bias – or, as he later put it, he became "the most detested villain in the drama of 'The birth of Israel.'"[31]

Although Truman pledged to uphold Roosevelt's promise to consult the Arab leaders, his decision to open the gates to Jewish immigration signaled an impending tilt toward Zionism, despite the dire warnings from the DOS. On August 16, 1945, Truman told the press. "We want to let as many Jews into Palestine as is possible." Warned that sharp increases in Jewish immigration would spur conflict within the British mandate, Truman ruled out the dispatch of US armed forces to help keep the peace in the region. At the same time, the president tried to reassure Ibn Saud that his humanitarian support for Jewish refugees did not signal a full-scale tilt toward Zionism.[32]

With the ethnic conflict in Palestine on the brink of eruption, the British government pursued collaboration with the United States in an effort to quell the rising unrest and achieve an ultimate settlement. In November 1945, Truman affirmed his support for the "quick evacuation of as many [Jews] as possible" to Palestine, but acceded to a British request to establish a joint Anglo–American commission to consider the Palestine question.[33] Beginning in January 1946, the 12-member Anglo–American Committee of Inquiry amassed data on Palestine and the refugee crisis and held hearings in Washington and in London before issuing its final report in April.

The six American members of the committee included committed Zionists James G. McDonald, who would become the first US ambassador to Israel, and journalist Bartley Crum, who became an active member of the lobby. The committee supported the admission of 100,000 Jewish refugees while trying to find additional destinations for other displaced European Jews. As to the future of Palestine, an international trusteeship should be established in which "Jew shall not dominate Arab and Arab shall not dominate Jew," the joint committee concluded; "Palestine must ultimately become a state that guards the rights and interests of Moslems, Jews, and Christians alike." The report called for the JA to support its recommendations, particularly those renouncing violence and illegal immigration. On June 11, 1946, Truman appointed a Cabinet Committee on Palestine to negotiate with the British on implementation of the special committee recommendations.[34]

While both Arabs and Jews rejected the Anglo–American trusteeship, the Committee's endorsement of the 100,000 refugees was a victory for the Zionists. They insisted, however, that the number was insufficient and there should be no limitations on Jewish immigration, land purchases, or any other roadblocks to the creation of a Jewish settler state. Both Palestinians and Arabs more broadly reacted bitterly over the rejection of a Palestinian state and perceived US collusion with Zionist expansion into the region. At a meeting in May with top DOS officials, the foreign ministers of Saudi Arabia, Egypt, Iraq, Lebanon, and Syria again complained that contrary to repeated promises they had not been adequately consulted, and, moreover, that "the introduction of 100,000 Jews would bring about a basic change of the situation" in Palestine. Saud warned that a massive influx of Jews and efforts to create a Jewish state in Palestine would require the forced relocation of the local Arab population.[35]

Intense pressure from the Zionist lobby prompted Truman to reject British Prime Minister Clement Atlee's request that he hold off on clearing the path for the admission of 100,000 new Jewish immigrants. The British had authorized an interim program of allowing 1,500 Jewish refugees a month into Palestine, explaining that before larger numbers could be admitted, "The illegal Jewish armies must be suppressed and there must be a general disarmament throughout Palestine. Otherwise the armies would be swollen by recruits drawn from the new immigrants," an action that "would cause serious repercussions throughout the Arab world involving additional military commitments which the British Government could not undertake alone." Under persistent pressure from the lobby, Truman told his British ally the United States was moving "without delay" in support of the influx of 100,000 Jewish refugees.[36]

AZEC launched "an all-out effort ... to impress the President with the fact that Americans generally" supported admission of the 100,000 Jewish refugees into Palestine.[37] Meeting directly with Truman, Wise and Silver also called on the president to condemn Britain over the arrests of Jewish resistance leaders in Palestine. Though he took a dislike to the

assertive Silver, Truman complied, declaring that he hoped the prisoners
"would soon be released." In July Truman reiterated there should be "no
delay in pushing forward with a policy of transferring 100,000 Jewish
immigrants to Palestine with all dispatch."[38]

Later that month, Zionist extremist groups, led by two-future Israeli
prime ministers, stepped up assassinations and attacks on British military,
police, and civilians. Irgun, led by the Polish émigré Menachem Begin,
worked with Lehi, which had revived under the Russian émigré Yitzhak
Shamir, in carrying out terror attacks against British targets. For a time the
Haganah collaborated with both groups. On July 22, 1946, Irgun took
out an entire wing of the King David Hotel in Jerusalem, headquarters of
the British general staff, killing 91 people in the terrorist bombing.
In 1947, after the British hanged three Irgun members, the Jewish group
killed two British soldiers and booby-trapped their bodies. Anti-Jewish
demonstrations erupted across Britain, including five days of rioting in
Liverpool in which more than 300 Jewish properties were attacked.[39]

Amid the 1946 midterm elections, neither major US political party
could afford to ignore the thousands of letters and telegrams pouring
into the White House from schools, synagogues, and businesses, among
other sources, behind the admission of the 100,000 immigrants as well as
unfettered Jewish land purchases.[40] AZEC and the APC denounced the
Arabs, the British, and the DOS for their opposition to the Zionist agenda.
In continuing to summarily dismiss Arab concerns and objections,
Zionists advised Truman, "the so-called Arab Higher Executive
Committee," the leading organization of Palestinians, was "in no sense
a responsible body" and had "no support in Palestine." Senator Wagner
declared it was "high time that British leaders gave heed to the urgent
promptings of the President of the nation that helped to keep the British
people themselves from being exterminated."[41]

With the majority of American Jews concentrated in New York, the
Empire State congressional delegation lobbied Truman intensively.
The congressmen "were becoming impatient," explained Brooklyn Rep.
Emanuel Celler (D-NY), an emerging stalwart of the Israel lobby.
"Democrats and Republicans alike were apt to give out statements to
the newspapers that the Administration was refusing to see them on the
Palestine question," he warned Truman's aide Matthew Connelly.
Truman subsequently met with the group of 30 congressmen and moved
toward embracing their agenda. In addition to New York, Chicago was an
emerging center of lobby activism. Rep. A. J. Sabath (D-IL) called
Truman's attention to a gathering of 19 Illinois congressional

FIGURE 4 Rep. Emanuel "Manny" Celler (D-NY), shown speaking in 1944, served for decades as an influential stalwart of the Israel lobby in the US Congress. New York Post/Getty Images

representatives who after attending a speech by a rabbi expressed their "insistence" that the administration pressure the British to end their policy of "delay and procrastination" on admission of the Jewish migrants.[42]

The Zionist lobby benefited from key White House insiders, especially David K. Niles, a longtime New Dealer from Boston who served as Truman's adviser on Jewish and other minority affairs. The son of a Russian Orthodox Jew, Niles countered the "biased" DOS advice and urged Truman to throw his weight behind the Zionist cause. Niles "was one of the trump cards held by the Zionists," Henderson recalled:

From his desk in the White House he could observe all developments relating to Palestine that were taking place in the United States and inform and advise his Zionist contacts ... If the President would make a decision displeasing to the Zionists, he would tell them that the 'career people' in the State Department had misled the President.[43]

Niles lobbied from within the White House on behalf of the 100,000 Jewish migrants, noting his own "personal interest in this matter." He strove to tamp down Zionist criticism of Truman while emphasizing the president's moral as well as financial support for the cause. In July 1946 he assured Gov. Herbert Lehman (D-NY), "The President's personal sympathies have been very deeply aroused by the plight of European Jewry."[44]

Pulled in opposite directions by competing wings of advisers, Truman continued to receive a steady stream of security-motivated anti-Zionist advice from the DOS and the Pentagon. The Joint Chiefs of Staff (JCS) warned against alienating both the oil-rich Arabs and the loyal British ally while spiraling the Middle East into ever-deeper turmoil. Many national security elites wanted to stand firm in response to the Zionist lobby. "If we yield to the pressure of highly organized Zionist groups just now," Undersecretary of State Will Clayton warned Truman, "we shall merely be encouraging them to make fresh demands and to apply pressure in the future."[45]

Although he had opposed creation of a Jewish religious state, and grew increasingly resentful of the relentless pressure of the Zionist lobby, Truman continued to give ground. The pivotal moment came in an announcement marking the Yom Kippur Jewish holiday just a month before the elections. On the advice of financier Abraham Feinberg – a skilled Democratic fundraiser who would serve for decades as a pivotal figure in the Israel lobby – Truman implied his support for the partition of Palestine into separate Jewish and Arab states.[46] In an acknowledgment of the impact of the lobby, Truman explained that the "widespread attention in the United States, both in the press and public forums," had led him to the conclusion that partition "would command the support of public opinion in the United States."[47]

Connelly later recalled that Truman backed the Zionist cause for "humanitarian" reasons, but also because it "was good politics," particularly with an election bid looming in 1948. On a number of occasions Truman privately alluded to the clout of the Zionist lobby on the one side and the dearth of political pressure on the other side of the issue. "I raised the question with Mr. Truman," Connelly recalled, "'How many Arab votes are there in the United States? Where does the Democratic Party get its financing from?' And the answer was apparent."[48] Truman's action gratified his former business partner and close personal friend, Edward Jacobson, a Jew from Kansas City who emerged as an important intermediary between Truman and the Zionist lobby. "Harry, my people need help and I am appealing to you to help them," Jacobson wrote on the eve of the president's Yom Kippur announcement.[49]

While the Zionists notched a crucial victory, Truman's decision left Atlee "astonished" that his ally forged ahead, thus "refusing even a few hours grace to the Prime Minister of the country which has the actual responsibility for the government of Palestine in order that he might acquaint you with the actual situation and the probable results of your action. These may well include the frustration of the patient efforts to achieve a settlement and the loss of still more lives in Palestine." Foreign Minister Ernest Bevin had "begged" Truman not to go ahead with the decision to admit the 100,000, which "had set the whole thing back" in the effort to keep the lid on the volatile ethnic conflict and move toward a settlement in Palestine. The British Parliament erupted with cheers when Atlee publicly condemned the American decision.[50] Wise, however, lauded Truman's decision "to overcome the obduracy" of the British. The JA similarly expressed "our profoundest satisfaction" with the president's decision.[51]

Not surprisingly for a provincial politician little experienced in foreign affairs, Truman understood American politics and public opinion more profoundly than he grasped the deteriorating political situation in the Palestinian mandate. The president dismissed Palestinian, Arab, and British arguments that the influx of immigrants and creation of a Jewish state would lead to violent dispossession and open warfare. Showing little appreciation for the drives that fueled the Zionist settler movement, Truman declared in January 1947 that the Jewish leaders had "no intention of expelling now or at a later date the indigenous inhabitants of that country." In view of how much Jews suffered in the war, he found it "inconceivable that responsible Jewish groups or leaders could be contemplating acts of intolerance and aggression against Arabs in Palestine."[52]

THE PARTITION OF PALESTINE

Truman's decision to side with the Zionists proved decisive for the British, who concluded that especially absent American cooperation the mandate was a lost cause. In February 1947 Great Britain turned over the mandate to the UN, which created a special committee on Palestine (UNSCOP). As the UN General Assembly (UNGA) took up the issue of partition, the Zionists feared that US diplomats would sabotage the decision while the Arabs hoped for that very outcome.

Niles warned Truman about the influence of diplomats "widely regarded as unsympathetic to the Jewish viewpoint," advising it was "important that at least one of the advisers" to the American UN delegation be someone in whom "American Jewry have complete confidence." Finding "some merit" in Niles's political advice, Truman appointed General John Hilldring, a proponent of Jewish immigration to Palestine, to advise Secretary of State George Marshall.[53]

As UNSCOP took up the fate of Palestine, AZEC stepped up the intensity of its campaign to fend off opposition and generate support of partition. Truman later wrote in his memoirs that he never had "as much pressure and propaganda aimed at the White House as I had in this instance."[54] The White House was "inundated with thousands of letters urging it to adopt a patently pro-partition stance."[55] Kenen noted that the lobby had been "instrumental in helping the Jewish Agency for Palestine receive official recognition" at the UN special session. He mobilized AZEC "to get members of Congress alerted again to the Palestine problem." AZEC urged Jews all over the country to "call on their respective Congressmen or Senators." American Zionists claimed to represent "the overwhelming majority of US Jews," adding that the "ideological disputes" that had previously "divided the Jewish community ... are no longer in existence."[56] By this time the APC had reorganized as the American Christian Palestine Committee (ACPC), and embarked on "a massive public relations campaign on behalf of the Zionist cause."[57]

The subsequent UNSCOP recommendation to partition Palestine into separate Arab and Jewish states elated the Zionists, whose long struggle was culminating with international sanction of a Jewish homeland. "To say Jews are pleased with the report is an understatement," an American reporter observed. Future Israeli Prime Minister Golda Meir (known as Goldie Myerson at the time) called the UNSCOP recommendation a "very good report" with "two serious drawbacks" – the exclusion of Jerusalem and the western Galilee from the proposed Jewish State.[58] Born in 1898 in Kiev but educated in Milwaukee, where she became a schoolteacher, Meir anchored Zionist fundraising and public relations in the United States for her close ally Ben-Gurion and the JA.

On September 17, in a pivotal speech at the UN, Marshall signaled acceptance of the partition plan by stating that the United States placed "great weight" on the majority UNSCOP report. The outraged UN delegates from Iraq, Syria, Lebanon, Egypt, and Saudi Arabia viewed Marshall's statement as "an all-out declaration of American support" demonstrating that the United States "would make every effort and wield its influence in favor of a Zionist solution for the Palestine problem." The Iraqi foreign minister declared that Washington has succumbed to "Zionist pressure" and that as a result violent conflict was inevitable.[59]

In October the Arab Higher Committee (AHC) rejected partition, declared a general strike, and demanded the withdrawal of British troops and the establishment of "an Arab democratic state." Lebanese diplomat Charles Malik outlined a plan to settle the Palestine issue based on recognition of a new Arab state with a capital in Jerusalem, but one that would constitutionally guarantee "full cultural freedom to all ethnic groups" and establish "safeguards for the religious freedom of Judaism, Christianity and Islam." Saud wrote directly to Truman on October 26 to condemn US support for the creation of a Jewish state, an "unfriendly act" that would deliver "a deathblow to American interests in the Arab countries." Saud declared Arabs would never accept a Jewish state in Palestine and would destroy it by force if necessary.[60]

The Arabs, among others, denounced the UN partition vote as corrupt, citing zealous Zionist efforts to sway votes in New York. Joined by several members of Congress, Zionists proffered inducements to small and malleable states such as Costa Rica, Guatemala, Honduras, Liberia, and Ethiopia, as well as allies Greece and China. The Zionist UN representative filibustered to delay a vote on partition until the required two-thirds vote could be mustered. The United States persuaded its newly liberated colony, the Philippines, to reverse its position to come out in favor of partition. On November 29, the UNGA voted 33–13, with 10 abstentions (including Great Britain), to partition the former British mandate.[61]

Poised to realize their dream, the Zionists immediately embraced Resolution 181 while all 11 of the Arab states voted against the nonbinding resolution. Most Jews celebrated the partition, but Zionist extremists condemned it. Begin declared, "The partition of Palestine is illegal. It will never be recognized ... Jerusalem was and forever will be our capital. *Eretz Israel* will be restored to the people of Israel. All of it and forever."[62] Maximalist American Zionists led by Silver also coveted control of Jerusalem and feared the implications of a Palestinian state, but they concluded that gaining international recognition of the new Jewish state outweighed such concerns for the time being.

Jewish settlers owned only 11 percent of the land that the UNSCOP plan turned over to them. UNSCOP awarded the Zionists the most fertile land, while some 400 Palestinian villages would be subject to Jewish authority. Some of the UN member states naively assumed the two states would peacefully coexist; hence, actual distribution of land was not critical, but this was a complete misunderstanding of Zionist ambitions and the drives that inhered in settler colonization. Thus, as Walid Khaladi explains, Resolution 181 was "a hasty act of granting half of Palestine to an ideological movement that declared openly already in the 1930s its wish to de-Arabize Palestine."[63]

The pivotal role played by the United States in the UN partition of Palestine was not lost on either the Zionists or the Arabs. Citing Truman's "personal hand" and "unflagging efforts," the ZOA leadership heaped praise upon the president during a "gigantic" celebratory rally in New York City. Frank Goldman, president of B'nai B'rith, declared Truman "would go down in history" as a hero to Jews worldwide. Weizmann expressed his "profound sense of gratitude" directly to Truman.[64] The Arabs, on the other hand, blamed the United States for the "mutilation" of Palestine, which reflected "a forthright commitment to wield American effort and influence to bring about a pro-Zionist settlement of the problems."[65]

Decrying the growing clout of the Zionist lobby, DOS career diplomats charged that the United States had expediently caved in to domestic political pressures at the expense of sound international diplomacy. They argued that the pro-Zionist policies, culminating in partition, betrayed the British ally, alienated the Arab states, and created opportunities for the Soviet Union to exploit in fomenting communist expansion in the region. In other words, they advised, all-out support for Zionism undermined the containment policy, damaged national interests, and promoted global instability.

DOS diplomats recognized that increased Jewish immigration and partition would ignite an explosive ethnic conflict. Even the Zionist settlers who might achieve their aims in the short term ultimately would not realize long-term security in such a hostile environment. At the same time, the oil-rich Arabs would be alienated by pro-Zionist American policies, which would strengthen communists and Muslim extremists. Finally, the diplomats argued that Washington undermined its international reputation by sacrificing the policy of self-determination in not allowing Palestine to transition from British rule into an independent state, as neighboring colonized states such as Iraq, Lebanon, and Syria had done.

The DOS specialists recommended pivoting to the establishment of an international trusteeship under some combination of UN, US, and British supervision. Under the trusteeship proposal, the Jewish irregular armies and Palestinian fighters would be reined in by occupation forces until such time as Jews and Arabs could be persuaded to adopt economic and social policies creating a framework of long-term coexistence within a unitary state. They noted that the Balfour Declaration called for a "Jewish national home," but not specifically a Jewish "theocratic racial state," as Henderson put it.[66]

Contention between Truman and the DOS climaxed in the months between the UNSCOP call for partition in the fall of 1947 and the Declaration of Independence by the new nation of Israel in May 1948. Henderson declared that the British were being driven out of the Middle East, where they were needed to help contain communism, and unfairly "castigated before the whole world" for seeking a reasoned settlement of the conflict. The combination of a British withdrawal and partition would open the floodgates to "wide-scale violence" in Palestine. In the absence of US or international police forces in the wake of the British pullout, "I wonder if the President realizes," Henderson mused, "that the plan that we are supporting for Palestine leaves no force other than local law enforcement organizations ... which will not be able to cope" with the violent unrest.[67]

Henderson proved correct, as a full-scale war erupted in the former British mandate. In the first phase of the conflict in November and December 1947, the well-schooled Zionist forces crushed the poorly organized Palestinian irregulars. Unlike the Zionists, the Palestinians lacked arms and central command, and had nothing comparable to the Haganah, which had trained under the British for years. Both belligerents conducted assassinations, killed indiscriminately, and resorted to public bombings and other acts of terror. The death on the battlefield of Abd al-Qadir al-Husaini deprived the Palestinians of their most effective and inspirational resistance leader.

In January 1948, the second phase erupted when neighboring Arab states intervened in an effort to head off the creation of the Zionist state in Palestine. The Haganah rallied with the aid of the irregular forces and decisively defeated the Arab states. In marked contrast to the highly unified Zionists, Iraq, Syria, Lebanon, Egypt, Saudi Arabia, and Transjordan pursued their own self-interests in the conflict rather than uniting behind the Palestinian cause. "Every attempt at coordinated action failed as a result of inter-Arab rivalry," Gudrun Kramer points out. Although Transjordan entered into the war against the Zionists, King

Abdullah remained opposed to a Palestinian state, as it would be rooted in territory that he sought to annex. "The other Arab states were all too aware of King Abdullah's ambitions," Eugene Rogan notes, "and they dedicated more effort to contain Transjordan than to save Palestine."[68]

Wracked by disorganization, internal conflict, and competing motives, the fledgling Arab states were no match for the well-organized and highly motivated Zionists. The Arabs subsequently blamed one another for their defeat in Palestine, propagated myths of heroic struggle, and have kept the archives of the war largely under wraps ever since. At the time, however, their humiliation was keenly felt. Within three years of the end of the debacle in Palestine, the leaders of Egypt, Lebanon, and Jordan were assassinated.[69]

Despite persistent Zionist claims that Arabs were the aggressors, it was only after the collapse of Palestinian resistance that the neighboring states intervened. Only Syria and Egypt attacked inside the boundaries of the new state of Israel. The most intense fighting had been the result of Zionist expansion beyond the UN-mandated boundaries. The Zionists were the stronger military force and became the aggressors in the 1948 war. As a CIA analysis pointed out, the Zionists possessed more fighters and were better organized, armed, and equipped than their Arab adversaries.[70]

An Israeli myth growing out of the war held that the invading Arabs had ordered Palestinians to leave their homes to clear the field for battle. Israeli schoolbooks have long incorporated the "sheer fabrication" that Jewish authorities attempted to persuade the Palestinians to stay in their homes.[71] Decades later the release of archival evidence enabled "post-Zionist" historians to show that "the consensus in support of transfer among the Zionist leaders helped pave the way for the precipitation of the Palestinian exodus of 1948," as Benny Morris put it. "Similarly, far more of that exodus was triggered by explicit acts and orders of expulsion by Jewish/Israeli troops" than was previously acknowledged.[72]

The 1948 war provided the opportunity to achieve the long-established "Zionist goal of obtaining as much of Palestine as possible with as few Palestinians in it as feasible," Ilan Pappé points out. Over the course of several months in 1948, the Zionists drove out about half the population of Palestine and destroyed more than 500 villages.[73] At the apex of planning was Ben-Gurion, who in 1937 had flatly declared, "We must expel Arabs and take their places." As prime minister, Ben-Gurion held ultimate authority over security issues, but he was not alone in advocating a sweeping campaign of removing the Arab population from desired areas of the new Israel. "Nearly all the founding fathers of the Israeli state," Nur Masalha points out, "advocated transfer in one form or another."[74]

The Israelis stepped up the removal campaign to create more facts on the ground before the war could be brought to an end under the UN ceasefire. Moreover, the Zionists accelerated destruction of villages "with the specific aim of invalidating any discussion on the subject of refugees returning to their houses, since their houses would no longer be there." As Ben-Gurion told the Cabinet in June 1948, "We must prevent at all costs their return." Areas such as the Galilee, once almost exclusively Palestinian, were now occupied by Israelis. Jewish forces also took villages in southern Lebanon and summarily executed scores of their residents.[75]

Calling upon the new Jewish state to seize the moment, ebullient Zionists urged annexation of the West Bank of the Jordan River. Following a Cabinet debate, the proposal failed by a vote of 6–6. One of the major arguments against the annexation was the incorporation of too many Arabs within the Jewish state. Amid the war in 1948, Transjordan became the Hashemite Kingdom of Jordan through integration of the West Bank and absorption of half a million Palestinian refugees.[76]

ANTI-ZIONISM'S LAST STAND

The Zionist lobby played a pivotal role in fending off an effort by the national security bureaucracy to revive trusteeship as a solution to the problem in Palestine. As Zionist forces began to drive out Arabs and create a de facto Jewish state in Palestine, opposition spread throughout the national security bureaucracy in Washington. In January and February 1948, George F. Kennan, the progenitor of the anticommunist containment policy, declared that, as a result of partition, "US prestige in the Moslem world has suffered a severe blow and US strategic interests in the Mediterranean and the Near East have been severely prejudiced." Although certain to "encounter strong opposition from the Zionists," a trusteeship would "probably have the support of the Arab states and of world opinion in general," and in any case should be implemented.[77] The National Security Council (NSC) endorsed Kennan's recommendations, declaring that the United States should "alter its previous policy of support for partition and seek another solution to the problem." The Pentagon, however, sharply opposed sending US military forces, already stretched thin by the global containment policy, to bolster a trusteeship in the Near East.[78]

As clashes between Jews and Palestinians intensified, Truman wavered in his support of the partition plan. Marshall backed the DOS and the CIA, which declared that the partition plan "cannot be implemented" in the face of opposition from the British and the Arab world. Citing Zionists who were unhappy with the UN-mandated borders, the CIA assessment added that "even among the Jews there is dissatisfaction over the partition." The CIA report concluded that the "only course open to the UN is to reconsider the whole issue." On February 22, Truman wrote, "I approve in principle this basic position. I want to make it clear, however, that nothing should be presented ... that could be interpreted as a recession on our part from the position we took in the General Assembly."[79]

Diplomats saw an opening in Truman's tepid endorsement and, with a nod from Marshall, directed the US ambassador to the UN to announce American support for a trusteeship rather than the partition of Palestine. On March 25, though privately he was livid over the effort to abandon partition altogether, Truman declared, "Unfortunately, it has become clear that the partition plan cannot be carried out at this time by peaceful means." With "open warfare just over the horizon," Truman endorsed the trusteeship as an effort to check the "bloodshed descending upon the holy land." The president reiterated, however, that trusteeship was an interim step until the formal dissolution of the British mandate in May, whereupon there could be a return to the UN partition plan. The DOS proceeded to draw up an extensive trusteeship proposal.[80]

Arab leaders reiterated support for the creation of "one independent state for the whole of Palestine whose constitution would be based on democratic principles and which would include adequate safeguards for minorities and the safety to holy places." Henderson urged Truman to attempt to persuade American Zionists to do their "utmost to prevail upon the Jews in Palestine to adopt a reasonable and conciliatory attitude." Diplomat Dean Rusk warned that "extremists like Dr. Silver" constituted a "formidable war party that complicated our task considerably." The UN called for an immediate ceasefire, which Rusk urged Truman to support even though it was likely "that the Arabs would accept the truce and that the Jews would not," which might "create problems" for the president.[81]

The Zionist lobby erupted in opposition to the trusteeship, condemning Truman for the "reversal of the American position regarding the partition of Palestine." American Zionists demanded that Truman reassert his support for partition and furthermore "lift the arms embargo" that had been instituted in an effort to contain violence in the region and come to the aid of the Jews against "the ever-increasing onslaughts from Arab marauders." Denouncing trusteeship as a "leap into the unknown," Weizmann insisted the Jews were at "risk of extermination," yet the United States would "not even grant them the arms to provide for their own defense."[82] Describing "the reversal on Palestine" as "a great shock to the American people," the ACPC claimed that about two-thirds of editorial comment in the US press was "adverse" to the shift to trusteeship.[83] Eleanor Roosevelt, a confirmed Zionist, publicly backed partition and called for the Jews to be "equipped with modern armaments" to defeat the Arab opposition in Palestine. The debate over the arms embargo precipitated more conflict among Truman's advisers, as Marshall and Henderson sought to maintain the freeze while pro-Zionist advisers, including Niles, Connelly, and Clark Clifford, called for ending the embargo.[84]

Working through Niles and other aides, as well as appealing directly to Truman, the Zionists told the president that DOS diplomats were undermining "your policy on Palestine." Liberals such as the longtime editor of the *Nation*, Freda Kirchwey, a staunch Zionist, told Truman it was apparent "with respect to the Palestine question the desire of the Near Eastern Division of the State Department to defeat your policy on this question and to make as its own the vicious policy of Foreign Minister Bevin of Great Britain." The criticism revived Truman's congenital suspicions of the "striped pants boys" and "tea hounds" in the DOS, long perceived as a bastion of northeast Protestant elitism. After the Zionist lobby subjected Henderson to what diplomats called "a new smear campaign," Truman reassigned the Near East division director as ambassador to India, thus removing a key anti-Zionist from the debate over Palestine.[85]

While ultimately accommodating the Zionist position, Truman at the same time resented their intrusions and viewed them as responsible for much of the unrest in the region. "We could have settled this Palestine thing if US politics had been kept out of it," he told Niles. The president blamed Jewish "terror and Silver" for exacerbating the Palestine conflict. "The Jews in this country," like "the Irish and the Latin-Americans," were "very emotional," Truman declared, which created problems that were then compounded by "the equally emotional Arabs." Truman claimed, "Nobody in the country has given the problem more time and thought than I have," adding that his "soul [*sic*] objective in the Palestine procedure has been to prevent bloodshed [but] we apparently have not been very successful."[86]

The Zionist lobby descended on Truman from myriad directions in opposition to the trusteeship proposal, but it was the combination of his

FIGURE 5 Freda Kirchwey, pictured here in 1944, was editor and publisher of *The Nation* from 1937 to 1955. Under her leadership, the influential liberal magazine was an ardent supporter of the Zionist movement and the new nation of Israel.
Constantin Joffe/Conde Nast Collection/Getty Images

old friend Jacobson and his increasingly close relationship with Weizmann that ultimately prompted Truman to act decisively on behalf of the new Israel. Truman later came to treasure his relationship with Weizmann, whose gentle temperament he contrasted favorably to Silver's abrasive personality. Described as an "irresistible political seducer" by his friend Isaiah Berlin, Weizmann charmed Truman. The president considered Weizmann "one of the wisest people I ever met." In the midst of the debate over the trusteeship, however, Truman initially put off

Weizmann's request for a meeting. Weizmann, who like other Zionists had begun to cultivate Jacobson for his access to the president, appealed to Truman's close friend to intervene. Jacobson responded, writing Truman, "Mr. President I have asked you for very little in the way of favors during all of our years of friendship, but I am begging of you to see Dr. Weizmann as soon as possible." He was "very old and heartbroken that he could not get to see you." Truman replied that the Palestine imbroglio "has been a headache to me for two and a half years," but he acceded to Jacobson's request for a meeting. On March 18, after Weizmann and Jacobson entered the White House secretly through the East gate, the three men held a "long, long conversation." By the time it was over Truman had essentially agreed to revert to partition and ultimately to recognize the new Jewish state. "You two Jews have put it over on me," he jocularly told them as they left the Oval Office. Left unaware of his decision were the DOS and the national security bureaucracy.[87]

In early March, Clifford – Truman's chief counsel, fellow Missourian, and cultivator of Jewish political support – denounced the shift to trusteeship. With the nation having originally embraced partition, "it was unthinkable that it should fail to back up that decision in every possible way." Clifford claimed partition "unquestionably offers the best hope of a permanent solution of the Palestine problem that may avoid war," but in fact war was already raging over the attempt to create a Jewish state. Clifford was on stronger ground with his claim that the opposition was being led by "those who never wanted partition to succeed, and who have been determined to sabotage it." Clifford dismissed as handwringing the oft-expressed concerns about a shutoff of access to Arab oil, declaring they would continue to sell the crude because "the Arab states must have oil royalties or go broke." Concluding with an Orientalist flourish, Clifford declared that the United States should not put itself in the "ridiculous role of trembling before the threats of a few nomadic desert tribes."[88]

At the decisive policy meeting in Washington on May 12, Clifford and Marshall grew "enraged" with one another. Marshall bluntly told Truman that Clifford was "wrong" and that support for partition and recognition of Israel were "based on domestic political considerations, while the problem which confronted us was international."[89] On May 14, the Israelis, having been assured by Clifford that Truman would proffer recognition, declared independence in the midst of a successful campaign to drive out the Palestinian Arabs. Within minutes of the Israeli declaration, Truman announced de facto US recognition of the new state of Israel.

The "reversal of US policy from truce plus trusteeship" to all-out support for the new Israel "deeply undermined confidence of other delegations in our integrity," UN Ambassador Warren Austin reported. Bevin denounced US policy as, "Let there be an Israel and to hell with the consequences!"[90]

A combination of factors lay behind the decisive American tilt toward Zionism: residual guilt over lack of response to the Nazi genocide; empathy for the Jewish refugees, and Orientalist perceptions of the Arabs whereas the European Jews were viewed as forces of modernity and settler progress; and not least the growing clout of the Israel lobby in an election year all lay behind Truman's decision. Clifford noted that Truman had been "under unbearable pressure to recognize the Jewish state promptly."[91] Much to the delight of the lobby, Truman named the dedicated Zionist McDonald as the first US diplomatic representative to Israel. Neither a diplomat nor a member of the wealthy elite, McDonald met none of the usual criteria for an ambassadorship, but he had the full support of Zionists who had funded him during the interwar period when he had worked in support of Jewish relief and immigration to Palestine. "There just could not have been a better choice," Kenen declared.[92]

Religious motives spurred the growing American support for Israel. Truman himself, like millions of Americans, was a devout Christian, a lifelong Baptist, and intimately familiar with biblical stories. The president claimed to have read the Bible "at least a dozen times" before age 15.[93] In going against Israel, Truman seems to have decided, he would be going against God. "Truman's biblical background at least predisposed him to favor prompt recognition," Irvine Anderson notes.[94]

Millions of Americans – "the most religious people in the developed world" – manifested the same "cultural disposition" to embrace the Bible as the word of God and the anchor of their support for the new state of Israel. Since the late nineteenth century, fundamentalists reacting to the theory of evolution had insisted that the Bible was the literal word of God. Millions of Americans learned the same lesson as a result of the Sunday School movement. Dispensational premillennial theology, which views the return of the Jews to the Promised Land as a prelude to the return of Christ and the beginning of New Times, had long been "deeply imbedded in American conservative religious circles." A Gallup Poll taken in 1945 found that 76 percent of Americans favored, and only 7 percent opposed, allowing the Jews to settle in Palestine.[95]

As in the Balfour Declaration, the Zionists had received decisive support from the world's leading power. The Arabs, by contrast, lacked powerful allies. Although he had expressed frequent frustration with the Zionist lobby, Truman called his announcement making the United States the first nation in the world to offer de facto recognition "one of the proudest moments of my life." In his view, the "long friendship of the American people for the Zionist ideal" made it "particularly appropriate that our Government should be the first to recognize the new State."[96] As the violence escalated in Palestine, the Israelis counted on the newly consummated special relationship, bolstered by the Israel lobby, to anchor a new and expanded Jewish homeland.

2

"New Forms of Propaganda Had to Be Found"

The Israeli War of Independence coincided with the 1948 presidential campaign, thus presenting the Zionist lobby with an extended opportunity to assert its influence within the American political process. Israel and its US backers lobbied to fend off international efforts to forge a ceasefire before their war aims could be achieved. The top priority for Israeli foreign policy, in growing collaboration with American Zionists, was to ward off efforts to force Israel to disgorge territory and allow for the return of Palestinian refugees. In addition to expanded borders, they also sought – and secured – de jure recognition, loans, and military assistance.[1]

Military domination on the ground, combined with increasingly powerful political support within the United States, enabled the Israelis to stymie UN mediation efforts led by Count Folke Bernadotte. The United States formally backed UN mediation, but within weeks the Swedish diplomat declared he was "very disappointed and discouraged" by the lack of US and UN forces to facilitate his efforts to forge a ceasefire and a settlement of the Palestine conflict.[2] In early June, the Israelis formally accepted a four-week ceasefire, but weeks later the CIA reported they were "greatly increasing their military potential under the cloak of a truce." The ascension to brigade commander of Moshe Dayan, known for his aggression, was a sign that the Israelis had little interest in compromise with an Arab opposition that they dominated on the ground. According to the CIA, Israeli military forces numbered some 97,800, compared to 46,800 Arabs under arms in and around Palestine.[3]

In August, Bernadotte declared he was "making progress" in talks with the Arabs, noting that he believed Transjordan, Lebanon, and possibly other states would acquiesce to the de facto if not the de jure recognition of Israel. He emphasized, however, that Israel first had to enforce the ceasefire and stop the ongoing campaign of driving Palestinians from their homes. Already, the UN diplomat explained, the "condition of 300,000 to 400,000 Arab refugees without food, clothing and shelter was appalling." The scenes of the elderly, pregnant women, small children, and other vulnerable people facing life-or-death situations after being driven from their homes clearly disturbed the UN mediator. While Bernadotte insisted that the removal campaign must be halted and Palestinian civilians allowed return to their homes, the new Israeli government was adamantly opposed to this.[4]

AZEC lobbied the two main political parties in opposition to the Bernadotte Plan and in favor of the expanded borders for the Jewish state. Having achieved a breakthrough in the 1944 presidential and congressional campaigns, Kenen spearheaded efforts to assert Zionist influence in the 1948 canvass. The Zionist lobby fully backed Israel as it sought to incorporate the Galilee, the Gulf of Aqaba, the Negev Desert, and Jerusalem. Effectively lobbied by AZEC, the Democratic Party platform declared that border modifications "should be made only if fully acceptable to the State of Israel." AZEC pursued "modifications" as a lobbying theme in an effort to secure the expanded borders and to oppose Bernadotte's proposed territorial compromise. The Republican platform was less specific on border modifications but condemned the Democrats for "vacillation," whereas the GOP had been "the first to call for the establishment" of the "Jewish Commonwealth" for which it promised "full recognition."[5]

While the lobby exerted its influence on both political parties, Bernadotte insisted Israel was attempting to exercise the "right of conquest" and "proving completely intractable" to his peace efforts. The Israelis, the UN mediator bluntly declared, were "showing signs of a swelled-head" in the wake of their ringing victory. US observers assigned to the UN were likewise "unanimous in disgust at Jewish actions" breaking the ceasefire that Arabs were attempting to observe.[6] A US general monitoring the military situation reported that it had become "routine" for the Zionists, who were "now far superior to all other forces combined," to commit "willful and premeditated violations of the truce." In mid-August Marshall advised Truman of "the apparent tendency of the Provisional Government of Israel to assume a more aggressive attitude in Palestine."[7] Marshall called attention to "strong if not violent Jewish demands," citing truce violations, expansive territorial claims including Jerusalem, "inflammatory speeches," and "evidence of hostility of Israelis in Palestine toward the military observers serving under Count Bernadotte."[8]

FIGURE 6 Count Folke Bernadotte of Sweden, shown here arriving in Rome on July 10, 1948, was given the thankless and ultimately fatal task of mediating the Palestine conflict under UN auspices. On September 17, 1948, the Israeli terror group Lehi, headed by future Israeli Prime Minister Yitzhak Shamir, assassinated the UN mediator at a roadblock in Jerusalem.
Hulton Deutsch/Corbis Historical/Getty Images

On September 16, Bernadotte proposed a peace plan based on formal Arab recognition of the State of Israel, negotiation of final boundaries, respect for all faiths and international authority over Jerusalem, and the right of return and otherwise meeting the humanitarian needs of the Palestinian refugees. The Arabs continued to balk at formal recognition of the Zionist state, which Ben-Gurion cited as justification for his refusal to enforce the ceasefire.[9] Israel adamantly opposed return of the refugees and rejected Bernadotte's proposed compromise on borders. As for Jerusalem, Ben-Gurion declared that the city "meant more to Jews than Paris to the French or London to the British."[10]

On September 17, as Bernadotte returned to Jerusalem to promote the peace plan, his UN-flagged convey was stopped at a roadblock at which time Lehi assassins shot him to death.[11] From the outset Bernadotte had called attention to the inability to control extremists and the lack of security for his mission. One of three men within the faction of Lehi that ordered Bernadotte's assassination was the future Israeli prime minister, Yitzhak Shamir. The Israeli government condemned the assassination, but no one was ever brought to justice for the murder of the UN mediator.[12]

Marshall and the DOS argued that Bernadotte's killing offered "a rare opportunity for settling this dispute if acted on decisively and promptly," but Truman, under strong pressure from AZEC amid the presidential campaign, rejected the advice. On September 28, journalist and ardent Zionist Bartley Crum complained to Clifford that Marshall "approved the Bernadotte Plan without prior approval of the President," adding in a reference to the presidential campaign, "Marshall is doing the President more harm than anything I can think of." The following day, as the campaign against New York Gov. Thomas Dewey entered the home stretch, Truman reminded Marshall of the Democratic Party Platform provision endorsing border modifications favorable to Israel.[13]

American Zionists took out full-page advertisements, launched a letter-writing campaign, and lobbied through Niles, Jacobson and other "friends in Government circles" to preclude Truman's support for the martyred mediator's UN peace plan, which Dewey and the Republicans also condemned. Silver worked to "mobilize our people all over the country" to support the expanded borders of the new Israel. "The pressure from the Jewish groups on the President was mounting," noted Clifford, who drew up plans for de jure US recognition of Israel, admission into the UN, as well as loans and assistance. Israel remained aggressive, using a pretext to launch an offensive that captured Beersheba, thus solidifying takeover of the northern Negev. On October 21, the Israelis accepted the UN ceasefire but rejected provisions calling for their return to the October 15 borders.[14]

Blaming the "boys at the State Department" for pressuring Israel to relinquish seized territory, Foreign Minister Moshe Sharett called for "recruiting everybody we've got" for "an all-out effort" to lobby the administration. Weizmann continued to work through Jacobson, telling Truman's former business partner, "I should be very happy if you could keep me informed about any further developments at your end." Weizmann urged Jacobson, who "made numerous trips to Washington" to meet with Truman "completely off the record," to tell "your friend" to oppose any plan that would "cut off Israel from the Negev." The DOS urged support for a UNSC resolution that would have required Israel to give up the Negev but Truman, as Peter Hahn notes, "caved in under pressure from Israel and its domestic supporters." Truman subsequently told Weizmann he "deplored any attempt to take away" the Negev and, moreover, would "oppose any territorial changes" that were "not acceptable to Israel."[15]

In December, the Truman administration sided with Israel and AZEC by rejecting a UN resolution affirming the Bernadotte Plan. Elated by the failure of the UN peace plan, the Israelis launched a new offensive on the southern Negev, crossed into Egypt, and shot down five British aircraft as they reconnoitered the battlefield. Britain threatened military retaliation and Truman privately branded Israel a "troublemaker, endangering the peace by flouting the UN." Shortly after the dawn of the new year, the Israelis pulled back and accepted the UN ceasefire. In the first half of 1949 Israel concluded bilateral armistice agreements with Egypt, Lebanon, Transjordan, and Syria, bringing an end to the first Arab–Israeli war.[16]

By the time of the ceasefire in January 1949, Israel had increased in size from 55 percent under the UN partition to take possession of 77 percent of the former British mandate. With some 750,000 Palestinians driven out, a census conducted in November 1948 counted 782,000 Jews to 69,000 remaining Palestinians within the borders of the new Israel. More than 6,000 Zionists and many more thousands of Arabs (the number is unknown) died in the conflict.[17]

The War of 1948 was an intensely emotional triumph for the Zionists, particularly in view of the long global history of anti-Semitism culminating in the Nazi genocide. For the Palestinians, by contrast, the *Nakba* was a catastrophic event against which they would struggle interminably.[18] Within the United States, the well-publicized scope of the Nazi genocide underscored Jewish victimization and left little cultural space available to perceive Zionists as aggressors or to view Palestinians as victims. Opinion polls showed that while most Americans were unaware of or indifferent in regard to the Palestine conflict, more than twice as many (28 percent to 11 percent) sympathized with the Zionists over the Arabs.[19]

Under the Declaration of Independence proclaimed by Ben-Gurion on May 14, citizens received full social and political equality with no distinction based on religion, race, or gender. Israel pledged to uphold the UN Charter, and specifically the equal rights of Arab inhabitants. While Israel began to trumpet its status as "the only democracy in the Middle East," the Palestinian residents of the Jewish state in actuality would live in a condition of marginality and inequality.[20] Ben-Gurion dominated the new state as the prime minister while the more moderate Weizmann assumed the presidency. The Haganah transitioned into the IDF, which became the most powerful institution in Israeli society.

In the wake of Israel's military triumph, an "ardent group of Zionists" lobbied for de jure recognition. A month before the presidential election Crum declared it was "imperative that the President speak out" on de jure recognition as well as an Israeli request for a loan, or Dewey would "beat him to it."[21] Working closely with Niles, American Zionists circulated to "members of Congress, editors, commentators, etc." a document pressing for de jure recognition. Truman pledged to proffer formal recognition following elections in Israel. On January 31, 1949, he did so, presenting as symbolic gifts pens from the signing ceremony to Niles and Feinberg.[22] A wealthy Democratic fundraiser and architect of the "whistle-stop" train tour of the country that spurred Truman's upset victory over Dewey in 1948, Feinberg had been under FBI investigation for evasion of the World War II draft as well as his orchestration of illegal weapons smuggling as director of "Americans for the Haganah."[23]

In January, under intense pressure from Israel and its American supporters, Truman granted Israel assistance totaling $100 million. When US diplomats opposed the loan in the midst of the removal campaign against the Palestinians, Truman responded that "a flat turndown" was untenable, as it would have "all sorts of implications."[24] Truman was being pressured by the new Israeli representative in the United States, Eliahu Epstein (later Hebraized to Eliahu Elath), who complained, "Repeatedly we have been put off on this matter ... the quota of empty words which we have received in this delaying action must set some kind of record." Jacobson again beseeched Truman at Weizmann's request and subsequently advised the Israeli patriarch that, after a "lengthy discussion," Truman had decided to make the loan.[25]

The lobbying effort helped to ensure that financial assistance was not tied to Israeli cooperation with ongoing international efforts to forge a formal peace accord. Contrary to orthodox accounts emphasizing implacable hostility to the Jewish state, the Arabs put out peace feelers

FIGURE 7 Democratic Party strategist, fundraiser, and longtime Zionist activist Abraham L. Feinberg, pictured here in 1943, became a focal point of FBI investigations into Zionist activities. Feinberg weathered the probes and played a crucial, mostly behind the scenes role in the growth of the lobby and especially in aligning the Democratic Party with Israel.
Toronto Star/Getty Images

following the military debacle. "After the sobering experience of military defeat at the hands of the infant Jewish state," Avi Shlaim points out, the leaders of the Arab states were, "prepared to recognize Israel, to negotiate directly with it and even to make peace with it. Each of these rulers had his territorial price for making peace with Israel but none of them refused to talk."[26]

Negotiations with Egypt, Jordan, and Syria after the armistice agreements thus might have offered the possibility of a full-blown peace settlement, but the Israelis were "in no mood to make territorial or any other substantial concessions."[27] Ben-Gurion eschewed negotiations with foes that he viewed as implacable and Nazi-like. "Israel has stiffened rather than modified her position," diplomat William Burdett noted. The armistice talks had "emphasized Arab weakness." Israel "gave at no point and the Arabs gave at every point where concession was necessary. Israel intends to exploit that weakness to the maximum."[28]

In 1950, as Transjordan formally absorbed the West Bank of the Jordan River and abbreviated its name to Jordan, all that remained in Arab hands of the former Palestine mandate was the Gaza Strip, a nominally self-governing territory under Egyptian trusteeship, and the West Bank including East Jerusalem. That same year the Knesset passed the Absentee Property Law, "the key piece of legislation in the de-Arabization of Israel." The law precluded refugees from returning to their property and broadened authority to seize designated areas for "security" reasons.[29]

With Israel dispossessing the former residents and controlling more than three-fourths of the former mandate, and Jordan absorbing the West Bank, little space remained on the map for the realization of Palestinian national ambitions. Instead hundreds of thousands of refugees who had been driven out during the war were dispersed into primitive camps in Lebanon, Syria, Jordan, Egypt, the West Bank, and Gaza.

Following rejection of the Bernadotte Plan, it fell to the Palestine Conciliation Commission (PCC), created under UN Resolution 194 on December 11, 1948, to seek "a final settlement of all issues outstanding" between the Arabs and the Jews. These included agreement on borders, demilitarization, and establishment of a "permanent international regime for the Jerusalem area." Resolution 194 also declared, "Refugees wishing to return to their homes and live in peace with their neighbors should be permitted to do so at the earliest practicable date and compensation should be paid for the property of those choosing not to return."[30] The DOS offered full support of the PCC agenda but remained blinkered on the creation of a Palestinian state in deference to Abdullah's plans to absorb the West Bank into Jordan.[31]

DONNING ISRAEL'S ARMOR

The end of the election season undercut the leverage that Israel and American Zionists could bring to bear, heightening the perceived need for a more permanent and structured lobby. Absent an aggressive and effective lobbying effort, Israel might be forced into accepting the UN proposals on borders, Jerusalem, and repatriation of refugees, all of which Zionists adamantly opposed. By March 1949, a month prior to the first formal conference of the PCC, the Truman administration had grown "disturbed over the uncooperative attitude being taken" by the Israelis. The US representative on the PCC, Mark Ethridge, a newspaper publisher from Louisville, quickly perceived that "without pressure placed by the United States on Israel there can be no good result from the work" of the UN commission.[32]

Israeli leaders and American Zionists mobilized a hasbara campaign to ward off efforts by the DOS, the Truman administration, and the PCC to compel a compromise agreement with the Arabs over borders, refugees, and the status of Jerusalem. Clearly, the most important locus for hasbara activities was the United States, the sole country that could make or break Israel's existence as a viable nation state. Despite their dependence on the Americans, Ben-Gurion and his colleagues were determined to assert control over Israeli foreign policy, including hasbara activities. Prominent Diaspora Jews such as Silver and the myriad Jewish organizations, accustomed to playing a central role in the Zionist movement, would have to learn to defer to the Israelis.[33] This transition created a great deal of tension and jockeying, but in the end a new Israel lobby replaced the "old" Zionist lobby, which had coalesced at the Biltmore Conference in 1942.

While the Truman administration and the PCC attempted to persuade Israel to accommodate a settlement, the Israeli diplomat Abba Eban labored to unite a fragmented American Diaspora and synchronize it with Israel's determined effort to stymie the UN negotiations. A child of Lithuanian parents but educated from a young age in Great Britain, Eban was an erudite scholar-diplomat ideally suited to coordinate the transition in relations between the new Israel and the American Jewish Diaspora. Eban, who had anchored the JA delegation in New York in brokering the partition of Palestine, intuitively grasped that mobilization of the American Diaspora could prove decisive in achieving Israel's diplomatic goals.[34]

In August 1949, Eban hosted a meeting at the Israeli consulate in New York with leaders of various American Jewish organizations. The purpose of the meeting, as Natan Aridan points out, was to emphasize "expectations of American Jews in influencing US policy and securing support for Israel." At the briefing, Eban emphasized that the PCC

FIGURE 8 Louis Lipsky, a veteran Zionist from Rochester, was a key architect of the early Israel lobby. "American Zionist political support," he declared in 1951, provided the "armor Israel cannot get along without."
Jerry Cooke/Getty Images

proposals would undermine Israel and the lives of Jewish people across the globe and should therefore be resisted at all costs.[35]

Eban found a key ally in Louis Lipsky, a veteran American Zionist from Rochester. Together with Kenen, these three men laid the foundation for the powerful national lobby that arose in the wake of Israeli independence. Sharing Eban's emphasis on the crucial role of the Diaspora Jews, Lipsky declared, "American Zionist political support" could provide the "armor Israel cannot get along without."[36] In his memoirs, Kenen wrote that the Israel lobby "owes a debt to Lipsky," whose vision paved the way for its ultimate success.[37]

Experienced in Washington since 1922, when he testified in Congress in support of the Balfour Declaration, Lipsky recognized that in the wake of the creation of Israel "new forms of propaganda had to be found."[38] Brandeis, Frankfurter, Silver, Wise, and other prominent Jews had generated vital support for creation of the Zionist state, but the time for the "great man" approach to American Zionism had passed. Now that Israel existed, a more methodical and persistent lobbying effort was required.

While the new state of Israel had to conduct foreign policy directly with the DOS, Lipsky emphasized that a dedicated domestic lobby could influence diplomatic relations by generating popular support and promoting financial assistance for the Zionist state. The Israel lobby in the United States thus could bypass the DOS in a continuous campaign to put pressure on the president and Congress to meet Israel's military and financial needs while staving off challenges to its foreign policies. Moreover, there would be no legal requirement to register as a foreign agent, as the organization would be American.

Displacing Silver, Lipsky became chairman of a new organization, the American Zionist Council (AZC), which replaced AZEC in 1949. AZC attempted to establish itself as an umbrella organization uniting the American Diaspora for the specific purpose of lobbying on behalf of Israel. In June, AZC announced that a four-member "presidium" of representatives from the ZOA, *Hadassah* (the Zionist women's organization), *Mizrachi* (a Zionist religious group), and the Zionist Labor Organization of America had replaced Silver, who was relegated to the role of "honorary chairman" of AZC. Over the ensuing months, AZC broadened its reach to represent a total of nine Jewish organizations.[39]

The effort to consolidate Diaspora support for Israeli policy encountered resistance from the AJC as well as the ACJ, the latter having opposed the creation of a Jewish state in the first place. While the ACJ became a pariah group, demonized and condemned by Zionists, the prestigious AJC, led by wealthy industrialist Jacob Blaustein, posed the greatest challenge to efforts to consolidate Diaspora support behind Israeli policies. Blaustein rejected the argument that American Jews should conform to a propaganda line set down in Tel Aviv, thus abjuring their rights to attempt to influence their government's foreign policy in ways they saw fit. Lipsky, who embraced the argument that within the Diaspora "the Zionist Organization exists for service to the State," condemned a "powerful minority" for forcing "the grave problems of American Jewry to be met by a fragmented, discordant community."[40]

Convinced that the American Diaspora was the key to "strengthen ties" and thereby get the United States "to grant Israel preferential treatment," Eban persisted over several months in the effort to close ranks within the American Jewish community. In November 1950 AZC assembled some 250 prominent American Zionists, but the meeting failed to produce accord on the central issue of the role of the Diaspora in relation to Israeli policies. At this point Eban, who had replaced Elath as ambassador to the United States in June 1950, suggested the creation of an advisory group that would convene on a regular basis for "utterly private and unofficial" consultations aimed at securing US support for Israel's security aims. The group included Lipsky, Niles, Feinberg, Blaustein, and representatives of several prominent Jewish organizations. In subsequent years the advisory group evolved into the Conference of Presidents of Major Jewish Organizations, which emerged as "one of Israel's most important accomplishments in cementing Diaspora cooperation."[41]

Pro-Israel propagandists faced pressure from the Truman administration on the issue of the Palestinian refugees. With the global cold war dominating national security policy, US officials advocated a viable resettlement plan for the displaced Palestinians out of concern that the "destitute, idle refugees" would make the area "highly vulnerable to Soviet exploitation."[42] The Israelis, however, had established a policy cornerstone that under no circumstances should the refugees be allowed to return to their homeland. Even though Israel supposedly accepted Resolution 194, including the return and/or compensation of refugees as a condition of its subsequent admission into the UN, Ben-Gurion and his colleagues never considered abiding by it.[43]

Striving for as much ethnic homogeneity as possible in the new settler state, Israel had flung open its doors to masses of Jewish immigrants, both Ashkenazi (Eastern European) and Sephardic (from Iberian and Middle Eastern countries). Israel sought to reinforce the minority status of Palestinians that remained within their boundaries through ongoing Jewish immigration, confiscation of property, and iron-fisted opposition to repatriation of refugees. Sharett, though decidedly more moderate than Ben-Gurion on other issues, was equally uncompromising on the refugee question. He bluntly told US diplomats it was "out of the question to consider the possibility of repatriation of any substantial number of the refugees." The quest to pressure the Israelis to compromise on the issue was further constricted, lamented a US diplomat, because the American public, while fully aware of the wartime assault on the Jews, was "generally unaware of the Palestine refugee problem."[44]

Meeting with Sharett in April, the new Secretary of State, Dean G. Acheson, explained that the "some 800,000" refugees "constitute[d] a serious political problem," adding that "a considerable number must be repatriated if a solution is to be found." Concerned about the Jewish state "impairing in any way its moral position" through diplomatic intransigence, Acheson advised that taking in possibly "a fourth" of the refugees would be "a statesmanlike move by Israel." Sharett responded by insisting that Acheson had inflated the number of refugees, which he put at closer to half a million; that the return of refugees "would disturb the homogeneity of Israeli areas"; and thus that "resettlement is the proper solution for refugees." Weeks later, Weizmann told Truman that the refugee problem was "not created by us" but rather by Arab aggression, a persistent propaganda theme of the new state. Affirming Orientalist perceptions of Arabs, Weizmann added, "These people are not refugees in the sense in which that term has been sanctified by the martyrdom of millions in Europe."[45]

Israel proved equally oppositional on proposed border settlements, as it ruled out giving up any territory seized beyond the partition lines. In the PCC negotiations, Israel added that it might rightfully lay claim to the Gaza Strip, which lay under Egyptian control. Sharett told Acheson that Israel "could not give up the minimum security which it had won with so much blood and expenditure." Weizmann reiterated the theme to Truman, declaring, "No fair-minded man will deny us the right to retain that part of our ancient land which has become ours at a terrible cost of blood and treasure in the course of a war forced upon us by others."[46]

From April to September 1949 the PCC met at Lausanne, Switzerland, but Israeli intransigence precluded a settlement. The PCC members – the United States, France, and Turkey – proved unable to move the Israelis toward compromise. In a personal letter to Truman, Ethridge – who had previously been assigned to assess postwar Soviet hegemony in Eastern Europe – declared, "This is by far the toughest assignment you have ever given to me." He explained, "The Jews are still too close to the blood of their war – and too close to the bitterness of their fight against the British mandate to exercise any degree of statesmanship yet." The traumatized Israelis thus acted on the precept "that their security lies in military might instead of in good relations with their neighbors." The Arabs, "shocked and stupefied by their defeat," and filled with "great bitterness toward the UN and the United States," nonetheless "have made what the

Commission considers very great concessions; the Jews have made none so far." Echoed the *New York Times*: "It seems to some observers that for the first time Israel is on the 'wrong' side of almost every point at issue in the eyes of world opinion, as expressed through the United Nations resolutions on Palestine."[47]

Israel blamed continuing Arab bellicosity for the diplomatic impasse, but US officials refuted the argument. Despite Israeli claims that they were under threat of renewed warfare, the "US Government does not believe the Arab states are preparing to resume conflict. Any public statement to the contrary is designed for internal consumption within the Arab states," and, moreover, could be "matched by corresponding Israeli public statements." On August 13, Truman told Weizmann that while he could appreciate Israel's security anxieties, "nevertheless, it seems reasonable to believe that the conclusion of armistice agreements with the neighboring Arab states should prove reassuring," especially with the UN and US standing behind them.[48]

At the end of May, a frustrated Truman informed the Israelis that the United States was "seriously disturbed by the attitude of Israel with respect to territorial settlement in Palestine," and notably "to the question of Palestinian refugees." If Israel refused to make a real effort to achieve a lasting peace, the "US Government will regretfully be forced to the conclusion that a revision of its attitude toward Israel has become unavoidable." The Israelis responded a little more than a week later, with Sharett again insisting the impasse was the fault of the hostile Arabs and refusing to budge on borders or refugees.[49] Ethridge complained of Israeli "press tactics," including leaking confidential information to undermine the PCC negotiations.[50]

By means of a formal "Aide-Memoire," the United States declared it was "regrettable that the Government of Israel did not respond more affirmatively with respect to the questions of Palestinian refugees and of boundaries." As solution of the refugee problem was "a common responsibility of Israel and the Arab states," Israel's obduracy on the issue was unacceptable. Moreover, "The United States Government could find no basis for a settlement" in the Israeli effort to "retain areas which it has occupied outside the 1947 partition lines, and to submit further demands as to territory in Arab Palestine." The war was over, the Americans declared, hence there was no place for "the renewal of hostilities or the threat of hostilities."[51]

Israel responded to US diplomatic pressure by openly declaring its intention to deploy the Israel lobby to go over the heads of the Truman administration. The Israelis "informed our representatives in Palestine that they intend to bring about a change in the position of the United States Government ... through the means available to them in the United States," Ethridge reported. The DOS responded to Israeli intransigence and the threat to unleash the lobby by urging the administration to make a "basic decision concerning our attitude toward Israel." If Israel would compromise, a Middle East peace could be achieved; hence, Washington should withhold economic assistance to force Israel to come around, though clearly such action would "arouse strong opposition in American Jewish circles."[52]

Declaring that US policy masked "nefarious designs behind the appearance of principle," the Zionist lobby charged that the DOS diplomats were seeking "revenge for the past failures of their Palestine policy." Speaking for the coalition of American Zionist groups who were in the midst of merging into AZC, Hyman Schulson told Niles, "Recent developments in Washington and Lausanne indicate that tendencies hostile to Israel have once more gained the upper hand" and "permeate the entire operating staff" of the DOS. Schulson accused Ethridge of attempting to "create a concerted Arab front opposed to Israel." The situation called for "drastic intervention by the President." Feinberg urged the removal of Ethridge from the PCC and accused diplomat George Wadsworth of "making unsolicited anti-Semitic remarks in many social meetings with various Arab representatives." Feinberg offered no examples or substantiation to back up the charge.[53]

Already "disgusted" by Israel's diplomatic intransigence over the border and refugee issues, Truman was livid over the deployment of the lobby to go over his head, which he viewed as a betrayal in view of his decisive support for the Zionist state. Truman responded by suspending the remaining $49 million of the $100 million Export-Import loan, as the dispute "shook US-Israeli relations to the core." However, as a result of stepped-up pressure from the lobby, Truman's anger proved short lived. Bowing to telephone calls, telegrams, and public criticism, the president restored the funding and the administration gave up on attempting to force the Israelis into making a settlement or accommodating return of Palestinian refugees. Instead, their fate would be turned over to the United Nations Relief and Works Agency for Palestine (UNRWA). "President Truman is still our staunch friend," a reassured Weizmann told Jacobson."[54]

As a result of the Israeli "take it or leave it" attitude, Acheson concluded "no real basis for conciliation appears possible at Lausanne." As the PCC conference, like so many diplomatic initiatives that would follow, collapsed in failure, postmortem analysis reflected a common theme. "If there is to be any assessment of blame for stalemate at Lausanne," Ethridge declared, "Israel must accept primary responsibility." As international efforts to forge a settlement proved feckless, the Israelis chalked up "more and more *faits accomplis* [that] cannot be changed," Britain's Bevin declared. "This has happened in the matters of Jerusalem boundaries and in territories."[55]

COVETING THE HOLY CITY

No issue incited more indignation from Israel and the lobby than efforts to mediate the status of Jerusalem. Under the UN partition resolution the JA had accepted the provision that Jerusalem would fall under an international regime. Nonetheless, Israel now sought to declare Jerusalem the "eternal capital" of the new Jewish state in direct violation of the partition resolution, as well as of UN Resolution 194, which had called for a "permanent international regime for the Jerusalem area." Referencing the biblical narrative of ancient Israel, Ben-Gurion declared the issue had been settled "3,000 years ago." Weizmann added, "Jerusalem has been our capital since the days of David and Solomon."[56]

The palpable Israeli desire to exercise unilateral authority over Jerusalem inflamed Roman Catholics as well as Muslims. Francis Cardinal Spellman, the Catholic archbishop of New York, sought Truman's "assurance" that international control would be established in order to safeguard the "Christian holy places" in Jerusalem. Condemning at the same time Israel's indifference to the plight of the Arab refugees, Spellman urged Truman to take a strong position in order to convey "the reaction of the Christian peoples of the world against the 'fait accompli' policies of Israel." Acheson advised Truman, "The Vatican has consistently advocated a stronger type of internationalization," prompting the president to assure Spellman of his support. In September 1949, the DOS affirmed US backing of Resolution 194 on the international status of Jerusalem.[57]

From New York, Eban and the AZC lobbied to ward off the internationalization of Jerusalem. In the midst of his campaign to forge a united front among American Diaspora Jews, Eban urged them to "enlighten" the Truman administration on the Jerusalem issue and to oppose efforts to internationalize the city.[58] On December 5, 1949, Ben-Gurion declared that Jewish-occupied portions of Jerusalem were now part of Israel. As the "impassioned" Israeli prime minister told the US ambassador in Tel Aviv, "Christianity still cannot accept nor tolerate the fact that the Jewish state now exists and that its traditional capital is Jerusalem." He guaranteed that Israel would safeguard "places sacred to all mankind," while vowing that "It would take an army to get the Jews out of Jerusalem."[59]

The UNGA reaffirmed the call to designate Jerusalem as a *corpus separatum* in accordance with the 1947 partition, but the United States voted against it. Truman directed Acheson to "take sides with the Israeli Delegation against the Arabs" in the UN. Resolution 303 was passed by the UNGA 38–14 with seven abstentions. Catholic nations and all of the Arab states except Jordan voted in favor of an international trusteeship overseeing the holy city, as did the Soviet Union and its allies. Great Britain joined Washington in voting against Resolution 303. Both nations cited the opposition of Israel and Jordan, the two countries that occupied the city. Contemptuous of the UN, Ben-Gurion responded within days by moving his office into the city.[60]

Although still officially opposed to establishment of the capital in Jerusalem, the United States had sided with Israel and the lobby against the majority of world opinion, a precedent that would play out repeatedly in the ensuing decades. Calling the UN resolution a "nightmare," Eban expressed his gratitude for "the harmony that had existed between the Israeli delegation and the US delegation in the assembly concerning the Jerusalem question."[61]

While fending off US pressure over borders and Jerusalem, Israel and its US backers mounted "a sweeping public relations campaign" to get military assistance from the Americans while denying the same to the Arab states. The campaign succeeded, as Truman overruled the Pentagon and the NSC, both of which had advised against military aid. They argued that Israel already had "the preponderance of striking power" in the region, hence the United States should not "increase Israel's offensive capabilities and give incentive to offensive planning." Once again deferring to the "many active sympathizers with Israel in this country," Truman chose to "arm the Jews appropriately." Bowing to the inevitable, the DOS devised the Tripartite Plan, under which Britain, France, and the United States could sell weapons to states that renounced aggression, enabling military assistance to go to the Israelis as well as the Arabs. In 1950–51 Israel received some $8.7 million in weapons, compared to about $4 million for the Arab states combined.[62]

Following a meeting in 1950, Henry Morgenthau and Ben-Gurion had urged Truman to incorporate a formal security alliance with Israel into cold war strategy.[63] Teddy Kollek, a close associate of Ben-

Gurion, emphasized that Israel "wishes to be a partner of the West in the defense of the Near East, and to participate in Western planning for this defense." Eban also forwarded "proposals on the possibilities of Israeli cooperation in western defense plans for the Near East."[64] The quest for a formal, NATO-style collective security pact with the United States and Europe became a staple goal of Israel and the lobby, but one they never realized.

Israelis and American Zionists made good on the threat to go over the heads of the Truman administration to mobilize public and especially congressional support behind Zionist policies. Acheson noted that Truman perceived the Zionists as attempting "to bring all the pressure on him." Acheson also complained to Elath about the absence of a "calm atmosphere" amid discussions on US relations with Israel. Acheson found it "particularly unfortunate" that the Israelis had circulated a press release based on his discussion of military assistance to Israel with lobby stalwart Rep. Jacob Javits (R-NY); "I would not do such a thing in Israel," he told Elath.[65]

TAPPING AMERICA'S "VAST FINANCIAL RESOURCES"

Successful in warding off US and UN efforts to achieve a settlement on borders and refugees, Israel and the lobby launched a campaign to tap into the "vast financial resources" of the US government. Israel needed the funding primarily to finance resettlement of the massive influx of Jewish immigrants.[66] In July 1950, the Knesset passed the Law of Return enabling any Jew in the world to relocate to Israel and gain citizenship. Three months later, Israel and the lobby collaborated in drafting a memorandum to Truman outlining the Zionist state's need for emergency financial assistance for resettlement of Jewish refugees.

Convening at a "national planning conference" in Washington, "more than 2,000 Americans, representing the organized Jewish community of the United States," focused on "the welfare of Israel, the world's youngest democracy, in relation to the established policy of the United States." Noting that 600,000 Jews were expected to arrive in Israel over the next three years, the group concluded that "The highest purpose of Israel's national life today is the absorption of mass immigration." The Zionist lobby not only would justify its efforts to secure US financial support on humanitarian grounds, but would also argue that it served American national interests as "a step towards consolidation of the defenses of the democratic world." Signatories of the memorandum to Truman included

Feinberg, longtime Zionist Nahum Goldmann, Jacobson, Lipsky, and Morgenthau.[67]

The campaign to garner US support for Jewish migration established the Israel lobby as the most potent perennial lobby of the US Congress for financial assistance to a foreign government in all of American history. While Kenen had grasped the critical role of direct political action since the 1944 election, the lobbying campaign now centered on securing financial support and thus homed in on the Congress. The elected officials were susceptible to public pressure, especially members of the House of Representatives, who had control of the purse strings and had to stand for election every two years. Kenen and his colleagues well understood that if they could get Israel in the financial pipeline by means of intensive lobbying of Congress, a regular program of funding would ensue. This scenario played out beyond their wildest expectations in the coming decades as Israel emerged as the leading overall recipient of US foreign assistance.

In 1950, AZC initiated the campaign by mobilizing local Zionist committees to "contact at once all incumbent Congressmen and Senators, as well as all candidates for Congressional and Senatorial offices." They should be approached "in a tactful manner," but the ultimate goal was to "secure their pledges of support in the coming Congress for direct financial aid to Israel." Formally embracing "the Jerusalem program" – under which the World Zionist Congress (WZC) in 1951 emphasized devotion to the consolidation of Israel as the central goal of the international Zionist movement – AZC called for "unifying all Zionist factions and submerging all party interests." AZC emphasized that unity within the Diaspora was "the only means for effectively carrying out" the congressional fundraising campaign.[68] "When the [Jewish] community is thus organized," Lipsky advised, AZC would then bring in "all our local Christian and liberal friends, representatives of labor organizations, and leaders of public opinion in the community." The third step in the campaign would be "distribution of educational material" on a local level as part of a united "nationwide effort."[69]

In consultation with Eban, Lipsky tabbed Kenen, who was then working directly for the State of Israel anchoring public relations in its UN office in New York, to coordinate the campaign. On February 12, 1951, Lipsky informed Kenen that AZC "has agreed to retain you as its public relations counsel to assume the general direction of all its activities in connection with securing US economic assistance for the State of Israel." Ten days later, Eban told Kenen that "The Government of Israel has a deep interest in your present assignment, the success of which is vital to its future."[70] Years later, Eban recalled that "In 1951, I asked Si Kenen to come to Washington ... to ensure a permanent atmosphere of sympathy for Israel in the Congress and the press."[71] Kenen was to "register in Washington as a lobbyist" for AZC, for which he would receive a salary of $1,050 a month (about $115,000 annually in 2018 dollars) plus expenses.[72]

By terminating his employment with Israel in deference to lobbying for AZC as a US citizen, Kenen and the lobby attempted to alleviate FBI scrutiny under the FARA. Since World War II the FBI had investigated Zionists, some with alleged communist ties and sympathies, and had placed bugs and wiretaps on Feinberg, Kenen, the JA, and other Zionist offices. In 1948, the Justice Department indicted nine men for attempting to supply US aircraft to the emerging Israel in violation of neutrality laws. With the FBI aware that Israel was attempting to "change the policies of the United States State Department," the establishment of a lobby comprised of US citizens was meant to relieve Kenen and AZC of federal scrutiny. In May 1951, Kenen informed the Justice Department that he no longer worked for the Israeli government and asked that his name be delisted from the foreign agents registry.[73]

Working closely with the ACPC, Kenen lined up Sens. Taft and Paul Douglas (D-IL) behind a $150 million grant-in-aid request for Israel. They did not expect to receive anywhere near that amount, but Taft urged the lobby to aim high with the $150 million figure. Senator Wagner, one of the founders of ACPC, weighed in, calling for "immediate and active support" of the aid bill. Working in concert with Eban and the Israeli government – his erstwhile employer – Kenen focused on "encouraging a number of Senators to agree to join in sponsorship with Douglas and Taft when the Bill is ready. Prior to its introduction, the Government of Israel shall make a formal request." Kenen explained that it was a more effective approach to "carry out this type of campaign in relation to legislation pending in Congress than in relation to the request made by the Government of Israel."[74]

Kenen spearheaded "propaganda activities" encouraging press stories, public statements in support of Israel, and mobilization of "Jewish congressmen" as well as "influential Christian leaders" behind the Taft–Douglas bill.[75] According to information later collected in a US Senate investigation (see Chapter 4), AZC spent several thousand dollars lobbying on behalf of "legislation for financial aid to Israel."[76]

In May, the publicity and fundraising campaign climaxed with the arrival of Ben-Gurion, who came to Washington to address the National Press Club and took the opportunity to meet with members of Congress to promote the aid package. "Never before have the Jews of America been so aroused for Zion," an ebullient Kenen declared. He counted hundreds of supportive groups backed by thousands of telegrams, articles, and letters, many circulated to "dedicated Christian readers" brought into the fold by the ACPC. Closely monitoring the effectiveness of the lobbying effort in a series of updates to Lipsky, Kenen reported in June, "It now appears that a majority of the membership in the House have indicated support for the Israel aid bill." His next report added that there was "no doubt today of a favorable majority in the Senate." The AZC and the ACPC culminated the campaign with a flood of last-minute telegrams to members of Congress and community leaders.[77]

Angered by the prospect of the United States underwriting Israel's rapidly growing population and territorial expansion, the Arab states vehemently opposed the Taft–Douglas bill. The DOS expressed concern about US officials showing favoritism to Israel by participating in "drives conducted by private organizations for funds to promote the immigration of persons of Jewish faith into Israel." The Arab states viewed "any action by the US favorable to Israel as proof that the US follows an anti-Arab policy," the diplomats observed. The Arabs cited "numerous statements of high US government officials tending to contrast them unfavorably with Israel." For instance, Vice President Barkley, a longtime member of the ACPC, described Israel "an oasis of liberty in a desert of despotism." The outbreak of anti-American demonstrations, including bombings of the US legations in Beirut and Damascus, underscored that the United States had become "the target of widespread adverse criticism in the Arab countries for alleged partiality towards Israel."[78]

Concerned about the ongoing potential of the Arabs to ally with the Soviet Union in the cold war, the DOS advised Truman to "reaffirm in public statements our friendship for the Arab governments and peoples" while avoiding "public statements which might appear to suggest partisanship by this government in the controversial Palestine problem." The JCS weighed in with concerns about alienating Saudi Arabia, as the generals "firmly opposed" any action that might jeopardize "our use of Dhahran air base."[79] Despite threats over US support for Israel, Saudi Arabia ultimately "aligned itself with the United States" as the kingdom "prioritized its partnership with Washington over Palestine."[80] By this time – in the wake of intensive lobbying spearheaded by Elath – US oil companies had abandoned as a "false assumption" the previously held view that support for Israel would undermine US access to Arab oil.[81]

Alarmed by the growing clout of the lobby, some of Truman's advisers openly condemned the budding special relationship with Israel. As Diplomat Richard Ford noted, "An informality not normally associated with the high-level political ties found between two sovereign states has characterized both the official and the public relations of the United States and Israel." Capitalizing on the "intimate, long-standing interest of American Jewry in the Zionist movement," Israel "freely tapped" the domestic political influence. Ford called for "an objective review of the situation and for the adoption of a rather more impersonal approach in our top-level official dealings with Israel."[82] With the "White House under pressure to send a message to the WZC [meeting in] Jerusalem," Acheson declared he was "not disposed to do so," citing concern about "severe and unnecessary political repercussions flowing from this act in Arab states."[83]

In March 1951 the NSC addressed the concern over Middle East policy with Paper 47/5, which formally proclaimed as official US policy "impartiality" in the Palestine conflict. The call for an impartial policy arrived in the midst of the AZC campaign for the Taft–Douglas financial assistance package. The congressional fundraising effort was "based upon an obvious claim for favoritism," the DOS observed. "The plea is based on 'special ties' between the two countries [yet] the potential impact of this proposal in hurting our position in the Near East is illustrated by the circumstance that four Arab states, Egypt, Jordan, Lebanon and Saudi Arabia, have already articulated their protests against it officially." The DOS sought to limit aid to Israel in deference to the policy of impartiality, with Acheson adding that Israel needed to keep in mind that the United States already underwrote the international aid and resettlement efforts for the Palestinian refugees.[84]

As the lobby intensified its efforts in Washington, Truman showed his wariness of the potential political impact of criticizing Israel. The president declared, "No one in the [DOS] should express views of any sort outside the department without further direction from me." On May 3 and 4, Ben-Gurion lobbied personally in Washington, taking lunch with Truman (no record was kept of the meeting) and meeting with the members of Congress. In June, with Niles suffering from cancer, Truman brought in Blaustein, the AJC president but also a member of Eban's Diaspora advisory group, to serve simultaneously as a presidential advisor on relations with Israel.[85]

"Distraught" over the intensity of the lobby campaign, Truman turned to Feinberg in hopes that he could make the "political Jews [keep] quiet for the time being." Working with Acheson, Feinberg became the fixer in the eventual compromise in the debate over the Taft–Douglas bill. In the end, Israel received $65 million for the Jewish immigrants. Congress also apportioned $65 million to the Palestinian refugees and Arab states in a transparent but ultimately empty gesture of parity insofar as the Arab states collectively dwarfed Israel in population and geographic scope.[86]

Israel and the lobby had won a "decisive victory," precipitating a "revolutionary change" ensuring "the inclusion of Israel in our country's foreign aid program," a triumphant Kenen declared.[87] In 1952, with the pro-Israel lobby well established and Washington "now aware of Israel's needs," Congress authorized another $73 million in resettlement assistance.[88] Kenen attributed the success of the lobby to an "effective coalition of Israel's friends – Jews and Christians, Zionists and non-Zionists – who united in unprecedented cooperation" and successfully countered "all the arguments in the Arab propaganda book." On September 10, 1951, Sharett sent Kenen "affectionate greetings on the remarkable achievement of which you may justly feel proud."[89]

Even as the lobby celebrated unprecedented success in its campaign, Ben-Gurion alienated some American Jews by suggesting that those who did not live in Israel were "exiles" from the faith. Blaustein rebuked the Israeli leader, declaring, "American Jews owe loyalty to the United States – and only to the United States."[90] Ben-Gurion's assertion that true Zionists should live in Israel left American Zionists vulnerable to charges of "dual loyalty" at a time of intensified American patriotic identification amid cold war crises replete with charges of communist sympathies and disloyalty. In an October 1951 AJC "Resolution on Israel," Blaustein wrote "America is our home," adding it was "completely false and unrealistic" to suggest that "Israel is the only place where Jews can live in security and dignity," and that Ben-Gurion should refrain from efforts to "interfere with the internal affairs of American Jews." Ben-Gurion responded with a clarification recognizing American Jews' loyalty to the United States, but he remained wedded to the notion that genuine Zionists should relocate to Israel; hence, the tensions with some US Jewish groups would resurface.[91]

The dissident ACJ called on Ben-Gurion to refrain from statements that encouraged charges of "dual loyalty on the part of American Jews," which might "impair the relationship of American Jews to their Government." The ACJ also resented being condemned by Zionists, as it demanded respect for "our program and our principles without being subject to charges" of being "detrimental" or engaging in "anti-Israel" activities.[92] Insisting that the ACJ was a minority fringe group, the Israel lobby condemned the rival Jewish organization for its "virulent activity" that was "continuing to becloud the issues respecting Israel." The AZC directed its local councils to "watch closely [ACJ] activities in your community and report to us on them" in order that they might "be noted and counteracted."[93]

Christians in the ACPC had emerged during the Taft–Douglas campaign as a crucial component within the growing clout of the Israel lobby. The ACPC and AZC were literally inseparable, as they shared the same New York address: 342 Madison Avenue. By effectively merging into the Israel lobby, the ACPC countered rival Christian groups, such as the Committee for Justice and Peace in the Holy Land, which formed in February 1948 in opposition to Zionism.

The ACPC "worked closely with Israel's Ministry of Religious Affairs" in crafting publications, conducting workshops, and responding to criticism of the Zionist state. The group countered articles in *Christian Century*, which had called for "self-determination and federalism among sub-states or cantons" rather than a Zionist state. An article by the Rev. William Sloane Coffin in *Christianity and Crisis*, arguing that Zionist actions were inviting the return of anti-Semitism, spurred a "furious" response from Zionist Christians. In addition to the Christian modernists, led by the strongly pro-Zionist Reinhold Niebuhr, Christian fundamentalists exalted the rise of Israel in the context of biblical prophecy as a momentous indicator of the imminent return of Christ. These groups dismissed Arabs and Muslims as backward, if not evil. Some condemned UN efforts to mediate the conflict as part of an effort to implant a "satanic one-world government."[94]

WINDFALL FROM WEST GERMANY

The ACPC and AZC backed a successful Israeli effort to secure a financial windfall from the newly created Federal Republic of Germany (FRG). Seizing the momentum of broadened awareness of the full scope of the Nazi genocide and attendant calls for atonement, Israel secured a massive long-term financial package of $845 million in reparations to Diaspora Jews. The United States brokered the negotiations between its new NATO ally and the Zionist state. Eban thanked Acheson for the "sympathetic assistance by the Secretary and his staff for bringing about the agreement."[95] The AJC endorsed the West German reparations deal as a model of "voluntary cooperation" between the United States, Israel, and American Jews.[96]

At one point during negotiations Sharett hinted that the German reparations might enable Israel to compensate Palestinian refugees, but no such payments materialized, leaving Arabs livid over the deal. They viewed the US and now West German funding as strengthening Israel against them while confirming that Washington was Israel's special ally rather than an honest broker of conflict resolution. Truman took Acheson's advice to avoid making a public statement about the reparations accord, but the Arab states were well aware of the financial arrangements and the US role in securing them. The United States received "the brunt of adverse criticism" in the Arab world, a US diplomat reported from Beirut.[97]

The Israelis thus secured financial resources for their rapidly expanding settler state while continuing to fend off international efforts at mediation. The PCC remained the official diplomatic platform in pursuit of a settlement, yet the Israelis maintained "basic hostility to the mediating initiative of the commission." While the Arab delegations had "agreed to discuss the substantive proposals," Israel continued to "refuse to make any substantial concessions" while insisting on "exacting from the Arabs a precisely defined bargain in return for possible Israel concessions."[98] In the fall of 1951, the PCC mediation efforts finally collapsed as a result of Israeli intransigence on borders, refugees, and the status of Jerusalem.[99]

Israel and the lobby maintained steadfast opposition to Truman administration efforts to address the issue of the Palestinian refugees, who were a living embodiment of the Nakba and a thus a source of simmering resentment across the Arab world. Indifferent to Palestinian suffering, Israel and AZC offered tendentious propaganda on the subject. Invariably placing "refugees" in quotation marks, the lobby denied all responsibility and blamed the Arab states for the catastrophe. "*The central and incontrovertible fact is that the Arab Higher Committee stimulated, organized and directed the mass exodus,*" the AZC asserted [italics in original]. "We regarded the flight of the Arabs as a disaster," Kenen told a congressman amid the Taft–Douglas lobbying campaign, "because we had been assuring the world that the Jews and Arabs could live together and that partition was possible." The lobby, including the ACPC, maintained a steady propaganda theme that Arabs actually cared little about refugees and only pursued repatriation as a tactic to undermine Israel from within.[100] In November 1952,

US diplomats countered that "responsible Arab leaders" understood that "large-scale return" of refugees to Israel was "out of the question." These Arab leaders thus might respond favorably to the admission of some refugees, "particularly farmers," as a gesture toward peace. Israel remained adamant in response. Sharett declared he was "taken aback" that Israel continued to be confronted with the refugee issue, as its position was "firmly fixed" that "no useful purpose would be served by increasing the number of Arabs in Israel."[101]

In the wake of the string of victories on blocking the return of refugees, expanded boundaries, funding for immigration, and the status of Jerusalem, Kenen grew concerned that the Israel lobby might be too successful. He cited the "view now prevailing that Israel is the favorite of the Administration and Congress and that the Arab states and the Arab refugees are discriminated against." To deflect such criticism, Kenen sought to link "aid to Israel and aid to the Arab states," explaining to Lipsky, "This is not really something new. We have always, in our Zionist propaganda, contended that the establishment of a Jewish state would be beneficial to the entire Arab world."[102]

Despite the putative desire to uplift the Arab world, the lobby maintained a steady stream of Orientalist stereotypes and frequently invoked the trope of "appeasement" to warn against US accommodation of Arab/Palestinian positions. The assertion by critics that support for Israel would undermine US "power and prestige" in the region was irrational and "reminiscent of the 1930s for this was the rationale of the appeasement policy," the AZC declared. Rather than manifestation of the broader conflict, Arab anger reflected "hyper-nationalism and xenophobia as a classic diversion, whereby feudal kings and pashas are enabled to stir up prejudices and animosity, turning the minds of hungry, underprivileged masses from domestic ills and maladjustments."[103]

Arab frustration was genuine, however, if often counterproductive. The Arab states provided Israel and the lobby with fodder for propaganda through a steady stream of pledges to destroy the Zionist state. Although unlike Israel the Arabs had been willing to negotiate through the PCC, lobby pamphleteers could overshadow diplomatic flexibility by emphasizing the Arab economic boycott against Israel, which had been put into effect in 1945 and remained active. Moreover, lobbyists rarely missed an opportunity to publicize statements put out for public consumption within the Arab states calling for the "liquidation of Israel," "Israel's disappearance," removal of the "cancer in the body of the Arab world," vows "[n]ever [to] make peace with Israel," that "Israel is destined to die," that "the Middle East cannot accommodate both nations," and that "reconciliation with Israel is a crime."[104]

Bluster notwithstanding, the Arab states not only could not destroy Israel, they were vulnerable to further "aggressive expansion" by the Zionist state. As the settler population doubled to 1.3 million from 1948 to 1951, Arab leaders perceived the rapid influx of migrants as evidence that Israel intended not only to hold captured territories, but also to expand further. "Arab doubts of the ability of Israel to maintain an expanded population within its present borders have a measure of validity," Acheson acknowledged.[105]

AGGRESSION AGAINST SYRIA

Following the armistice agreement, the UN sought to keep borderland demilitarized zones (DMZs) under international control, but Israel "embarked on an energetic and ruthless policy of creating facts on the ground in the DMZs." The border assaults furthered the settler project of expanding the area available for the accelerating Jewish population while renewing the "transfer" policies pioneered in the 1948 war.[106]

Only a handful of Jewish settlements existed along the border with Syria, as compared with a much larger resident Arab farming population, prompting Ben-Gurion's move "to squeeze the Syrians out of the DMZs even if this was not in line with the spirit or the letter of the armistice agreement." The more moderate Sharett, the UN, the United States, and of course the Syrians opposed what Shlaim describes as unprovoked and "amazingly aggressive" Israeli actions forcibly removing hundreds of Arabs from villages in the DMZ and blocking the UN from entering the area. Early in 1951, as Israel initiated a development project draining Lake Huleh, troops entered Syrian territory, thereby provoking a violent clash in which seven Israelis were killed. Several Knesset members condemned the IDF for initiating the conflict, but Ben-Gurion secured Cabinet approval to destroy three villages inside the DMZ in an action that included use of airpower for the first time since the armistice agreements. In the first week of May, scores of Israelis, Syrians, and villagers died as fighting with heavy artillery raged along the DMZ.[107]

Cavendish Cannon, the US minister in Damascus, reported that an "organized campaign to eliminate indigenous Arab inhabitants of the demilitarized zone to bolster Israel's claim to the area" lay behind the aggression. The Israelis mendaciously asserted that the Arabs had attacked Zionist settlers, but Cannon reported in May 1951 that an

"aggressive attack on Israel is wholly out of keeping with the demonstrated Syrian policy of restraint and is not in accord with UN observer
reports."[108]

The United States sponsored a UNSC resolution that brought an end
the fighting and condemned Israel for its militarism by a vote of 10–0.
Asserting that Washington had "appeased Syria," the AZC launched
a "tremendous letter and telegram approach" to the administration,
Congress, and the media. Jacobson, Niles, Weizmann, and Kirchwey
publicly decried the US failure to back Israel in the conflict. The lobby
response succeeded in generating public support for Israel.
"The nationwide press campaign showed an almost universal approval
of Israel's position," Lipsky declared, and "drainage of the Huleh swamp
continues."[109]

Despite the Israeli provocations, Syria subsequently undertook
"impressive moves toward reducing tension" and offered "pragmatic
and constructive" terms for a settlement of the border conflict in US-
and UN-brokered negotiations. Israel ultimately rejected the opportunity
to stabilize the Syrian border in deference to securing "exclusive and
unfettered rights over the lakes and the Jordan River."[110]

While Truman enabled Israeli aggression in the Huleh dispute, the
lobby displayed growing anxiety over his imminent departure from the
White House and the uncertainties about his successor amid the 1952
presidential campaign. Lipsky was determined to "have our cause embodied in the efforts of both political parties," a strategy that would succeed
beyond expectations in the ensuing years as the Israel lobby became
a dominant force in Congress as well as the White House.[111]

Manifesting its powerful influence over US Near East policy, the Israel
lobby essentially wrote the planks of both the major American political
parties in the 1952 campaign. Kenen and Feinberg crafted the Democratic
plank calling for "continued assistance" to Israel, which the party's nominee Illinois Gov. Adlai Stevenson duly embraced. On the other side of the
aisle the lobby had the backing of "Mr. Republican" Sen. Taft, who
ultimately failed to get the nomination, as well as Sen. Richard Nixon of
California, who would become vice president, and Javits, among other
prominent Republicans. Silver had alienated Truman with his assertive-
ness and thereafter became increasingly linked with the Republican Party
of his fellow Ohioan Taft. After he "requested the [Israeli] Embassy's
suggestions as to contents," Silver drafted the framework for what became
a pro-Israeli Republican Party platform in the 1952 campaign. While less
specific about financial assistance to Israel than the Democratic plank, the

Republican platform nonetheless emphasized the Party's historic support for Zionism and its "friendly interest" in bolstering Israel.[112]

The lobby also appealed for support from the leading Republican internationalist of the era, John Foster Dulles, as well the ultimately successful candidate, the hero General Dwight D. Eisenhower. To the AZC Eisenhower was a complete unknown, as he had "never, to our knowledge, made a statement on Israel." After Eisenhower received the nomination, Silver played a key role in lobbying the Republican candidate, who finally responded on October 18 with a statement on Israel drafted by Silver that declared, "Every American who loves liberty must join in the effort to make secure forever the future of this newest member in the family of nations."[113]

Less than reassured by the vague and belated endorsement, the AZC recognized that Eisenhower and Dulles, who became secretary of state after Eisenhower's landslide victory, would present challenges that they had not faced under the Democrats. "Last Tuesday's election will make it much more difficult to secure economic and political assistance for Israel," Kenen mused to Lipsky, if only because the Republicans had pledged to lower taxes and cut government spending, including foreign assistance. After an initial burst of effusive praise following Eisenhower's election, Kenen advised, "We ought to stop the flow of statements extolling Eisenhower," explaining that "If we protest too much about it" the new president "will begin to wonder."[114]

Truman left the presidency fully aware that he had played a pivotal role in cementing the US–Israeli special relationship. Mired in the Korean stalemate and long stymied in his domestic Fair Deal agenda, Truman was unpopular at home yet revered in Israel. The Zionist state had honored the president by naming a new settlement for him (Kfar Truman) in territory located beyond the 1947 partition line on the site of a former Palestinian village of Bayt Nabala. The Israelis had showered Truman with gifts, including a plaque of the Israeli Declaration of Independence and an elaborate Torah scroll written in Hebrew.[115]

Many Israelis, as well as American Jews and Christians, told Truman he had fulfilled a divine mission to reunite the Jews with the holy land. In 1949 Israel's chief rabbi told him: "God put you in your mother's womb so that you would be the instrument to bring about Israel's rebirth after two thousand years." Truman often quoted from one of his favorite Bible passages, Deuteronomy 1:8: "Behold, I have given up the land before you. Go in and take possession of the land to which the Lord has sworn unto your fathers, to Abraham, to Isaac, and to Jacob." In his

FIGURE 9 Israeli diplomat Abba Eban presides as President Harry Truman confers with Israeli Prime Minister David Ben-Gurion at the White House in May 1949. Although frequently angered by Israeli recalcitrance as well as the intensity of the burgeoning Zionist lobby, Truman nonetheless provided the new nation of Israel with decisive political and economic support.
Mondadori Portfolio/Getty Images

farewell address Truman declared that as a result of US support, "Israel can be made into the country of milk and honey as it was in the time of Joshua." Truman embraced the mantle of the modern day Cyrus, the Persian king who in the sixth century BCE ended the Babylonian captivity and authorized the rebuilding of the Jewish temple in Jerusalem. Believing that he had been part of a divine plan to establish the new Israel, Truman proclaimed, "I am Cyrus, I am Cyrus."[116]

3

"We Should Not Be Deterred by Political Pressures"

The Israel lobby's concerns that the Eisenhower administration would be less amenable to its advocacy were well founded. The Republican administration sought to contain Israeli border aggression and forge a Middle East peace, and vowed not to be intimidated by Zionist political action. The lobby confronted a series of wrenching crises during the Eisenhower years, but emerged even stronger with the help of key political allies, especially in the US Congress.

Perceptions centered on the cold war largely dictated the Eisenhower administration's foreign policy, including the Middle East. Geographic proximity to Europe and the Soviet Union, as well as vast oil supplies, added to the region's importance. Economic issues and the legacies of colonialism posed challenges for US policy under any circumstances, but relations with the Arabs had deteriorated as a result of Truman's tilt toward Israel and establishment of the special relationship. By the time Eisenhower assumed office, as Peter Hahn has noted, "US policy toward Israel seriously aggravated tensions" with the Arab world.[1]

Although it had promptly recognized Israel in 1948, the Soviet Union had since broken off relations with the Zionist state. In the months leading up to his death in March 1953, Stalin launched anti-Semitic purges, citing a fictional "doctor's plot" to topple him. In February, Lipsky told Dulles that the break in relations with the USSR "gravely increases Israel's peril" and heightened the need for a closer security arrangement with the United States. Javits advised Dulles, "It would be a good time to establish US bases in Israel" to counterbalance the Soviet tilt toward the Arabs.[2]

Rather than pursue a formal security alliance with Israel, which they believed would only drive the Arabs into the Soviet camp, Eisenhower and

Dulles determined to assert the "impartial" policy and to confront Israel over its diplomatic intransigence. Despite trumpeting revival of the "balanced" approach, Eisenhower and Dulles "had no intention of returning to the 1947 partition plan or of forcing Israel to repatriate large numbers of Palestinian refugees."[3] They did, however, strive to restrain Israel's aggressive tendencies. Eisenhower recalled a conversation shortly after World War II with some young Zionists who "belittled the Arabs in every way," insisting that they would be easy to dominate because of their alleged "laziness, shiftlessness and lack of spirit." Eisenhower recalled telling them they were "stirring up a hornets' nest" and they should resolve the clash "peacefully and without doing unnecessary violence to the self-respect and interests of the Arabs."[4]

Dulles believed the timing was "propitious" for a Middle East peace accord because "the Arabs felt that President Eisenhower and the Republican Administration would not, on political grounds, be unfair to them." The Truman administration had created "the present jam" because it had "tried to meet the wishes of the Zionists in this country and that had created a basic antagonism with the Arabs." Dulles advised Javits that "Any overall settlement must involve some bitter elements for the Israelis and I particularly mentioned the internationalization of Jerusalem as foreseen by the 1948 UN Resolution."[5]

In February, Kenen concluded it was "too early to forecast" the approach Eisenhower and Dulles would take, but he feared that allegedly pro-Arab diplomats, specifically naming Henderson, would attempt to reassert control over DOS policy. Kenen forwarded to Dulles a report reputedly backed by "considerable research" to advance the argument that perceived "Arabist" influence over policy "adversely affects the prospects of peace in the Near East by fortifying Arab intransigence." Working through Taft, who "made use of our suggestions," Kenen warned against adoption of a rumored "new approach" by the administration of "paying more attention to Arab countries" and cutting financial assistance to Israel.[6]

Eisenhower, a Kansan whose career arose within the segregated armed forces, was uncomfortable around minorities – African-Americans and Hispanics, but also Jews.[7] The administration brought in Maxwell Rabb, an attorney and a Jew, as an adviser on minority affairs, and also turned to a Jewish friend of Dulles, Bernard Katzen, who focused on minority affairs for the Republican National Committee. The two – supporters of Israel, but not active as lobbyists – arranged a meeting between Eisenhower and a group of Jewish leaders at the end of March. Kenen and Lipsky were among those who met with the president in the off-the-record session, but the meeting did not allay their fears that the administration would tilt back to the Arabs.[8]

Believing that "[t]he administration has been subjected to an extraordinary offensive to bring about a change in American foreign policy in the Middle East, favoring the Arab states," Kenen mounted a campaign "to stimulate our people to greater activity to counter the pro-Arab offensive." He mobilized local Jewish councils linked with AZC and dispatched hundreds of "Dear Friend" letters, which declared "Those who seek a new Middle Eastern foreign policy profess the doctrine of 'equal' treatment, but they actually mean reduction of support and aid for Israel." The missive advised countering arguments about repatriating Arab refugees by placing emphasis on funding Jewish migration to Israel. The letter also urged opposition to the Arab economic boycott, emphasizing its "serious impact on Israel's economy."[9]

ACPC members and other supporters including Eleanor Roosevelt took up the campaign, using the arguments and often the same language as the "Dear Friend" letter. Alarmed by the "rumor that there is to be a change in our government policy toward Israel," Roosevelt advised Eisenhower and Dulles to maintain financial and diplomatic support of Israel. "The Arab states do not espouse the cause of the free world that Israel does," she declared, adding that the root of the problem in the region was their failure to "cooperate with Israel." Eisenhower responded he intended to be "fair and friendly," and anticipated roughly maintaining the $73 million level of financial support in aid to Israel, noting that it would exceed the funding for all of the Arab states combined.[10]

In May, Dulles became the first secretary of state to visit the Middle East, a trip that included a meeting with the charismatic leader of Egypt, Gamel Abdel Nasser, who assumed power in the wake of a nearly bloodless military coup that ousted the monarchy in 1952. Dulles discussed the prospects for US economic and military aid to Egypt and confided, "The Republican administration does not owe the same degree of political debt as did the Democrats to Jewish groups." Upon returning stateside, Dulles delivered a speech advocating a balanced Middle East diplomacy, including the need for Israel to integrate into the region.[11]

As Dulles attempted to implement the impartial approach, "there was a vigorous reaction by Israel's friends in this country," as Kenen put it. AZC condemned the administration's references to "territory under Israel's control," which implied a rejection of the expanded 1949 borders, as well as a "tendency to apologize to Arab states for past American

FIGURE 10 Eleanor Roosevelt (right) was a longtime champion of the Zionist cause. Here she is shown on September 18, 1961, receiving an award for her work on behalf of the sale of Israel bonds from Israeli Foreign Minister and former Milwaukee schoolteacher Golda Meir.
Hulton Archive/Getty Images

friendship to Israel and their constant innuendos that there has been something wrong with our past policy."[12] From Israel, Sharett ungenerously complained of a "steep descent" from Truman to Eisenhower "with respect to the heart," and from Acheson to Dulles "with respect to the brains."[13]

In August 1953, a National Intelligence Estimate (NIE) established the administration's policy toward the Middle East – one that was sure to provoke opposition from the Israel lobby. "The Arab-Israeli dispute has seriously damaged the US security position by increasing area instability, by adding to the difficulty of organizing area defense and by posing a continuing threat of armed conflict," the NIE declared. "The Arabs believe that the US favors Israeli interests," spurring a "decline of US prestige and influence in the Arab world." Israel commanded influence "out of proportion to its size, population and resources" because it "has the political and financial support of the Zionist movement and many influential groups and persons in the western nations[,] particularly the US." There was "no prospect of a full peace settlement in the present highly charged atmosphere," hence "war could break out" at any time.[14]

QIBYA AND THE LOBBY'S RESPONSE

Borderland assaults, mostly instigated by the Israelis, showed that the NIE concern about the possibility of renewal of open warfare was well founded.[15] Some 200–250 Zionist settlers died from attacks by infiltrators in the period between the 1948 and 1956 wars, but often-indiscriminate Israeli attacks killed an estimated 3,000–5,000 Arabs. Israel authorized a "free-fire" policy, under which the military, police, and civilians shot "anything that moved," especially at night; "The vast majority of those killed were unarmed." Rapes, summary executions, and collective punishment were common, especially in the years immediately following the War of 1948. No Israeli settlers or military figures were confronted with criminal charges.[16]

The July 1951 assassination of Abdullah, who had collaborated with the Israelis to control the West Bank, provided Ben-Gurion with a pretext to authorize attacks on the long border with Jordan. Several villages and communities were located directly on the armistice line, which made them targets. Despite their enmity for the Israelis, "The Arab governments and armies opposed infiltration into Israel and attacks by infiltrators against Israel, primarily because they feared reprisals," Israeli historian Benny Morris explains.[17] Though the Israelis knew that the Arab governments were trying to restrain infiltration, they nonetheless charged that Jordan was sponsoring *Fedayeen* guerrilla raids.[18]

The borderland instability heightened US concern about Jordan's vulnerability to communism following the death of Abdullah, who had been, as the CIA put it, "a resolute anti-Communist, pro-Western ruler."[19] US diplomats feared that "acts of terrorism carried out by uniformed Israeli soldiers" would encourage the growth of radicalism in the kingdom. The US ambassador to Israel, citing "recent excursions into Arab territories" as well as "bombing of settlements in Jordanian territory," conveyed the "deep concern of the US Government over the ill effects both in the Middle East and abroad of the policy now being followed." The Israelis insisted the tensions were "a direct result of unrestrained infiltration by Arab marauders." US officials knew this charge was exaggerated; moreover, they argued that reprisal raids would only serve to embitter the neighboring Arab states and further undermine the quest for

a settlement. A diplomat concluded that within Israel a "dominant military clique obviously takes a cynical view" of peace efforts and "pursues
its own policies."[20]

The Israelis shrugged off US and international criticism while carrying
out violent assaults that Ben-Gurion and other hardliners believed would
send the appropriate message to the Arabs, viewed as primitive and
implacable foes. Ben-Gurion and Dayan, the eye-patched war veteran
and architect of the settlement attacks, had no hesitation in launching
aggressive raids and in deflecting criticism, both internally and from
abroad. Ben-Gurion mocked the UN and frequently averred, "Our future
does not depend on what the Gentiles say but on what the Jews do." Ben-
Gurion and the militarists ignored the more cautionary approaches of
Sharett and Eban. Israel thus persistently pursued aggressive border
assaults that undermined Arab sovereignty, reinforced humiliation, and
intensified enmities in the region.[21]

The most atrocious event occurred on October 14, 1953, in the West
Bank village of Qibya. Citing an attack that killed an Israeli mother and two
children, Colonel Ariel Sharon's commando Unit 101 went on a rampage
through the Jordanian village, blowing up occupied homes and killing 69
residents, mostly women and children. A US analysis of the event reported
that "Jordan authorities seemed to have admitted Arab guilt" in the killings
of the woman and the two children, and thereafter "assisted Israel authorities in tracking the criminal across the border into Jordan. This assistance,
however, apparently did not satisfy the Israelis," who unleashed a massive
attack with 400 troops and mortars, destroying 45 homes.
The disproportionate Israeli assault came in the context of "a long series
of incidents which appear designed to provoke some rash act on the part of
the Arabs" who have "thus far restrained themselves from any serious
reprisal, both to maintain their position in the UN and because they are
not militarily capable of either attacking Israelis or defending themselves
against attack." The analysis concluded: "Hotheads among the Israeli politicians and military forces are getting the upper hand."[22] Ben-Gurion
responded with a campaign of disinformation, declaring that after "a
searching investigation it is clear beyond doubt that not a single army unit
was absent from its base on the night of the attack on Qibya."[23] This
assertion "was not Ben-Gurion's first lie for what he saw as the good of
his country," Shlaim notes, "nor was it to be the last, but it was one of the
most blatant."[24]

Israeli borderland aggression, culminating with the atrocity at Qibya,
created a crisis for the lobby, which nonetheless ultimately responded

adroitly. AZC condemned a DOS statement expressing "deepest sympathy for the families of those who lost their lives in and near Qibya during the recent attack by Israeli forces."[25] The lobby accused the professional diplomats of "obvious bias, in disregard of the traditional friendship between America and Israel." The DOS had "hastened to single out one side for rebuke," Kenen declared, whereas the "basic cause" of the "tragic incidents" at Qibya was "the refusal of the Arab states to make peace with Israel."[26]

The Qibya assault coincided with Israel's defiance of the UN and international law through unilateral diversion of the Jordan River. Together these events created a crisis within the special relationship, spurring AZC to accelerate its defense of Israeli interests. Danish General Vagn Bennike, the UN truce supervisor, had demanded a halt to the diversion of the Jordan, which flowed through the demilitarized zone north of Lake Tiberius, into the lake, and then southward where it constituted the (pre-1967) border with Jordan. "Rather than comply the Israel government speeded up construction on the diversion dam," the DOS reported in October 1953.[27] Backed by Ben-Gurion, Dayan spearheaded the diversion of the river as part of an ongoing campaign to drive the Syrians out and "establish complete Israeli control over the DMZ and the water sources in the north of the country."[28]

Determined to confront the Israelis over their aggression and defiance of international law, Dulles announced that the United States was withholding millions of dollars in Mutual Security funds scheduled for allocation to Israel "in view of the problems that exist in that area between the United Nations and Israel."[29] The administration thus sought to use economic assistance as leverage to rein in Israeli aggression. A DOS position paper described Israel as "not a viable state," as it "has been largely sustained by United States contributions private and public."[30]

Clearly alarmed, AZC denounced the funding cutoff as "an unwarranted act of duress" that would compel Israel to "suspend economic development in surrender to its enemies." Working in concert with the Israeli Embassy, AZC sent out an "emergency bulletin" emphasizing "Urgent Action Required at Once!" The lobbyists condemned the "misguided course of policy undertaken by the State Department towards Israel," which, if not halted, would produce "tragic consequences." By "applying economic sanctions against Israel" while the Arabs "continued guerrilla warfare," the DOS was "encouraging their intransigency and the formation of new anti-Israel accusations." Amid the crisis, Kenen relocated from New York to Washington to facilitate direct lobbying of Congress and the White House.[31]

The lobby letter-writing and press campaign targeted Dulles directly and subjected the nation's top diplomat to a withering assault that left him "feeling terribly pressured and misrepresented." On October 26, Javits brokered a meeting between Dulles and a group of executives of Jewish organizations mobilized by Eban and the AZC, including the United Synagogue of America, B'nai B'rith, and the Council of Jewish Federations and Welfare Funds, among others. A devout Presbyterian, Dulles informed the group that he "had been nurtured on the Old Testament" and claimed he had been "instrumental" in getting Israel established, and was therefore "disturbed" that "Jewish people have not appreciated what he did for them" and "continued to criticize him over the years." It had been necessary to suspend the economic aid "to support the UN" and to "dispel the Arab notion that the United States backs Israel right or wrong." Dulles took "strong exception" to the "various inaccuracies and distortions" circulated by the Zionists. Instead of condemning US efforts, Dulles suggested that the "Jewish fraternity" should turn its attention toward "the Israeli government to try to change their policy of presenting the world with *faits accompli*. Cooperation seemed to be a one-way street as far as Israel is concerned." Dulles added that the United States "had been working very hard with the Arabs but no one in the group seemed interested in that."[32]

Two days later, Dulles restored the funds earmarked for assistance in return for Israel's pledge to end the unilateral diversion of the Jordan waters. The understanding averted an immediate crisis, but failed to resolve the long-term conflict over the borderland waterways. At the time, to get the funding restored, the Israelis agreed to the administration's alternative plan for multilateral resource development of the Jordan River valley. Named for Eisenhower's envoy Eric Johnston – who was an ACPC member, as the Arabs pointed out, and thus hardly out to undermine legitimate Israeli interests – the Johnston Plan established a framework for sharing the waterway and producing hydroelectric power.[33]

Tensions remained acute as the administration backed the UNSC, which issued the "strongest censure" of Israel on November 24 in response to the Qibya attack. The UNSC directive to Jordan to "continue and strengthen the measures it is already taking" to impede infiltration was mild by contrast.[34] AZC condemned the censure resolution, adding "It is deeply regretted that the US Delegation associated itself with the unfair and one-sided action."[35]

Assessing the tumultuous events of the fall, Kenen declared that "Relations between Israel and the United States have reached their lowest point since 1948." Writing privately to Lipsky amid the censure debate, Kenen acknowledged that Qibya had "undermined the moral position of the Jewish people ... discredited the premises of our propaganda and has given the color of truth to Arab propaganda." But instead of becoming bogged down with "introspective brooding," the "American friends of Israel, Christian and Jewish, Zionist and non-Zionist," had rallied behind the cause "and were able to impress upon the Government that an anti-Israel program would be deeply resented by large sections of American opinion." Local councils had shown they could "spring back to life and action in a crisis." The DOS had been "overconfident and did not anticipate the vigor and breadth of public reaction to its anti-Israel measures."

Thus, ironically the most significant outcome of Qibya was to affirm AZC's ability to thwart US efforts to rein in Israeli aggressiveness, reclaim the initiative, and fend off the effort to assert the "impartial policy" in the region. The crisis had shown the need for "intensification of our work in the field of public relations" with emphasis on Congress, churches, and college campuses, which became the key constituencies over the ensuing history of the Israel lobby. The task at the time was to "resume the offensive[,] ... restore and reinvigorate" the local councils and to "draw in young people." The lobby would continue to cultivate its base within the organized Jewish and sympathetic Christian communities, but it needed to reach out to the broader public as well.[36]

Under the direction of Eban, working in collaboration with Kenen and the leaders of the major Jewish organizations, the Israel lobby underwent a major reorganization to achieve the post-Qibya goal of "intensification of our work in the field of public relations." Under Eban's direction, the ad hoc group of Jewish leaders became formalized as the Congress of Major Jewish Organizations, also known as the Presidents' Conference. Many of the American Jewish leaders traveled to Israel to meet with officials there to discuss their policy goals in relations with the US administration and Congress. By 1959, the Presidents' Conference had established a Park Avenue office with a budget and staff.

A key organization with the Israeli-backed US lobby, the Presidents' Conference acted as a representative body of American Jewish opinion on the Palestine conflict and Middle East policy. With Eban, Kenen, and bipartisan groups of lobby stalwarts in Congress – notably Celler and Javits – often acting as facilitators, the Presidents' Conference arranged to meet periodically with policymakers to discuss US decision-making on matters related to Israel. By organizing and adding permanence to the group, Eban avoided having to meet separately with the individual Jewish groups. Ironically, the DOS and US national security elites also grasped the utility of having a centralized group of Jewish leaders rather than having to respond to the demands of myriad Zionist groups.[37]

While the group of prominent American Jewish leaders could appeal directly to US national security policymakers, Eban and Kenen reorganized the lobby at the grassroots level, all the while fending off federal scrutiny. AZC came under renewed threat of federal investigation into the illegal use of tax-exempt contributions to lobby for a foreign government. Kenen and Lipsky attributed the threat of federal intervention to the "acrimonious clashes with the Eisenhower-Dulles regime."[38]

In March 1954, Kenen, Eban, and the lobby orchestrated another bureaucratic reorganization by creating the American Zionist Committee for Public Affairs (AZCPA). The new entity, detached from the AZC, would solicit *taxable* contributions, a move designed to deflect federal scrutiny. In a 1954 report mandated under federal law governing lobbies, AZCPA reported engaging in "activities related to the conduct of our foreign policy in the Middle East ... The committee approached members of Congress as part of its general program to inform American public opinion on these matters, but its activities did not relate to any legislation either pending or proposed." The next year AZCPA branded itself a "non-profit association interested in foreign policy."[39]

The CIA as well as the FBI closely monitored the restructured Israel lobby and sought to counter its growing effectiveness. In 1951, the American Friends of the Middle East (AFME) was launched to counter the influence of the Israel lobby. AFME was organized and illegally financed by the CIA under the leadership of the secretary of state's brother, Allen Dulles. Under the National Security Act (1947), it was illegal for the CIA to infiltrate or provide financial assistance to domestic organizations, but the spy agency covertly broke the law in an effort to counter the Zionist lobby. The illegal funding remained secret until revealed in a 1967 exposé on the CIA in *Ramparts* magazine.[40]

AFME and the DOS strove to maintain executive authority to direct foreign policy by countering the Israel lobby's growing clout in Congress and with the public. AFME, the CIA, and the DOS sought to cultivate pro-Western regimes to prevent communist or radical Islamists from coming to power in the oil-rich region by tapping into popular resentment over the history of European colonialism, racism, economic inequality, and Zionism. In 1953, the CIA fomented a successful coup against the Iranian nationalist Mohammad Mossadegh and intervened in Syrian politics as well. The interventions backfired, ultimately fostering a "legacy of instability, authoritarianism, and anti-Americanism."

Israeli aggressiveness heightened popular resentment across the Middle East, destabilizing the region, thus prompting the covert support for AFME and other groups. Journalist Dorothy Thompson, who appeared on the cover of *Time*, which judged her the most influential female American public figure after Eleanor Roosevelt, was the leading spokesperson for AFME. Thompson and other AFME members were not puppets of the CIA – though they apparently knowingly took funding from the spy agency; rather, they shared the same perceptions on Middle East diplomacy.

AFME also worked closely with the ACJ, the anti-Zionist Jewish organization led by Rabbi Elmer Berger, who had "consulted extensively with the CIA as AFME was set up," Hugh Wilford points out.[41] The ACJ continued to reject the idea that "being Jewish means belonging to some special 'nation' or 'people' or 'race.'" The ACJ emphasized the

> moral and ethical side of Judaism as a religion – not as a nationalist loyalty that demands that we buy Israel bonds, or give money to help finance national plans of Israeli officials, or send our children, with their technical skills, to help build the 'Jewish' homeland, or to teach our children all about the geography and national problems of Israel.[42]

By this time the ACJ was the bête noir of the Israel lobby, which accused the rival organization of echoing Nazi propaganda and promoting anti-Semitism.[43]

Working closely with Thompson, Berger, and other counterlobbyists was Henry Byroade, a DOS assistant secretary for the Near East region. A diplomat who served in the army in the Pacific theater of World War II, Byroade assumed the hot seat as head of the Near East division and was thus the chief DOS adviser on the region. Secretary Dulles "would have liked" to have returned Henderson to the post, but he well knew that "the Jews feel he is pro-Arab."[44] As it turned out, Zionists felt the same way about Byroade, who, like Henderson, would eventually be driven out of the post under pressure from the Israel lobby.

Byroade offered a sweeping critique condemning the "sudden series of border incidents perpetrated by Israel," the "demand for complete control of the Jordan River," and "refusal to cooperate" flowing from "arrogant

FIGURE 11 Journalist Dorothy Thompson became a leading spokesperson for AFME, created in 1951 as part of a broad CIA campaign to counter the growing influence of the Israel lobby. Thompson later declared that her counter-Zionist activism cost her myriad friends and undermined her standing in public affairs. Bettmann/Getty Images

and obstructive attitudes toward the United Nations" and truce supervision personnel. While acting "to preclude a reasonable settlement, Israel has made considerable progress in the propaganda battle to convince the American public of the justice of her case." Publicly claiming to adhere to a "vision of peace of the prophets of Israel," the Zionist state had instead acted "to counter United States endeavors to stabilize conditions in the area." Fueled by "an almost mystical belief" in their destiny, "the Israelis appear unable to show the realism required for a successful adjustment into the Near Eastern environment."[45]

In April 1954, the Israel lobby lashed back when Byroade went public with his criticisms in a speech before the Dayton World Affairs Council. Declaring that Israel was "behaving like a conqueror," Byroade emphasized concerns about the erosion of US influence in the Arab world. Eban lodged a protest against the speech, and the AJC's Blaustein arranged

FIGURE 12 Rabbi Elmer Berger, pictured in 1956, was for many years the leading voice of the anti-Zionist ACJ, which opposed creation of a "Jewish state." For years Berger and the ACJ labored, ultimately unsuccessfully, to stymie efforts by the Israel lobby to make American Jewish identity synonymous with support for Israel.
Denver Post/Getty Images

a meeting with Dulles "to express his apprehension that the 'impartial policy' was going a little far in certain respects." Byroade responded, "The American people have a right to be informed of the fundamental causes of tension in the Middle East which affected their security."[46]

Byroade showed "a tender solicitude for the sensibilities and feelings of the Arabs," Kenen charged after a meeting with the diplomat, but "did not show a similar concern" for Israel or American Jews. The lobby bitterly resented Byroade's close relationship with Berger and his collaboration with the ACJ, "an organization whose sole reason for existence is an unnatural hostility" toward Israel. Kenen condemned Byroade's advocacy as "bewildering and incomprehensible," filled with "insubstantial" arguments.[47] Byroade clearly had replaced Henderson "as the Zionists' most hated figure in the State Department."[48]

Dulles initially defended Byroade against the lobby attack, telling Lipsky that the diplomat's argument was "basically sound, and I am not disposed to repudiate it."[49] However, as the clashes with the Zionist lobby intensified, Dulles concluded that Byroade's "perception and judgment are good but he is brittle, jerky, and prone to antagonize. Also I feel he is inclined to make presentations going beyond his instructions and usual diplomatic procedure." Byroade was "too personally identified with issues" and his "morale" was declining amid the clash with the Israelis and their American backers. Dulles sympathized, explaining to Nixon, "Unless you adopt an all-out Zionist policy, it is hard," but he decided nonetheless to reassign Byroade as ambassador in Egypt, and subsequently in 1956 to South Africa.[50]

Asserting its growing influence in Congress, the Israel lobby fended off challenges from the DOS, AFME, ACJ, and other non-Zionist groups. Berger averred that opposing the Zionist lobby was akin to navigating against the flow of a massive holiday parade. Fading from public influence, Thompson declared that her criticism of Israel "lost me thousands of previous admirers and scores of personal friends." While the anti-Zionist groups had virtually no members of Congress in their ranks, the ACPC counted scores of senators and representatives as members. Thus, "mainline Protestants outmaneuvered the anti-Zionist liberal Protestants," while fundamentalists remained solidly behind Israel.[51]

Endeavoring to advance an ambitious peace plan code-named Project Alpha, Dulles realized he had no choice other than to improve relations with Israel and the domestic lobby, hence the decision to reassign Byroade. Under the Alpha proposal, which Dulles developed in concert with Great Britain in 1954, Israel would acknowledge the Arab refugee issue by taking in 75,000 returning Palestinians over a five-year period. The Arab states would take in the remaining hundreds of thousands of refugees, recognize Israel, end the maritime blockade and economic boycott, and all concerned would embrace Johnston's Jordan River Valley plan. Border adjustments would provide a corridor connecting Jordan and Egypt through the Negev Desert, which Israel would nonetheless retain. Finally, the United States would contribute generous financial inducements to accommodate refugees of all stripes and sweeten the agreement for all concerned.[52]

In order to generate Israeli as well as Arab support, the administration would have to ameliorate "the rapidly deteriorating Israel situation with its inevitable repercussions on the American Jewish fraternity." Rabb and Katzen undertook "some missionary work" in an effort to address the "tremendous dissatisfaction among friends of Israel in this country." Dulles was hopeful about Alpha but fully aware of the challenges, as he told Dewey. Israel, "aggressive and well-armed" and with a penchant for "roving into neutral territory," would be hard to bring to the table, whereas for their part the Arabs "talk big and don't seem to work for peace."[53]

As the 1954 Midterm elections loomed, the Israel lobby, homing in on the Congress, mounted a campaign against military aid to Arabs and in favor of economic and military assistance to the Zionist state. In March, some 20 members of Congress arranged a meeting in the DOS to object to arms sales to Arab states and promote arming Israel instead.[54] Dulles declared that the United States "does not exclude the possibility of arms sales to Israel," but he added that security in the Middle East "cannot rest upon arms sales alone but rather upon the international rule of law." As he reminded the legislators, "The Arab refugees remain perhaps the most important single source of bitterness existing between the Arab States and Israel," hence the issue had to be addressed in the peace plan.[55]

Israel and its supporters appealed for aid, citing the high cost of settling new Jewish migrants, but received little support from Dulles. "Whether Israel should have an immigration policy which could create economic problems might be a matter for Israel to decide," the nation's top diplomat declared. He added that Arab resentment spiked when the United States "provided financial support for such immigration" while doing nothing to repatriate the displaced Palestinians.[56]

The administration tried to stand firm against increased pressure from the lobby and Congress. In April Eisenhower affirmed, "We should continue our present policy of impartiality and should not be deterred by political pressures which might generate in connection with the forth-coming elections."[57] Dulles vowed he would "not allow himself to be stampeded" into arming the Israelis, explaining that it would "be inter-preted throughout the Arab world that we have capitulated again. All we have tried to do will be lost." The diplomat wanted to "try to do some-thing, but the Israelis themselves in speeches have been urging the Jews in this country to put the heat on us."[58]

At the end of October, Dulles summoned Eban to a confidential meet-ing, arranging his arrival through a "private elevator." Dulles advised Eban that "He ought to know that we knew that there were Israeli Embassy activities which seemed clearly to go beyond the bounds of what was proper for a foreign government in that they involved domestic political action." Dulles asked the Israeli diplomat to take "proper steps" to rein in activity that went "beyond the bounds of propriety." Eban promised to "look into the situation," which merely reflected a "natural desire on the part of his Government and his Embassy to develop friend-ships on the part of the American people." Four days later, AZCPA announced that more than 300 candidates for Congress from 36 states and 25 Senate nominees "have declared their opposition to the sending of arms to the Arab states under present conditions."[59]

ISRAEL LASHES OUT

Ignoring US calls to exercise restraint, Israel maintained "a deliberate Government policy" of "aggravating the border situation ... at the risk of open warfare." However, in the wake of international condemnation over Qibya, Israel confined attacks to bases and police outposts across the borders with Egypt and Jordan in an effort to minimize victimization of women and children. Israel justified the "retaliatory raids," but US diplomats noted, "The evidence indicates only individuals or small groups are responsible" for episodic infiltration across the border. They reiterated that Jordan as well as Egypt had not authorized – and indeed had tried to impede – Palestinian returns and Fedayeen attacks on Jewish settlements.[60]

Increasingly focused on Nasser as the exemplar of rising Arab nationalism, Israel stepped up pressure on Egypt over the continuing closure of the Suez Canal to Israel-flagged ships since the War of 1948. In 1951 the Truman administration supported a successful UNSC resolution in opposition to the Egyptian restrictions on canal traffic, but the lack of enforcement angered the Israelis. Egypt also established a blockade in the Gulf of Aqaba, a move supported by the Saudis and a position for which the Arab regimes could claim some legitimacy under international law. The DOS "considered Egypt's blockade legal since both channels lay within three miles of Egypt or the Egyptian-occupied Tiran Island."[61]

Ben-Gurion and his militant colleagues adopted a worst-case scenario of Nasser as an implacable foe dedicated to uniting the Arab world behind the destruction of the Jews. They assumed war with Egypt was inevitable. "Yet," as Israeli historian Motti Golani notes, "this attitude seems to have been more a state of mind than the result of a systematic evaluation of the situation, and consequently requiring no concrete proof." The Israeli leaders began to speak of "preventive war," adds Shlaim, though "there was no evidence that Egypt planned to attack Israel."[62]

After replacing Ben-Gurion as prime minister in the wake of Qibya, Sharett wanted to pursue a "quiet and deft diplomacy" that included establishing the "first and only link Israel has ever had with Egypt," the CIA noted. He had "hoped to negotiate a lasting peace between the Arabs and the Jews" and to work with Nasser accordingly.[63] The Israeli hard-liners believed, however, that aggression rather than diplomacy represented the best course of action. Taking up the slack for Ben-Gurion in his abbreviated retirement was Dayan, who became the IDF chief and routinely ignored orders from Sharett, thus undermining the moderate prime minister's ability to govern. Also contemptuous of Sharett's authority was Pinhas Lavon, the new minister of defense but a man of "unstable character," and the architect of an audacious false-flag espionage operation in July 1954 that entailed bombing US Information Service libraries and other Western targets in Cairo and Alexandria. The terror attacks would then be blamed on the Muslim Brotherhood in an effort to desta-bilize Nasser and to "damage US–Egyptian relations," but the failed plot was exposed.[64]

In concert with Ben-Gurion, ostensibly in retirement, Lavon, Dayan, and Shimon Peres plotted to detach Gaza from Egypt, renew aggression on the Syrian border, and partition Lebanon in order to forge a Maronite Christian state that might ally with Israel. Sharett opposed and tried to contain all of these schemes, but absent Ben-Gurion's support he was outflanked and eventually forced from office in 1956.[65]

In addition to the effort to provoke war with Egypt, Israel resumed aggression on the Syrian borders. In December 1954, five Israeli soldiers were captured inside Syrian territory. A year later, Israel attacked Syrian positions on Lake Tiberius, killing 50 compared with 10 Israeli dead, and taking another 30 prisoner. The UNSC condemned the Israeli aggression as a "flagrant violation" of the armistice agreement as well as the UN Charter.[66]

Viewing Sharett as weak, and determined to overthrow Nasser, Ben-Gurion stormed back from retirement in February 1955 and promptly launched Operation Black Arrow, a cross-border assault on Egypt. The attack, led by Sharon, targeted Egyptian army headquarters outside Gaza City and killed some 40 Egyptian soldiers and wounded about 30, compared with 8 Israeli dead and 9 wounded. Isolated and irregular Fedayeen raids had been initiated from Gaza in the past, but claims that Sharon's assault on the military outpost came in response to an Egyptian attack against Israel were "patently untrue."[67] The UNSC unanimously condemned the "prearranged and planned" Israeli attack in Gaza.[68]

Recognizing that Nasser "cannot take another Gaza-like attack by the Israelis lying down," Dulles labored to keep the lid on the Israeli–Egyptian border conflict and to keep the Alpha peace plan alive. He failed at both. The DOS at the time and historians since have argued that the Lavon affair and the Gaza raid stemmed from Israel's "calculated attempt to antagonize Nasser and strangle the Anglo–American peace plan in its cradle."[69]

With Ben-Gurion and Dayan actively trying to provoke war and regime change in Cairo, the Israelis attacked across the border in late August. Dulles told Eisenhower the Israelis knew "Egypt's cease-fire order was genuine," but rather than "respond in kind" they had "struck across the border."[70] Aware that Nasser planned to unleash a commando attack in retaliation, the DOS tried to head it off at the last minute, but some of the attackers went forward, killing 17 Israelis. The action played into the hands of the Israeli hardliners. In November the IDF attacked Egyptian territory along the DMZ on orders from Dayan, killing 50 Egyptian soldiers and capturing 50 more in the largest military assault since the end of the 1948 war.[71]

Nasser cited the aggression in Gaza as the driving force behind the major arms deal he signed with Soviet-allied Czechoslovakia in September 1955. Much to the alarm of the Israelis and the Americans, Egypt would receive MIG fighter jets, tanks, and armored personnel carriers from the Soviet bloc. The move – precisely what Dulles and the DOS had hoped to preclude by pursuing the "impartial policy" – disturbed the nation's top diplomat. Dulles kept the faith about his Alpha peace plan, to which he gave maximum publicity in a speech before the Council on Foreign Relations in New York on August 26 amid the border conflict. The diplomat called for a "spirit of conciliation" to overcome mistrust and to address the "tragic plight of 900,000 refugees who formerly lived in the territory that is now occupied by Israel." Days later he told Eisenhower that the Arab reaction was "not as violently against as we feared," but the Israelis remained unmoved. Eban summarily dismissed Alpha, declaring that "The whole proposal smacks of Munich." Meanwhile, Ben-Gurion and Dayan wanted war, not peace.[72]

With the Israelis actively seeking to provoke war, Nasser rejected the US suggestion that Egypt had within its power the ability to forge a peace settlement. "You continue to talk of the problems with Israel as if they were my problems which I have to settle," Nasser told Eisenhower's envoy Robert Anderson. "They are in fact your problems and you must settle them. You will have to solve the problem of Israeli aggressiveness."[73] The momentum toward open warfare accelerated with the failure of the Anderson mission combined with the subsequent breakdown of negotiations over US efforts to win over Nasser by financing construction of the Aswan high dam in Egypt.[74] The reason for the reversal was Dulles's anger over Nasser's recognition of "Red" China the previous week. The United States, he explained on May 22, 1956, "could not look with favor" on the Egyptian leader's actions that served "to promote the interests of the Soviet Union and Communist China."[75] In Cairo, Byroade, soon to be exiled to Pretoria, criticized "negative thinking" about Egypt and noted the imbalance of policy in cutting off assistance to the leading Arab state even as "other countries including Israel continue to receive economic aid."[76]

Israel wanted armaments in addition to economic assistance, and when Washington demurred Ben-Gurion and his colleagues turned to France. "The Israeli military wanted a war," Golani explains, but needed "the support of an external power that would supply Israel with arms and give backing in the international arena." France, believing incorrectly that Nasser was playing a critical role in the war of independence being waged against the French settler colony in Algeria, supplied the arms and the alliance the Israelis needed. When the British entered into the alliance with France and Israel, planning began for the attack on Egypt that was to culminate in the overthrow of Nasser.[77]

The trigger for the invasion was Nasser's announcement in July that he was nationalizing the Suez Canal Company, which controlled the waterway constructed under British and French colonialism in 1869. Nasser's nationalization of the Suez Canal had not been aimed at Israel, yet Ben-Gurion saw an opportunity to overthrow the Egyptian leader and deliver a blow to the perceived threat of rising Arab nationalism while at the same time internationalizing the canal, expanding Israel's borders, and reaping the security benefits of the reassertion of Western influence in the Middle East. As an added bonus, amid planning for the Suez invasion France secretly agreed to assist Israel in constructing a nuclear reactor at Dimona in the Negev Desert.[78]

The United States condemned Nasser's nationalization of the Suez Canal, but tried to achieve a diplomatic solution to the crisis short of war. In tripartite talks held with the British and the French in London from July 29 to August 2, Washington encountered a pair of belligerent yet insecure allies reeling from a sweeping postcolonial decline. Complicating the matter, nationalization of the canal was sanctioned under international law when accompanied by the compensation that Nasser pledged to pay. The Egyptian leader also pledged to allow international monitoring. Egypt sought the revenues and the right to supervise the canal as other countries did in other waterways, including the United States in the Panama Canal located some 1,000 miles from US shores.[79] The belligerent allies were not interested in such comparisons, nor would they be impeded by international law.

UN Secretary General Dag Hammarskjold sought to affirm a pledge made by Ben-Gurion that Israel would not "do anything to disturb the peace." The Israeli leader struck Hammarskjold as "almost a solitary dictator," and, moreover, "almost totally in the wrong" on the crucial issues of the Arab–Israeli conflict. Hammarskjold urged Ben-Gurion to abandon his penchant for aggressive "retaliation," which he found both "immoral and expedient," and "expressed regret that so far the UN have been ignored" on the Suez affair that was instead taking on a lamentable "Europe v. Asia complexion." Hammarskjold reminded Ben-Gurion, as well as the British and French, that use of force against Egyptian territory would be clear violation of the UN Charter.[80]

As the Suez Crisis approached a boiling point, the lobby focused on the 1956 election campaign. In June, AZCPA hosted 17 national Jewish organizations at a strategy conference in Washington. The lobby sharply opposed the Alpha proposals, including summary rejection of Israel taking in Palestinian refugees. The Jewish leaders also rejected the proposed Arab corridor through the Negev, declaring, "We have heard with regret that there are proposals that Israel be asked to yield vital territory of her small area to the Arab states." Condemning the administration for following "the road to appeasement," AZCPA declared, "The American people will not tolerate anything so immoral as the sacrifice of Israel to Communist infiltration of the Near East. The time to act is now."[81]

Working closely with Rep. Celler, Kenen mounted a successful pressure campaign urging existing members and candidates for Congress to sign a letter in support of arms for Israel. At the time, amid the escalating crisis with Egypt the administration had held up a shipment of helicopters, half-tracks, and machine guns while urging Canada to delay a supply of F-86 jets for Israel. The AZCPA letter, declaring that it was "vital that our Government act decisively" by arming Israel "strictly for purposes of self-defense," advised local councils to send a "congratulatory message" to members of Congress who signed the letter in support of military aid to Israel: "If your Congressman did not sign, please wire or write him" to do so, it urged, pointing out that the list of signatories would be published. In August, Kenen reported that the "eight-week campaign involving Congressional and community leaders all over the country produced 151 signatures to the letter." That same month Dulles released the weapons package to Israel.[82]

In the 1956 campaign, the lobby again succeeded in lining up both Democratic and Republican platforms strongly in support of Israel. Kenen celebrated the "psychological impact on the Arab world" of US political support, which made it "clear that the US does not intend to let Israel down." Republicans emphasized unquestioning support for Israel, while the Democratic plank declared that a "dangerous imbalance of arms" in favor of the Arabs required "supplying defensive weapons to Israel." Once again the Democratic nominee for president, Stevenson, repeatedly called into question the commitment of Eisenhower and Dulles to Israeli security. In October, following an attack by infiltrators from Jordan killing 13 Israelis, the IDF launched a disproportionate retaliatory assault, killing 69 soldiers and destroying three army posts. Vowing that he would "not be influenced by domestic politics" amid the presidential campaign, Eisenhower warned the Israelis that the United States would not tolerate a general assault on Jordan.[83]

THE SINAI WAR

On October 29, despite Ben-Gurion's pledge not to "disturb the peace," the Israeli military struck the ill-prepared Egyptian positions in an assault orchestrated by Dayan. Two days later, Israel's allies joined the campaign, which quickly subdued Egypt. Backed by allied air power, which "effectively decided the war for Israel," the IDF dominated Egyptian forces on the ground, seizing the Gaza Strip and the Sinai Peninsula, sweeping across the canal, and taking some 6,000 prisoners and substantial military equipment in the process.[84] Fulfilling a major goal of Dayan's war plan, Israel occupied Sharm el-Sheikh, a city on the strategic point at the tip of the Sinai Peninsula overlooking the Gulf of Aqaba, in an effort to ensure unfettered Israeli access through the Straits of Tiran to the Indian Ocean.[85]

While the Israelis celebrated, the Eisenhower administration feared the destabilizing global impact unleashed by the largest international military confrontation since the Korean War. Eisenhower, whose brilliant military career had centered on trust and cooperation among allies, condemned the aggressors for their mendacity and resort to war. Adding to the insult, the action came in the final days of his re-election campaign and, moreover, detracted international attention from the coinciding Soviet invasion of Hungary. The administration had to consider the possibility of a wider war in which the Soviets, allied with "Red" China, might come in on the side of Egypt in an effort to force the United States to side with the colonial powers, thus undermining its standing with Third World nations.[86]

Determined to rein in the Israelis as well as the European allies, Eisenhower declared, "We must make good on our word" to defend legally established international boundaries; "We should let them know at once of our position, telling them that we recognize that much is on their side in the dispute with the Egyptians, but that nothing justifies double-crossing us."[87] Israel proved by far the most recalcitrant of the three allies. Moreover, "Britain and France took the brunt of international pressure and superpower outrage," Golani points out, "and this was one of the most important kinds of help they gave Israel in the Sinai War."[88]

After bludgeoning Britain and France into accepting a ceasefire on November 6, the administration turned its attention to Israel. The Zionist state accepted the ceasefire, but proved congenitally resistant to relinquishing its conquests.[89] In a victory speech before the Knesset on November 7, Ben-Gurion rejected the call for UN troops to replace the invasion force in Egyptian territory. The Israeli leader declared that the Egyptian armistice agreement and the 1949 boundaries were "dead and buried." At the same time, Hammarskjold reported that Israeli troops were forcing UN observers out of Gaza. Silver, among others, called for Israel summarily to annex Gaza, but Ben-Gurion responded that Israel would be unable to "digest" the Strip with its large predominately Palestinian and refugee population.[90]

Refusing to appease Israel, Eisenhower employed diplomatic language that barely veiled threats to cut off funding and to sponsor UN action to censure, sanction, or even expel the Zionist state. Eisenhower expressed his "deep concern" about "statements attributed to your government to the effect that Israel does not intend to withdraw from Egyptian territory." He added, "It would be a matter of the greatest regret to all my countrymen if Israel policy on a matter of such great concern to the world should in any way impair the friendly cooperation between our two countries."[91] With the UN and the United States aligned, Ben-Gurion had little room to maneuver and eventually would be forced to pull back. Privately, he lashed out at the US ambassador to Israel and accused the UN of dispensing "perverted justice."[92] In Washington, Eban claimed that Egypt had planned to "destroy Israel," adding that it was a "great mistake" to stop them from toppling Nasser and instead putting him "back on his feet."[93] Dulles told Meir, Sharett's replacement as foreign minister and an acolyte of Ben-Gurion, that Israel should have made peace with its "Arab neighbors," but instead "what Israel had done in Egypt had deferred this possibility for perhaps a generation." Meir responded by blaming the Arabs exclusively for the unrest.[94]

The Israeli attack and the Eisenhower administration's determined response created another crisis for the Israel lobby. The American Zionists were taken by surprise by the attack and placed in the unenviable position of backing a popular president and their own government or siding with Israel and risking the dreaded charge of "dual loyalty." The Conference of Presidents of Major Jewish Organizations convened in emergency session and held a series of follow up meetings. American Jews were divided in their response, prompting Eban to observe, tellingly, that "for the first time in our memory there was reluctance" of Jewish leaders "to justify Israel's actions without reserve."[95]

Although polls showed that most Americans, including many Jews, had responded negatively to the tripartite invasion, AZCPA was able to regain equilibrium and build popular support behind the effort to fend off sanctions and bolster the Israeli claim to maritime rights and security guarantees. With the Israeli Embassy promoting "comprehensive hasbara" activities, AZCPA sent out letters urging "friends" to "form committees of your local Zionists councils – together with all Jewish organizations willing to cooperate – to visit leading officials, clergymen, editors, teachers, labor leaders, and others." As always, the lobby campaign homed in on Congress, with Kenen and his aides carefully tracking the statements and positions of representatives and senators on proposed sanctions and the US demand for withdrawal from Gaza and the Gulf of Aqaba.[96]

The lobby effort received support from several influential representatives and senators, but none more vital than Senate Majority Leader

Lyndon B. Johnson (D-TX). Using his notorious powers of persuasion, known as "the Johnson treatment," the Texas Democrat and lifelong friend of Israel (see Chapter 5) carried the congressional debate in Israel's favor. Thus, as Olivia Sohns argues, the rejection of sanctions was "largely due to Johnson's intervention."[97]

Johnson criticized Eisenhower for allegedly being harder on Israel for invading Egypt than on the Soviet Union for invading Hungary. The prospect of sanctions against the "little State" of Israel "disturbed" Johnson, who held Egypt and the surrounding Arab states largely responsible for the Middle East conflict. He viewed as a "double standard" that there had been "no suggestion in the United Nations that economic sanctions should be applied against Egypt that force that state to agree to permanent cessation of hostilities from those areas." Johnson, who had not previously challenged Eisenhower–Dulles foreign policy, declared that "justice and morality" ruled out any sanctioning of Israel.[98]

Citing its intensive lobbying efforts in Congress, AZCPA took credit for unleashing the "uproar on Capitol Hill that deterred the Administration from imposing sanctions."[99] Dulles remained keenly aware of the lobby's clout, noting, "Israel's principal outside support came from the United States" and that "many American citizens were loyal supporters of Israel." The nation's top diplomat complained that the "pressure of the Jews" was causing a "very nasty situation on [Capitol] Hill." Dulles indulged in a familiar stereotype, as he complained of "the terrific control the Jews had over the news media." In the end, however, the mainstream press, while sympathetic to Israel and critical of Egypt, nonetheless urged Israeli withdrawal from the Sinai.[100]

On February 20, 1957, Eisenhower delivered a televised address to express his "keen disappointment" over the continuing occupation and his insistence on an Israeli withdrawal. The president declared bluntly that it was wrong "that a nation which invades another should be permitted to exact conditions for withdrawal." Under intense pressure, Israel finally agreed to withdraw from the Gaza Strip as well as the Sinai Peninsula. "While US pressure was certainly the most powerful agent," a US diplomat averred, "expulsion from the UN and Israel's isolation were almost equally strong incentive factors" in finally forcing the Israeli withdrawal.[101]

Crucially, Israel's withdrawal was not unconditional. The Israelis claimed the right to re-intervene in Gaza if the UN occupation forces failed to preclude Fedayeen attacks. Moreover, committed to securing access to the Indian Ocean through the Straits of Tiran, Israel agreed to withdraw from Sharm el-Sheikh only on the basis of a US guarantee that a UN occupation force would ensure continuing Israeli maritime access. The Israelis planned to develop the adjacent port city of Eilat for Indian Ocean trade, which required unfettered access to the Gulf of Aqaba. The US guarantee, stipulated in an aide-mémoire, served that purpose but angered the Arabs, who condemned the Americans for taking the "Israeli side."

The Arab states claimed the Gulf of Aqaba was "a narrow closed gulf governed by Arab territorial waters" rather than an international waterway. Saudi Arabia, which assumed responsibility for ensuring access for Muslim pilgrimages to Mecca, asserted Israel was now in a position to disrupt such traffic and in essence was being rewarded for its aggression in Egypt with new maritime rights and claims. "Greatly disturbed," King Saud lodged an official protest, insisting "there should be merely a return to the status quo ante" and that "any alteration would be seriously objectionable." In July 1957, Dulles reported, "The situation in the Gulf of Aqaba was acute and that according to Naval intelligence reports was being exacerbated by the presence of Israeli war vessels."[102] A decade later the dispute over the gulf and the Straits of Tiran would trigger yet another Middle East war.

Arguably more than any American president before or since, Eisenhower had confronted Israeli aggression and forced the Zionist state to relinquish seized territory. Although the forced withdrawal was anomalous in the history of the settler conflict, and even though many Zionists were "sincerely disturbed" that "the fruits of victory have been given away too cheaply," Israeli aggression had produced critically important new security guarantees from the United States endorsing their position on the international status of the Gulf of Aqaba.[103]

Nasser's defiance of Israel and the Western powers and his rising popularity threatened to unleash a "strongly running flood" of Soviet-allied Arab nationalism, Dulles feared.[104] Accordingly, in January 1957 Eisenhower propounded his "doctrine" pledging US economic and military support to help Middle Eastern countries fend off communism, but the initiative was also designed to contain the spread of Nasserism.[105] The JCS insisted, however, that the support of Arab states could be "achieved and retained only by decisive US political and diplomatic action to solve the present Arab-Israeli dispute." The nation's top generals called for agreements on resettlement of Palestinian refugees, the status of Jerusalem, and Arab recognitions of Israel in return for a "Western guarantee that Israel will not thereafter expand territorially." The United

FIGURE 13 President Dwight D. Eisenhower and Secretary of State John Foster Dulles, shown here discussing Egyptian nationalization of the Suez Canal in a radio address on August 3, 1956, tried but failed to reassert the "impartial" policy and forge a Middle East peace accord. Following the tripartite invasion of Egypt, Eisenhower forced the aggressors to withdraw prompting an embittered response from the Israelis who nonetheless received important security guarantees on access to the Gulf of Aqaba.
PhotoQuest/Getty Images

States "should take this action now," the JCS advised, before the Soviet Union further exploited the conflict to make inroads in the region.[106]

The generals bluntly declared that the Israel lobby should not be allowed to stand in the way of the nation's broader foreign policy aims: "The threat to US security inherent in failing to take the initiative and solving this problem is so great as to transcend the interests of any minority group within the United States."[107] Having been down this road with his own Project Alpha, fended off by Israeli aggression and the formidable defense mechanisms of the lobby, Dulles dismissed the Pentagon push for a settlement as "simply not realistic."[108]

Fears of metastasizing, Soviet-backed Arab radicalism lay behind another CIA coup attempt targeting the pro-Nasser government in

Damascus. The failed operation backfired, as it facilitated the decision by Egypt and Syria to fuse into the United Arab Republic (UAR) in 1958. In July of that year a brutal military coup unfolded in Iraq, shattering the Baghdad Pact and creating a perceived threat to Western access to Mid-east oil. Fearing that he might meet a similar fate, Lebanon's Christian President, Camille Chamoun – who had come to power in an election rigged by the CIA and was "not representative of Lebanon's population" – requested US intervention.[109] Within 48 hours of the Baghdad coup, Eisenhower invoked his doctrine and the United States launched its first direct military intervention in the Middle East, as some 5,000 Marines landed in Beirut. Operation Bluebat, eventually comprising some 14,000 US military personnel, ended after a few months following the election of a new president and some reduction in the sectarian strife in Lebanon. However, like previous US interventions in the region, it left a legacy of distrust and broadened anti-American popular sentiments.[110]

Eban had encouraged US military intervention in the region months before the Marine landing in Lebanon. He told Dulles the administration should consider establishing a US "military presence," noting that an American "defensive arrangement" with neighboring Lebanon would be "a source of great assurance" to Israel.[111] The Eisenhower administration continued to fend off Israeli requests for alliance membership and permanent stationing of US forces in the Middle East. Dulles offered reassurance, however, "that if Israel should be the victim of unprovoked aggression to extinguish its sovereignty our response would be just as good as it was in the Lebanese case." Such US support provided "a real sense of security" while also serving "as a deterrent to Israel's enemies."[112]

THE LOBBY RESPONDS TO NEW CHALLENGES

In 1957, AZCPA faced a financial crisis as a result of the loss of tax-exempt status and the high cost of lobbying to defend Israel in the Sinai crisis. As revenues "fell sharply," the lobbying organization "would have gone bankrupt" if it took no action, Kenen declared. "I don't have a dime," he mused, "and cannot possibly continue putting up my own money" to bolster lobbying activities. Kenen had absorbed a substantial pay cut in his official salary to just over $9,000 (about $80,000 in 2018 dollars). Thus, on both personal and professional grounds, Kenen expressed concern about the solvency of the entire lobbying enterprise.[113]

Kenen and benefactors responded adroitly by launching the signature publication of the Israel lobby, the *Near East Report* (*NER*). On the advice of counsel, the lobbyists established the *NER* as a separate corporation. "Our organizations have always felt they could not legally contribute to the AZCPA because they did not want to endanger their tax exemption," Kenen explained. "But there is nothing to prevent them from subscribing to the *Near East Report*" as long as it had "no corporate or organizational connection with the AZCPA."[114] Kenen noted, for example, that the Zionist women's organization Hadassah was making a substantial contribution by purchasing multiple copies of the *NER*, whereas it "would not make such a payment to the AZCPA because of the Committee's lobbying activities." Asserting that the *NER* "fills a very great need," AZCPA undertook a "systematic effort" to circulate it "to all Congressmen and many editors," as well as Jewish organizations, college professors, libraries, and churches. Within months, *NER* circulation topped 5,700, with a goal of 20,000 by 1959.[115]

Noting that "Journalism is my first love," Kenen brought a high level of "excitement and enthusiasm" to his role as the editor of *NER*. He claimed the newsletter reflected a "sincere effort to present the facts objectively." Given the lobby's mission and the newsletter's contents, the claim can hardly be taken seriously, but what Kenen understood was that the "news"-letter would be most effective if it presented itself as a "concise and authoritative record of all significant happenings in the Near East."[116]

After less than a year of publication, Kenen exulted that "The *Near East Report* has caught on" and "proved to be a godsend."[117] Circulating widely in Congress, the *NER* featured speeches and resolutions by Javits, Celler, and other lobby stalwarts, thus rewarding their pro-Israeli advocacy with favorable publicity and prompting other representatives and senators to climb on the bandwagon. The well-edited newsletter's regular features included "Heard in Washington," "Propaganda Pressures" (decrying *Arab* propaganda), and "Viewing the News." The *NER* relentlessly pursued a handful of staple propaganda themes, most prominently economic and military assistance for Israel while opposing the same to the Arab states; hostility to Arab leaders, especially Nasser; and condemnation of the Arab states' economic blockade and "blacklist." As the newsletter evolved, Kenen began to publish 30-page special supplements, took in advertising, and added book reviews and other features.[118]

As the end of the Eisenhower presidency neared, the special relationship remained firmly intact despite the sharp tensions that had erupted over Israeli aggression, from Qibya to the Suez conflict. In October 1958,

Meir declared that Israel was "very happy with the course of developments between the United States and Israel in the past year. She felt there
was no basic difference of views between the countries regarding the
situation in the Middle East." Kenen concurred, noting, "American
friendship for Israel is at a peak and that American-Israel relations were
never better than they are at this moment."[119]

Israel had successfully parried the Palestinian refugee issue, laid claim
to Jerusalem, held onto its expanded boundaries while carrying out
aggressive border attacks culminating in a full-scale war with Egypt, and
had solidified US guarantees of its security in the process. When disputes
arose the Israel lobby was quick to intervene and to mobilize its growing
support in the Congress. When Eban complained that he had "been
unable to obtain information" about a hold-up of an Israeli loan request,
AZCPA fueled protests from Celler and Javits, who were joined by Reps.
Kenneth Keating (R-NY) and Hugh Scott (R-PA). Washington had held
up financial assistance after the Sinai invasion, in lieu of US requests for
Israeli cooperation on the Palestinian refugee issue, and over concerns
about the costs of the rapid rate of growth of ongoing immigration to the
Jewish state. In April 1959, AZCPA, Israel's supporters in Congress, and
Eban decried "political conditions" being "attached" to the loan.
The DOS backed off, advising "that it was certainly not the
Department's intention to deny aid to Israel, or to put ambassador Eban
on the spot." Once again, the financial flows promptly resumed.[120]

By this time Kenen had amassed extensive files on the voting records of
all members of Congress. The lobby compiled data categorizing elected
representatives as "active champions," or merely "sympathetic," "leaning
toward Israel," "indifferent," and "leaning away," and then used the
information to spur supporters and pressure others. Working with Eban
and Kollek, among other Israelis, the lobby sponsored "a series of dinner
parties," each attended by scores of House members and Senators: "private functions at which Ambassador Eban" and other featured guests
could "present [their] country's views."[121]

Kenen was determined to secure increased US financial assistance for
Israel but "did not want to inflate this question into a public controversy
which might impair US-Israeli relations." In March 1959 a "Dear Friend"
letter to supporters in local councils and other organizations nationwide
advised that, with Congress adjourning, many representatives "will be
home for the next week. This offers an opportunity to let your
Congressman know" of the need to vote in favor of aid to Israel:
"We want letters written by Christians as well as Jews." The local councils

were advised that "Letters should be original and personal. Please do not send mimeographed appeals – they provoke an adverse reaction."[122]

After securing renewed US financial assistance for Israel, the lobby spurred a "revolt on Capitol Hill" in opposition to a World Bank loan to Egypt. They failed to block the loan, which funded postwar repairs and improvements to the Suez Canal, but claimed a "splendid paper victory" by securing passage of an amendment to a foreign aid authorization bill expressing the "sense of Congress" that the president should deny assistance to any nation that waged "economic warfare" such as blockades or boycotts. Eisenhower condemned the amendment, which targeted Egypt yet had no teeth.

The debate over the "freedom of the seas" bill, as the amendment was dubbed, marked the emergence of Sen. J. William Fulbright (D-AR) as a formidable foe of the Israel lobby. Fulbright used his chairmanship of the SFRC to block the amendment, and when that failed he sought to attach provisos that would apply sanctions simultaneously to nations that were defying UN peacekeeping efforts or impeding resolution of the Palestinian refugee issue. The measures clearly targeted Israel. Despite the "violent reaction" and much "unpleasantness" amid the debate over the amendment, the "outcome was healthy," Kenen advised Eban. The important point was that Congress had rallied behind the campaign, passed the amendment, and fended off opposition from a prominent senator as well as the president.[123]

Irritated by the growing clout of the lobby, and stonewalled by the Israelis on a host of issues, the Eisenhower administration was left soured on the special relationship. Perpetually concerned that the Arab–Israeli conflict created instability that heightened the prospects for the spread of Soviet influence throughout the Middle East, the administration had hoped to receive a higher degree of cooperation from its special ally. "Except for Israel," Eisenhower complained privately in July 1958, "we could form a viable policy in the area." Once the architect of an ambitious Middle East peace initiative, Dulles had come "reluctantly to the belief that a formal overall plan for the solution of the entire Arab-Israel dispute would be difficult of achievement."[124] Dulles "had been reading the Old Testament and they had the same problems as we have today . . . It did not make sense to think that he could solve problems which Moses and Joshua with Divine guidance could not solve."[125]

4

"What Kind of Relationship Was This?"

As the 1960 presidential campaign loomed, the lobby orchestrated a decisive restructuring with the creation of a new entity, the American Israel Public Affairs Committee (AIPAC). The reshuffle reinforced efforts to fend off federal scrutiny while better positioning the lobby for fundraising and exerting political influence. On August 11, 1959, Kenen registered AIPAC with the Department of Justice. Removal of "Zionist" from the lobby's name was a deliberate effort to broaden support, especially among non-Jews. The change was, Kenen explained, a reflection of "the fact that many non-Zionists were supporting its work, both with contributions and in public action." The AIPAC executive committee was simultaneously expanded "to co-opt leading American Jews. It also established a National Council in order to stimulate fundraising."[1]

As the 1960 campaign heated up, AIPAC manifested its growing political clout, hosting the first in a series of what were to become its signature annual policy conferences. The conference attracted politicians from both parties and "served to inform American Jewish leadership, as well as the public at large." AIPAC followed up by securing a Democratic plank in 1960 in support of direct negotiations with the Arab states, a longtime goal of Israeli policy. The Republican platform was more restrained but in the end both parties once again signed off on "strong pro-Israel declarations." With AIPAC quickly established as the dominant domestic champion of Israel, Kenen proudly proclaimed, "We speak for the American Jewish community as a whole."[2]

KENNEDY AND THE LOBBY

Israel and AIPAC celebrated the return of the Democrats to the White House in the closely contested 1960 election in which John F. Kennedy narrowly defeated Nixon, but dominated the Jewish vote. Kenen had "preferred Kennedy to Nixon," as the Massachusetts senator had developed into a strong supporter of Zionism whereas Nixon was tarred with the Eisenhower–Dulles legacy.[3] After returning from his wartime service in the Navy and promptly winning election to the House of Representatives in 1946, Kennedy realized that Zionists would scrutinize his views because of the association of his father, Joseph P. Kennedy Sr., with appeasement of Germany during his tenure as Roosevelt's ambassador to the Third Reich in the 1930s. Advisers Hirsh Freed and Lewis Weinstein were Zionists who had little doubt that Jack Kennedy would have a prominent political career, hence they encouraged him to embrace Israel. Kennedy initially turned down Weinstein's request that he address a Zionist convention meeting in Boston in June 1947. Weinstein, Freed, and other Zionist advisers concluded that Kennedy had been exposed to "Arab propaganda" and thus lacked a proper understanding of the issue. After a series of briefings and arranged meetings with proponents of Zionism, Kennedy embraced the pro-Israeli position. "Lew, you convinced me," Weinstein quotes Kennedy as saying; "I think every doubt has been erased." Kennedy agreed to address the Zionist convention, where he delighted some 1,000 delegates by declaring his support for "a free and democratic Jewish commonwealth in Palestine."[4]

Assisted by Freed and Weinstein, who was a "close friend" of Kenen, Kennedy successfully combated the efforts of Republican Henry Cabot Lodge to use the association of Kennedy's father with Nazi Germany against him in the 1952 Massachusetts senatorial campaign. Monitoring the campaign, Kenen noted that Kennedy "repeatedly affirmed his friendship with Israel."[5] Noting that he had passed through Palestine in 1939, Kennedy intoned during the Senate campaign, "The tragic plight of the Jewish people in Europe and the daring fight that was being made to build a new home in Israel under the guns of the British and the Arabs stirred me deeply." By that time Kennedy had revisited the area and toured the new Israel, which he described as a critical outpost of democracy. He also supported US economic assistance to the Zionist state.[6]

Throughout the 1950s, the Massachusetts senator spoke regularly before Jewish groups, prompting Kenen to observe that Kennedy "grew up in Boston, among Jews" and "feels at home with a Zionist audience."

In April 1956, Kennedy spoke at the "America Salutes Israel" program at Yankee Stadium. Kennedy melded his Zionism with recognition of rising Arab nationalism and the bitter legacies of colonialism. Though he condemned the Eisenhower–Dulles handling of the Middle East, Kennedy opposed the tripartite invasion of Egypt in 1956 and called for Israel to vacate the Sinai Peninsula. However, in February 1957, he rejected the Eisenhower administration's threat to enforce sanctions.[7]

Kennedy affirmed his Zionist credentials in a series of speeches before Jewish groups leading up to the 1960 presidential campaign. Indulging in familiar Orientalist stereotypes, Kennedy averred, "When the first Zionist convention met in 1897 Palestine was a wasted, neglected land" that had since been transformed, like the "Great American Desert," by "determined settlers" into a "a miracle of progress." Israel was "one of the youngest republics but one of the oldest of peoples," which through "miraculous rebirth and growth" had come to embody "all the characteristics of Western democracy." Kennedy sought to "dispel a prevalent myth . . . that without Israel there would somehow be a natural harmony throughout the Middle East and the Arab world." Endorsing modernization and development, Kennedy declared that support for Israel should not "foreclose any effort that promises a regeneration of a much wider segment of the Middle East." He assured that the Gulf of Aqaba would remain an open international waterway, and signed on as one of the sponsors of the "freedom of the seas" amendment.[8]

Kenen expected Kennedy to be "more receptive" than Eisenhower to support of Israel, but the lobbyist grew alarmed as the new president-elect considered appointing Fulbright as secretary of state. An outspoken critic of Israeli policies as well as a proponent of resettling some of the Palestinian refugees in Israel, Fulbright posed "a great danger," Kenen declared.[9] Kennedy chose Dean Rusk, a veteran DOS diplomat who had criticized Israeli policy in the past but was a much lower-profile personality than Fulbright.

Rusk would have to contend with Myer "Mike" Feldman, a Philadelphia businessman and attorney, who had joined Kennedy's staff in 1958 and played a central role in the 1960 presidential campaign. Kennedy's adviser on all matters Jewish, Feldman helped fend off Lyndon Johnson and Hubert Humphrey (D-MN) – both with impeccable Zionist credentials – in the Democratic primaries. Working with Kennedy ally Connecticut governor Abraham Ribicoff during the campaign, Feldman organized a large gathering of "the leaders of the Jewish community" for a meeting in Feinberg's New York apartment. The group included prominent Jews from Chicago

FIGURE 14 Philadelphia attorney and deputy special counsel Myer "Mike" Feldman, working in close liaison with the Israel lobby, served as President John F. Kennedy's top adviser on American Zionism and the Middle East conflict. JFK Library Photo by Abbie Rowe

and the West Coast as well as the East Coast. Kennedy reassured the gathering of his support for Israel as well as his embrace of liberal causes that were popular within the American Jewish community, including civil rights. Feldman judged the meeting a success and believed it "contributed to the enormous support he got from the Jewish voters" in the fall campaign.[10]

A deputy special counsel to the president, Feldman functioned essentially as a member of the Israel lobby inside the White House. He perceived his identities as "a Jew, as an American, as a Government official" to be in "harmonious relationship." Feldman recalled that he told

Kennedy "quite frankly that I had an emotional sympathy with Israel, and I was sure this would color any advice that I gave him, and maybe he would want somebody else. And he said to me, 'No', he said he would expect that I would have those sympathies" and that he wanted to be "advised in anything that was happening that he ought to know about. So I felt perfectly free to go to him at any time."[11]

Rusk expressed frequent frustration over Feldman's access to the president and his ties with the lobby, which included regular communication with Kenen and a close friendship with Avraham Harman, a veteran of Israeli hasbara efforts who had replaced Eban as ambassador in 1959. Rusk complained that it was "improper for an Israel diplomat to call on [Feldman]," thus bypassing the DOS. US diplomats complained that Feldman had become "the primary White House staff influence" on the Middle East conflict. "Actions dealing with Israel and Arab-Israeli matters and which could have a domestic political impact must now be cleared with the White House."[12]

Feldman played a central role in Israel's successful quest to achieve a breakthrough in securing advanced US military hardware, namely, Hawk surface-to-air defensive missiles. Rusk opposed sale of the Hawks, warning the president against encouraging a "Fortress Israel" mentality. The DOS argued the Hawks would "usher in a new and more dangerous phase of an already desperate arms race." They wanted Israel to adopt a more cooperative approach to the disputes over the Jordan River water diversion, resettlement of Arab refugees, and to avoid destabilizing King Hussein. "If we are to regain some degree of Arab confidence in us," Rusk advised, "there must be a significant unilateral concession by Israel."[13] Rusk's goals provoked determined opposition from Israel and the lobby.

Fending off DOS opposition, the Democratic fundraiser and lobby stalwart Feinberg persuaded Kennedy to meet with Ben-Gurion during his trip to New York in May 1961. Ben-Gurion had been forced to resign as prime minister amid the revival of controversy over "the Mishap": the botched false-flag operation targeting American facilities in Egypt in 1954. While the "censored Israeli press" described the Lavon affair as a mere "security mishap," the CIA noted, Ben-Gurion had waged but lost an intense domestic political fight over Lavon's responsibility for the incident.

Coincident with controversy over the Lavon affair, leaks in 1960 revealed the existence of the Israeli nuclear program, which Ben-Gurion had initiated without Cabinet authorization – and moreover without informing Israel's special ally. Ben-Gurion capped off the spate of controversies that led to his resignation with another round of polarizing statements about the duty of the world's Jews to migrate to Israel.[14] In December 1960, Ben-Gurion offended many American and other Jews when he declared before the Zionist Congress in Jerusalem that "the fate of Israel ... whether it will be a state that radiates light to the entire Jewish people ... or will become – Heaven forbid – a Levantine state" depended on in-migration of Jews. As a result of "creeping assimilation ... the Judaism of the Jews in the US and similar countries is losing all meaning." Two days later, the AJC reacted sharply, declaring that Ben-Gurion had violated the "explicit understanding" made with Blaustein a decade earlier "that the government and people of Israel fully respect the right and integrity of Jewish communities in other countries to develop their own mode of life."[15] The ACJ continued to reject the view that "all Jews, regardless of their legal citizenship, are part of a body politic called 'the Jewish people'" and should be dedicated to the 'Jewish national home,' now the State of Israel." Feldman derided the ACJ as "the anti-Jewish Jewish group."[16]

Amid the Lavon and nuclear reactor revelations, Kenen wrote privately that Ben-Gurion "has done us a great deal of damage" and "has begun to outlive his usefulness." Noting Ben-Gurion's penchant for secrecy and "obduracy," the AIPAC leader declared that "Israel should have let our government know" about the secret reactor program. Kenen had tried to learn about the Lavon affair in order to spin it as positively as possible in the *NER*, but "no one connected with the Israel government ever told me the real story." Moreover, "Harman was insistent that I observe their censorship regulations ... Now the whole story has come out in the [*New York*] *Times*," which "discredits Israel in the eyes of many Americans, who attach so much importance to freedom of speech and the freedom of the press."[17]

By meeting with Kennedy amid the Israeli political crises, Ben-Gurion hoped to revivify his lagging domestic political standing as well as to lobby for the Hawks. In New York Ben-Gurion did not secure Kennedy's agreement to sell the Hawks, but he nonetheless left the May 30, 1961, meeting encouraged. The Israeli patriarch recalled being "shocked" when Kennedy "took me to a corner far away" from the assembled aides and diplomats and declared, "You know I was elected by the Jews. I have to do something for them."[18] Once again displaying his considerable political tenacity, Ben-Gurion subsequently returned to power as prime minister.

Kennedy intended to support Israel, but he wanted cooperation to stabilize the region in order to pursue a development agenda, which he

FIGURE 15 Although temporarily ousted as prime minister, Israeli patriarch David Ben-Gurion nonetheless secured a meeting in New York in May 1961 with the new American president John F. Kennedy. Ben-Gurion initiated lobbying for the sale of Hawk missiles to Israel, which Kennedy approved the following year.
New York Daily News/Getty Images

believed would contain the threat of Soviet-backed communism in the Middle East. Preoccupied with cold war hot spots from the Caribbean to Indochina, the Kennedy administration did not make the thorny "Arab-Israeli dispute" an early focus of its attention. When it did formulate a comprehensive approach to the region, the DOS proposed continuing to "contribute heavily in money or money equivalents to enable Israel to meet its security and growth (including immigration) objectives without directly implicating the United States" in the Jewish migration;[19] "Direct US support would alienate Arabs who associated spikes in Jewish immigration with Israel territorial aggrandizement."[20]

Washington would "frequently reassure Israel" by emphasizing "that it has in effect an unwritten but effective security guarantee from the US" and was "thus in a position to conduct a policy of restraint." The United

States would continue to oppose Israel's demand for direct negotiations with the Arab states even though "opposition to this resolution has been a source of continuing criticism of the US government, to a limited extent by Israel officials but on a considerable scale by Israel's American sympathizers." Kennedy hoped to forge a new relationship with Nasser and to find a solution or at least amelioration of the plight of the Palestinian refugees. The DOS well knew that "considerable pressure will be mounted against the administration domestically" on those issues; nonetheless, a "delicate balance" had to be maintained in relations with the Arabs.[21]

Israel and the lobby continued to mount "considerable pressure" on the status of Jerusalem. While Israel had aroused the anger of the Arabs by moving the Foreign Ministry and other government offices to Jerusalem, the United States had long urged countries not to move their embassies to the holy city. In March 1959, Meir called on Washington to adopt "a more passive role than in the past with other governments on the question of locating diplomatic missions" in Jerusalem. The Netherlands and some Latin American nations were among the few that had located in the holy city. Meir complained that others "would move there too if they were not afraid that to do so would incur the displeasure of the United States." In 1962 Israel closed the Foreign Liaison Office in Tel Aviv, another "step in a pattern of [Israeli] efforts to whittle down the current stand of the majority of nations regarding Jerusalem," the DOS noted.[22]

Israel and the lobby worked through Feldman to challenge US diplomatic efforts to discourage other countries from moving their embassies to the holy city. The pressure paid off in June 1962 when the DOS announced it would not take "further actions to dissuade other governments from establishing diplomatic missions in Jerusalem."[23]

AIPAC DEFENDS ATTACK ON SYRIA

Israeli expansionist pressures accompanied by bursts of conflict characterized the borderlands between the Sinai War and the War of 1967. In October 1957, Dulles, citing "increased tension between Israel and Jordan," called on the Israelis to "suspend, without prejudice[,] tree planting activity being carried out by Israel in the area between the lines of Jerusalem." Israel terminated the tree planting without relinquishing the associated territorial claims. Tensions simmered over Israeli challenges to UN administration of Mt. Scopus in northeast Jerusalem. Other incidents included Israeli shots fired at a Jordanian airliner, which had seven Americans aboard but resulted in no injuries.[24]

Serious border conflict erupted when Israel took aggressive actions in the DMZ, renewing efforts to divert water from the Jordan River, which Syria and Jordan also coveted for agriculture. Despite opposition from the Arab states, Kennedy "steadfastly supported the diversion of the Jordan Valley water to Southern Israel."[25] The Syrian border comprised only a fraction of Israel's borders with Arab countries, but the area was especially volatile because of the water diversion as well as deep mutual enmities. Syria, which in 1961 renewed its independent status by terminating the UAR linkage with Egypt, had emerged as the most vituperative anti-Israeli Arab society.

In March 1962, much to the "dismay" of US diplomats, Israel launched an attack inside Syrian territory, citing as justification the wounding of two Israeli policemen in a boat on Lake Tiberius. The characteristic asymmetrical Israeli assault included bombing and artillery blasts, killing "probably around two dozen" Syrians. "For the first time in several years Israel has crossed international frontiers and applied force of much greater magnitude than that directed against Israel," Phillips Talbot, Rusk's top Middle East adviser, reported. Rusk reminded Harman that the United States "has constantly opposed any Israeli use of retaliatory raids, and we believe Israel must understand it cannot continue to take the law into its own hands." Harman responded that the lake was "100% in Israel's territory – the whole lake and its shore," but he was told in return that the United States did "not accept this Israel assumption of unlimited sovereignty." The Israelis shrugged off criticism of the raid, arguing that borderland militancy sent the desired message to the Syrians.[26]

The assault resulted in an acrimonious UNSC debate in which the United States joined the Soviet Union in a 10–0 vote (with France abstaining) that found Israel in "flagrant violation" of the armistice agreements. Pointing out that Israel had violated previous resolutions that forbad retaliatory assaults, UNSC Resolution 171 called on Israel "scrupulously to refrain from such action in the future."[27]

The direct US role in the UNSC resolution incensed the Israelis and AIPAC. The *NER* decried the resolution censuring Israel as "one-sided and unjust" and "a disservice to peace, to America's own interests, and to the authority of the UN." The AIPAC newsletter publicized a spate of "criticism from major newspapers, members of Congress and leading Jewish organizations."[28] Much of the opprobrium focused on UN Ambassador Adlai Stevenson, who had already come under attack the previous year for urging Ben-Gurion to help resolve the Palestinian refugee issue.[29] Israel had responded to that threat by prompting its African allies to introduce a rival UN initiative, known as the Brazzaville resolution for the capital of the Congo, which called for direct negotiations with the Arab states. The DOS backed the longstanding posture of the Arab states opposing direct negotiations in deference to working through the UN toward a settlement. In response to the US sponsorship of the UNSC resolution over the assault on Syria, Israel threatened to revive the Brazzaville resolutions. When the Americans "made it clear that we would regard such a resolution at this time as an effort to embarrass the United States," the Israelis withdrew the threat.[30]

AIPAC accused Stevenson and the administration of "appeasing" the Arabs. Stevenson explained that the clash with Syria had been the most serious borderland conflict since the Sinai War. Rather than "raising the scale of military action in violation of the Armistice," Israel had an obligation to support the peacekeeping machinery and resolve disputes through diplomacy. Stevenson added that he had refrained from direct "condemnation" of Israel even though the United States had been "repeatedly abused" by Israel and AIPAC for backing the UNSC action and for opposing the Brazzaville resolution.[31]

Kennedy came under bipartisan attack from Israel's stalwarts over the borderland clash with Syria. Javits blamed Syria, which the UNSC had let off "scot free" while "denying Israel the right to defend itself." Kennedy's "apparent change in policy" favoring the Arab states was "disillusioning and disturbing," the New York Republican declared.[32] On the Democratic side, Humphrey perceived a lack of "equal-handedness," explaining it was "a serious mistake to condemn Israel more energetically than Syria." Celler declared that "the aggression began with Syria" and that Israel was merely "taking action to defend itself."[33]

Javits, Humphrey, Celler, and other lobby stalwarts also stepped up condemnation of the Arab boycott of Israeli products as well as restrictions on Jews traveling within various Arab countries. Javits chastised Kennedy for inaction against "the Arab boycott of Israel, blacklisting of American business firms by the Arab League, and discriminatory practices against American citizens." In a letter to Kennedy, Rep. Seymour Halpern (R-NY) accused the DOS of "appeasement" of Saudi Arabia, which retained the prerogative to bar Jews from traveling to the kingdom.[34] Feldman assured Celler that the administration was "dealing firmly with the problem of Arab discrimination against American citizens of the Jewish faith," but did not want to publicize its "modest successes" on the issue. A "claim of victory will lead to" a backlash from the Arab states, he explained.[35]

FIGURE 16 Senator Jacob Javits (R-NY), shown here with Senator Robert
F. Kennedy (D-NY) and Rabbi Isaac Alcalay in a 1964 event, anchored the
Israel lobby in the US Senate.
Bettmann/Getty Images

Aided by the spiraling circulation of the *NER*, AIPAC pressured the
Kennedy administration to advocate squarely for Israel. Before Kennedy
had completed his first year, the *NER* asked "Has There Been a Change?,"
suggesting that Kennedy had not followed through on campaign promises
or in fulfilling the Democratic platform planks, notably on direct negotiations. Beginning in 1962, the *NER*, which began as a "semi-monthly,"
shifted to biweekly publication as its circulation continued to grow.[36]

While Feldman and Celler arranged a private White House meeting
enabling Kennedy to reassure a group of prominent Jews of his support
for Israel, DOS diplomats labored to keep afloat diplomacy cognizant of
Arab interests.[37] Robert Komer, who advised national security adviser

FIGURE 17 Diplomat and counterinsurgency specialist Robert W. Komer urged President Kennedy to confront Israeli aggressiveness in the Middle East and to rein in the domestic lobby. In the end Komer had little to show for his efforts, as Kennedy proved reluctant to take on the lobby.
Bettmann/Getty Images

McGeorge Bundy on the Middle East, recalled that he played the role of "middle man" representing the views of the professional diplomats and Arab specialists. He recalled they were "pathetically grateful" for his efforts to counter lobby influence. Komer described Feldman as "Israel's lawyer," adding that "Mike would, more often than not, try to sneak around end [*sic*] and get this word in to Kennedy and get a decision on something that was wanted without the foreign policy view being ground in."

Komer insisted it was "one thousand percent legitimate" for the State and Defense departments forcefully to represent Arab positions. Such advocacy facilitated "our strategic and economic interests" because the Arab states constituted a much larger geographic bloc than the small Zionist state. The DOS had to "counter to the great domestic pressures from the Israeli constituency on the White House" and ensure that the Arab states did not tilt toward the Soviet bloc in the broader cold war context. At the same time Komer, who was Jewish, met regularly over lunch with diplomat Mordechai Gazit, and believed he had the respect of the Israelis for his refusal to back down to them.[38]

Komer, Rusk, Talbot, and other diplomats countered Zionist efforts to forge a close strategic and military alliance with the United States and to give Israel an aggressive free hand along its borders. In the midst of the debate in May 1962, Shimon Peres, deputy minister of defense and a rising star in Israeli politics, toured the United States to raise money for Jewish migrants and to gain support for Israeli border policies. Rejecting US analysis that showed Israeli military superiority over the Arabs, Peres lobbied for the sale of the Hawk antiaircraft missiles and a formal military alliance with the United States. Despite American objections, he defended retaliatory raids as a "valuable instrument of Israeli policy."[39]

Komer countered by urging Kennedy "to talk Israel into a less belligerent attitude along its frontiers. The Israelis, as you know, believe the only way to deal with the Arabs is to be tougher than they are. Hence the retaliatory raid policy." The Israelis, he advised, "have been less than cooperative with the UN truce teams and mixed armistice commissions around the borders. They're also engaged in a quiet bit of territorial aggrandizement in the 'no man's land' between Israel and Jordan in Jerusalem." If the administration hoped to achieve a settlement, or at least to avoid another Middle East war, it would require "restraint on the part of Israel as well as the Arabs."[40]

In August, Kennedy told Ben-Gurion: "Both Syria and Jordan have given the United States categorical assurances that they wish to avoid trouble on their borders with Israel and cooperate fully with the United Nations instruments."[41] However, the borders remained volatile. Following an incident in December, Ben-Gurion, citing Syrian "obduracy and insolence," threatened to unleash the IDF on Syrian soil "with all force at its command." Noting "clear evidence of increasing military preparedness and troop movements," the US Embassy in Tel Aviv warned that Israel was "capable of seizing Syrian positions on the heights."[42] Talbot declared that Ben-Gurion's threat violated pledges to "avoid actions along the border" and was "scarcely in keeping with efforts to tone things down."[43]

FENDING OFF THE REFUGEES

Much to the chagrin of Israel and AIPAC, the Kennedy administration renewed an ultimately futile US effort to generate Israeli cooperation on the Palestinian refugee issue. As Israel's population soared in its first decade from 800,000 to more than two million, Arabs charged that US financial assistance to Israel was enabling Israeli economic progress and border aggression while the dispossessed Palestinian refugees continued to languish in the makeshift camps. Hammarskjold recognized the centrality of the issue, noting that he was "surprised by the universal interest in the refugee problem wherever he went." The UN leader declared that the issue of the refugees was the "toughest one facing him in the Middle East."[44]

In March 1960, Ben-Gurion told Eisenhower in Washington, "As far as Israel is concerned there is no possibility for repatriation." The Israeli leader tendentiously asserted that the refugees "had fled of their own volition" and "therefore are not Israel's responsibility." Moreover, he averred, the Palestinians were "not capable" of fitting into Israeli society. They would constitute "an injection of poison," hence it would be "suicide for Israel to accept the refugees." Ben-Gurion charged that the Arab leaders were merely "using the refugees as a political weapon."[45] A US diplomat declared in 1961, "The sum impression of the Israeli position is that the present unhappy situation should endure for a very long time with the US continuing to bear the brunt politically and economically."[46]

By the end of the Eisenhower years, some members of Congress had become increasingly vocal in opposition to continued US funding for the UN program of humanitarian relief for the refugees. At the time, the United States covered about 70 percent of the cost of providing for the refugees, spending some $23–25 million annually and more than $300 million in total.[47] In June, citing "criticisms recently heard in Congress over of lack of progress in the Palestine refugee situation," the DOS called for a "new approach to this problem."[48]

Despite Israel's intransigence and threats to retaliate with the Brazzaville resolution, the Kennedy administration floated a new plan for resettlement of the Palestinian refugees. To spearhead the initiative, Kennedy selected Joseph Johnson, an academic serving as president of the Carnegie Endowment for International Peace. Appointed as a UN special envoy, Johnson spent months traveling in the region, consulting Arabs as well as the Israelis and ultimately producing a plan that allowed Palestinian refugees a choice on where to resettle yet built into the plan "several 'disincentives'" to them choosing a return to Israeli occupied territory. The envoy insisted that "security for Israel" was the paramount consideration throughout the planning process.[49]

Briefing Kennedy on the Johnson Plan in August 1962, Rusk explained that the proposal constituted the "thin edge of the wedge" to jump start resolution of the refugee issue.[50] The Kennedy administration attempted to revive the longtime US approach of resettling the vast majority of refugees in Arab states, along with a small percentage in Israel. Rather than securing a homeland, Palestinians could live in Israel or the surrounding Arab states. US officials preferred the conservative solution of resettlement as a means to contain perceived radical alternatives of communist-tinged national liberation and the threat of violent conflict. "Our concern," Rusk explained, "is that in the absence of progress, extremist elements in the Arab states might seek to 'Algerianize' the Arab-Israel dispute" – a reference to the violent anticolonial conflict that ultimately forced French withdrawal from its former North African colony.[51]

Before committing to the Johnson Plan, Kennedy wanted to "find out what Israel will do. I don't want to get into a costly fight without getting something." Referencing AIPAC's public condemnation of Stevenson for his previous advocacy of a resettlement plan, Kennedy emphasized that he did not "want to live with the residue of another fight for years and years." Johnson, the special envoy, warned, however, that seeking prior approval from the Israelis could scuttle the entire plan. "If word gets around that this is cleared with the Israelis," he advised, "this will kill the plan" with the Arabs.[52]

In an effort to offer "incentives" to generate support for the Johnson Plan from Israel as well as "Israel's friends" in the United States, Kennedy fundamentally altered US arms policy by offering to sell Israel the Hawk missiles.[53] Just before Kennedy took office, the Defense Department declared there was "no valid military reason to accede at this time to Israel's request for military assistance from the United States," absent "compelling political reasons."[54] While fending off Israeli requests for tanks and jets, Kennedy opened the door to US arms sales to the Zionist state by opting to sell the Hawks. Citing stepped-up Soviet bloc arms supplies to Egypt, the State and Defense departments fell into line. In the wake of the assault on Syria, diplomats held out hope that the sale of the Hawks "would strengthen the weak link in Israel's defenses and thereby reduce any temptation Israel may have to take preemptive offensive action. From the domestic standpoint," the Near East division diplomats added in June 1962, "American supporters of Israel would be pleased and would be less critical of US policy."[55]

The Kennedy administration thus banked on hopes that the sale of the Hawks would placate the Israelis and AIPAC, while the dependence of many conservative Arab states on Washington for financial assistance would mute their criticism. The Arab states remained chronically disunited, particularly as Nasser intervened militarily in Yemen in an escalating proxy war with Saudi Arabia. The administration hoped to win over the Israelis and AIPAC with highly favorable financial terms for the sale of the missiles, arranged by Feldman, and by presenting the decision in two White House meetings: one with prominent American Jews, and a follow-up with key congressional members of the lobby.[56]

Kennedy and his advisers acquiesced to Feldman's advice that making the Hawk sale directly conditional on resettlement of refugees would constitute an insult. Rather than confronting the Israelis with a straight quid pro quo, Feldman proposed instead that the United States would offer the Hawk missiles and invite Israeli reciprocity on the Johnson Plan. For "press guidance" once the news broke, the Hawk sale was to be described as "entirely unrelated" to the refugee plan.[57]

"I hardly need stress," Rusk declared in August 1962, "that it would be most unfortunate if the Israelis were to end up with the Hawks and strength and security assurances while being responsible for derailing the Johnson Plan before it could even be given a good try."[58] Precisely what Rusk feared would occur did occur, as Israel took possession of the Hawks and torpedoed the Johnson Plan. Although "ecstatic" when Feldman told them during a secret trip to Israel in August 1962 that "You're going to get the Hawks," Ben-Gurion and Meir maintained Israel's inveterate opposition to repatriation of Palestinian refugees.[59] On August 20, Ben-Gurion wrote Kennedy of his "profound appreciation" for the decision to sell Hawks, and then summarily rejected the Johnson Plan. Given the Arabs' professed desire to destroy Israel, he avowed, settlement of the refugee problem was "feasible only if the Arab refugees are integrated in the Arab countries." Ben-Gurion emphasized to Kennedy that the plan was dead, adding, "We shall fight against it to the last man."[60]

At follow-up meetings in New York in September with both the Israelis and their domestic supporters, Feldman reported the "unalterable opposition" of Meir, Harman and Feinberg. Meir threatened to revive the direct negotiations resolution through the African surrogates at the concurrent UN meeting if the Johnson Plan was formally introduced.[61] To Talbot, Rusk's top adviser on the Middle East, it was apparent that Israel was "making an all out effort to scuttle the plan." Tel Aviv's criticisms of the Johnson Plan were "unjustified and contrived ... Having now received assurance of the Hawk missile the Israelis feel free to take a hard line" and remain "adamant on the one issue on which we seek reciprocal cooperation."[62]

Komer believed Israel's uncompromising rejection of the Johnson Plan doomed the quest for progress toward an Arab–Israeli settlement.

"The hell of it is that initial Arab reactions suggest they may buy the plan," he declared. John Badeau, the US ambassador in Cairo, reported Nasser to be "not as negative I expected" and to have shown "some disposition to consider the merits of the plan." Meetings with other Arab leaders, including Jordan and Saudi Arabia, were equally encouraging, but in early October Syria rejected the Johnson Plan as a violation of Resolution 194 by compromising the absolute right of return. However, after consultation with the United States and other Arab countries, the Syrians backed off from their outright rejection. On November 11, Rusk told Kennedy, "No Arab action taken thus far either public or private would conclusively preclude acquiescence in the Johnson approach."[63]

AIPAC pressured Kennedy and Congress to bury the Johnson Plan. "A large delegation of Jewish leaders called on me today expressing concern about the situation," adviser Arthur Schlesinger reported on September 21. "We ought to avoid a repetition of last year's problem with Adlai [Stevenson]," he added. Briefed by AIPAC, several members of Congress publicly denounced the plan. Talbot declared that "distorted descriptions" of the Johnson Plan had been "put into the minds of congressmen and of Israel's American supporters" to obscure the fact that Israel "is still seeking, as it has done for 14 years, to avoid repatriating any significant numbers of Palestine refugees."[64]

Originally charged with selling the Israelis on the Johnson Plan, Feldman actually acted as a lobbyist against the resettlement proposals. He argued that the plan could "flood Israel with refugees," and thus had caused "considerable furor in the Jewish community." Noting he did not "see a prayer" of the Israelis accepting the plan, Feldman advised Kennedy that he could not "stress too strongly his firm conviction that the faster you disengage from this plan the better." Years later, Talbot averred that Feldman "was being used as a pipeline not just by American Jewry but by the Israeli embassy" and that "his contacts with the Israeli ambassador were considerably closer than either of them talked about in public."[65]

While Kennedy had been hopeful but not optimistic about the plan's prospects, some of his advisers were bitter that the Israelis had shot down a proposal that might have kick started a process in which other issues could begin to "fall into place," generating momentum toward an overall settlement. Instead, "the Israelis have mounted a pressure campaign with which it is almost impossible" to cope, Komer observed. "Since this is an issue where our foreign-policy goals must necessarily be formulated with an eye to our domestic flank, they take full advantage of this fact." The "tactical handling" had been bungled, he added, by providing "the

Hawk assurances beforehand." As a result, "We have gotten nothing for our efforts."[66]

Komer charged that Israel was rejecting diplomacy and, moreover, that the special relationship had become noticeably one-sided. The former CIA counterinsurgency specialist initially proposed to "gin up" an explanation in which the Arabs would "take the onus" for the failure of the Johnson Plan, but Komer ultimately placed the blame squarely on Israel. "Circumstances have never been more propitious for a refugee initiative if only we could get the Israelis off the dime," he advised. "To do so, however, we have to do something we have never done before, except briefly at Suez. We have to pressure Israel to come around."[67]

Dubbed "Blowtorch Bob" for the intensity of his advocacy on foreign policy issues, Komer called for a showdown with the Israelis: "If we cave in too precipitously under Israeli pressure this time (especially after just offering Hawks) they'll think they can lead us around by the nose." Komer continued to push for a "tougher line toward Israel," explaining, "Only if we can convince the Israelis we mean business will we be able to restrain them when necessary; only this in turn will give us the necessary leverage to do the same with the Arabs." In the absence of US pressure, Israel would continue to "pursue a hard policy demanding that any settlement be on the basis of the essential maintenance of the status quo," or an Arab capitulation to Israeli terms.[68]

The DOS urged Kennedy to take a harder line in direct talks with Meir. "Despite our extreme care to assure the protection of Israel's sovereignty and security," relations were "badly out of alignment," a briefing paper argued; "So far, it has been 'all give and no get' from our standpoint." Washington had provided the Hawks, sided with Israel in the dispute over the Jordan River, and provided financial assistance. Israel responded by not only rejecting the Johnson Plan, but also "leak[ing] US-Israel background talks on the refugees, presumably to generate Arab animosity against the US." Israel threatened to sponsor a direct negotiations resolution and continued to fend off US efforts to inspect Israeli nuclear facilities, an issue Feldman had neglected to broach in his trip to Israel.

The briefing paper urged Kennedy to confront Meir about the coordinated political pressure brought to bear by the close association between AIPAC and Israel. "Contrary to proper diplomatic procedure," the DOS continued, "the Israel Embassy here has actively sought in dealing with American newspapermen, members of the Congress and others to undermine our policy." Kennedy should confront Meir with the need for "greater reciprocity" in US–Israeli relations, but because she was "less intellectually flexible" even than Ben-Gurion, a meeting of the minds with the Israel foreign minister would require "a determined persistence in discussion to persuade her to hear out or accept an opinion contrary to her own."[69]

On December 27, 1962, Kennedy met with Meir in Palm Beach, Florida, at which time he offered the historic acknowledgment that the United States and Israel shared a "special relationship . . . comparable only to that which it has with Britain." Kennedy lamented Israel's rejection of the Johnson Plan, insisting that the "great majority" of refugees would have resettled outside of Israel. The United States intended to continue its support of Israel, but "by the same token we believe that Israel should consider" American interests, including "recognition that this partnership we have with it produces strains for the United States in the Middle East." Israel should try to "lessen collisions" in the region, not provoke them. After all, thanks to US support "Israel does not have to depend wholly on its own efforts for security." True to her reputation, Meir gave little indication that Kennedy's words made much of an impact, observing she was "not really surprised when people do not see Israel's security problems as the Israelis do."[70]

While the Israelis celebrated receiving the Hawks even as they fended off a potential refugee settlement, the Arabs were correspondingly bitter. The DOS monitored public responses in Arab countries, concluding that perceptions of the United States were at the lowest since 1957. Badeau condemned the "unwillingness of the Israelis to make minimal gestures to assist the USA in its Arab relations or even to desist from deliberately stirring up trouble between the US and the Arabs." He added: "Having chosen this mess of potage we should not be surprised at the bitter taste."[71]

UNDERCUTTING RAPPROCHEMENT WITH NASSER

Israel and AIPAC accused the Kennedy administration of pursuing pro-Nasser diplomacy. Upon taking office, Kennedy sought rapprochement with Nasser in an effort to keep Egypt out of the Soviet camp and to head off a burgeoning arms race in the Middle East. The administration had its work cut out, aides advised, because Nasser and other Arab leaders "believe the previous Democratic administration under President Truman was strongly partial to Israel." Despite the challenges, Kennedy initiated a "personal correspondence" that established a rapport with the Egyptian leader.[72]

The initiative "gave Nasser the feeling that Kennedy really cared about relations" and produced positive results, Badeau recalled. Nasser appreciated the Americans informing him personally of the decision to sell Israel the Hawk missiles, declaring, "Of course, I don't like this. You knew I wouldn't like it, but I'm grateful to have been told."[73] The Egyptian media response to the Hawk sale was muted, and unlike in the past no significant public demonstrations were orchestrated. Monitoring anti-Israeli propaganda emanating from Egypt, US officials reported that "The amount of attention and degree of virulence employed appears to have been substantially less than in preceding years."[74]

The administration discussed plans to invite Nasser to a summit in Washington, though such a meeting was sure to provoke a hostile response from Israel and AIPAC. The DOS proposed to exploit Feldman's "wide contacts with leaders of the Jewish community ... to lay the groundwork for a Nasser visit without too much fallout."[75] Kennedy aide Chester Bowles met with a group of prominent Jews to discuss the prospect of cultivating a new attitude toward Egypt.[76]

Using Feldman and public relations to generate acquiescence by Israel and AIPAC to a rapprochement with Nasser proved to be a nonstarter. Talbot pointed out that Ben-Gurion and his colleagues viewed Nasser as the "root of all evil ... some sort of new pharaoh or new Hitler." Ben-Gurion confirmed Talbot's analysis, recalling in a letter to Kennedy his memories of "Arab leaders praising Hitler as the liberator of mankind and praying for his success. Knowing them I am convinced that they are capable of following the Nazi example." Whereas he had "lived for decades with the Arabs," the Americans could not understand the situation because "it is difficult for civilized people to visualize such a thing," Ben-Gurion wrote. "As a Jew I know the history of my people, and carry with me the memories of all it has endured over a period of three thousand years." The Israeli hostility to Nasser, as Talbot pointed out, obscured that "anti-Israel feelings are even stronger in the Arab world outside Egypt than in Cairo, and that even were Nasser to disappear from the scene Arab resentment of Israel would remain undiminished."[77]

Israel and AIPAC floated the specter of "a new Nazism" in Egypt by trumpeting the issue of German scientists working in the Egyptian armaments industry. US diplomats shot down spurious accounts of German scientists working on the manufacture of chemical and nuclear weapons inside Egypt. "The Israelis would come up with these stories, usually indirectly through the American community," Komer recalled. Intelligence analysis revealed that the "threat" actually consisted of "old weather sounding rockets made by a couple of fourth rate German scientists who used to work for the French." It was a "tempest in a teapot," added Badeau, noting that most of the German technicians worked on aircraft rather than rockets, and that, if anything, Egypt turned to the Germans to avoid becoming dependent on Soviet assistance.[78] The Kennedy administration summoned veteran New York politician and diplomat Averell Harriman, but despite his "high standing with the Jewish community" the efforts to downplay the German–Egyptian nexus "ha[ve] been attacked by almost every Anglo-Jewish newspaper," Feldman reported.[79]

In May 1962, McGeorge Bundy shot down the proposed summit with Nasser, noting that the vehement opposition from Israel backed by the "American Jewish community" could "create quite a political backlash."[80] Despite sending Egypt some $177 million in aid by 1963, the attempted US rapprochement was never consummated. Egypt stopped short of allying with the USSR, but continued to receive advanced weaponry from the Soviet bloc, including fighter jets, bombers, and tanks. Nasser insisted that Egypt needed to be able to defend itself from Israeli aggression, but the Egyptian leader actually deployed his military in Yemen, including 40,000 troops by 1963. Egyptian forces, battling Saudi-backed Islamic conservatives in Yemen, became bogged down in the inter-Arab conflict. The Kennedy administration came to the defense of the oil-rich Saudis, condemning the Egyptian intervention and terminating the attempt at rapprochement with Nasser.[81]

Kennedy again received no return – other than to incur the wrath of the Israelis and the lobby – on a major initiative in the Middle East. Kennedy had been "a disappointment to AIPAC," Kenen declared, citing a litany of failures. These included, in reference to the clash with Syria, a "continuing policy that tends to coddle and pamper Arab belligerence while severely censuring Israel for replying to that belligerence." AIPAC "sharply attacked" the Johnson Plan, condemning the opening of dialogue with Nasser as well as the failure "to take strong action against the Arab boycott and blockade" or to support direct negotiations, which had been embraced by the Democratic platform. Kenen did acknowledge that the sale of the Hawks was a "major breakthrough" needed to combat Soviet military aid to Egypt.[82]

At its annual meeting in May 1963, AIPAC emphasized the threat posed by Nasser and the German scientists, condemned US aid to Egypt, and demanded a formal US military alliance with Israel. The lobby depicted a unified Arab world committed to the destruction of Israel, but, as US diplomats pointed out, citing the war in Yemen and tensions between Nasser and Hussein, among other fissures, "The Arab unity movement is confronted by strong divisive forces that will not be overcome for years, if then."[83]

"With Israel and the Zionists no logical arguments will be effective," advised the diplomat Robert Strong. "The Zionists will keep the maximum pressure on senators and congressmen until they achieve their principal objective." Kennedy considered making a direct presidential appeal on Middle East diplomacy to a predominately Jewish audience, directing Feldman to "explore the possibility of making a major address at Yeshiva University, or some similar forum," but the speech was never delivered.[84]

AIPAC and the Israelis stepped up their pressure in the spring of 1963. On May 1, the *New York Times* reported that members of Congress from both parties, led by Javits and Humphrey, "have begun attacking the administration's allegedly pro Nasser and pro Arab policy in the Middle East." Charging the DOS with "appeasing Nasser ever since he came into power," Sen. Ernest Gruening (D-AK) offered an amendment to the Foreign Assistance Act of 1963 complementing a House version introduced by Javits targeting US foreign aid to Egypt. The amendment passed overwhelmingly, making aid to Egypt (including food supplies) vulnerable to cut off.[85]

Asserting that the United States had been guilty of appeasing Nasser, Israel and AIPAC spurred a resolution by Rep. Leonard Farbstein (D-NY) calling on the United States, Britain, France, and other nations to form a collective defense treaty with Israel. The proposal was anathema to American diplomats, who were committed to preserving the "delicate balance" in the Arab–Israeli conflict.[86] Feldman, however, emphasized the "growing unrest among members of the Jewish community over American policy in the Near East." He argued that the provision of "vast amounts" of US and international assistance to Egypt enabled Nasser to carry out "his adventures," including efforts aimed at the "encirclement" of Israel.[87]

Desperate to take "the domestic political cutting edge off these Congressional Zionist-inspired attacks," the administration was "wishing that there was some liberal senator who felt differently and who could therefore defend the administration but even Arthur Schlesinger can think of no one in this category." Komer continued to urge taking a tougher line with Israel. Such ideas were "well and good," Bundy responded, but "the president simply did not believe in laboriously and publicly marching up some steep hill in order to get pushed down" by Israel and its domestic supporters.[88]

To many diplomats, "it has become increasingly clear that the White House is under steadily mounting domestic political pressure to adopt a foreign policy in the Near East more consonant with Israeli desires," as deputy assistant secretary James Grant put it. The Israelis were "determined to use the period between now and the 1964 presidential elections to secure a closer, more public security relationship with United States." The Kennedy administration faced the prospect of "seeking some form of accommodation to domestic pressures flowing from this Israeli desire without seriously impairing our other interests in the area. At best this would be extremely difficult to accomplish."[89]

During one of their regular lunch meetings, Komer confronted Israeli diplomat Gazit regarding the "hullabaloo" playing out over US–Israel relations. "He said flatly that this hullabaloo was likely to get worse unless we did something to meet Israeli security requirements," Komer reported:

I asked him if this meant we were being threatened with an increase in the already substantial Israeli pressure on us for new security guarantees etc. unless we caved. Gazit replied that their concerns were a fact of life with which we would have to live; that the Israelis had not inspired in any way the current noises from Javits et al on the Hill.

Komer again condemned the "alarmist" rhetoric about threats to Israel's security and appealed to Gazit for a "moratorium on propaganda maneuvers," but this was an exercise in wishful thinking. He concluded that Israel was determined "to press us for all the traffic would bear. Its consistent policy seems to be to force us into an openly pro Israeli stand despite our protest that this would undermine us with the Arabs and give the Soviets a field day." Komer was left wondering: "What kind of a relationship was this?"[90]

FULBRIGHT CONFRONTS THE LOBBY

One senator who was not afraid to challenge Israel and the lobby was Fulbright. The maverick Arkansan, famous for sponsoring the acclaimed overseas educational exchange program that bore his name, had long since concluded that Israel and AIPAC exercised undue influence over US policy. Since the Sinai War he had used his influence in the SFRC to challenge

FIGURE 18 Senator J. William Fulbright (D-AR) emerged as one of the few members of Congress who proved willing to challenge the Israel lobby. Fulbright urged Kennedy to pressure Israel to compromise as a quid pro quo for US financial and military assistance. In 1963 he held closed-door hearings into the lobby's questionable fundraising activities.
Corbis Historical/Getty Images

various aspects of the special relationship, including the effort to block the "freedom of the seas" and the Farbstein amendments. Carefully tracking the actions of all members of Congress, Kenen warned in 1961, "Fulbright cannot be appeased. He is simply anti-Israel and will show it."[91]

In 1962, Fulbright complained directly to Kennedy over the "policy reversal" of selling the Hawks despite the "intransigent" Israeli government's refusal to "receive and discuss in a forthcoming spirit" the Johnson proposals on refugees. "Were this policy decision regarding the missiles accompanied by a *quid pro quo* – possibly in the form of a reasonable Israeli position on the Johnson Plan – I would not be troubling you with this letter." Kennedy subsequently discussed the issue privately with Fulbright, but took no action.[92]

The next year, Fulbright stunned AIPAC by conducting two days of closed SFRC hearings, which revealed evidence that Israel, working through the JA, had funneled millions of dollars into the domestic lobby to promote favorable public opinion of Israel. By means of indirect

funding – or, less charitably, money laundering – the JA had funded Kenen
and his activities, underwritten the *NER* as well as the Jewish Telegraphic
news agency, sponsored speakers, and promoted myriad other pro-Israeli
"public information" initiatives, including efforts to influence Congress
and divert attention from Israel's nuclear reactor research. Drawing on
FBI wiretaps and subpoenaed documents, the investigation revealed abundant evidence of the lobby's fundraising, which included contributions
from mobsters Aaron Weisberg and John Factor, known as "Jake the
Barber."[93]

Delving into the financial dealings of the lobby, the FBI had become
aware that the JA – headquartered in Jerusalem but with an "American
section" office in New York – was purchasing subscriptions of the *NER*
and diverting revenues to the lobby. The JA was also making $5,000 direct
quarterly payments to Kenen. From January 1, 1955 through the end of
1962, the JA made more than five million dollars in payments in support
of lobbying, without proper itemization in its filings as required under
federal law.[94]

In separate one-day hearings in May and August 1963, Fulbright
grilled representatives of the JA as well as attorney Maurice Boukstein,
who had provided the legal advice leading to the creation of AIPAC.
Fulbright homed in on Kenen's activities, demanding to know "why he
shouldn't register" as a foreign agent. In 1951 Kenen had been registered
as a foreign agent for lobbying purposes, but in subsequent years declined
to do so on the grounds that the lobby was a domestic enterprise and did
not represent the Israeli state. However, the SFRC investigation showed,
as Fulbright pointed out in the hearings, that "In order to insulate him,
you took the indirect way of paying him."[95]

The revelations emerged in the midst of a broader SFRC probe into
foreign agent violations by the Dominican Republic and several other
countries, but Fulbright did not shy away from including Israel and
AIPAC despite pressure from Kennedy, Vice President Johnson, and
several senators and representatives. Feldman had informed Kennedy of
the "detailed investigation of the interconnection between the various
Jewish organizations in the United States and the use of the funds they
raise," adding that "The Jewish community is very uneasy about this
investigation."[96] By contrast, the ACJ, while insisting that it took "no
sadistic or vindictive pleasure in these developments," expressed its
approval of AIPAC being subjected to "responsible analysis and govern-
mental scrutiny." The ACJ's Elmer Berger predicted that "Almost certainly the Zionist apparatus will trot out its most lethal political blackmail

to 'call off the dogs.'" Berger cited a front-page story on May 28 in the *Wall Street Journal*, which reported that the White House, noting "the importance of Jewish voters in key states," was "working backstage to persuade" Fulbright to drop the investigation.[97]

Under pressure from domestic supporters of Israel, Fulbright agreed to hold the hearings in closed session, but he planned to have them read into the Senate record. He desisted only after Johnson focused his notorious powers of persuasion on the Arkansas senator. Transcripts of the hearings remained classified for decades. The hearings produced substantive modifications of federal law, including new provisions requiring registration by agents of foreign interests and full disclosure of financial arrangements.[98]

Fulbright's investigation exposed and shut down the indirect funding "conduits" to AIPAC and compelled the American Zionist Committee to register as a foreign agent. By that time AIPAC had separated itself legally from the AZC, had registered with Congress in accordance with laws governing domestic lobbies, and had recovered from the financial challenge of the late 1950s. The *NER* published a detailed account of the hearings, insisting that JA funds had been used for "religious and cultural education" rather than "lobbying or political action," and that no laws had been violated. The *NER* wanted to know "whether Sen. Fulbright now intends to investigate the activities and expenditures of the pro-Arab organizations."[99]

In 1965 the FBI followed up with AZC director Philip Bernstein, who told them "Our Committee raises its funds entirely from contributions," with "not a penny from Israel."[100] The challenge from Fulbright put the Arkansas senator in the crosshairs of AIPAC, which targeted him for attack and eventually celebrated his re-election defeat in 1974.[101]

DISINFORMATION ON ISRAEL'S NUCLEAR PROGRAM

On December 8, 1960, CIA Director Allen Dulles reported that overflights by U-2 spy planes and other intelligence sources revealed that the Israeli nuclear complex at Dimona probably included a reactor capable of producing weapons-grade plutonium. The following day, Eisenhower summoned Harman and confronted him with photographs from the U-2 flights. Secretary of State Christian Herter alluded to the high cost of the facility, noting acidly that it had "not been mentioned in recent discussions of Israeli economic development plans and possible US financial assistance" for them.[102]

On December 20, Harman "reassured the Secretary regarding the peaceable purposes of the reactor."[103] However, CIA and Atomic Energy Commission (AEC) experts believed "the Israeli nuclear complex cannot be solely for peaceful purposes," and that the Soviets and the Arabs would come to the same conclusion. Expressing its "disappointment," the outgoing Eisenhower administration found Israel's secrecy and evasiveness "difficult to reconcile with the confidence which has traditionally characterized US-Israel relations."[104]

Backed by the DOS, which called for "persistent but quiet diplomatic approaches," the Eisenhower administration demanded expert inspections of the Dimona facility. The administration received backing from "Congressional leaders" who were "unhappy" that the Israelis "deliberately misled" the United States by keeping "a development of this importance secret ... when they were operating on the basis of special confidence to press a highly sensitive request for arms and economic assistance." On January 17, 1961, the DOS informed Congress that the United States had been "assured categorically at the highest level of the Israeli Government that Israel has no plans for the production of atomic weapons ... We have been assured that Israel will be glad to receive visits by scientists from friendly countries at the Dimona reactor when public interest has quieted down."[105]

Despite repeated assurances that they had no such intentions, the Israelis continued to develop a nuclear weapon and proved "adept at concealing their activities" at the Dimona facility. Israeli secrecy "was aimed primarily at the United States," which posed the "greatest threat" to impede the drive for nuclear weapons capability. At least rhetorically, Washington championed international control of nuclear weapons and was a driving force behind the creation in 1957 of the International Atomic Energy Agency (IAEA). Until 1964, only four powers – the United States, Britain, France, and the Soviet Union – had nuclear weapons.[106]

The Kennedy administration directed "intelligence agencies to maintain a continuing watch on Israel as on other countries to ensure that nuclear weapons capabilities are not being proliferated." The new administration "is very much interested in this matter," Rusk declared, calling for "an early visit" of qualified inspectors to Dimona. Because Israel and the United States were "such close friends," the Americans emphasized, an inspection could take place "very quietly and without publicity."[107]

Responding to the new administration, Harman declared he "could not conceive why there should be continuing interest in Dimona in the United

States or anywhere else," as Israel had "no intention of manufacturing the bomb." During their May 30, 1961, meeting in New York, Kennedy secured Ben-Gurion's pledge that Israel had no plans "for the time being" to develop a bomb, and would only consider doing so if Egypt should attempt to obtain nuclear weapons. After being granted access to the Dimona site, two US scientists found no evidence of Israeli plans to develop the bomb. However, the "informal" visit was a "window-dressing exercise," according to Ambassador Walworth Barbour. The initial Israeli response to US inquiries into the nuclear program was "this is not your business." Thereafter, the Americans "had considerable difficulty making arrangements for periodic visits," during which the Israelis would strive to "appear as forthcoming as possible, at the same time without revealing anything to us." Barbour later recalled, "It was all a very unrealistic exercise that went on for many, many years and then finally just petered out when even the United States realized it wasn't getting anywhere. And it became ridiculous."[108]

The DOS advised that Israel continued to pursue the bomb while planting stories in the press about the peaceful benefits of atomic energy in an effort "to obviate further need for a visit by United States scientists." US diplomats reported that the Israeli Cabinet, "under the influence of Dayan and Peres, decided the United States would do no more than display an angry attitude."[109] Although a staunch advocate of developing the bomb during Israeli Cabinet debates, Peres gave the Americans his "unequivocal assurance" that Israel would not seek nuclear weapons "unless it [found] that other countries in the area" were doing so.[110]

Kennedy's decision in 1962 to sell Israel the Hawk missiles stemmed in part from hopes that if Israel received advanced conventional weapons it would refrain from pursuing a nuclear capability. However, on his secret trip to Israel to hand over the Hawks Feldman had not raised the subject of nuclear research, despite a DOS request that he do so. In his meeting with Meir, Kennedy framed his acquiescence to Israel's rejection of the Johnson Plan as a quid pro quo for renewed Israeli guarantees on nuclear non-proliferation. Reminding the Israeli foreign minister that the special relationship was a "two-way street," Kennedy called on Israel to take full account of "our problems on this atomic reactor. We are opposed to nuclear proliferation. Our interest here is not prying into Israel's affairs but we have to be concerned because of the overall situation in the Middle East." A US diplomat reported that "Mrs. Meir reassured the president that there would not be any difficulty between us on the Israeli nuclear reactor."[111]

Less than three months after receiving Meir's reassurances, intelligence sources revealed that Israel remained in active pursuit of a nuclear weapon. On March 6, 1963, the CIA advised that Israel sought the bomb to "exploit the psychological advantages of its nuclear capability to intimidate the Arabs," and that its "policy toward its neighbors would become more rather than less tough." An Israeli nuclear capability would wreck US nonproliferation policies and provoke "dismay and frustration" among the Arabs, who would blame the United States as "the one power which could if it chose prevent the development of an Israeli nuclear capability." Finally, the Arabs could be expected to turn immediately to the Soviet Union for armaments, including nuclear weapons of their own.[112]

The Israeli nuclear development program undermined longstanding US efforts involving a "highly secret" working group from State, CIA, and arms control agencies to head off a Middle East atomic weapons race. Washington lacked "positive evidence" of nuclear weapons development, but "The size of the program, what we know of its nature, and the amount of uranium concentrate acquired all suggest that Israel intends at least to put itself in a position to be able to produce a limited number of weapons relatively quickly." By contrast, Egypt either "alone or in combination with other Arab states, does not have the capability of producing a nuclear weapon in the foreseeable future."[113]

On the brink of achievement of a historic limited nuclear test ban treaty with the Soviet Union, Kennedy wanted "clearer assurances" that the bomb would not be introduced into the Middle East. The president ordered "As a matter of urgency that we undertake every feasible measure to improve our intelligence on the Israeli nuclear program." In addition, he ordered "the next informal inspection of the Israeli reactor complex to be undertaken promptly and to be as thorough as possible."[114]

Citing Feldman's ties to the lobby, Komer and Bundy informed Kennedy they were excluding the Jewish affairs adviser from deliberations "because of the extreme sensitivity" of the nuclear issue.[115] In Tel Aviv Barbour refused to be put off by the Israelis, insisting "We need to see Dimona." Ben-Gurion demurred that Israel preferred "that Nasser be a little afraid" rather than relieved of the threat through an open declaration that Israel would not seek to develop nuclear weapons. Barbour reiterated that "We urgently want a reply to our specific request" for twice-annual inspection of Israeli nuclear research facilities. He concluded, Israel "intends to strike a hard bargain for visits."[116]

Committed to nuclear nonproliferation in the wake of the Cuban Missile Crisis and the Limited Test Ban Treaty, Kennedy declared,

"We should attempt to get every country that is not yet agreed to inspection to accept some form of international inspection." Nasser rejected inspections, but pointed out that, unlike Israel, there was no nuclear site under construction in Egypt to inspect. Nasser, who reacted "in a restrained manner" to revelations of the Israeli nuclear program as well as to the Hawk sales, reassured the Americans he "had no intention whatsoever" of seeking nuclear weapons and also "no intention of attacking Israel." On July 22, 1963, Nasser pledged in a public speech that Egypt was not planning to attack, nor seeking to destroy, the Zionist state.[117]

Kennedy stepped up demands for a new round of inspections, insisting in a letter to Ben-Gurion, "There is no more urgent business for the whole world than the control of nuclear weapons." Ben-Gurion would only agree to annual rather than semiannual inspections, to be conducted only by Americans rather than the IAEA. The Israeli leader affirmed that he considered the pledge to develop nuclear power solely for peaceful uses to be "absolutely binding." Maintaining a determined pose in reply, Kennedy warned, "This Government's commitment to and support of Israel could be seriously jeopardized if it should be thought that we were unable to obtain reliable information" on Israel nuclear activities. US national security elites concluded, however, that the offer of annual inspections "failed to meet our minimum requirements." A reactor of the size at Dimona required "two inspections yearly with far more complete controls than the Israelis are prepared to allow us. A visit before the reactor goes critical is essential."[118] At the end of June, Levi Eshkol replaced Ben-Gurion as prime minister and overcame Cabinet opposition to formally accede to the US demands for renewed inspections at Dimona. Barbour reported that Eshkol "has not had an easy time in obtaining the agreement of his colleagues" on the nuclear issue, and that Meir "probably is not personally wholly sympathetic."[119]

As the United States pressed for more stringent and semiannual inspections, the Israelis appeared to regard inspections at Dimona "as a bargaining card" to which they might consent in return for a "full-fledged alliance, with all the trimmings."[120] Kennedy considered but ultimately rejected Israel's quest to propel the United States into a "defensive alliance with close joint planning" along the lines of NATO. The Americans rejected repeated Israeli claims of vulnerability to a "growing Arab threat," especially with the Arab world disunited and Nasser's army bogged down in Yemen. On August 7, 1963, the Joint Chiefs of Staff, declaring that "The Israeli forces have the capability of defeating aggression by any combination of Arab states which might oppose them," deemed a formal security alliance with Israel unnecessary and provocative.[121]

The Kennedy administration enlisted Blaustein to reassure the Israelis that in terms of security the United States was committed to "meet Israel's requirements for the foreseeable future." The AJC president met with both Ben-Gurion and his replacement, Eshkol. He found the latter "reasonable and conciliatory," but noted that Eshkol had "a real problem on his hands" as he faced pressures from "a younger group of politicians, as exemplified by Mr. Peres." The younger cohort were willing to embrace "the 'go it alone school' and could be much more militant in their actions."[122]

By the time of Kennedy's assassination in November 1963, Israel and AIPAC had solidified the now officially proclaimed special relationship the United States. While AIPAC focused on the Congress and the public, Feldman worked effectively from inside the Kennedy White House to fend off efforts by Fulbright, the State Department, and advisers such as Komer as they sought to balance Middle East policy by bringing pressure to bear on the Israelis to compromise. Thus, "Despite the inflexibility displayed by Israel," as Shlaim points out, the Kennedy administration had "continued to tilt America's Middle Eastern policy in Israel's favor."[123]

Deftly managing its special ally, the Israelis achieved a breakthrough with the Hawk missiles even as they rejected a quid pro quo on resettlement of Palestinian refugees, dissembled and evaded US efforts to rein in the budding nuclear weapons program, and weathered challenges posed by federal scrutiny of the lobby itself. Successful as they were in managing the Kennedy administration, Israel and the lobby anticipated even brighter days ahead under his successor, a longtime friend of Israel, Lyndon Baines Johnson.

5

"The Best Friend that Israel Could Have"

In a memorandum "not for publication or circulation," written four days after the Kennedy assassination, Kenen anticipated growing support for Israel from the new administration. "President Johnson took a front-rank pro-Israel position" as Senate Majority Leader in 1957 when he "sharply criticized [Eisenhower] Administration threats to impose sanctions against Israel" over its refusal to withdraw from Egyptian territory. Personally lobbied by Eban and Kenen amid the Suez Crisis, Johnson had been "emphatic and persistent" in his support of Israel's position.[1]

Kenen noted that in response to his stand on Israel, Johnson had "received thousands of letters from his constituents and we saw many of his replies." Johnson told a group of San Antonio constituents in 1953, "You can be sure I have always been pro-Israel and will continue to be so."[2] In 1958, Johnson sponsored a congressional resolution commemorating Israel's tenth anniversary, praising the Zionist state as a haven of displaced refugees and for having "developed democratic institutions, in the Near East and played a constructive role in the family of nations." A grateful JA "paid the expenses of Johnson and his entourage at the 1960 Democratic National Convention," according to the Fulbright SFRC investigation.[3]

While the lobby freely tapped into Johnson's pro-Israeli sentiments, it did not manufacture them. Johnson's support for the Zionist state was longstanding, deeply felt, and, as with many Americans, rooted in religion and culture. Johnson came from "very religious stock" and "'inherited' some of that influence," recalled the Rev. George R. Davis, Johnson's minister at the National City Christian Church in Washington, DC; "He was a man of great faith and prayer." While Johnson "did not wear his religion on his sleeve," it nonetheless influenced his political views. "He truly believed that his religion could most sincerely be worked out and expressed through the political field," Davis declared. "His underlying motivation was religious."[4]

The popular evangelist Billy Graham prayed with Johnson in the White House on several occasions, recalling that Johnson "liked to have the Bible read to him."[5] In 1964, Johnson expressed to Jordan's King Hussein his "deep interest in the Bible."[6] Although Johnson had been raised a Baptist, and his great grandfather, George Washington Baines, Jr., had been "one of the best-known Baptist leaders in the early history of Texas," Johnson decided of his own accord, after attending a revival meeting as a young man, to join the Christian Church.[7] According to several observers, including Davis and Graham, Johnson's religiosity influenced his desire to uplift disadvantaged social groups, notably African-Americans and Hispanics. In the midst of the Civil Rights Movement, which he advanced with crucial executive support, Johnson told another religious leader, "Almighty God has blessed our nation with a new opportunity to redress the grievances of the past and to heal our regional and racial divisions."[8]

With respect to the Jewish experience, especially influential was Johnson's favorite aunt, his father's sister Jessie Hatcher, who advised him:

Lyndon, always remember this, don't ever go against Israel. Because Israel ... was given to them by God. That's the only nation in all the land that God ever recognized as His own ... the Jews are God's people, and they are always going to be ... that's their land ... and nobody is going to take it away from them.

Both Hatcher and Johnson frequently recounted this exchange and acknowledged its lasting influence. Johnson recalled to Graham, among many others, his aunt's admonition: "Lyndon, don't forget the Jews, God's chosen people."[9]

Johnson also linked the settlement of Israel with romanticized Texas frontier history. During a state visit by Eshkol to the Johnson ranch in 1968, the toast at the formal dinner linked the Alamo with the ancient fortress of Masada, overlooking the Dead Sea. "Our western settlers and Israel's *kibbutzniks* were imbued with ... the same indomitable spirit." Johnson declared, "We are both pioneers."[10]

Johnson identified and empathized with Israel while at the same time developing close personal relationships with Jews, both American and Israeli. In his memoirs, Johnson expressed his admiration for Israel "gallantly building and defending a modern nation against great odds and against the tragic background of the Jewish experience," all while being forced to live in a "harassed and beleaguered fortress." Within weeks of taking office, Johnson spoke at the Eighteenth Annual Weizmann Institute Dinner in New York, where he lauded the Israeli patriarch, who died in 1952, for his efforts to "restore to the Jewish people the land of their forefathers, a land that for centuries had been a barren, dry desert, infested with disease."[11]

One of Johnson's closest personal advisers, Harry McPherson, recalled, "I've always felt that someplace in Lyndon Johnson's blood there are a great many Jewish corpuscles." Noting Johnson's identification with Israel and his "affection for a great many Jews," McPherson declared he that he considered Johnson "part Jewish, seriously." Johnson pledged in the wake of the assassination to carry on with Kennedy's policies, but he would take the special relationship to a higher level. Johnson would confirm the conviction of Israeli diplomat Ephraim "Eppy" Evron, a friend of the president. McPherson declared that Evron "genuinely loved" Johnson and trusted that the president "would do nothing that ever hurt Israel and was the best friend that Israel could have." Johnson's sympathies lay with Israel, but at the same time he counted on American Jews, among the most liberal groups in the nation, to support his Great Society domestic reform program.[12]

With a friendly president in power and his party in control of Congress, the lobby seized the moment to mount a campaign behind securing advanced weaponry for Israel. Having received the Hawks from Kennedy, Israel and AIPAC set their sights on securing offensive weapons, notably tanks and supersonic jets. The quest proved successful: by the end of the Johnson presidency the United States had become Israel's chief arms supplier.

Acquainted with Mike Feldman since the 1950s, Johnson retained him as his "prime minister on the question of Israel." Prior to the Weizmann dinner speech, Feldman advised Johnson to use the term "resettlement" in any reference to the "so-called refugees" and to avoid the term "Palestine," which "went out of existence in 1948." Feldman urged support for the ongoing Israeli diversion of the Jordan waters and for increased US military assistance. In May 1964, Johnson sent Feldman to Israel to brief Eshkol on the administration's plan to supply Israel with tanks, but to do so indirectly through West Germany, so as not to enflame anti-American sentiment in the Arab world. Warning Johnson that "I have rarely been exposed to as much pressure as I have recently on the question of tanks for Israel," Feldman urged pro-Israel stalwarts in Congress and "the Anglo-Jewish press" to rein in public pressure on the sale of tanks until Johnson could orchestrate a third-party transaction.[13] Eshkol, the increasingly influential Labor Party leader Peres, and "responsible leaders of the Jewish community" all agreed to low-key arrangements for indirect sale of the tanks.[14]

On June 1, 1964, Johnson received Eshkol in the first formal summit with an Israeli leader hosted by the United States since Weizmann visited in 1949. Johnson and Eshkol got along well, and the president pledged that he was "foursquare behind Israel on all matters that affected their vital security interests." Unlike his predecessors, the appreciative *NER* declared, Johnson had shown no fear that "overt display of friendship" with an Israeli leader "would antagonize the Arabs."[15] In addition to the bimonthly newsletter, the *NER* began to publish special supplements, including "Arab Propaganda ... Line and Apparatus" (October 1964). The 32-page supplement emphasized Arab efforts to "weaken American commitment to Israel" by propagating "myths" such as the notion of "expansionist Zionism." The supplement credited the Johnson administration with "emancipation of US policy from blackmail," citing the green light for Eshkol's state visit and rhetorical support for "Israel's desire for peace with its neighbors."[16]

Eager to keep Israel and AIPAC in his corner, Johnson expressed his appreciation to Eshkol that "the tank matter had not been made a public issue and had been kept discreet." He added that Israel should not be "too worried about primitive Egyptian weapons." In addition, Johnson emphasized, "We back Israel fully on the Jordan water." Eshkol shot down any prospect of Israel taking in refugees, dismissing the stateless Palestinians with the standard Israeli discourse as "not people within the classic meaning of refugees. They are used by the Arab nations to develop enemies against Israel." Johnson and Eshkol issued a joint statement in support of territorial integrity, effectively sanctioning the expanded borders attained by Israel in the 1949 armistice agreements.[17]

As Johnson girded for election in 1964, the Democratic Party delighted AIPAC by going "far beyond its 1960 statement," notably in suggesting resettlement of Palestinians "in lands where there is room and opportunity." As the first speaker in the Democrats' platform committee deliberations in Atlantic City, Kenen orchestrated the provision. Clearly in sync with the Democrats, AIPAC expressed disappointment with the Republicans, who "decided to meet the objections of the liberals over Goldwater conservatives" and thus offered only an anodyne plank to "maintain stability in the region." The Middle East did not factor heavily in the race, in which Johnson crushed Goldwater in a landslide.[18]

Retained as secretary of state, Rusk expressed ongoing State Department concerns that US partiality to Israel, including rejection of the refugee plan and unilateral diversion of the Jordan waters, put relations with the Arabs "in increasing jeopardy."[19] In response, Johnson told King Hussein he wanted to "assure all the Arabs that Johnson is just a much their friend as Kennedy was." In a letter to Nasser, Johnson emphasized his desire for "constructive cooperation," adding his "assurance," in a veiled reference to the Dimona reactor, that Washington opposed "nuclear proliferation" in the region. In response, Nasser told the US ambassador that Egypt had no major issue in bilateral relations with Washington; rather, the problem was that the "US had always supported Israel and had supported the status quo. The Arabs could not accept this."[20] It would soon become apparent, however, that "the personal rapport that Kennedy had managed to establish with Nasser in 1961–62 eluded Lyndon Johnson."[21]

While Israel and AIPAC played up the theme of vulnerability, US analysts viewed an Arab attack on Israel as highly unlikely. In his meetings attempting to address the refugee issue, envoy Joseph Johnson reported, "All the Arabs had told him in various ways that war on Israel by the Arabs would be folly and he believed they were sincere. On the other hand they had serious fears of Israeli expansion or aggression." In April 1964, an intelligence estimate advised that "Attitudes toward Israel remained basically hostile, but a fair proportion of Arabs have gradually come privately and reluctantly to accept the fact that Israel will exist for many years to come." In late 1965, Egypt offered to conduct high-level talks with Israel, a proposal that Israel rejected despite the oft-expressed Israeli desire for direct negotiations with the Arab states. The Syrian regime condemned Egypt for weakness and called for a pan-Arab assault, culminating in the liberation of Palestine. However, Hussein opposed movements that called for the West Bank – then under Jordanian control – to become part of a new Palestinian state. The Arab world thus remained far from united or positioned to mount an assault on Israel.[22]

Despite its military superiority, Israel's congenital security anxieties surfaced powerfully in response to the growing Palestinian national liberation movement. *Al-Fatah*, a Palestinian national liberation group founded in the late 1950s, stepped up incursions and calls for resistance to Israel. Fatah drew inspiration from the successful Algerian revolt against France, as well as other "Third World" national liberation movements ranging from Cuba to Vietnam. During the tumultuous 1960s, the Palestinian diaspora and liberation movement gained increased visibility, organization, and growing international support, but at the same time spurred Israeli countermeasures.[23]

In May, after years of Israeli blocked efforts to address the refugee issue, the Palestine Liberation Organization (PLO) held its inaugural meeting. Later that year the Arabs united behind the liberation of Palestine, which they endorsed at a summit in Alexandria. Egypt precluded Fatah from mounting assaults from either Sinai or the Gaza Strip. Hussein opposed Fatah but could not control the group, which benefited from a teeming refugee population in Jordan as well as the long border with Israel from which to launch sporadic incursions. Syria cheered such incidents, which were typically small operations of harassment, hit-and-run assaults, or homemade bombings.[24]

Growing Arab radicalism and cross-border incursions heightened Israeli insecurities and spurred expansive tendencies. As many in the Arab world suspected, some Israelis contemplated moving into the West Bank of the Jordan River, an action they might justify as providing security against the cross-border incursions emanating from Jordanian territory. Although Meir had told Kennedy in December 1962, "Israel is perfectly prepared to live within its present borders," Arabs and American diplomats did not believe Israeli policy was purely defensive. "Israel's policy is basically expansionist and it would not hesitate undertake aggression to achieve its aims if at any time it felt this could be accomplished with impunity," an Egyptian diplomat warned the Americans.[25]

In October 1962, Ambassador Barbour had reported on the basis of a "reputable source" that an aggressive younger generation of Israeli political leaders "believes the only solution to the Arab-Israeli dispute is a decisive Israeli military victory over the Arab states, followed by a dictated peace." If the Arabs mounted the appearance of a threat, "the group would regard preventative war as desirable." While no action was imminent, Barbour warned presciently that such a war could become Israel's "national policy" in the future.[26]

Although Ben-Gurion had given way to the more moderate Eshkol, militant leaders Dayan and Peres were increasingly influential. In an effort to fend off criticism that he was insufficiently militant, Eshkol cultivated support from the hardliners. The Israeli prime minister "initiated a public rehabilitation of the Irgun, bringing the remains of Jabotinsky back to Israel and adding to the image of national legitimacy to be granted to [Menachem] Begin and the Irgun."[27]

Pressures from the Israelis as well as from Arab rivals underlay concern about the political stability of the Jordanian monarchy. Committed to bolstering Hussein as a moderate, anticommunist Arab leader, the United States diverted naval forces into the region and prepared to intervene if necessary to keep the king in power. While the United States and Great Britain bolstered Hussein, Israel undermined the king through the water diversion and punitive raids into Jordan. These actions encouraged radical opponents who sought to overthrow Hussein, with rhetorical support from Nasser's regime. The Egyptian pressures against Hussein in turn prompted Israel to threaten to seize the West Bank.

Israeli officials told US diplomats that Hussein's overthrow would delegitimize the 1949 armistice agreement and give Israel the right to redraw its boundaries with Jordan. "You know, they are very good at words, these guys," McGeorge Bundy responded to the dubious Israeli claim. Seemingly anticipating – and perhaps even encouraging – Israeli aggression, however, Bundy continued: "I don't see the president going to war with Israel to recover the West Bank. I wonder if anyone is in a position to say that to the Israelis."[28]

Komer suspected the Israelis of seeking "to take advantage of current tensions" in the Arab world to position themselves to annex Jordanian–Palestinian territory. As he pointed out, "The West Bank is such a cul-de-sac that Israel could pinch it off in 24 hours." Israel's apparent defense of Hussein over more radical Arab leaders was in actuality "a kiss of death to the brave young king." Komer suspected that the "Israelis want him to fall so they could take West Bank ... while half of Nasser's army is locked up in Yemen."[29] Hussein held on to power but remained under siege from Arab radicals, especially as Jordan proved powerless against Israeli cross-border assaults.

THE LOBBY CAMPAIGN ON US ARMS SALES

Israel and AIPAC mounted a campaign against proposed US military assistance to Jordan, which was designed to ensure that Hussein did not turn to the Soviet bloc for weapons. Washington had been "subsidizing Jordan for years, in order to keep King Hussein – the most sober of the Arab leaders – out of Nasser's clutches," as Komer put it, but Israel insisted the armaments heightened its vulnerability to Arab aggression. "All our estimates continue to show Israel as maintaining its military superiority over the Arab states for the foreseeable future," Rusk replied.[30] To Komer it was "crystal clear" that Johnson's hesitation on the proposed Jordanian arms package, which had the full support of the national security bureaucracy, stemmed from "his concern over the US domestic reaction."[31]

Agitated due to being pressured by the lobby on the issue, which he viewed as little short of betrayal given his long-term support of Israel, Johnson asked the Democratic fundraiser Feinberg – considered an asset by the Israelis, who referred to him by the code name *Andre* – to intercede with Eshkol.[32] "The only reason I'm helping Jordan is on account of Israel," Johnson declared. "Our judgment is we oughn't let this little King go down the river," he told Feinberg; "If you want to turn him over and have a complete Soviet bloc we'll just have to … We think it would be better to give 'em as little as possible and control it. And all of our defense people think it would be."[33]

Showing both fear of the lobby's political clout as well as frustration with its tactics, Johnson made the extraordinary statement that he would simply leave up to the Israelis and the lobby the decision on the US arms sales to Jordan. "I'm not prepared to take on the *New York Times* and Mike Feldman and everybody else. And I'm gonna let them make the decision," he told Feinberg. "We don't want it laid on to a man from Johnson City … If anybody is pro-Israel" it was he, the president declared, recalling his decisive opposition to Eisenhower's proposed sanctions after the Sinai War: "Back when they were in real problems and getting ready the sanctions I just came down here and said 'Hell no, that can't be,' and I stopped it … I'm not gonna get in the middle of these clashes and have one of them leak it on me that I want to join up with the Arabs."[34]

American diplomats fumed that Israel was effectively working to "discredit our entire Near East policy." By "mounting a wide-ranging campaign to stop all aid" to Arab countries, Israel impeded US efforts to promote stability and arms control, and to curb Soviet influence. Lucius Battle, the US ambassador in Cairo, cited a lobby campaign of disinformation in which "Israel and its friends in the United States have been able to establish widespread credence in an upside down world where Syria is the trigger-happy party in the demilitarized zones, Nasser is dedicated to the destruction of 'peace loving' Israel, and the plight of the Arab refugees is somehow the fault of the Arab host governments." He called for a firm diplomacy, emphasizing that "Israel's interests (as determined by Israel) do not at all times and in all respects coincide with those of the United States."[35]

The professional diplomats resented being bypassed by "backdoor negotiating with the White House through unofficial emissaries," notably

Feldman and Feinberg.[36] Bundy described Feldman as "an unreliable channel," but noted that, on the other hand, "the trouble with the rest of us is [the Israelis] don't trust us."[37] Continuing to play its role as a thorn in the side of Israel and AIPAC, the ACJ condemned "the maintenance of 'Jewish presidential advisers'" as well as the expectation that "Jewish leaders" could deliver "Jewish votes."[38]

Rusk condemned an "attempted end run through friends of Israel in the United States" to generate political opposition to the Jordanian arms package. "We have now made this point clear on about five occasions," he declared, "and we are not pleased by continuing efforts to use these side channels." In February 1966, Johnson appealed to Eban, who had replaced Meir as prime minister, to urge "well-meaning friends of Israel ... to stop coming in the back door, or writing, or sending telegrams, or talking to the newspapers," and instead allow the two governments to "handle these matters" diplomatically.[39]

Israel and AIPAC exploited the sale of tanks and planes to Jordan to step up their own demands for direct supply of US weaponry. Feinberg questioned whether "he could reassure various groups of US Jewry who were hearing about arms to Jordan and wondered how Israel could be protected." After a "violent initial reaction" the Israelis acquiesced to the Jordanian arms deal, but only after ensuring that "certain other measures [we]re taken to enhance their security position," as Komer put it.[40] An informal quid pro quo thus emerged wherein Israel acquiesced to the Jordanian arms deal in return for purchase of tanks directly from the United States rather than from a third party. Kenen signaled AIPAC's approval of the arrangement, declaring that the arms deal with Jordan was "justified."[41]

While the Hawk missiles were defensive weapons, the direct sale of offensive battlefield weapons to Israel was something the Americans had wanted to avoid. US officials did not want to heighten Arab insecurities and resentment, and they also did not trust the Israelis not to put the offensive weapons to use in border disputes. "I think there is some difficulty about our making a flat commitment on numbers of tanks," Johnson told Rusk, "when we're on notice [that] they are going to take preemptive action on that Jordan water business."[42]

It was for these reasons US officials had arranged – or, rather, "kind of forced," as Johnson put it – the West German ally to supply Israel with the tanks.[43] However, growing publicity on the third-party tank deal as well as concern inside the Federal Republic about alienating the oil-rich Arab states prompted the West Germans to cancel the supply program, placing the onus back on Washington to provide Israel with the offensive weapons. Claiming that the FRG had "surrendered" to Nasser, the *NER* condemned West Germany for its "breach of commitment to the Jewish survivors of Hitler," an act that went "beyond the call of appeasement."[44]

In July 1965, the United States and Israel signed off on the deal providing Israel with 210 M-48 Patton tanks.[45] Kenen credited a congressional lobbying campaign led by Celler for "the decision of the Department of State to announce publicly that the United States has been supplying tanks to Israel."[46] Asserting "The Arabs remain committed to destroy[ing] Israel," Celler secured the signatures of 76 House members in a letter to Rusk demanding additional efforts "to strengthen Israel's defenses in order to deter those who menace her security." The *NER* published and praised Celler's letter.[47]

As Israel and AIPAC mounted a campaign emphasizing their vulnerability in the face of an implacably hostile Arab world, the Israelis submitted a "sizable request for military assistance" in 1966. Israel continued to press for "as close to 100% military identification with the United States as it can get" while refusing to be assuaged by repeated US assurances that it would defend the Zionist state against any threat to its security. Johnson responded by approving "a military aid package for Israel, far more ambitious than Kennedy's" already elevated levels of assistance.[48]

Having achieved a breakthrough establishing the United States as its chief supplier of battlefield weapons, Israel lobbied its special ally to become "the prime Israeli Air Force supplier." The Johnson administration initially demurred, but the Israelis refused to take "no" for an answer. They urged Feldman to appeal to Johnson, "probably to pass on a complaint about how poorly we're treating Israel," as Komer sarcastically put it; "Such gambits are part of a standard Israeli effort to put pressure on us for more military and economic help." The Johnson administration relented, offering 24 planes, but the Israelis responded with a request for 210 aircraft. In February the administration countered by "siccing [Robert] McNamara on the Israelis." After the defense secretary set Eban straight in "20 no-nonsense minutes," Israel settled for 48 A4E Skyhawk fighter jets in return for acquiescing to the sale of 36 secondhand F-104 jet aircraft to Jordan.

Sale of the Skyhawk jets was a major triumph for Israel and the lobby. The "most significant arms sales to date" was the direct result of "an intense public relations campaign launched in conjunction with AIPAC and Israel's supporters." AIPAC downplayed the offensive capability of the Skyhawk, insisting that the purpose of the jets was "to increase Israel's deterrent capacity." The sale of the tactical aircraft was of "both military and psychological importance," advised the *NER*, but should not "lead to false complacency" as Israel still had additional military needs. The AIPAC newsletter dubiously claimed the sale of the Skyhawk "has no connection" with sale to Jordan of the F-104 Interceptors.[49]

Acting on "requests" from Feinberg, National Security Advisor Walt W. Rostow got busy "canvassing new things we might do for Israel." Announced on May 20, the sale of the Skyhawk jets "will probably stand out as the major US-Israeli event of 1966," he reported, adding, "We will not crow about it because we do not want to invite any more Arab reaction than is inevitable."[50] Following the tank and plane sales, "The Israelis have agreed to try to do all they can to keep their most vocal supporters under control, but that's easier said than done," NSC adviser Harold Saunders declared.[51]

Johnson provoked the ire of some American Jews when he linked support for Israel with support of South Vietnam amid the escalating Indochina War. Liberal Jews were among the growing chorus of critics of the war. "The President could never understand why there were so many Jews who were anti-Viet Nam," McPherson recalled, noting that Johnson viewed Israel in the same way he viewed South Vietnam: as "a small country fighting aggression."[52]

Speaking to a group of Jewish war veterans in September 1966, Johnson described both South Vietnam and Israel as small "free world" countries that were vulnerable to external aggression. He made the same comparison in a public appearance the previous month at a dedication in Ellenville, New York, declaring, "If you turn the other cheek in Vietnam ... what do you do when little Israel calls on you for assistance and help? I'll tell you what you do. You do what is right. You keep your commitment. You stand up for freedom, whatever the price."[53] In response, the Israeli-financed Jewish Telegraph Agency reported that some Jews resented Johnson for intimating that his assistance to Israel was conditional on American Jews getting behind the administration's war effort in Vietnam.[54]

Alarmed by the criticism of Jews over what he viewed as a legitimate comparison of his commitment to defend small nations, Johnson insisted, "I never made any statement that indicated that I wanted to force Jewish leaders to do anything." Johnson expressed "gratitude for the Jewish veterans' war resolution supporting us ... I couldn't understand those that didn't support us." The president declared that he did not link "my

commitment to Israel [to] what the Jews did for me in this country."
Invoking the need to maintain credibility, Johnson emphasized that the
administration sought "to defend freedom everywhere[,] and if I pulled
out of Vietnam" and reverted to "Fortress America I could never defend
the freedom of any little country anyplace – Africa, Middle East or any
other place."[55]

Johnson followed up by "speaking at some length with Mr. Feinberg"
to emphasize that his support for Israel was not conditioned on the back-
ing of American Jews for the war in Southeast Asia. AIPAC subsequently
backed the president, denouncing as "innuendo" the suggestion that
Johnson held support for Israel hostage to his Vietnam policy.
The "misunderstanding" was regrettable, the *NER* declared, because
"US support for Israel has never been as clear or as certain as under the
Johnson Administration."[56]

In the wake of the "rhubarb over the Jewish War Veterans interview,"
the Johnson administration strove to establish "better liaison" with
American Jewish groups. In March 1965, Feldman left the administration
to private legal practice in partnership with another Israel lobbyist, David
Ginsburg. Feinberg alluded to "the need for the President to set up some
apparatus which will provide a continuing relationship between him and
the Jewish Community."[57] On September 28, 1966, Johnson, following
the tradition of his predecessors, met "off the record" with "a select group
of Jewish leaders – from 30–40 people." The President then tabbed
McPherson, one of his most trusted aides, though not Jewish, to serve as
liaison for "continuing contact with the Jewish community."[58]

Johnson shored up relations with Israel and AIPAC through loans and
a report sent directly from the president to Feinberg "for your personal
use" detailing what the administration "has done for Israel over the past
three years. The depth and breadth of these programs are impressive,"
Johnson told the financier and lobby go-between; "So is the fact that our
total aid to Israel last year was higher than in any previous single year
because of significant military credits." The report cited the "important
sales to Israel of tanks and combat aircraft in 1965 and 1966."
At Johnson's behest, on October 10 Rostow informed Feinberg that the
administration was adding a $6 million Export-Import Bank loan to the
Industrial Bank of Israel. "This comes on the heels of 28 September
approval of a $5.6 million loan to help finance El Al Airlines' seventh
Boeing jet," Rostow advised. "The President wishes you to be notified."[59]

The report that Johnson forwarded to Feinberg, entitled "US Help for
Israel, 1964–1966," opened with the statement "Perhaps the best way to

characterize US-Israeli relations in this period is to say that they are closer today than ever." Eban concurred, characterizing the Johnson years as "a high point in the evolution of American-Israel friendship." The lobby patriarch added that Johnson personally had "contributed in abundant measure to the reinforcement of Israel's strength and spirit." Such comments, publicized in the *NER*, were reassuring to Johnson, who feared American Jews might rally behind Republican hopeful George Romney as the 1968 presidential campaign got under way.[60]

CONTINUING DECEPTION OVER DIMONA

The Johnson administration, like its predecessor, hoped in vain that US conventional military assistance could deter the Israeli nuclear program. Like Ben-Gurion, Eshkol had consistently denied any intention to develop nuclear weapons even as he sought to delay inspections of the Dimona facility. In November 1964, Johnson told Eshkol that it was "imperative that these semi-annual inspections go forth." The Israelis eventually acceded to another informal US inspection while continuing to reject more rigorous international supervision of the IAEA. Eban complained that Washington was unfairly forcing inspections on the Israelis and not the Egyptians. US officials responded that while Israel had a nuclear research program, the "paucity of nuclear facilities" in Egypt made the question of inspections there "academic at this time."[61]

Rusk accurately suspected Israel was "closer to nuclear weapons capability than we supposed." By 1964 Canadian intelligence sources had informed the United States that Israel had secretly acquired 80–100 tons of Argentine uranium oxide, or "yellowcake," to fuel the Dimona reactor and enable production of weapons-grade plutonium.[62] Israel stonewalled US inquiries into the yellowcake purchase. Although a 10-hour US tour in January 1965 found no conclusive evidence of an early weapons development program, the DOS remained "concerned that Israel may have succeeded in concealing a decision to develop nuclear weapons."[63]

In March 1965, Israel declared that it "will not be the first to introduce nuclear weapons into the Arab-Israel area," but US officials remained skeptical. Noting that Israel "deliberately misled us initially about the nature of the nuclear facility at Dimona," Rusk advised Johnson, "We must assume Israel intends to make its decisions on whether to produce nuclear weapons without consulting us." Citing the "great urgency about this matter," Rusk urged the president to "press Israel now for acceptance of IAEA safeguards." In a letter to Eshkol

FIGURE 19 The photograph offers a partial view of the Dimona nuclear power plant in the Negev Desert in 2002. Israeli officials repeatedly misled their American benefactors about the nuclear research program, rejected international inspections, and refused to sign the Nonproliferation Treaty of 1968 in deference to becoming the first and thus far only nuclear weapons state in the Middle East. Thomas Coex/Getty Images

on May 21, Johnson duly requested that Eshkol agree to place all nuclear facilities under IAEA control. Israel again rejected IAEA supervision in deference to the "bilateral arrangement" of periodic informal and inconclusive US inspections.[64]

In February 1966, Rusk warned Israeli diplomats that "The only major question that could have a disastrous effect on US-Israeli relations was Israel's attitude on proliferation." Rusk called for more stringent inspections and warned that the United States could not sell Israel jet aircraft without cooperation on nonproliferation. Eban responded mendaciously, declaring that Israel had no intention of producing nuclear weapons, "so we will not use your aircraft to carry weapons we haven't got and hope we will never have."[65]

The United States found the Arab states and the Soviet Union more cooperative than the Israelis toward its efforts to keep the Middle East free of nuclear weapons. Despite his actual distrust of the Israelis, in 1966 Rusk had assured the skeptical Soviets that Israel had no intention of developing the bomb. The Soviets reiterated they had no intention of supplying any Arab country with nuclear weapons. In July 1966, Rusk expressed gratitude for an Egyptian statement of "willingness to accept international controls on nuclear activities." He called it an "important development" in the effort to preclude "the introduction of nuclear weapons in the Middle East," adding that the United States "would see what we could do to make it of significance."[66]

Two weeks later, Rusk informed Israeli diplomats of the "Soviet interest in denuclearization and said that if Israel would agree to IAEA safeguards, he believed its Arab neighbors would also agree and the USSR would go along." Israel's UN Ambassador, Gideon Rafael, replied that Israel "was not giving any thought to it" because a nuclear ban would not redress Israeli claims of an imbalance in conventional weapons in the region. "This means then you want to hang on to the threat of nuclear weapons," Rusk challenged in response; "Either this card is in your deck or it is not. If it's not then get it out of the way by accepting safeguards." Rusk thus confronted the Israelis with the double game they were playing, but Raphael responded simply by reiterating that Israel would not be the first to introduce nuclear weapons to the region.[67]

The Israelis kept a veil over their nuclear weapons program, which reached the threshold in 1966. Throughout 1967, Israel continued to deny any intention of developing a nuclear weapon, which it had already done in all but testing. Johnson's advisers, including Eugene V. Rostow, understood that "Israel has never leveled with us on its nuclear intent." Evidence that Israel "was quietly but steadily placing itself in a position to produce nuclear weapons" was mounting, he added. Israel remained "unwilling to tell us what happened to 80–100 tons of unsafeguarded uranium concentrate that they bought from Argentina four years ago."[68]

Rostow urged Johnson to withhold an economic aid package for Israel "until we get the report on our Dimona inspection" in order "to demonstrate that you're serious about nuclear non-proliferation." Johnson, however, would not risk the wrath of AIPAC that was bound to ensue in response to any delay of US aid to Israel. Another in the series of dubious informal US inspections in April 1967 found "no evidence that Israel is producing or intends to produce nuclear weapons material," but acknowledged the "possibility that the team may have been deliberately deceived by the Israelis."[69]

The Johnson administration attempted, but ultimately abandoned as futile, an effort to head off the Israeli nuclear program by financing a program of nuclear desalination. Under the proposal, Washington would provide Israel with a nuclear reactor to desalinate water in return for acquiescence from Tel Aviv to international inspections of its nuclear facilities. The effort began in 1964, but by the end of the Johnson administration four years later it had become obvious that "Israel would under no circumstances bargain over its nuclear progress," and the proposal was abandoned.[70]

ISRAEL LASHES OUT

In March 1965, a US National Intelligence Estimate warned: "The Arab-Israeli dispute is heating up." Despite their military superiority over the Arab states, Israelis displayed continuing anxiety about the growing Palestine liberation movement. Israel was becoming "increasingly firm and even provocative in border patrolling, and the number of military incidents along its borders is rising," US diplomats reported: "Responsible Israelis do not now rule out the possibility of a preemptive or punitive strike against Arab targets."[71]

After "repeated veiled and not veiled references to the need for preemption," the Israelis struck in May 1965 with attacks against Syria and Jordan. Syria was the primary target as Israel sought to impede water diversion north of Lake Tiberius, punish Damascus for its support of Fatah raids, and establish a new border more favorable to Israel. Years later, Dayan admitted that the Israelis initiated at least 80 percent of the provocations by baiting the Syrians through intrusions into the DMZ. These actions would eventually provoke a response, which Israel then used as a pretext to attack construction sites connected with efforts to divert water from Arab territories north of the lake. Meanwhile, Israel had been diverting water from the lake into its territory. In the end Dayan's strategy worked, as Syria abandoned the diversion effort and Israel effectively won the water war.[72]

The Syrian regime backed episodic guerrilla attacks by the Palestine liberation movement, but Israel was the main aggressor in the mounting border conflict. Dissatisfied with the 1949 armistice line, and as contemptuous of the Syrians as the Syrians were of them, the Israelis engaged in "aggressive and provocative behavior and local skirmishes that eventually culminated with a full-scale Arab-Israeli war."[73] The DOS condemned Israel's aggression, rejecting claims that the cross-border attacks were purely retaliatory responses to Fatah raids and Syrian provocations. The assaults, including the use of artillery and aircraft, prompted a US warning that "if such actions lead to Security Council consideration the US will not be able to support Israel."[74]

The Israelis shrugged off the American protestations and stepped up their provocations on the border with Syria. In mid-July 1966, Israel again bombed the Syrian water diversion project.[75] After summoning the Israeli ambassador, Rusk declared that the militant response "to alleged *Fatah* actions was out of proportion to the damage of those raids, and appears to us ill advised." In view of Israeli military superiority over the Arabs as well as US backing, Israel was a country "whose security is essentially, if not absolutely, assured," Rusk continued. Thus, Israel's posture should be "characterized more consistently by calm, confidence and restraint"; instead, the Zionist state "acted as if its existence was in immediate jeopardy." The United States perceived "real opportunities to make large strides toward peace and stability in the Near East," he added, but cross-border attacks served instead to increase tensions while "detracting from Israel's image as a country sincerely devoted to peace with its neighbors."[76]

Rather than exploiting divisions within the Arab world, Israeli actions facilitated reconciliation between Syria and Egypt. Under pressure as the recognized leader of the Arab world to combat or at least condemn Israeli aggression, Nasser restored diplomatic relations with the Syrians. Nasser, who in 1965 had offered to meet with Israeli leaders and had downplayed the issue of Palestine, now declared that he would seek "to liberate Palestine in a revolutionary manner." In November 1966, the Egyptian leader signed a mutual defense treaty with the Syrian Ba'thist regime, which had seized power in a coup earlier that year.[77]

American professions of friendship, provision of sophisticated weaponry, and financial assistance produced no commensurate influence over Israeli policy. The Israelis went on the attack against their foes without informing, much less seeking the consent of, their special ally in Washington. Having gone all-out to support Israel and placate the domestic lobby, the Johnson administration was rewarded with a cross-border assault that laid the groundwork for the subsequent outbreak of a third Arab–Israeli war.

On November 13, 1966, the Israelis launched a major military assault on the West Bank. Citing the deaths of three Israeli soldiers in a land mine incident along the Jordanian border, Israel sent a large invasion force backed by tanks and aircraft into the town of Samu, south of Hebron. Several Jordanian and Israeli soldiers died in Operation Shredder. In an act of collective punishment, the IDF admitted to destroying 41 houses; a subsequent UN assessment counted 125 homes destroyed. The West Bank villagers had been herded into the town square to witness the destruction of their homes. No evidence surfaced connecting Samu and surrounding villages with the mine incident for which they paid the price exacted by the IDF. Evidence suggested the mine had been planted by the revolutionary Palestine Liberation Front.[78]

What made the Samu attack shocking was that it targeted Jordan even though Hussein had been secretly collaborating with the Israelis as well as US diplomats in an effort to contain Fatah and keep the West Bank border as calm as possible. The Samu attack "shattered the *modus vivendi* which had lasted for several years along the Israeli-Jordan border," a CIA analysis recounted a few days after the attack. "During this period, King Hussein had made a sustained effort to avoid provocations to Israel." Hence, the Israeli attack "badly damaged Hussein's position at home."[79]

The Samu assault was a watershed moment for Hussein, and thus "proved to be a decisive moment in the march to war" in the Middle East. The Israeli assault spurred Hussein's fears that Israel coveted the West Bank and could not be trusted or compelled by the Americans to respect Jordanian security. Driven to "seek alternative solutions to secure the volatile West Bank," Hussein "sought an alliance with Nasser." Clea Bunch argues that in the wake of the Israeli incursion Hussein came to the conclusion "that war was inevitable and that the American government would not act decisively to defend Jordanian territory."[80]

Considered by the CIA "the worst single incident since Suez," the Samu assault "set back progress for long-term accommodation with the Arabs," Walt Rostow noted. "It makes even moderate Arabs feel fatalistically that there is nothing they can do to get along with the Israelis no matter how hard they try. It puts a premium on extreme Arab chauvinism." The West Bank invasion "undercut Hussein," Rostow advised Johnson, after Washington had "spent $500 million to shore him up as a stabilizing factor on Israel's longest border." The Samu assault was all the more galling, Rostow added, because, "We have been cautioning Israel against just such a step."[81]

Johnson's advisers advocated confronting Israel over the incendiary assault. Two days after the Israeli attack Rostow told Johnson he was "concerned we haven't reacted strongly enough against Israel's massive raid into Jordan." While Rostow could "sympathize" with the Israeli view that it could not ignore "cross-border raids of Arab terrorists," the Samu attack was "out of all proportion to the provocation and was aimed at the wrong target. In hitting Jordan so hard, the Israelis have done a great deal of damage to our interests and to their own."[82] Israel offered no regrets over the Samu assault, which hardliners publicly defended in contrast to "passive" defense measures that would fail to dissuade Israel's Arab foes.[83]

Saunders, Rostow's top adviser, called on the administration to seize the opportunity offered by the Samu assault to "spell out what we want" and compel the Israelis to "face up to the consequences of their present course and listen to the prophets of reconciliation." Noting that "We may never be in a stronger position vis-à-vis Israel," Saunders advised telling the Israelis, "We've invested energy and treasure in stabilizing Israel's borders. Now Israel has deliberately destroyed the fruits of that investment and raised the costs to us besides. We can't go on investing unless Israel itself begins moving toward long-term coexistence with Arabs." Saunders urged Rostow and Rusk to emphasize with Johnson, "The President wants to make progress on the Arab-Israeli stalemate, and we can't let this pass."[84]

The DOS followed up, directing the US Embassy in Tel Aviv to convey a clear message: "We do not believe that the Israelis should be allowed to believe that they can practice their version of realpolitik with neighboring Arab states at this critical juncture."[85] Acting on Saunders' recommendation, Rostow advised "putting out the line with our Jewish friends here that the US can't go on supporting Israel's interests" unless it made a genuine effort to achieve accommodation with the Arabs.[86] Condemning "Israel's ill considered and grossly excessive strike," Komer told Feinberg "to pass the blunt word that Israel was 'going too far' in striking Jordan and had better lay off."[87]

The lobby put the best possible face on the Johnson administration's sponsorship of a resolution of censure in the UNSC. The *NER* explained that Washington had to support the censure resolution otherwise the USSR would have reaped the benefits of posing as the sole defender of the Arab world. In other words, "The resolution did not mirror the views" of many UNSC members that voted for it, including the United States. AIPAC praised UN ambassador Arthur Goldberg, a dedicated Zionist, who condemned the Samu assault, but in what the *NER* called an "even-handed American reaction," Goldberg added, "We also deplore the terrorists incidents" that provoked it.[88]

As massive demonstrations erupted across Jordan, with its teeming Palestinian population embittered by Hussein's effort to placate the Israelis only to have them unleash the military at Samu, US officials feared the monarch would be overthrown. "Grim … obviously under pressure," and "with tears in his eyes," Hussein told US diplomats he felt besieged from all sides: the Israelis as well as the Syrians and Palestinian militants who called for his ouster. Noting that his own military "no longer has confidence in me," Hussein pleaded for increased US military assistance to bolster his regime. Otherwise, he added, Jordan might like Syria "turn to the East" for Soviet arms and assistance.[89]

The subsequent modest boost in military assistance intended "to meet King Hussein's political requirements" in the wake of the Samu attack prompted a predictable outcry from Tel Aviv and AIPAC. While rejecting out of hand Jordan's "stupendous $200 million request" for military support, Washington accelerated delivery of F-104 aircraft and added anti-aircraft weapons and other military equipment to the Jordanian pipeline. Still simmering over the Samu attack and focused on the "very dicey" political turmoil in Jordan, Rostow observed, "No matter what we do, the Israelis and their friends will object."[90]

"Forewarned is forewarned," Rostow ominously advised Johnson of the anticipated Israeli backlash against increased US military aid to Jordan in the wake of Samu: "The package will be minimal and will not seriously affect the Israeli–Jordanian military balance. However, we will have to reckon with an Israeli reaction."[91] On December 9 Komer told the president, "I called Abe Feinberg pronto ... so he could head off [a] developing problem which otherwise could cause nothing but trouble all around." Komer added, "We were working day and night to overcome a crisis which Israel itself had created. As usual, we had to pick up the pieces."[92]

Although Israel had launched the Samu attack with no advance warning to its special ally, Eban complained that the United States had not "taken into confidence" its Israeli ally before deciding on the arms supplement to Jordan. Eban condemned the UNSC censure as "insensitive and intemperate" and as having an "adverse impact on Israel's psychological atmosphere." Noting that the administration was receiving "a lot of back flap" from Israel and AIPAC, Komer advised Feinberg "to tell his friends to keep their shirts on, and not start telling us how to handle Jordan again. Their credentials were hardly very good on the subject."[93]

Once again Israel and the lobby exploited the modest US shipments to Jordan to step up pressure for additional arms supplies to Tel Aviv. "The entire US Jewish community felt it was isolated after Israel's censure by the US," Feinberg explained, thus it was "extremely important" to resupply the Israelis "in order to give a sense of security in the face of continuing Syrian raids." Ever wary of AIPAC's clout, the Johnson administration dispatched top US diplomats in Washington "to rush off to New York on a blizzardy afternoon" leaving the DOS "headless" in order to hold to an emergency meeting with prominent American Zionists.[94]

As had occurred in the past, Israel and AIPAC thus parlayed their protests about arms sales to Arabs – which had been provoked by an Israeli military assault – into US promises of new military assistance to the Zionist state. Although the Americans had threatened to "reexamine" arms sales to Israel, especially after US-supplied tanks were deployed in the Samu attack, no follow through materialized. Instead, the United States went ahead with the supply of the Skyhawk attack aircraft, thus affirming Israel's goal of establishing its special ally as the chief supplier of a rapidly modernizing Israeli air force. In addition, Israel requested 200 armored personnel carriers (APC), spare parts, credits, and other military assistance.

The DOS recommended a sharply lower level of assistance for 1967 after the sale of the Skyhawk had catapulted US aid to Israel to the highest-ever level in 1966. To Rostow the larger issue was "whether we're still willing to draw the line somewhere to preserve some balance between our Arab and Israeli policies. They think they've made a breakthrough with you on the tank and plane sales," he advised Johnson, "and they're trying to exploit it to the hilt."[95]

McNamara and the JCS opposed a new round of military assistance to the Israelis. On February 2, 1967, the JCS reiterated, "Israel's present military forces are capable of defending successfully against any individual or collective Arab attack." Moreover, new military provisions would obviate criticism for the Samu assault, increase tensions with Arabs, fuel the Middle East arms race, and move the US closer to being Israel's main arms supplier. McNamara reminded Johnson that the Israelis were informed that the Skyhawk sale did not constitute a precedent for future US arms sales and that Israel had been told to look to Europe for additional military provisions.[96]

Johnson, however, after a meeting with Feinberg, placed Goldberg in charge of the Israeli arms request. The task of arbitrating an arms supply decision hardly fit his job description, but Johnson had promised Goldberg an expansive role in foreign policy when in 1965 he persuaded him to step down from the Supreme Court in order to vacate the seat for another close Jewish friend of Johnson (and of Israel), Abe Fortas. Both were dedicated Zionists and intimate advisers, and Fortas had been one of Johnson's closest friends since the 1930s. "Under continuing pressure in New York" from American Zionists, Goldberg put together a compromise plan for Israel of military equipment, credits, loans, and other support. A month after the

"Goldberg proposals" on new arms supplies went into effect, Israel launched the third Middle East war.[97]

As the United States solidified its role as Israel's main arms supplier, Washington delighted AIPAC by withholding food aid to Egypt, precipitating a bitter rupture in US relations with the Nasser regime. Pro-Israeli members of the House and Senate had long decried food aid to Egypt, arguing that the assistance had failed to ameliorate Nasser's behavior. As 1966 came to a close, Washington again attempted to use US food aid as an incentive in hopes that Nasser "might moderate his revolutionary policies." The quid pro quo failed, in the eyes of US diplomats, as Nasser had: "continued clandestine organization against the more moderate, oil rich monarchies; ventured into the Congo rebellion; became increasingly draconian in Yemen"; continued to "agitate Arab 'nationalism'"; operated a "propaganda machine" that "has King Hussein on the ropes"; and generally pursued policy that "often parallels Moscow's." On the other hand, "within the Arab world he has been a restraining force vis-à-vis Israel," tried to hold back the Syrians, and had done nothing to impede Western access to Middle East oil supplies.[98]

AIPAC opposed the renewal of food aid, explaining that it enabled Egypt to divert resources into its military.[99] In January 1967, Cairo's ambassador to Washington insisted "Egypt must have wheat. Failure to get it would cause great repercussions on all our relations."[100] Surveying the situation, Rostow declared, "We're rapidly sliding into a showdown." US economic aid "has shrunk to a little technical assistance and school feeding." A decision on food aid was the "toughest" and "most important decision facing us in the Middle East today," as Nasser was "still the most powerful figure" in the Arab world and was viewed paradoxically as both a troublemaker and a force of restraint in the region.[101]

As Egypt's patience wore thin, Nasser and his colleagues contrasted all-out US support for Israel with the denial of assistance in feeding his rapidly growing population. They declared US–Egyptian relations were "at their lowest ebb since 1952," and the current US policy was "even worse than that of John Foster Dulles," as Anwar Sadat put it.[102] In a February speech, Nasser condemned unswerving US support for Israel and Arab "reactionaries" – a euphemism for the Saudi Arabian monarchy. In what the US ambassador called a "tirade," Nasser declared he would not appeal to Washington, "begging on knees," hence he withdrew the request for American wheat. Convinced that the Americans were out to undermine him, Nasser accused the CIA of plotting a coup to secure his overthrow. "Unfortunately," Saunders acknowledged, "there is just enough truth to make it difficult to refute" Nasser's charges. He cited hostile "Congressional statements" and a public comment by McNamara that Middle East tensions had been "sparked" by Egypt. Another US diplomat acknowledged CIA machinations in Yemen supporting the anti-Nasser forces, as well as inside Egypt. "Nostalgic hostility towards the Nasser regime," he added, "can only give us more trouble in Egypt." By March the wheat deal had collapsed, and so had US–Egyptian relations.[103]

AIPAC celebrated the termination of the aid program to Egypt and the general direction of US policy in the Middle East. "American policy has become more independent of Arab pressure in recent years," the *NER* approvingly noted. Kennedy and Johnson had committed the United States to come to Israel's defense in the event of attack, taken a "firm stand" on water diversion, and had armed the Zionist state with Hawk missiles, tanks, and warplanes. Finally, as the withdrawal of food aid to Egypt showed, Washington had "abandoned the quixotic notion that we should give aid to countries like Egypt without strings."[104]

As US policy tilted more heavily than ever in favor of Israel, the Arab regimes sought clarification from Washington of its intentions in the event of Israeli aggression and annexation of territory. In February 1966, Rusk declared it was "inconceivable" that the United States "would ever support an Israeli attempt at territorial expansion."[105] The American statements reassured neither Nasser nor Hussein. The Jordanian monarch was "not at all convinced that the Israelis have accepted the status quo as a permanent solution," reported the US ambassador in Amman in mid-May; "Israel has certain long-range military and economic requirements and certain traditional religious and historic aspirations which in his opinion they have not yet satisfied or realized." Hussein believed Israel's goals could only be achieved through "alteration of the status of the West Bank of the Jordan. Thus in the King's view it is quite natural for the Israelis to take advantage of any opportunity."[106]

Israel curbed attacks on Jordan in the wake of the fallout from Samu, but tensions with Syria did not abate. Having won the water war, Israel coveted the Syrian Golan Heights, overlooking the Galilee (Lake Tiberius). Control of the heights would dramatically improve the Israelis' strategic position vis-à-vis Syria as well as neighboring Lebanon. The Israelis thus continued to make aggressive thrusts in an effort to provoke the Syrian regime. "Israel's strategy of escalation on the Syrian front," Shlaim flatly declared, "was the single most important factor in driving the Middle East to war in June 1967."[107]

In February 1966 the Ba'th regime took power in Syria and embarked on "a fierce anti-Zionist ideological offensive."[108] US officials perceived Syria as "the most bellicose of the Arab states." The regime encouraged "*Fatah's* violent anti-Israel line" while providing the Palestinian movement with "a base for its operations, training facilities, and a propaganda outlet." Although most incidents of border infiltration emanated from Jordan and Lebanon rather than Syria, in the wake of the Samu attack Israel focused primarily on Syrian-backed "terror attacks," for which it threatened to retaliate. In January 1967, US officials warned the Syrians that the potential for conflict was "dangerously close" and that they "should not overestimate the US ability to influence the Israeli Government against military reaction to acts of terrorism."[109]

As the Israelis threatened another round of military intervention, Washington attempted to steer them toward a defensive policy of bolstering anti-infiltration technology along the borderlands rather than launching "massive retaliatory raids of which Samu is the most recent example." An Israeli military attaché dismissed the "passive defense" proposals as reflecting "a fundamental US failure to understand the true nature of the threat Israel faces." The Israelis were "particularly disturbed" that the anti-infiltration measures could be considered as an "alternative" to military reprisals, an approach that would only succeed in "encouraging the aggressor" rather than demonstrating that "terrorism" would be "self-defeating."[110]

On April 7, 1967, Israel again initiated a major military conflict by sending agricultural equipment into the DMZ, knowing that the Syrians would, as Dayan explained years later, "get annoyed and shoot." In this case, the provocation precipitated a one-sided battle rather than a minor skirmish. When the Syrians shelled Israeli settlements, the Israelis called in tanks and air power, escalating the clash into a full-scale military assault. The battle raged "most of the day and involved mortar, artillery and tank fire and several aerial dogfights," the DOS reported. In a harbinger of the war to come, Israel commanded the air, shooting down six Soviet-made MIG fighter aircraft, including two on the outskirts of Damascus, a humiliating blow to the Syrian regime. After displaying dominance in the air over the Syrian capital, all the Israeli jets returned safely to their base.[111]

Blaming Syria for "harassing Israel's frontiers," the *NER* explained, "Israel's patience ran out." The newsletter called the clash the "most critical Arab-Israeli military engagement since 1956."[112] Like the Samu assault, the Israeli attack on Syria spurred an angry response across the Arab world. Humiliated by past defeats and ongoing aggression, masses of Arabs longed to strike back and deliver Israel a dramatic defeat, if not all-out destruction. While Arab publics, encouraged by a global discourse trumpeting "wars of national liberation," grew increasingly militant, the Israelis came to the conclusion that the sooner a general war came, the better, while they enjoyed military superiority over the Arab world and an accommodating president in Washington.[113]

In May, as tensions mounted, the United States hoped to dissuade the Israelis from unleashing more violence. Viewing Syria rather than Israel as the aggressor in the border conflict, Rostow advised Johnson, "We sympathize with Eshkol's need to stop these raids," but "you would be justified in letting these gentlemen know that a miscalculation causing a Mid-East blow-up right now would make life awfully hard for you." On May 17, Rusk advised Eshkol "in the strongest terms [of] the need to avoid any action on your side which would add further to the violence and tension in your area." At the same time, the Johnson administration completed negotiations for 100 APCs, military spare parts, and other assistance totaling $72 million.[114]

While the Americans sought simultaneously to reassure as well as to contain the Israelis, Nasser came under increasing pressure to respond to the Israeli cross-border assault. US diplomats sought to reassure Nasser that the United States had "urged restraint in the strongest terms and at the highest level of the Israeli government," and reiterated that it "would never tolerate unprovoked aggression by Israel against its Arab neighbors."[115] However, Arab critics joined Syria in subjecting Nasser, the putative leader of the Arab world, to "taunts of cowardice." CIA Director Richard Helms declared the Egyptians were "embarrassed because they had not helped the Syrians in April" when they got "trounced" in the Israeli attack.[116]

Nasser responded to the pressure with a series of provocative decisions that facilitated Israel's subsequent decision to go to war. He put Egyptian military forces on alert. With 50,000 Egyptian troops tied down in Yemen, Nasser summoned reserve units. The Egyptian leader ordered his army across the Suez Canal to amass near the Sinai border with Israel. Nasser's actions precipitated the withdrawal of UN forces, which had served as peacekeepers since the Sinai War. Reoccupation of the Sinai was within Egypt's legal rights and thus not a casus belli, but Nasser understood that his next act – closing the Straits of Tiran to Israeli shipping – likely would provoke Tel Aviv to go to war. Nonetheless, the

Egyptian leader "succumbed to the pressure" of Arabs who were demanding a more militant response to Israel.[117]

On May 22, Nasser announced that the Straits of Tiran would be closed to Israeli shipping, returning the waterway to its status prior to the Sinai War. Israel had withdrawn in the wake of the Sinai War only under intense pressure from the Eisenhower administration, and only then upon receiving assurances that UN troops would remain, which they did for a decade, to ensure that the Straits of Tiran and the Gulf of Aqaba remained open to Israeli shipping. Maritime access facilitated Indian Ocean trade and development of the Israeli port city of Eilat, from which Arab residents had been ousted in 1949.

Engaged in an ultimately fatal game of brinkmanship, Nasser declared in a public speech on May 26 that war was "inevitable" because the Israelis could not be expected to acquiesce to his actions closing the Straits of Tiran. If the Israelis resorted to war, the Arab world would unite against them "and our basic objective will be to destroy Israel," Nasser declared. Despite the bellicose rhetoric and his claim that the Arabs would unite and "God willing" prevail in a war, Nasser made it clear that he would not initiate an armed conflict. Egypt had "exercised power" and achieved its objectives "without resorting to arms," but as a result of those actions it could now "expect the enemy to deal us the first blow in the battle."[118]

As leader of the Arab world, Nasser was drawing a line by insisting on a return to the status quo ante the Sinai War. Reoccupation of the Sinai was Egypt's unquestioned right, but Nasser had not anticipated that in response to his initiative UN General Secretary U Thant would remove all UN occupation forces, including those occupying Sharm el-Sheikh. U Thant explained that he interpreted the "unexpected" Egyptian request for the withdrawal of UN forces as "tantamount" to a request for "total withdrawal."[119] Nasser later told an American envoy that "the Egyptians had been surprised both with the speed with which U Thant acted on their request and also on his action in withdrawing all of [the UN force] although it had only been asked to withdraw it from certain areas."[120]

Although Nasser anticipated that Israel would go to war over the issue, he did not believe that it had a right to do so. Nasser, supported by the Arab states – including his rival, Saudi Arabia – viewed his actions in the gulf as legitimate because Israel's navigation rights had been achieved through aggression in the Sinai War. Nasser's actions in the Straits of Tiran were thus aimed at "removing the last vestige of the tripartite aggression, in consonance with the moral principle that no aggressor be rewarded for his aggression."[121]

The status of the Straits of Tiran was not only contested by the states involved, but was also ambiguous under international law. Despite its name, experts disputed the designation of a "strait" because an open sea existed on only one side rather than a body of water connecting two seas (such as the Strait of Gibraltar). The Arabs argued that the waterway constituted a closed gulf rather than a strait open to international shipping. As a DOS legal expert advised Rusk, "The exact status of this body of water is still a matter open to controversy."[122] Despite the ambiguities of international law, the United States backed Israeli navigation rights in the dispute over access to the Gulf of Aqaba. US officials cited Nasser's provocative alteration of the status quo reversing the arrangement entered into under Eisenhower to secure Israeli withdrawal at the end of the Sinai War.[123]

THE LOBBY CAMPAIGNS FOR FULL US SUPPORT

As the crisis with Egypt unfolded, Israel and the lobby launched an intensive pressure campaign designed to secure unstinting US support in the mounting confrontation with Nasser. Working through Ginsburg and Feinberg, Rostow attempted to get the Israelis to hold off at least "for a short while" in pressuring Johnson to provide Israel with full backing. The Israelis refused, informing the go-betweens that the request was "unrealistic." Instead, the Foreign Ministry authorized a campaign to "create a public atmosphere that will constitute pressure on the administration in the direction of obtaining our desired goals, without it being explicitly clear that we are behind this public campaign."

Israel collaborated with AIPAC in "organizing ... in a variety of styles" a campaign of letters, telegrams, and public statements condemning the UN, warning of Nasser's malevolent intentions and rising prestige, and emphasizing the need for decisive US support of Israel. "Our purpose," the Israeli directive explained, "is to create a public atmosphere (Jews and non-Jews) that will strengthen our friends within the administration and lessen those who treat us with disdain" – the latter specifically including Rusk.[124]

AIPAC flooded Congress and the White House with telegrams and phone calls demanding unequivocal support for Israel. "This is a time when lobbying might mean life or death for Israel," Kenen declared, as he "sounded the alarm" in spurring the nationwide publicity campaign.

B'nai B'rith mobilized "telephone squads" and organizers urged that "as many individual members of your group as possible send wires to President Johnson." The Jewish group called an "EMERGENCY MEETING" in Washington, emphasizing that "<u>A Mass Turnout is Essential!</u>"[125]

American Zionists exerted pressure on the Johnson administration to convene another meeting with Jewish leaders and to side squarely with Israel in the dispute over the Gulf of Aqaba. On May 22, ZOA President Jacques Torczyner sent a telegram to Johnson declaring it was a "very opportune time for the President to see a delegation of Jewish leaders, similar to the meeting called by Ambassador Goldberg several months ago." Torczyner explained that the group sought to hear Johnson "reaffirm unequivocally that we are committed to Israel's security and territorial integrity" and "not to place too much reliance on the United Nations."[126]

In a public speech the following day Johnson responded to pressure from the lobby by tilting US policy in the dispute in Israel's favor. Referencing the Gulf of Aqaba unambiguously as an "international waterway," Johnson declared that a "blockade of Israeli shipping is illegal" and had raised a "new and grave dimension to the crisis." The statement implied that a full-blown blockade existed, which was not the case. Johnson did not allude to the history of disputation over the legal status of the gulf or Israel having been the first to alter the status quo during the Sinai War.[127]

Johnson's response elicited gratitude from Israel and the lobby, but the publicity campaign did not abate. Evron, the Israeli minister in the Washington Embassy who had developed a close friendship with Johnson, conveyed his "deep personal gratitude" to the president. Evron told Johnson that the Israeli Embassy "was flooded with telephone calls from people we both respect that were deeply gratified by your statement."[128]

Nasser responded by condemning the United States as well as "America's lackey," Great Britain, for their "hypocrisy" in siding decisively with the Israelis in the dispute over the Gulf of Aqaba after having responded less decisively to Israeli aggression in Jordan and Syria. Nasser declared that the United States, by confronting Egypt while backing Israel, would provoke the hostility of the Arab world leading to, as US diplomats put it, "a complete loss of influence in the area for the indefinite future."[129] In his May 26 public speech, Nasser declaimed, "Nobody spoke about peace or threats to peace" when the Israelis carried out aggression against Syria, but when Egypt acted in pursuit of its "legitimate rights" the Western powers "turn[ed] the world upside down and sp[oke] about threats to peace and about a crisis in the Middle East."[130]

While siding with Israel in the dispute in the Gulf of Aqaba, Johnson asserted that the United States "strongly opposes aggression by anyone in this area, in any form, overt or clandestine." He added, "I wish to say what three Presidents have said before – that the United States is firmly committed to the support of the political independence and territorial integrity of all the nations of the area."[131] While Johnson had sided with the Israelis, the president's reiteration of US support for territorial integrity in the region was a clear warning to them against a renewed campaign of cross-border militarism. Thus, as of May 23 the Johnson administration, while blaming Nasser for the growing crisis, did not believe Egyptian actions constituted a casus belli.

The Americans – backed by the UN, the British, the French, and the Soviets, indeed virtually the entire international community – insisted that diplomatic solutions had not been exhausted and Israel should refrain from unleashing war. Working through allies and the UN, the Johnson administration pursued an international declaration designating the Straits of Tiran as an open waterway. The administration also explored the feasibility of sending ships through the Strait under escort or securing an agreement allowing non-Israeli flagged ships to carry oil and cargo to Israel. Nasser did not rule out arbitration by the World Court, but at the same time declared he did not trust international authorities, citing US domination of them. Egypt did, however, relax enforcement of the restrictions on shipping, and refrained from instituting a full-blown blockade. On June 1, Rostow told the Israeli ambassador "There is no sign yet that Nasser is bent on enforcing" the edict against Israeli ships passing through the straits.[132]

Despite US efforts to restrain them, powerful forces within Israeli society and the American lobby longed to deliver Nasser and the Arabs a devastating military defeat. While insisting that Israel "had no intention of taking initiatives," Eban declared that his government remained "disturbed because it had not sensed the kind of identification, the kind of special support that it had hoped to receive."[133] As Eban flew to Washington for direct consultations, Johnson expressed "anxiety about the pressure building up around the meeting," including the stepped up lobby campaign. Evron assured Johnson that the Israeli government wanted "sober talk not inflammatory drama." He told Rostow that the Israelis "know President Johnson well enough – and trust him so deeply" that they would not do anything "counter-productive." Despite such assurances, Harman rejected the administration's request to tone down the hasbara effort. "Of course we are continuing it," he reported back to the Foreign Ministry.[134]

On May 26, Eban advised Johnson in a secret White House meeting, "We are sitting on a time bomb." The diplomat explained that an "apocalyptic atmosphere" prevailed in Tel Aviv as Israel faced "imminent attack" and thus a stark choice of "surrender or fight."[135] Johnson and his top national security advisers rejected the apocalyptic scenario, which Eban also knew was not true. The administration emphasized that intelligence showed that Nasser's troop movements were primarily defensive and that he had no intention of attacking Israel. Moreover, the JCS had reiterated that Israel was militarily superior to its Arab adversaries and would prevail in war if attacked. "Our best judgment is that no attack on Israel is imminent," Johnson told Eban, adding, "if Israel was attacked our judgment is that the Israelis would lick them."[136]

Irritated by Israeli suggestions that the United States was "retreating" in the face of Arab aggression, Johnson emphasized that he would work with the UN, Congress, and US allies to reopen the Straits of Tiran, obviating the need for aggression. There was no need for Israel to launch a war. "We will pursue vigorously any and all possible measures to keep the Strait open," Johnson pledged, adding that "At the same time Israel must not make itself responsible for initiating hostilities." With "emphasis and solemnity," Johnson repeatedly declared, "Israel will not be alone unless it decides to go alone."[137]

The CIA accurately predicted that, in the event of an Israeli attack on Egypt, the USSR would not enter the conflict, despite Soviet warnings that "a new hotbed of war must not be permitted to develop" in the Middle East. Asserting on May 27 that Israel was on the brink of undertaking a "reckless act," Soviet Premier Alexi Kosygin urged Johnson to exercise "a restraining influence." Johnson immediately sent a telegram to Eshkol, noting, "The Soviets tell me they have information that you were preparing to take military action against your Arab neighbors." Writing "as your friend," the president reiterated, "Israel must not take any preemptive military action and thereby make itself responsible for the initiation of hostilities." The American and British ambassadors to Israel lobbied intensively against the counsels of war.[138]

On May 28, the Israeli Cabinet convened in an atmosphere of "hysteria and utter confusion that was symptomatic of the mood of the entire country." Eshkol had been amenable to a diplomatic solution, but the hardliners and a coterie of IDF generals were in the process of forcing the prime minister's hand. The IDF leaders had come to the conclusion that their credibility was on the line, and hence they needed to respond with aggression to the Egyptian provocations. The confrontation between Eshkol and the military was so contentious that a virtual coup atmosphere prevailed on "the night of the generals." From that point forward the IDF established its dominance, and has since remained "the most powerful institution in Israeli society."[139]

Under extreme domestic pressure, Eshkol had no choice but to name as the new Minister of Defense Dayan – "the most devious, manipulative, and power hungry" of the pro-war cohort.[140] Dayan and the generals demanded war, insisting that otherwise the Arabs would be emboldened to take the offensive and ultimately would seek to destroy Israel. The Israeli public broadly supported the IDF, showing that, as the CIA noted, "Eshkol has suffered a setback and must adapt his policy to the views of the tough-minded military that Dayan represents."[141] On May 28 the Cabinet stopped short of a decision to go to war, but just barely.

6

"Let the Israelis Do This Job Themselves"

In the last days of May and early June 1967, the Johnson administration came under stepped-up pressure to unleash Israel to launch a third Arab–Israeli war. By reoccupying the Sinai and declaring his intent to close off the Straits of Tiran, Nasser had "won a major skirmish," the *NER* declared on May 29, and this was "the fruit of appeasement." Warning against "another Munich," the newsletter declared that if Nasser's actions were allowed to stand, "The cost of US surrender would be incalculable." The good news was that Congress was rallying, and "There is sympathy for Israel throughout the country."[1]

Israel benefited from broad support in the Congress, especially the House, where "the clear majority sentiment," Walt Rostow advised Johnson, was "pro Israel. They feel Israel is being 'pushed around' by Nasser." Echoing one of the themes of the lobby publicity campaign, he added, "They are worried about the effects of the passage of time on Israel with the respect to the build-up of Egyptian forces in the Sinai and the debilitating consequences for the Israel economy."[2]

AIPAC grew concerned as Fulbright and other "doves" in the Senate, already alarmed over the long and inconclusive Indochina War, warned against direct US involvement in the Middle East. On May 26, AIPAC circulated a letter on Capitol Hill declaring it was "deeply disturbed by the attitude of a number of senators who have prematurely issued statements barring unilateral action by the United States if that should become necessary." Javits warned that under no circumstances could the United States "let the valiant people of Israel be driven into the sea."[3] He advised Johnson that it "might be reassuring to members of the US Jewish community if you were to have some members of Congress with special interests in Israel in for a briefing."⁴

Sen. Gruening, a Vietnam War dove famous for opposing the 1964 Tonkin Gulf Resolution, was a hawk on behalf of Israel. Citing "definite commitments to Israel ... given repeatedly in no uncertain terms" since the Truman administration, Gruening declared (ironically, given the *Egyptian* food shortage) that the United States should not "stand idly by and permit Egypt to starve Israel."⁵ Fulbright, however, called for Israeli restraint and a multilateral solution to the conflict. "If ever there was a case where the UN should be brought in," he declared, "this is it."⁶

While AIPAC worked the Congress, Israeli officials continued to press the Johnson administration to unleash Israel in a Middle East war. Memories of the Nazi genocide, only a generation removed at the time, and Orientalist perceptions of Arabs as savage and implacable foes, served as powerful tropes enabling aggression. "Israel will not be prepared for any deal or a 'Munich,'" Harman emphasized to Rusk. The ambassador insisted that, despite pledges to the contrary, an attack by Nasser was "inevitable" and that Israel was "threatened not with aggression but with genocide." Rusk reminded Harman, "We have been told categorically that Egypt will not attack." He added that if in the event of high tensions the Soviet Union were to assure Washington that it had no intention of launching an attack, the United States in response "would not rush into confrontation." Harman replied, "The Soviets were a different people from the Arabs," who could never be trusted. The response reflected what the CIA described as a "general belief that only the Israelis know how to deal with the Arabs."⁷

Wary of the prospect of a Middle East war, US officials nonetheless empathized with the special ally and lamented Nasser's short-term triumph. The Egyptian leader had "won the first round" and "vastly enhanced his own prestige" while confronting Israel with "dismaying choices," a CIA analysis asserted. Despite US efforts to restrain the Israelis, "Instant military counteraction might have been the most effective response," as in its absence Israel had suffered a "political setback" and the Arabs would be "encouraged to undertake new and still more dangerous harassments."⁸

Long critical of the tilt toward Israel, DOS diplomats believed the United States was now "reaping the full harvest of a 20-year area policy" of siding with Israel, as Hugh Smythe, the ambassador to Syria, put it. Washington was backing a "client state whose ties and value to the US were primarily emotional" at the expense of the overarching strategic interest of stable relations with the Arab world.[9] Israel was "the big winner" as the "evenhanded" approach had been progressively compromised, Harold Saunders, the top NSC adviser on the Middle East observed; "Now we are committed to side with Israel and, in opening the Straits of Tiran, even to wage war on the Arabs."

Although he believed the long-term US policy of enabling Israel had undermined the national interest, Saunders paradoxically concluded that the situation could be salvaged only through allowing the Israelis to carry out their aggression unilaterally. "At this point," he advised on May 31, the better policy would be "*to let the Israelis do this job themselves* [italics in original]. We ought to consider admitting we have failed and let fighting ensue." Rather than alienating the entire Arab world by joining the Israelis in war, Saunders advised "backing off just enough to keep our hand in there."[10] The Johnson administration ultimately followed a policy that closely paralleled this advice from Saunders.

Rusk, who long had been unequivocal in his efforts to contain Israeli aggression, appeared reluctantly to accept that the march to war was irreversible. "You cannot assume that the United States can order Israel not to fight for what it considers to be its most vital interests," he advised on June 3 in a circular telegram to US ambassadors in the Arab world; "The 'Holy War' psychology of the Arab world is matched by an apocalyptic psychology within Israel." With the militant Dayan taking over as minister of defense, Rusk accurately predicted it would "be impossible to hold the Israelis."[11]

While Johnson appeared to remain opposed to war, his sentiments and those of several key advisers lay unambiguously with Israel. Johnson's admonition to Eban, which he had emphasized through repetition – "Israel will not be alone unless it decides to go alone" – carried no shortage of ambiguity.[12] The president may well have meant to dissuade Israel from going to war, but Goldberg later claimed to have provided Eban with a very different interpretation.

Goldberg, who was considered an asset by the Israelis, who referred to him under the code name *Menasheh*, believed that Israel had a legitimate right to launch a war and that it inevitably would do so. In a 1983 interview, he recounted telling Eban that Johnson's "go alone" comment meant to convey that the president could not be expected to ask for or receive congressional authorization for the United States to enter a Middle East conflict. "They interpreted that to mean that the United States would be at their side and straighten it out" while avoiding direct intervention, Goldberg explained.[13] Whether Johnson meant what Goldberg said is uncertain, but the explanation complemented the advice from Saunders and the NSC to tacitly back the Israelis while they waged the war on their own. To his close friend Harman, Abe Fortas (code-named *Ilan* by the Israelis) conveyed the same message – that Johnson would avoid direct involvement but otherwise would have Israel's back.[14]

The Pentagon endorsed "unleashing Israel against Nasser," thus providing crucial support to the mounting prowar consensus. General Earle Wheeler, the hawkish chairman of the JCS, asserted that if war broke out a prolonged conflict "would hurt the Israeli economy," hence the United States should "give Israel military aid and all the support it needs for long-term military operations." Wheeler and CIA Director Helms expressed confidence in Israeli military superiority, but advised nonetheless that if war broke out Washington "should back them down the line and rely on Arab inefficiency and lack of homogeneity to weaken the Arab cause."[15]

On June 2 General Meir Amit, head of the intelligence agency Mossad, arrived in Washington to secure US backing as Israel was on the brink of launching a war. During a 40-minute meeting with McNamara, Amit, who served as an aide to Dayan in the Sinai War, made it clear that Israel intended to attack Egypt. He sought assurances of US "political backing," continuing arms supplies, and protection in the event of Soviet intervention. Amit asserted that Washington should not be concerned about a hostile reaction in the Arab world, as the "US is already damned in the eyes of the Arabs no matter what" it does. Amit recalled years later that McNamara responded by asking how long the war might last while making no effort to dissuade him. On the following day, Johnson again urged restraint in a message to Eshkol, but at the same time referenced his awareness of the "fully exchanged views with General Amit."[16]

During Amit's visit, Rostow told Johnson that Evron had proposed a scenario in which the Israelis would provoke a clash in the Tiran Straits in order to prompt Egypt to fire the first shot in war. "I believe we should most urgently consider the track he suggests," Rostow advised the president, even though the course of action "risks a terrible blood bath."[17] Based on his discussions with Evron and others, Rostow averred on June 3 that "about a week" remained before the eruption of conflict, but the following day the Israeli Cabinet voted secretly to initiate the war on the morning of June 5.[18]

By the first week of June, the Johnson administration, knowing that war was coming to the Middle East, chose not to engage in an all-out effort to head off the conflict. Helms, Wheeler, DOS, and NSC officials confirmed that war was likely to erupt.[19] On June 2, British PM Harold

Wilson added his "somber" assessment to the growing consensus that "war between Israel and the Arabs could not be avoided, despite the efforts we had been making and discussing."[20]

Even as the Israelis moved toward war, the Johnson administration received assurances from Nasser and from diplomats speaking "on behalf of all Arab ambassadors" that "no Arab state wanted to start a war." On May 31, the Arab diplomats told Rusk they were "united on the Palestine problem and against Israel," but that Nasser's actions sought to restore the situation that prevailed before the Sinai War, not to start a new war. With good reason, the Arab diplomats worried that "Zionist pressure" might prompt the United States to approve an Israeli first strike. At the time Rusk ruled out such a scenario, but added that the US position was that the Straits must be reopened.[21]

As Amit weighed the US response to the impending Israeli strike, Nasser reiterated to the US envoy Robert Anderson that the Arabs had no intention of attacking Israel. "He kept reassuring me that he was not going to start a war," reported Anderson. In a follow-up letter to Johnson on June 2, Nasser emphasized that his actions in the Tiran Straits needed to be viewed within the context of the broader Arab–Israeli conflict, notably "the rights of the Arab people of Palestine. In our view, this is the most important fact to be recognized." The second of the "two basic facts" Nasser wanted Johnson to consider was the history of border aggression. He cited the "constant violation" of armistice agreements, which had escalated to the point that Israel "has gone so far as to deny" the validity of the armistice lines and to "refuse to adhere to them."[22]

Professing a desire for "friendship" with the United States, Nasser arranged to send his vice president, Zakaria Mohieddin, to Washington to "discuss the totality of the Palestine problem, resolution of which would permit regulation of the Tiran Strait issue."[23] Nasser thus made clear his quest to use the current impasse over the Tiran Straits to spur broader discussions on the Middle East conflict, not to provoke a general war with Israel. If these issues could be addressed diplomatically, Nasser suggested, the issue of the Tiran Straits could be resolved and Egypt could coexist with Israel. The Egyptians informed the DOS that Mohieddin would depart Cairo on June 7 for high-level talks in Washington.

Despite Nasser's repeated assurances that no Arab state would initiate armed conflict, Israel, as in 1956, was determined to go to war. With voices of moderation pushed to the margins, Israeli militants recognized that US and international efforts to resolve the Tiran Straits crisis might undermine Israel's justification for going to war. The impending summit with Mohieddin threatened to ensconce diplomacy in the path of war, including the possibility of opening up the broader issues of the Middle East conflict to discussion. On June 3, the CIA discerned a "rising chorus of sentiment that sees Washington as holding Israel back and thereby selling the Israelis out."[24]

Within the DOS, a "contingency work group" continued efforts to devise a possible modus vivendi on the Tiran Strait issue. Proposals included tacit agreement enabling non-Israeli-flagged oil tankers to pass through the strait, thereby meeting Israel's economic needs without Nasser being forced publicly to back down. On June 4, the group's chairman described the task as one of "persuading Israel to forego action in the Gulf until all reasonable efforts toward a peaceful effort have failed."[25]

It was becoming increasingly clear, however, that the Tiran Strait crisis offered the Israelis an opportunity to launch a war that they wanted, rather than being the actual cause of the June 1967 war. Israel did not face an immediate economic or security threat, but was instead choosing war to strike a blow at the Arabs and deliver Nasser a defeat from which they assumed this time he could not recover. Amit had already made clear that the issue of the straits was "not crucial" to the Israeli economy or security, but was rather more of a "political symbol." Months later, General Yitzhak Rabin confirmed that the status of the Gulf of Aqaba was not a "life or death" issue, and, moreover, that the IDF knew that the forces Nasser sent into the Sinai "would not have been enough to unleash an offensive against Israel. He knew it and we knew it." IDF General Matitiahu Peled added, "All those stories that were put out about the great danger that we faced" were "an insult to the intelligence of any person capable of analyzing this type of situation." In 1982, Menachem Begin confirmed there was no fear of an imminent attack by Nasser. "We must be honest with ourselves," Begin acknowledged; "We decided to attack him."[26]

The crisis in the Gulf of Aqaba was "symptomatic of the basic confrontation ... over the so-called Palestine problem," Findley Burns, the US ambassador to Jordan, pointed out. "Both Israel and the Arabs regard it this way." Thus, there could be no compromise solution on the Straits of Tiran apart from resolution of the broader Arab–Israeli conflict. Noting "The only thing that can prevent war in the Middle East is settlement of the Palestine problem," Burns advised Johnson to declare that the larger issue of Palestine was the root of the problem and convene an international meeting to address the matter. "Wars result in peace conferences," he explained, "so better to have the conference as the first rather than the last step." The American president should declare further, Burns advised, "Pending the convening and conclusion of this convention, any state in the Middle East that initiates military action against a neighbor, the US will move for immediate UN intervention to stop the military action."[27]

Rather than flashing a red light of the sort recommended by Burns, the Johnson administration flashed a yellow, if not green, signal to the Israelis, who preferred in any case to obey traffic signals of their own choosing. There is no evidence that Johnson himself gave the green light to an Israeli attack, but the Israelis had been reassured by their "assets" that the president would not intervene to stop them, and could be counted on to deter the Soviets and prevent Israel from suffering a devastating defeat if the attack went badly.[28]

The Israelis knew that Johnson sympathized with Israel, which he viewed as a small state under siege rather than an aggressive settler state. They had also made the president fully cognizant of AIPAC and its vocal allies in Congress. Noting that many critics of the Vietnam War were encouraging a strong stand on behalf of Israel, adviser Benjamin Wattenberg added the dubious argument, "To some extent ... the Mideast crisis can help turn around ... the domestic disaffection about Vietnam."[29]

Johnson's religious faith, including the conviction that the Jews belonged in the Promised Land, provided a foundation for his attitudes and actions in the Middle East conflict. Johnson invoked his faith in a note to Eshkol a few days before the outbreak of war, avowing "May our God give us strength and courage to protect both liberty and peace."[30] In the end, the Israeli diplomats Harman and Evron had accurately gauged the American president. They told Eshkol it was their "personal assessment" that Johnson "intended to see this through even if, in the end, the United States was the only nation standing behind Israel."[31]

SIX DAYS OF WAR

Militarily superior to its Arab rivals and unrestrained by its special ally, Israel initiated a war that dramatically changed the course of history for the next half century and beyond.[32] Israel did not go to war with a blueprint or secret plans for defined territorial expansion, which instead evolved in "piecemeal, confused, and contradictory fashion" as the war unfolded. The war thus created the historical moment that ignited the expansionist drives that inhered in the settler state. Long unhappy with its borders, even though these had been dramatically extended by the War of 1948, Israel seized the opportunity to expand its narrow waist between the Mediterranean coast and the West Bank, to take control of access to the Western Wall and Jewish quarter of the Old City of Jerusalem, to retake the Sinai Peninsula and the Gaza Strip, and to seize the Syrian Golan Heights, overlooking the Galilee.[33]

In less than three hours on the morning of June 5, the Israeli air force destroyed all of Egypt's bombers and the overwhelming majority of its fighter aircraft, radar systems, runways, and other vital installations. Israel attacked Iraqi air bases as well as troops based in Jordan, and seized Tiran Island at the entrance to the Gulf of Aqaba from Saudi Arabia. The war was quickly decided in Israel's favor. Had the reverse been the case and Nasser in a position to overwhelm the Zionist state, the Israelis had discussed plans to detonate a demonstration nuclear device in the Sinai as a means of checking the Egyptian advance.[34]

After effectively neutering Egyptian airpower, Israel invaded the Sinai Peninsula with some 70,000 infantry backed by hundreds of tanks. After fierce fighting against an Egyptian force of some 100,000, Israel took command on the ground in the Sinai and much of the Gaza Strip. Ordered to "annihilate" the enemy, the IDF engaged in indiscriminate slaughter.[35] The Arab armies, "built to ensure the survival of the regime," failed as effective fighting forces against external aggression.[36]

On the eve of the Israeli attack, Nasser had brought both Jordan and Iraq into an Arab coalition to fight with Egypt in the event of Israeli aggression. With its forces placed under Egyptian command, Jordan entered the war following the Israeli attack, which led to the prompt destruction of its air force. Of far greater long-term consequence for Hussein and the Palestinians, Israel seized the West Bank and East Jerusalem. Prior to the Samu assault of November 1966, Hussein had collaborated with the Americans and the Israelis before turning to the Egyptians in an effort to ensure Jordan's security as well as its control over the West Bank. In the end, he failed on all fronts.

Although Syria sought to avoid the war, it too had a defense pact with Nasser, prompting an Israeli assault that took out two-thirds of the Syrian air force and concluded with the seizure of the Syrian Golan Heights. Despite much talk about striking back for the losses and humiliations since 1948, the Arabs instead suffered another, even more devastating and consequential defeat at the hands of the Israelis. Overall, in less than a week the IDF took territory inhabited by more than a million people from four Arab countries, and in so doing laid claim to land more than three times the size of Israel prior to the war.[37]

Although Johnson knew that the Israelis wanted to go to war, he believed that "we had at least a clear week for diplomacy."[38] Rusk declared that he had "looked forward to the scheduled visit of Vice President Mohieddin" of Egypt in the ongoing effort to manage the crisis short of war.[39] Given the close ties between the Mossad and the CIA – anchored by the legendary counterintelligence overlord James Jesus Angleton, a dedicated champion of Israel – it remains possible (but unproven) that US military and intelligence officials had advance knowledge of the impending attack.[40]

The Israelis struck at about 9 a.m. Cairo time, or 2 a.m. in Washington, when the Americans would be sleeping and unable to respond with alacrity. Once he had been alerted to the outbreak of the war, Rusk relied on his instincts, which proved accurate. While the situation was "a little hard to sort out," he told Johnson in an early morning phone call, "My guess is that the Israelis kicked it off."[41] Rostow suspected Egypt of initiating the conflict, with the impending Mohieddin visit perhaps constituting a "good cover" for an Egyptian "put-up job," a view he said McNamara was "inclined" to share. Rostow added that the Israelis were "drafting a message to you" that would explain that "Israel is the victim of Nasser's aggression," but had "no intention of taking advantage of the situation to enlarge territory [and] hopes peace can be restored in the present boundaries." Johnson authorized a statement drafted by Rusk stating that the United States was "deeply distressed that large scale fighting has broken out in the Middle East" and feared "tragic consequences will flow from this needless and destructive struggle if the fighting does not cease immediately."[42]

The Soviet Union promptly called for a ceasefire as well. On the morning of June 5, Kosygin sent the first ever substantive message from the Kremlin to the White House via the "hotline" established in 1963 in the aftermath of the Cuban Missile Crisis. With Johnson not yet available, Rusk responded by reiterating an earlier telegram that declared, "We are astonished and dismayed by preliminary reports of heavy fighting between Israeli and Egyptian forces." The administration had been "making the maximum effort to prevent this situation" and had received "assurances from the Israelis that they would not initiate hostilities pending further diplomatic efforts."[43]

Mostafa Kamel, the longtime Egyptian ambassador to the United States, complained bitterly that "The Arabs had kept their word" and avoided war, whereas Israel had unleashed the attack in violation of international law. He also "upbraided leading US newspapers, as well as senators and congressmen, for the constant repetition of the theme that 'time was working against Israel,'" arguing that "Such behavior could only be interpreted as either encouragement or endorsement of the Israeli attack."[44]

Israel persisted with the false claim to have responded to an attack by Egypt. Just after 8 a.m. on June 5 Israeli state radio announced "Egyptian forces opened a land and air offensive this morning," adding "Egyptian jets [were] approaching the coasts of our country." Days later, the *NER* perpetuated the fiction that the Arabs, "intoxicated by their battle cries," initiated the conflict out of their desire to achieve the "'final solution' for the 2,650,000 Israelis." Believing they had the backing of the USSR and that the United States was "hamstrung by Vietnam," the *NER* argued on June 13, the Arabs "thought they could take out Israel." Israel had merely "struck back swiftly," a propaganda line that Eban carried over into UN deliberations. On June 19 and again on June 26, well after it had become obvious to all that Israel started the war, Eban perpetuated before the UN the canard that "On that fateful morning ... Egyptian forces moved by air and land against Israel."[45]

Eban told McPherson, who was in Israel when the war broke out, that the Israelis "were attacked by the Egyptians, and they had counter-attacked." However, from their observations on the scene it quickly became clear to McPherson and Ambassador Barbour that Eban was misleading them, and that Israel "had begun the war," a fact they promptly reported to Washington. Continuing a pattern of generally accurate reporting on the Middle East crisis, the CIA quickly concluded that "Israel fired the first shots today."[46]

Eshkol wrote to Johnson that Israel was "repelling the aggression" of Egypt, which had been pursuing its "basic aim to annihilate Israel." As the UN had failed to thwart a "ruthless design to destroy the state of Israel," it was taking matters into its own hands. "Israel appeals, Mr. President, for your friendship, your fidelity and your leadership," especially to "prevent the Soviet Union from exploiting or enlarging the conflict." Expressing support for maintaining "territorial integrity of Israel and other nations," Eshkol declared Israel sought "nothing but peaceful life within our territory." After forwarding the message to Johnson, Rostow summoned Evron, who reiterated there was "no question": Israel had not attacked for the purpose of annexing new territory.[47]

Amit, who three days earlier had journeyed to Washington to test the waters on the Israeli decision to go to war, now followed up with justifications and requests for US assistance. Having "exercised maximum restraint" despite Nasser's "master plan to dismember" the Jewish state, Israel would now "punch all the buttons" to defeat its Arab foes. Amit chided the United States for discouraging an immediate response to Egyptian actions in the Gulf of Aqaba, a diplomacy that had "assisted Nasser at least to some extent in forming his encirclement and would make Israel's task much more difficult now than if hostilities had occurred earlier." The IDF did not seek direct US intervention, but Amit requested "money and weapons" as well as US efforts to "isolate the Soviets from the area." Ultimately, with the battlefield almost instantly well in hand, what Israel needed most was American "political backing."[48]

Gathering for an emergency meeting in the Cabinet Room, Johnson and his advisers expressed relief that the worst-case scenario – an imminent Israeli defeat on the battlefield accompanied by a request for US intervention – had not materialized. Former NSC Adviser McGeorge Bundy, summoned by Johnson to head an executive committee to manage the crisis, recalled that the "crucial issue" with which the group was "mainly concerned" was "the awful shape we would be in if the Israelis [had been] losing." He recalled it "was in a way reassuring when it became clear that the fighting was the Israelis' idea and that the idea was working. That was a lot better than if it had been the other way around."[49] Ironically, Rostow later recalled that Clifford, who had championed the Israeli cause during the Truman administration, condemned the Israelis for having "jumped off on minimum provocation" and chosen "to deal with the crisis by initiating war." Truman's former secretary of state, Acheson, Rostow recalled, "looked back on the whole history of Israeli independence and, in effect, said it was a mistake to ever create the state of Israel."[50]

Relieved that the Israeli special ally appeared to be dominating the battlefield, Johnson and his advisers pursued an immediate ceasefire in order to contain the conflict and attempt to forge a comprehensive settlement in its wake. However, on the evening of June 5, Goldberg, drawing on his contacts in Israel, told Rusk, "The Israelis have a frigid attitude toward any declaration supporting withdrawal." Rather than being compelled to back off, as in the aftermath of the Sinai War, this time the Israelis were determined not only to secure "freedom of passage through the Gulf of Aqaba," but were "out to get Nasser" as well.[51]

As the UNSC deliberated over a ceasefire resolution on June 6, Goldberg assumed a prominent role in which he substantially merged American and Israeli interests in managing the conflict. In a 1983 interview, Goldberg offered an extraordinary claim that Rusk "disqualified himself since he had been an assistant secretary of state and made some anti-Israeli statements. The President thereupon asked me to take charge. So the State Department did not handle the 1967 war, I handled it." In actuality, many US officials "handled" the war, but clearly Goldberg, a close confidant of the president as well as the Israel lobby, exercised substantial influence over US policy in the June war and its aftermath.[52]

Goldberg later dismissed as "poppycock" the notion that his Jewishness or pro-Israeli sympathies played a role in his handling of the crisis, but beyond doubt he was a dedicated Zionist, a self-described "firm and committed friend and supporter of Israel." Speaking at an AIPAC dinner celebrating Israel's 17th anniversary in 1965, Goldberg declared he believed in "the truth of the Old Testament prophecy that God selected *Eretz Israel* to be his Holy Land." About the same time, on one of many trips he made to Israel with his wife Dorothy, Goldberg explained he was "a Zionist in a two-fold sense ... I believe in the reunion of the people of Israel and the land of Israel. But, of course, I am a Zionist for more personal reasons as well. I am a Jew, and I believe in the brotherhood that unites all Jews." Goldberg added that he came "to reaffirm in *Eretz Israel* the heritage of *Am Yisrael*" (the people of Israel)."[53]

The son of Russian-Jewish immigrants, throughout his adult life Goldberg engaged in fundraising for Israeli immigrants and pressured the Soviets for more liberal Jewish emigration policies. Goldberg did not perceive a conflict between his support for Israel and his American patriotism, explaining on one occasion, "Both America and Israel have a pioneering beginning and pursue common ideals."[54] Dorothy Goldberg shared her husband's devotion to Israel, rejecting the concept of "dual loyalty" by averring, as it was American "national policy" to support Israel, there was no conflict in loyalty.[55] After leaving the administration in 1968, Goldberg was named president of the AJC. In 1972, Goldberg became honorary president of *Neot Kedumim*, the Gardens of Israel, a project centered on recreation of the biblical landscape of ancient Israel in an area between Tel Aviv and Jerusalem.[56]

In the UNSC debate on the evening of June 6, Goldberg sought to avoid discussion of both the origins of the conflict as well as Soviet and Arab demands for an immediate Israeli withdrawal from newly occupied territories. Although the United States knew by this time that Israel had started

FIGURE 20 Jurist and diplomat Arthur Goldberg, pictured here in 1975, was a lifelong Zionist and key figure in the Johnson administration's decisions enabling Israeli expansion in the June 1967 War. As UN ambassador, Goldberg fended off efforts to investigate the initiation of the war and sanctioned continuing Israeli occupation of newly conquered territories.
Washington Post/Getty Images

the war, Goldberg did not acknowledge Israel's aggression before the UN, and he opposed efforts to determine responsibility for the outbreak. As a result, as John Quigley points out, "The question of legal responsibility for the June 1967 war disappeared from the international agenda in the years after 1967." Moreover, on the evening of June 6, the ceasefire resolution adopted by the UNSC (Resolution 233) stopped short of demanding a pull back, instead calling upon "the Governments concerned to take forthwith as a first step all measures for an immediate cease-fire."[57]

Goldberg's actions marked the beginning of a decisive shift away from Johnson's prewar policy, emphasized in his May 23 speech, of guaranteeing territorial integrity as the bedrock of American and international diplomacy in the Middle East. Goldberg collaborated with the Israelis, who ordered their UN delegation "to stall for as long as possible, to allow the IDF to complete its work."[58] Delaying UN action was "very much in Israel's interest," a US diplomat pointed out, "so long as Israeli forces continue their spectacular military success." Indeed, as the UNSC debated, the IDF wrapped up the indiscriminate campaign in the Sinai.[59]

THE LOBBY WEIGHS IN

The Johnson administration came under immediate pressure from the lobby to give full backing to Israel in the conflict. A pivotal moment underscoring the impotence of the "balanced approach" to the Middle East conflict came at noon on the same day that the war erupted. In a press briefing at that time, DOS spokesman Robert J. McCloskey declared, "We have tried to steer an even-handed course through this. Our position is neutral in thought, word, and deed."[60]

The press statement spawned an outburst from the Israel lobby. Johnson, Bundy recalled, was "driven up the wall" by the DOS announcement "that we were neutral in thought and deed and word, which was not what his friends in New York wanted to hear. So he heard about that from the Arthur Krims and Abe Feinbergs of the world."[61] Krim, Feinberg, and Ginsburg feared that any actual invocation of neutrality could preclude fundraising and US military resupply of Israel. Fortas expressed the same concern in a call to presidential aide Joseph Califano.[62]

A few hours after the DOS press briefing Califano told Rusk that the neutrality statement was "killing us with the Jews in this country." He urged Rusk to "swamp McCloskey with a statement of his own."[63] Rusk promptly released a statement and met with reporters to emphasize that neutrality was merely a legal framework in time of war and was "not an expression of indifference." While still denying that the administration knew which side had initiated the fighting, Rusk emphasized, "The key problem is to get the shooting stopped."[64]

AIPAC and its affiliates launched a massive pro-Israel publicity campaign to coincide with the war. Thousands of letters and telegrams poured into the White House, government agencies, and the mailboxes of Congress. "During the period of June 9–12, we processed some 9,000 pieces of public mail commenting on the Middle East crisis," a DOS public affairs officer informed Rusk. "About 98 per cent of the mail was pro-Israeli." The other 2 percent "opposed American intervention in the

Middle East," and "only a handful of writers supported the Arab states."
He added that the White House had received "an additional 120,000
letters, which will all be answered."[65]

Invoking the "Munich analogy," a Jewish citizen, Irving Moskowitz,
declared that the "appeasement of Nasser" in 1956 was "directly responsible for the present dangers . . . Nasser must be stopped now . . . Only one
country, Israel, in the entire Middle East can be counted on as an ally of
the United States."[66] Members of Congress received similar letters from
individuals – some spontaneous, others spawned by AIPAC and Jewish as
well as Christian organizations, many invoking memories of the Nazi
genocide. "Has President Johnson, has Congress, has the World forgotten
Hitler and the six million Jews?" a citizen wrote to a Massachusetts
congressman.[67]

As the administration labored to secure a UN ceasefire, Israel's domestic supporters pressured Johnson to give full backing to rapidly expanding
Israeli war aims. On June 7, domestic advisers Larry Levinson and
Wattenberg informed Johnson that the "reaction from the Jewish community in America" was one of "sharp disillusion and dismay at the
McCloskey statement concerning 'neutrality in word, thought and
deed.'" While not blaming the president directly, American Jews believed
that McCloskey's statement suggested "a real feeling in the State
Department that Israel was just another country on the map and that
there was little concern for the humanity of the situation there."[68]

The actual "human situation," however, was domination of the battlefield by the Israelis, who were in the midst of transforming a war ostensibly fought in self-defense into one of territorial aggrandizement.
The Israelis and AIPAC backed US efforts, led by Goldberg in the UN,
to fend off Arab- and Soviet-backed ceasefire proposals demanding the
withdrawal of Israeli forces to the armistice lines established in 1949.
Buoyed by the limited nature of the UN ceasefire resolution, the Israelis
and their American backers reasserted their demands for expanded war
aims. In their memorandum to Johnson, Levinson and Wattenberg
reported that American Jews, though distressed by the McCloskey statement, were "pleased so far with the American position in the UN regarding the cease-fire and the fact that no withdrawal was stipulated."
The "major concern today among Jewish leaders," they continued, was
"that Israel, *apparently having won the war may be forced to lose the
peace (as in 1956)*" [italics in original]. Jews who remained fearful that
"the UN" would attempt to "sell Israel down the river" were "looking to
the president for assurances of a real guaranteed meaningful peace in the

Middle East and that Israel not be forced to a roll back as they were by the Dulles-Eisenhower position in 1956."[69]

Levinson and Wattenberg made it clear that Israel might well seek lasting territorial aggrandizement from the war, and that Johnson might pay the costs or reap the political benefits depending on his response. They reported that a B'nai B'rith leader "feels that Israel will not withdraw from some parts of the newly occupied territory no matter who demands what." They advised Johnson "ought *not* to mention 'territorial integrity'" as a basis for a ceasefire. "From a domestic political point of view," they concluded, it would be "highly desirable" to acquiesce on these points, in order to "neutralize the 'neutrality' statement."[70]

Clearly feeling the pressure of the Israel lobby, Johnson thundered in response that Levinson and Wattenberg were "Zionist dupes in the White House! Why can't you see I'm doing all I can for Israel!" he roared. The "hypocrisy" of many liberal Jews, who condemned him for the Indochina War yet supported the war in the Middle East, angered the beleaguered president, who nonetheless eventually pursued a path much along the lines outlined by Levinson and Wattenberg.[71]

Johnson had his own close ties to the Israel lobby, including Mathilde Krim, who was sleeping in a White House guest room when the war erupted. Swiss-Italian by birth, Mathilde Krim converted to Judaism and became a member of the Irgun terror underground during the mandate era. First married to a resistance fighter, she helped run guns to support Israel against the British and the Arabs, then worked at the Weizmann Institute outside Tel Aviv, where she met Arthur Krim. Divorced by that time, Mathilde in 1958 married Krim, a Wall Street attorney, the head of the United Artists motion picture company, a leading Democratic insider, and Johnson's top fundraiser. The Krims had a daughter, who served in the Israeli military. Observers typically described Mathilde as "very, very pretty ... a blonde beauty" who was also "very bright and competent." Indeed, Mathilde earned a PhD in the sciences and went on to a prestigious career as a cancer researcher at the Sloan Kettering Institute before becoming an early and leading AIDS relief activist.[72]

The Krims became among the closest friends of Johnson and his wife Claudia "Lady Bird" Johnson, and were regular visitors to the White House and the presidential ranch in Texas. In the days leading up to the June war, the Krims spent the Memorial Day weekend with the first family in the Texas hill country. Throughout the Johnson presidency the couples frequently ate, traveled, and stayed together, exchanging gifts, cards, and letters along the way. "There are no words to describe how

FIGURE 21 Arthur and Mathilde Krim with their daughter Daphna are flanked by
Lyndon and Lady Bird Johnson at a reception at the Krims' New York City home
near the end of the Johnson presidency. The Krims were close friends of the first
family and key advisers to the president on Israel and the Palestine conflict.
LBJ Library Photo by Frank Wolfe

much we cherish the friendship with which you have honored us,"
Mathilde wrote the Johnsons in October 1965. "We hope you know
how much it means to us to share these family days with you and how
much we treasure the warmth of your friendship," she added two months
later. On March 29, 1968, Johnson summoned the Krims from New York
to the Texas ranch where he told them (while receiving a massage in his
bedroom) that he did not intend to seek re-election, a decision they
opposed. "We remonstrated, protested vigorously," but could not change
Johnson's mind, Arthur recalled.[73]

The Krims were not only close friends but also advisers to Johnson,
who shared with them his innermost thoughts as well as top-secret documents and key decisions he was mulling, from civil rights to Vietnam and
certainly including the Middle East conflict. "Krim's the best man, the
smartest ... as pure as any man I ever saw," Johnson told Fortas in
a telephone call in 1968. "I see [Krim] damn near every week ... because
I just like to listen to him. He's so soft and sweet and kind and soothing.
I let him see every damn document that comes in, he reads anything."[74]

Underscoring "the intimacy of their special relationship," Johnson, who had received as a gift an amphibious automobile, once took an unsuspecting Krim for a drive on the ranch "and then took outrageous delight in plowing across the field straight into the Pedernales River."[75]

Arthur and Johnson "worked together on virtually every important part of my father's agenda in those eventful years," recalled the president's daughter, Lynda Johnson Robb. "There was no one whose company Daddy treasured more, and I imagine that was true of his advice and counsel as well." Lady Bird Johnson declared that Krim "broadened Lyndon's life and understanding about many things as well as warming his heart." The couples spent "many wonderful talking evenings – very philosophical – with deep responses from questions Lyndon asked."[76]

Johnson cherished the company of Mathilde as well as her husband and the president – who cultivated at least one longtime mistress (Alice Glass) – clearly found Mathilde attractive. "Dear Mathilde, Your letters are almost as stimulating as you are in person," he wrote her in 1971.[77] When the war broke out on the morning of June 5, Johnson went to the guest bedroom and told her the news.[78] Johnson left for the Oval Office but soon heard from Mathilde, who was concerned both about the potential for lack of support for the Israeli position as well as Johnson's standing with American Jews.

On June 7 she conveyed the message that "The President's position has been greatly misunderstood based chiefly on the unfortunate remarks of Mr. McCloskey concerning US neutrality." She observed that a rally planned the next day by American Jews in New York might become an "anti-Johnson rally" because of the widespread view that Israel had won the war despite lack of support from the United States. The Krims urged Johnson to insist on a comprehensive peace settlement entailing formal Arab diplomatic recognition before Israel was forced to withdraw from newly seized territory. They also urged a public commitment to regime change in Egypt through the issuance of "a Presidential statement saying that the United States would not resume relations with Nasser's government." Rostow passed on the "plea from Mrs. Krim" to Johnson, who read portions of the note to Rusk in a phone call on the afternoon of June 7.[79]

From the outset, the Johnson administration thus faced the formidable task of reining in Israeli aggression while simultaneously striving to manage the Israel lobby on the home front. Rostow feared "the average US Zionist doesn't understand" how supportive the administration actually was. Fortas weighed in, advising the president that the "Jewish community" had "deep reservations" about American policy as a result of the DOS announcement. He advised giving Israel a free hand: "We should let the Israelis and the Arabs negotiate this out, and save ourselves until the last half of the ninth inning." Fortas added: "The post-ceasefire situation is going to be the trickiest from the viewpoint of domestic politics."[80] Califano collaborated with Ginsburg in an effort to ensure that the theme of the rally being organized in New York would be "solidarity with Israel, combined with declarations that the President is doing a magnificent job in the Israeli crisis."[81]

Within 48 hours of the outbreak of the war, pressure from the Israel lobby had orchestrated a crucial shift in US policy away from preservation of "territorial integrity" and toward redefining the terms of the Middle East conflict in favor of an expanded Zionist state. The sweeping Israeli triumph on the battlefield conjoined with the Johnson administration's pro-Israeli sentiments and both were bolstered by the exertions of AIPAC and individual members of the lobby. The United States thus transitioned to a new policy of abandoning commitment to territorial integrity, which had been intact since 1949, in favor of allowing Israel to hold new territories taken in the war, ostensibly until gaining diplomatic recognition from the Arab adversaries.

The Arabs, who had every reason to feel aggrieved over the Israeli military onslaught, compounded their agony with diplomatic ineptitude. Radio Cairo angered the Americans as well as the British by claiming to have "proof" that the two powers had taken part in the attacks. On June 6, both Egyptian and Syrian radio broadcasts called on the "Arab masses" to lash back against US and British "imperialist" outposts within the "Arab homeland." Several attacks on American and British diplomatic facilities ensued. The administration directed the DOS and the US Information Agency to combat the "Big Lie" of direct American involvement in the attack. In contrast to the mendacious charge of direct US involvement, Arabs pointed out accurately that the United States had armed Israel and would have come to its aid had the war gone badly for the Zionist state. In any case, as a Lebanese diplomat averred, "Arab-American friendship" was clearly a casualty of the June war.[82]

While working with the Soviet Union in an effort to contain the Middle East conflict, the Americans at the same time took some satisfaction in the fact that the USSR had suffered a strategic defeat with the military humiliation of its Arab allies. "The Russians had badly miscalculated, even more so than in the Cuban Missile Crisis," Helms declared.[83] The CIA continued to predict, accurately, that the Soviet Union would not enter the conflict unless the Israelis went beyond the Sinai with a direct assault on Cairo or Damascus. From June 5 to 10, the United States and the USSR exchanged some twenty hotline messages, with the Soviets pushing for a complete Israeli withdrawal to the 1949 armistice lines and the Americans enabling the Israeli aggression in lieu of a comprehensive settlement of the conflict.[84]

ISRAEL STAYS ON THE OFFENSIVE

Israel held up debate for as long as possible, and then ignored the UN ceasefire resolution passed on the evening of June 6. "The shooting continues despite the UN cease-fire resolution," Johnson was briefed on June 7. "Early this morning Israeli planes were hammering Jordanian positions outside of Jerusalem. There was also some firing in the city last night." Hussein reported that his military "was in [the] process of destruction" and pleaded with the Americans: "unless the Israelis stopped their attack on Jordan immediately, Jordan and his regime would be finished."[85] Early on June 6, Hussein asked for a ceasefire, which the United States supported but the Israelis rejected. Continuing the war enabled the Israelis to seize East Jerusalem and the West Bank of the Jordan River – territory recognized as under Jordanian authority and also desired as the centerpiece of a Palestinian state.

Israeli militants led by Dayan, Yigal Allon, and Begin drove the policy of seizing and incorporating the Old City of Jerusalem and the West Bank into Eretz Israel before the UN ceasefire could stop them. On June 7, Dayan announced that Jerusalem had been "liberated" for the Jews and that Israel was henceforth "never to be parted from the holy places."[86] Euphoric in the midst of their shattering military triumph, many Israelis concluded that the biblical land of Israel was being delivered unto them.

Under US and UN pressure, Israel agreed to the ceasefire with Jordan only to continue the attack on the pretext that Jordan had violated it. That claim was "hardly supportable," according to Burns, who pointed out that acceptance of the ceasefire had been broadcast on Radio Amman. Burns concluded that the "IDF goal may well be total destruction of the Jordanian army."[87] The Jordanians certainly thought so, as they charged Israel had "agreed to the ceasefire to entrap the Jordanian army," adding that "150 Israeli tanks were moving through northern Israel toward the Jordan border, apparently en route to Syria."[88]

Israel's expanded war aims had become apparent in Washington. On June 7, Rusk declared "Israel was riding high and its demands will be substantial."[89] Rostow told Johnson the Israelis were in "position to dominate militarily the region," including taking "the West bank of the Jordan River, the whole Jerusalem area, and the whole of the Sinai Peninsula." A Defense Department analysis concluded "It is quite clear that the Israelis will hold fast to all of the territory gained during their remarkable military victory." As a result, the United States would be subjected to "great pressure, generated by our real interest in creating the preconditions for a fresh start in the Middle East and by our domestic political situation."[90]

At an emergency meeting of the NSC on June 7, Rostow informed Johnson that Eban had confirmed that Israel would not withdraw from newly occupied territory in the absence of a "definitive peace." Eban added that Israel would be appealing to Goldberg for "US support" in the UN. Eban sent this message through Feinberg/*Andre*, who advised Johnson that acquiescing to the Israeli war aims "was the way for the President to retrieve his position after the McCloskey statement."[91]

By the time of the NSC meeting, the Johnson administration had summoned Bundy from the Ford Foundation to head a special committee to spearhead American policy. The move brought in an experienced former national security adviser – with a track record of acquiescing to Israel – to manage the Middle East crisis while freeing Rostow to focus on the escalating Indochina War.[92] At the same time, questions had arisen about the pressures being placed on Rostow, who along with his chief aide Saunders received regular direct contacts from AIPAC and were asked to provide "fairly frequent briefing sessions" with Jewish members of Congress.[93] George Christian, Johnson's press secretary, acknowledged, "There is a definite ripple of speculation that Bundy was brought in to save the situation, that Rostow is Jewish and can't be effective in this, etc."[94]

The new NSC executive committee, modeled loosely on the committee assembled amid the Cuban Missile Crisis, quickly determined to pursue a comprehensive settlement of the Middle East conflict: "We recommend that the United Nations be the venue for seeking a settlement" encompassing Arab recognition of Israel, territorial integrity, resolution of the refugee question, and efforts to promote economic development in the region. The United States would "insist upon restoration of previous frontiers," but with free maritime access in the Gulf of Aqaba and assurances of Jewish access to the Western Wall in the Old City of Jerusalem.[95] Thus, as Rostow had urged, "Israeli concessions" on the refugee issue, territorial integrity, and the status of Jerusalem would be required along with Arab recognition for achievement of a permanent peace.[96] US officials recognized, however, that Israel's "leverage in US domestic politics can limit our flexibility."[97]

On June 8, Israel continued the assault on Jordan, in violation of the ceasefire, prompting Rusk to order the Embassy in Tel Aviv to "immediately contact the highest available Israeli official to convey that ... we had understood Israel had accepted the ceasefire and that it was effective on June 7." Johnson's daily brief reported that US-made "Israeli tanks were moving into northwestern Jordan," in violation of a previous agreement not to use them in the West Bank. Masses of new refugees were streaming into Amman, exacerbating the longstanding crisis. Meanwhile, Arabs were attacking US installations in Saudi Arabia and Syria. On June 9, Rusk declared "The position of Israel at the UN is deteriorating rapidly because of a general impression that Israel is not throwing itself fully behind the Security Council to obtain a ceasefire." The Israelis need to "demonstrate by actions on the ground" that their protestations of peace are real.[98]

Rejecting the pleas of its special ally to cease firing, the Israelis instead continued to "punch all the buttons," as Amit had avowed, including an attack on a defenseless US naval vessel and the opening of a ground offensive into Syria. A coalition of generals and settlers – the latter admitted to a Cabinet meeting "with the lust for land on their faces" – spurred an attack to seize the Syrian Golan Heights.[99] Syria had been "remarkably passive during the critical first two days of fighting."[100] Dayan feared the prospect of Soviet intervention, but the decision to invade Syria nonetheless went forward. US officials Angleton, Rostow, and Bundy appeared as eager as some of the Israelis to topple or at least discredit the Ba'th regime in which the CIA had previously initiated a series of failed coups. Meanwhile, the assault on the US naval vessel shocked the Americans and placed unprecedented strains on the special relationship.

ATTACK ON THE USS LIBERTY

The stunning Israeli assault on the USS *Liberty* remains one of the most neuralgic events in the history of the special relationship. On May 23, the National Security Agency, citing the "present situation in the Middle East," ordered the *Liberty*, a "technical research" vessel – a euphemism for a spy ship – into the eastern Mediterranean, where it would be positioned to monitor the escalating Arab–Israeli crisis. The NSA noted that the "excellent collection, processing, and reporting capabilities and her ability to remain on station for extended periods" made the *Liberty* ideal for the mission of gathering signals intelligence on all sides of the conflict.[101]

At 8:03 a.m. (Washington time) on the morning of June 8, hours after conducting a series of over-flights, Israeli fighter aircraft carried out six

FIGURE 22 A US Navy officer looks on at the battered remnants of the USS *Liberty*, which had been towed to Malta following the attack by Israeli aircraft and torpedo boats on June 8, 1967. The unprovoked assault on the intelligence vessel embittered US officials, many of whom rejected the official Israeli explanation that the *Liberty* had been misidentified as an Egyptian warship. Keystone/Hulton Archive/Getty Images

strafing attacks on the *Liberty*, firing rockets and napalm, as the spy ship cruised in international waters some 13 nautical miles off the Sinai Coast. Twenty minutes later three Israeli torpedo boats resumed the attack, with one torpedo blasting a direct hit to the hull in a clear effort to sink the ship. The lightly armed intelligence vessel offered virtually no resistance, as 34 crewmembers died in the attack and 171 were wounded. Following a "May Day" call from the *Liberty's* wounded captain, who gave the ship's position and declared, "I am under attack," the Navy's Sixth Fleet commander ordered eight fighter aircraft from the carriers *Saratoga* and *America* to go to "the defense of USS *Liberty*." The Soviets were advised by a US diplomat in Moscow, and then by Johnson directly, that American combat aircraft had been scrambled to the region in response to an attack on the "auxiliary ship" *Liberty*.[102]

By 11:25 a.m. on the morning of the attack, the Johnson administration recalled the fighter jets after an IDF officer informed the American naval attaché in Tel Aviv that Israel had been responsible for the attack on the *Liberty*. The Israelis explained that the assault had been a result of mistaken identity in which they believed the *Liberty* to have been an Egyptian ship. "Israelis obviously shocked by error and tender sincere apologies," Barbour wired from Tel Aviv. "Israelis do not intend to give any publicity to incident. We urge strongly that we too avoid publicity." The *Liberty* was towed to Malta and crew-members told not to discuss the incident. Many of them ultimately received medals and commendations, including the awarding of the Congressional Medal of Honor to the ship's injured commander William McGonagle, which he received in an unprecedented private ceremony.[103]

Eban declared he was "deeply mortified" by the attack and Eshkol sent his "deep condolences" and "sympathy to all the bereaved families," but the statements did not mollify the Johnson administration, the US Navy, or many members of Congress.[104] While Johnson fumed in private but said little in public, other members of the administration disputed the Israeli explanation of mistaken identity. US officials could not understand "how trained professional naval officers could be so inept to carry out yesterday's attack," especially as the Israeli navy "must be well drilled in identification of Egyptian ships."[105] At an NSC meeting on June 9, officials were skeptical of the explanation that the attack "resulted from trigger-happy eagerness to glean some portion of the great victory." Many of the American officials found it "inconceivable that it was an accident." The NSC demanded a full explanation, with Clifford insisting the incident should be treated in the same fashion "as if Arabs or USSR had done it … my concern is that we are not tough enough."[106]

On June 10, the United States demanded a complete "explanation of how the attack on the USS *Liberty* occurred." Harman's response that Israel "deeply regrets this tragic accident" and would "make amends for the tragic loss of life and material damage" did not placate the Americans.[107] Outraged by the attack, Rusk sent a sharply worded note pointing out that the *Liberty* should have been readily identifiable at open sea in the daylight (many crewmembers were sunbathing at the time of the attack). The ship flew an American flag (though the Israelis denied this), sported identifiable numbers and marking, and was much larger and readily distinguishable with its "elaborate antenna array" and communications equipment from the Egyptian class military vessels for which it was said to have been mistaken. Asserting that the attack was "quite literally incomprehensible" and "an act of military recklessness reflecting wanton disregard of human life," in addition to compensation Rusk demanded "disciplinary measures" for the "wrongful conduct" by Israeli military personnel.[108] "Finally, please tell Eban that I have spent the morning with the Senate Foreign Relations Committee and that there is very strong feeling here about the incomprehensible attack on the USS *Liberty*."[109]

On June 12, the official response further roiled the waters of the special relationship, as the Israelis adopted a defensive tone that left the Americans frustrated and angered. The note pointed out that Israel "immediately assumed responsibility for this error and conveyed its apologies and deep regret," as well as offering compensation. The note added that the United States bore some of the responsibility by sending the ship into a war zone without informing the Israelis of its presence or intentions. The NSC committee considered the Israeli response a "terrible note" that should be retracted.[110] "After reviewing the Israeli Government's reply to our note protesting the attack on the USS *Liberty*," Bundy recounted, "the Committee decided (a) to clear up our own preliminary understanding of the facts surrounding the attack and (b) to suggest unofficially to the Israelis that they take back their note and rewrite it in a more moderate vein."[111]

The Israelis refused to retract their note, continued to object to the description of the attack as "wanton," and stated that they were "greatly disturbed" by a leaked account in *Newsweek* magazine in which unnamed US officials suggested the attack may have been deliberate. The *NER* condemned the "absurd report" of a deliberate attack in *Newsweek*, reiterating that the assault on the ship was a "tragic blunder." After Evron complained about the public charge of deliberate attack, Rostow "explained to him that there was a good deal of strong Congressional feeling about the matter."[112]

On June 18, an Israeli court of inquiry came to the unanimous conclusion that the attack was "not in malice"; rather, it was an "innocent mistake."[113] The Americans remained troubled by "incongruous statements" in the official Israeli explanation. Although the *Liberty* sailors readily identified as Israeli the planes and torpedo boats that were attacking them, "Israeli boat commanders apparently failed to identify the much larger and more easily identifiable *Liberty*," a CIA analysis pointed out; "In six strafing runs it appears remarkable that none of the aircraft pilots identified the vessel as American." The alleged misidentification was all the more remarkable because "IDF headquarters had identified the *Liberty*, probably more than four hours before the attack," though the Israelis explained that this information was never communicated to the subsequent attack forces. At the very least, the CIA concluded, the incident reflected "questionable military policy" and "an extraordinary lack of concern on the part of the attackers as to whether the target was hostile."[114] A Defense Intelligence Agency study found "no available evidence" to show "conclusively" that it was a "premeditated attack on a ship known to be American." A US Navy Court of Inquiry led by Admiral John S. McCain (father of the future Arizona senator) held closed-door hearings and toured the *Liberty* in dock at Malta before ultimately accepting the official explanation.[115] Issuing a report in July, Clifford cast doubt on Israeli explanations, but based on "the available facts" could only conclude that the attack was "a flagrant act of gross negligence" for which Israel should pay compensation and punish the guilty parties.[116]

In subsequent years Israel paid several million dollars in compensation, but no one was blamed or punished for the *Liberty* attack. Americans ranging from Rusk and Helms to the *Liberty* survivors never accepted the official explanation. The Israelis argue they had no motive to launch a direct attack on the American ship, which had instead resulted from the fog of war, but various scholars, journalists, and military officials have argued that Israel attacked deliberately to preclude the *Liberty* from monitoring and possibly then preempting the impending attack on Syria, to cover up nearby executions of Egyptian captives, or to stop the *Liberty* from jamming Israeli communications. Declassified CIA documents, as well as transcripts from the Israeli military showing that the attackers had identified the ship as American, suggest a deliberate attack. Rear Admiral Isaac C. Kidd, who toured the ship and carried out the naval inquiry, was among many who swore the crewmen to silence to bolster the official explanation of an accident while holding privately to the conviction that the Israeli attack had been deliberate. In the absence of full declassification of documents on all sides and an all-out congressional investigation – long advocated by the *Liberty* survivors and their supporters – the incident is likely to remain disputed more than a half-century after the fact.[117] In any case, as Eugene Rogan points out, "The fact that such an unprovoked attack, incurring so many American casualties, could so easily be forgiven reflected the nature of the new special relationship between Israel and the United States."[118]

With the *Liberty* put out of service, US officials found it "difficult to obtain information on how fighting along Syrian borders was going."[119] On the morning of June 10, it became clear that the IDF was "smashing ahead" in defiance of the ceasefire, which Syria had accepted, and was poised for a possible drive on Damascus. Kosygin informed Johnson via the hotline that "a very crucial moment has now arrived" in which the USSR might be compelled to intervene in behalf of its ally. "These actions may bring us into a clash, which will lead to grave catastrophe," he warned. Kosygin called on the United States to "demand from Israel that it unconditionally cease military action in the next few hours."[120]

Israel's secrecy and aggression now threatened to embroil its special ally in a superpower conflict, as the Soviets drew the line over Israel's threat to drive on the Syrian capital. In response to the menacing Soviet note, Johnson accepted a recommendation to turn the Sixth Fleet around and sail toward the eastern Mediterranean, an action that Soviet submarines would assuredly detect and report back to the Kremlin. Combining diplomatic reassurance with the show of force, Johnson replied on the hotline to Kosygin that Israel had agreed to meet with UN representatives "to make all arrangements for ceasefire with Syria." Five minutes later Kosygin fired back with a "saber rattling" response, reporting that the Israeli assault was "intensifying" and that the Kremlin would intervene to thwart an "offensive towards Damascus." The Israelis, however, settled for seizing the Syrian high ground and stopped short of marching on the capital. With Israel's belated acceptance, all sides had embraced the ceasefire and the "six-day war" came to an end.[121] The Israelis, as Barbour put it, had "played for time" in the UN and taken matters to the "hair rising proximity of the brink" – and had "gotten away with it."[122]

THE OCCUPATION BEGINS

With the fighting at an end, focus shifted to determining the scope of Israeli ambitions with respect to the newly occupied Arab territories. Meeting with Goldberg in New York on June 8 in the midst of the war, Eban "made no specific commitments" and offered few details. However, he "implied" Israel would seek a peace treaty with Jordan. While making no promises about the status of Jerusalem, Eban sought to "assure all religious groups concerning holy places." Israel would demand free navigation and possibly some control over the Tiran Strait. The diplomat made no mention of Syria, which Israel attacked the next day. Goldberg reported that he conveyed the official US position that Israel should not seek to "emerge from the current situation as a power with designs to infringe on the territorial integrity of other countries."[123]

Eban's pledge that Israel did not seek territorial aggrandizement and had no "colonial" aspirations did not stand the test of time. Neither did Goldberg's alleged support for maintenance of territorial integrity, the cornerstone of Johnson's May 23 address on the Middle East. Once the war began, the Israelis and their domestic supporters launched a campaign against UN and international efforts to force withdrawal. As Rusk suspected, the Israelis were "buoyed up by the successes and it's not clear yet that their mood will be one of peaceful reconciliation."[124]

Historical memory played a critical role, as the Israelis and AIPAC determined to avoid a repeat of the outcome of the Sinai War in which the Eisenhower administration had forced an Israeli withdrawal from occupied territory. In this quest they anticipated support from Johnson, whose intervention as Senate Majority Leader had compelled Eisenhower to back off on the threat to sanction Israel for maintaining its occupation of Egyptian territory. Having acquiesced to the Israelis' initiation of the 1967 war, the Johnson administration determined to forge a permanent settlement of the Middle East conflict in its wake. With that aim in view, and under pressure from the Israelis and the lobby, the Americans shifted policy into acceptance of the argument that a permanent solution of the Middle East conflict would be a precondition of withdrawal from seized territory.

Back in Tel Aviv on June 13, Eban sounded an entirely different note than he had in New York, vowing that Israel would not "return to the straight jacket of 1957." The Israelis were now demanding direct negotiations with the Arabs on final borders, while declaring in addition that Jerusalem would not be administered internationally. Determined to fend off calls for Israeli withdrawal from Arab territory, Eban advocated "a holding action" and urged the Americans not to bow down to the UN nor "be intimidated by the Soviets."[125]

Eban attributed the prior "lack of precision in Israel's thinking as to detailed policies" to "the dramatic, rapid change" that "had raised opportunities which were inconceivable before and for which Israel was unprepared." Evron echoed to his friend Rostow that "euphoria and relief at the military victory" had left little opportunity "to think through their position."[126] But now that the situation was clarified, Eban emphasized, "an intermediate status between war and peace is no longer feasible." The Arabs would have to come to terms directly with the victorious Israelis in order to inaugurate "a new era for new Arab-Israel relations."[127]

Eban's new terms brought clarity in Washington, where US officials had been trying to dissect Israel's postwar position, "realizing that there are soft and hard liners in Tel Aviv."[128] The sweeping and emotional military triumph confirmed the ascendance of hardliners who meant to remain ensconced in the occupied territories. On June 13, a CIA assessment determined that Eshkol was "a weary man who has suffered two heart attacks [and] has been presiding over a weak coalition government. He has borne the brunt of a deteriorating economy and an increasingly precarious security situation during the past several years, culminating in the outbreak of hostilities." Viewed as "weak, compromising leaders," Eshkol and Eban had been forced to accommodate the hardliners but also "the public, in particular the average Israeli citizen-soldier, i.e., the younger generation which feels neglected and ignored by the aging Old Guard ... This criticism has been sharpened in the present crisis."[129]

Within the Johnson administration a consensus to accommodate Israel's territorial ambitions ultimately prevailed over the opposition of DOS diplomats. The latter tried to breathe fire into the ashes of the "balanced approach" in order to encourage moderates over extremists in the Arab world, contain Soviet influence, and "protect oil and US investment." A purely pro-Israel position, they argued, would close off options and "make the US a prisoner of Israeli initiatives."[130] From Amman, Burns urged a policy of restraining Israeli territorial expansion if there was to be "any semblance of peace with the Arabs." Israel should pursue its water rights, border security, and access to the Old City, but "must not further humiliate the Arabs ... Israeli magnanimity with the Arabs would be Israel's best means of obtaining real gains."[131]

The "most imperative" step in achieving peace was to ensure "that Israeli forces withdraw to the previous armistice lines." Burns advised, "Unless we weigh in" behind Israeli withdrawal, the hardliners led by "Dayan, rather than Eshkol, will call the tune." Rusk backed this position, declaring on June 16 that he took "at face value" the Israeli pledge of "no territorial ambitions and that it is prepared to withdraw to the frontiers if a condition of peace could be arranged."[132]

By this time, however, Bundy had steered the NSC special committee away from its original commitment to "insist upon restoration of previous frontiers." He now "oppose[d] those officers in the State Department who want to underline the territorial integrity clause of the May 23 statement." Bundy urged Johnson to reject the advice of DOS specialists because of their pro-Arab "bias." Bundy advised Johnson that, as Rusk was "mildly responsive" to the biased DOS view, he was not "right for you" in setting policy for the conflict. Rather, Bundy, who planned to return to the Ford Foundation, recommended that McPherson, a close adviser but not a trained diplomat, should serve as the president's main "Middle East watcher" and counterbalance to the professional diplomats, while still working with them.[133]

The ultimate decision, of course, rested with Johnson, who rarely sided against Israel and the lobby.

7

"Israel Will Remain Where She Is"

On June 12, the day after the 1967 war ended, Si Kenen clashed with lobby stalwart Senator Javits over a congressional resolution that "talks about guarantees and the political integrity of all states in the area." The draft resolution included "references to withdrawals." Kenen "complained bitterly," precipitating a "crisis with Javits" that left the New York Republican "terribly angry and insulted." But Kenen felt he had little choice, explaining, "When he puts in a resolution most people think he is reflecting our views." Israel and AIPAC sharply opposed maintenance of "territorial integrity" as well as "references to withdrawals"; "This is not what we wanted at this stage," Kenen explained. "What we really want is fluidity," hence Javits' resolution would have been "disastrous."[1]

On the same day, in the White House, Johnson revealed a shallow grasp of the Middle East territorial issues in a telephone call with Sen. Everett Dirksen (R-IL). "The Jordan thing we hope is negotiable," Johnson declared, apparently in reference to the West Bank and possibly East Jerusalem:

The Israelis have said in effect that they are not after this Syrian territory, Egyptian territory, they just want to live and let live and they I think would be pretty willing to follow recommendations to give that back, get out of there. But on Jordan they hope that's negotiable ... this little area there, they hope they can do that to the satisfaction of the Jordanians themselves. Our people think they can. So I think we have some chance on it.[2]

In the ensuing weeks, months, and years, it would become clear that Israel was in no hurry to "give back" territory seized in the war. Contrary to the president's expectations, Israel held on to the Syrian Golan Heights as well as the Sinai and the Gaza Strip. Rather than "live and let live," Israel carried out removal operations to make way for new Jewish settlements in the West Bank and East Jerusalem. Amid the euphoria of victory, Israel declined to pursue opportunities for peace accords with Jordan and/ or with a new Palestinian entity. Israel retained the Sinai and Tiran Island through another war in 1973, not relinquishing them until the aftermath of a peace treaty with Egypt in 1979.

Under pressure from Israel and the lobby in the days immediately following the war, the United States made the watershed decision to abandon its prewar position on the maintenance of territorial integrity embodied by the armistice lines of 1949. Asked at a press conference on June 13 whether he continued to support the borders recognized by the three presidents preceding him, Johnson responded, "That is our policy," but added, "It will depend a good deal upon the nations themselves ... what their views are, what their proposals are." Pressed about the Israeli occupation, the president replied, "If you can live with it until the nations can adjust themselves to their position and give their stories, I think it would be better for our country and for them."[3]

Israel and AIPAC perceived the June war as a historic opportunity to expand the Zionist state. "The crushing Arab defeat has changed the map of the Near East," the *NER* declared in its first issue after the war. "Much of the territory that Israel captured last week is strategically important to her security and to the exercise of rights denied in the past," the newsletter explained, citing Gaza, the West Bank, Jerusalem, and Bethlehem. Israel "will not return to UN armistice lines that offered no defense against Arab snipers and terrorists in the past."[4]

The lobby invoked Eisenhower's intervention in the wake of the Sinai War to argue that the American decision to force Israel out of occupied territory had perpetuated a conflict that otherwise could have been resolved. "It should never be forgotten that in 1956 we might have brought about a peace settlement," the *NER* asserted, "if we had not taken the one-sided position that Israel had to withdraw forthwith without the blessings of a permanent peace settlement." Now, after another war, "No American diplomat could justify pressure to roll back Israel."[5]

In the days immediately following the June war, AIPAC worked the telephones on Capitol Hill to gauge the attitudes of "as many senators as possible." Kenen feared that the attack on the *Liberty*, "alleged mistreatment of Egyptian prisoners," expulsion of Palestinian refugees, and efforts to absorb Jerusalem would undermine support for Israel. However, on June 14, after speaking with some 35 senators, "The report we get is that just about everybody is voting in support of Israel's position, that it cannot withdraw prior to a peace settlement." An Associated Press poll found that 365 out of 438 responses from members of Congress "were opposed to withdrawal without peace." A "roundup of American editorial, columnist and magazine opinion" revealed "considerable comment favoring Israel retaining strategic territory."[6]

Israel and the lobby thus enjoyed commanding support from Congress and, by extension, much of the American public, which sided overwhelmingly with the Zionist state. While there had been no shortage of divisions and disagreements within the "Jewish community" throughout Israel's history, no doubt most Jews shared the emotions of Rabbi Jay Kaufman, who vividly described at a convention of B'nai B'rith how "the terror in all our hearts at the onset of hostilities" gave way to "the fantastic joy and incredulous pride" as the "gallant Israeli army" delivered "the sweetness of victory."[7]

Backed by considerable popular support, Israel and AIPAC pressed Johnson to clarify US policy in Israel's favor, and he soon obliged. On June 19, the president delivered a decisive address confirming US support for a continuing Israeli occupation. Johnson listed recognition of each nation's right to exist as the first of five principles to achieve peace in the region. The fifth principle he cited was "political independence and territorial integrity," but the actual boundaries could be determined "only on the basis of peace between the parties." Israel thus would be under no US pressure to carry out a prompt withdrawal, but rather could hold out until the Arabs entered into direct negotiations. "Security against terror, destruction, and war" could only be achieved through "recognized boundaries," meaning that the 1949 armistice lines were no longer binding. Johnson called vaguely for "adequate recognition of the three great religions" in determining the status of Jerusalem, but did not make the status of the holy city one of the five vital principles. The other three principles were "justice for the refugees," maritime rights, and curbing the arms race in the region. The United States would assist in every way but the parties had to come to peace terms on their own, which meant that Washington would not compel an Israeli withdrawal.[8]

Johnson's speech delighted Israel and AIPAC, both of which had called for, as Bundy had advised the president, a "serious public statement . . . from your own mouth" establishing "basic guidelines . . . toward the future."[9] Feinberg declared that the speech was "wonderful" and that

"Jewish leaders all over the country" were "high in their appreciation" for the president's support.[10] "President Johnson has taken a position that is both firm and right," the *NER* declared on June 27, and "should be strongly commended and reassured of the support of the American people."[11]

Virtually powerless in comparison with AIPAC, the New York–based Arab Higher Committee for Palestine was "greatly disappointed" by the speech, writing to Johnson in condemnation of "a Zionist imposed peace permitting the treacherous aggressors to retain the fruit of their criminal war in violation of the United Nations Charter and international law."[12] Johnson's speech demanded Arab recognition and direct negotiations and bolstered maritime rights, all of which echoed Israeli positions. As to the other two principles of the speech, Israel and AIPAC would have little trouble getting the arms flow to Tel Aviv restarted, whereas "justice for the refugees" would continue to be ignored.

Johnson's speech on June 19 marked the full flowering of the special relationship, and the final internment of the "impartial" policy. It enabled an open-ended occupation and irresolution of the "Middle East crisis" for generations to come.

Kenen knew in the wake of Johnson's address that Israel and the lobby had prevailed, their path cleared to reap the spoils of victory by retaining the occupied territories (OT). Johnson had "learned the lesson so well in 1957 ... He is now in position to carry out what he was urging on Ike," Kenen wrote. Goldberg was effectively containing threats in the UNGA, the Congress was overwhelmingly behind the US policy of endorsing the occupation, the "annexation of Jerusalem" was imminent, and, to top it off, there had been a sharp increase in the "flow of contributions to AIPAC." Kenen concluded, "Everyone likes a winner, and Israel is a spectacular one. Also, Congress was relieved of the need to take action," and the Soviet Union "had suffered a setback." In sum, "Nothing has happened like this since 1947."[13]

From June 23 to 25, at a summit meeting in Glassboro, New Jersey, the Soviet Union pushed back against Johnson's decision to enable a long-term occupation. Kosygin accurately predicted that in the absence of an Israeli pullback "hostilities were certain to break out again."[14] Although the shooting had stopped, the occupation was a continuation of belligerence, which would have to be ended to achieve a final settlement. Johnson rejected the Soviet argument while stressing that Washington had less influence than was generally presumed over the Israelis and thus could not force them out. The president also chided the Soviets based on "alarming reports of new arms shipments to the Arab countries" in the wake of the war. Ultimately, the support for withdrawal by the American cold war adversary only reinforced the US and Israeli opposition to it.[15]

US–Soviet discussions continued within the UNSC, but the Israelis rejected international mediation of the conflict, in which they now held all the cards. The Israelis "feel time is on their side and no early move should be made in the Security Council," Rusk observed. At the same time, the Israelis opposed "any Moscow-Washington accommodation," Bundy noted, adding that "the Friends of Israel may try" an end-run to the White House" to pressure Johnson against a UN settlement. However, with strong international support behind mounting an effort to mediate the conflict, neither the Israelis nor AIPAC could head off UN involvement.[16]

The talks in New Jersey and heated debate in the UN created a "deluge of words," the CIA observed, yet "Nearly all mediatory efforts are focusing – and foundering – on the question of withdrawal of Israeli forces from the occupied territory."[17] Initially guarded about Israeli expansion, Eban now told Rusk: "The natural thing was for Gaza to be in Israel" and "there should be some kind of association between the West Bank and Israel."[18] Goldberg, who in the midst of the war on June 9 had warned against Israeli "designs to infringe on the territorial integrity of other countries," now championed the occupation in the UN. "Clearly Israel will not abandon a military advantage it has won in war if Arabs contend that a state of war still exists and refuse to recognize Israel has a right to national existence," the jurist declared.[19]

The Israeli demand for de jure recognition and direct negotiations – opposed for decades but now backed by the reversal in US policy – was a recipe for the perpetual occupation that ensued. Lebanese President Charles Helou explained the issue to the American diplomat John J. McCloy. A self-described "westernized Arab," Helou

stressed the need to understand basic Arab psychology ... No Arab leader could sign any agreement which would, in effect, give up what the Arabs hold to be the right to reclaim Palestine. As a direct consequence of this basic factor of life, real 'peace' in the judicial sense of the word is not attainable; there can be no Versailles-type peace treaty.

Helou added, "Since the Israelis understand this aspect of Arab thinking their persistent demands for direct negotiations leading to the signing of a peace treaty are considered only a pretext to retain the newly acquired territories."[20]

JERUSALEM

The US-backed Israeli demands for de jure recognition and direct negotiations had no chance of gaining support, particularly as they coincided with an Israeli campaign to annex Arab East Jerusalem. Jerusalem was sacred to Jews, Christians, and Muslims. The Muslim holy sites the Dome of the Rock and the Al-Aqsa Mosque were located in the heart of the now Israeli occupied Old City. Israeli aggression driving Muslims from authority in the Old City thus laid the foundation for decades of strife.

Israeli attitudes toward Jerusalem reflected a "convergence between religious and secular Jewish nationalism" that crystallized in the June war. In the early days of the conflict Evron "reported vividly" to his friend Walt Rostow on the "euphoria" that reverberated throughout Israel after the capture of Jerusalem.[21] Securing the Western or Wailing Wall surrounding the Temple Mount, the holiest site in Judaism, ignited a celebration throughout Israel. Bolstered by broad popular support, Israeli leaders vowed to maintain control of Jerusalem while preserving access to Christian and Muslim holy sites.

Zionist fundamentalists perceived the capture of the holy city as the fulfillment of biblical prophecy. "The land was promised to us by the Almighty, and all the prophets foretold its return to us," Chief Rabbi Yitzhak Nissim declared in an official ruling published in the *Jerusalem Post*. "Therefore it is forbidden for any Jew to even consider returning any part whatsoever of the land of our forefathers." The Israeli government did not formally endorse this position, but Dayan, Begin, and other hardliners stated publically that Israel had won authority over Jerusalem as well as the holy cities of Hebron and Nablus, which collectively comprised the "heritage of forefathers."[22]

As the ceasefire took effect on June 11, the Israeli Cabinet authorized the annexation of East Jerusalem. Employing euphemisms such as "municipal fusion" rather than annexation, the Israelis took charge, as they displayed an "aversion to UN presence in areas under Israel's control." In view of the "very strong international interest in Jerusalem," the holy city "should be recognized by some form of discussions, not treated unilaterally," Rusk declared.[23] "We understand the strength of the Israeli attachment to Jerusalem," the top US diplomat noted; "Other peoples also have strong feelings with regard to the holy places of Jerusalem, equally rooted in history." He added that with the destruction from the recent war and Israeli removal operations "likely to linger in memories of [a] wide Arab audience, much as do a few cases of Israeli brutality and destruction of villages during [the] war of 1948–49," it was all the more important for Israel to consider Arab as well as Zionist emotional attachment to the holy city.[24]

The Israelis remained "adamant" in response; Jerusalem was non negotiable, a position the Israel lobby fully supported. Ginsburg told Vice President Humphrey it was "inconceivable" that Jerusalem would ever again become a divided city. Acknowledging opposition from the Vatican and the Muslim world, the *NER* avowed, "Israel will resist pressures to internationalize the Jerusalem territory." The newsletter quoted novelist James Michener – author of the epic story of the ancient Jews, *The Source* – military historian Samuel Eliot Morison, and others declaring that Israel should keep Jerusalem as well as other territories.[25]

Ignoring the protests of the United States, Great Britain, the USSR, the UN, and the Arab world, Israel annexed not merely East Jerusalem but an area 12 times the size of the Jordanian sector of the municipality. Israel subsumed in whole or part 28 Palestinian villages, with the lines drawn in such a way as to incorporate as few Palestinians as possible. The Israelis left little doubt that their actions meant to present a fait accompli fore-closing the possibility that the newly defined boundaries of Jerusalem could be considered in negotiations regarding any potential settlement of the overall conflict.[26]

The United States offered detailed plans for at least "partial internatio-nalization" of the city, but declined to join the overwhelming majority of nations in condemning Israel's actions.[27] On July 4, the UNGA voted 99–0 with 20 abstentions, the United States among the latter, in favor of a Pakistani-sponsored resolution that condemned Israel for actions designed to "alter the status of Jerusalem."[28] The US abstention reflected its position that the status of Jerusalem was contingent on an overall settlement of the conflict. As Goldberg told Johnson: "We said that the whole kit and caboodle has to be settled" prior to Israeli withdrawal. The administration in effect acquiesced to the annexation.[29] When the UNGA adjourned on July 21 with no resolution of the conflict, Eban expressed his elation over the "favorable impasse."[30]

Affirming the clout of the lobby, especially on the emotional issue of Jerusalem, Goldberg acknowledged that "The Jewish community here would be up in arms" if the United States had supported the UN resolu-tions. Placating Israel and AIPAC came at a price, thus, Goldberg noted, "We have taken our lumps in the General Assembly and the international community on this issue." By abstaining, the Johnson administration also sided against multinational oil companies, which had expressed "acute concern" about a potential Arab oil boycott in response to the US position on Jerusalem. The CIA, however, had come to the conclusion, which proved accurate until 1973, that "a number of the Arab states – particularly the oil exporters – realize that their interests are not served by taking anti-Western positions."[31]

The Israeli quest to establish unilateral authority over Jerusalem virtually ensured there would be no peace settlement while simultaneously empowering Muslim fundamentalism. Anderson, the longtime US envoy to the Arab world, emphasized this prospect to Rostow, noting that many Arabs considered

the Syrian heights as a Syrian problem; the West Bank as a Jordanian problem; Gaza as an Egyptian problem; but the Old City of Jerusalem is capable of stirring the mobs in the street to the point where the fate of our most moderate friends in the Middle East will be in jeopardy and the basis laid for a later holy war.

He warned that "Anti-Americanism is rising due to our abstaining on the Pakistan resolution on Jerusalem."[32]

While united on incorporating Jerusalem and determined to fend off pressure to return to the June 4 boundaries, Israel only gradually defined the full scope of its postwar expansionist ambitions. Israeli officials showed virtually no concern for Arab land rights; rather, they were preoccupied with the issue of "the bride and the dowry," as Eshkol famously put it.[33] Congenitally driven toward expansion, the Israelis wanted to annex Arab territories – "the bride" – but balked at "the dowry" – the incorporation into Israel of the large Arab populations of the West Bank as well as the Gaza Strip and the Syrian Golan Heights, the last of which had not been part of the original Palestine mandate. Incorporating masses of Palestinians and other Arabs would "completely transform Israel's national existence," Eban explained. Thus, Israel "would like to have the territory without the population but did not see how that could come about."[34]

Israeli plans evolved haltingly with regard to the West Bank, the hilly region west of the Jordan River, controlled by Jordan since the 1949 armistice but long coveted by many Israelis as the heart of Eretz Israel. During the six days of war, Israeli forces razed hundreds of homes in the West Bank and the approaches to Jerusalem. On June 6, Dayan had ordered the IDF to "lay into the houses of Qalqilyah" after Israeli forces took the West Bank town just across the 1949 armistice line. The IDF drove out residents and destroyed some 850 homes before international outcry brought the removal campaign to a halt after "Israel strove unsuccessfully to conceal the expulsions and the destruction." Israeli forces conducted a similar operation in the strategically significant Latrun Salient controlling Western access into Jerusalem, again failing in efforts to cover up the campaign.

Despite international criticism, removal operations continued after the war. "Hundreds of houses were ruined in the West Bank after the hostilities had ceased," Israeli historian Avi Raz points out, "and thousands of Palestinians lost their homes and properties. All these acts of destruction were war crimes." Even as Dayan acknowledged that "The Palestinians on the West Bank had not taken part in the war," he promoted the expulsions to expand Israel territory. "I hope they all go," Dayan declared, adding it would "be a great blessing" if hundreds of thousands of Palestinians and Syrians could be forced from their homes in the West Bank, the Syrian Golan Heights, and the Gaza Strip.[35]

Militants led by Dayan overwhelmed moderates who might have considered "the possibility of an autonomous Arab state," perhaps "federated with Israel, and of comparable status to the Gaza Strip." Eban acknowledged discussions with West Bank Arabs about a "new Palestinian entity," yet Israel feared that "creation of [a] Palestinian state might simply increase irredentist desires. There would be yet another Arab state," creating the "danger that it would simply become for Israel what Algeria became for France." Evron told Rostow that "holding the West Bank was quite attractive although, in the long run, it might be well judged less so."[36]

Even as they debated the demographic implications of "the bride and the dowry," Israel's removal policies in the aftermath of the war "clearly attested to its resolve to keep the West Bank."[37] After driving the Palestinian residents out of their homes, Israel put in place a policy of "shoot to kill with no early warning" to impede them from returning. "Unwilling to allow any return of West Bankers from the East, Israeli troops regularly ambushed those attempting to cross back over the river," killing "many dozens" in the process.[38] Israel followed up with repression of the local population, including arrests, censorship, closure of shops, and "attempts to enlist local politicians as collaborators."[39] The Palestinians continued to eschew violence, responding with civil disobedience instead. In reply to a general strike, Dayan ordered a "punitive campaign" centered on Nablus, which included intrusions into educational and religious affairs of the historic West Bank city.[40]

FIGURE 23 Moshe Dayan, shown on June 23, 1967, advocated retention of the occupied Arab territories and a neocolonial framework for the West Bank and the Gaza Strip. At the apex of his political influence as the architect of the "Six-Day War," Dayan could virtually dictate Israel's expansionist policy, which nonetheless enjoyed broad support from an ebullient Israeli public as well as American Zionists.
Hulton Archive/Getty Images

By mid-July, the CIA concluded that with "hardliners, represented by Dayan," holding the upper hand, Israel would "remain largely impervious to external pressures to withdraw from occupied areas for months to come." According to his biographer, "The power and prestige that Moshe Dayan enjoyed after the Six Day War gave him the political authority to shape Israel's security policies as he saw fit." The militants had "the advantage of being identified by many Israelis as the architects of Israel's victory," the CIA explained, "and their positions have strong domestic appeal because they emphasize what Israel wants and feels it has won, with little regard to what might have to be conceded in the face of international pressures or opinion." The chances for a postwar settlement in the Middle East were thus "dim indeed."[41]

THE LOST PEACE

As Raz demonstrates in a thoroughly grounded recent study, "Israel preferred land to peace" and thus bypassed "a real opportunity for a settlement with its eastern neighbors" in the wake of the June war.[42] The annexation of East Jerusalem cut off the Old City, which had been "the hub of the West Bank," thus foreclosing the prospect of creating a viable "Palestinian entity." Long desirous of their own state, West Bank Palestinians – who had refrained from fighting during the war – were open to negotiations with Israel as an opportunity to realize their nationalist ambitions while getting out from under Jordanian control. However, the "Palestinian option" was "never regarded seriously by the Israeli leaders," as it ran counter to Zionist territorial ambitions as well as the "widespread disdain for the Arabs among the Israelis."[43]

Just as it had summarily dispensed with the Palestinian nationalists, "Israel did not take the Jordanian option seriously either."[44] King Hussein desperately sought a settlement that would preclude a long-term Israeli occupation of the West Bank and East Jerusalem. Feeling double-crossed by the Americans, who now explained that "Our guarantee of territorial integrity applied essentially to final boundaries rather than to current armistice lines," the King nonetheless proved willing to come to terms.[45] On July 13, the United States received a "most urgent and private message from King Hussein" offering to negotiate a settlement. Moreover, the Jordanian monarch had received the endorsement of Nasser, who simultaneously asserted that he wanted "to reestablish good relations with the United States."[46]

Hussein thus attempted to transcend Israeli barriers against engaging in diplomacy through third parties or on any terms other than the Arabs coming directly to Israel in defeat. While Syria matched Israel's hostility, displaying no interest in negotiations despite the Israeli occupation of the Golan Heights, Nasser, like Hussein, showed signs of flexibility. The Egyptian leader reiterated that any Arab leader would appear weak and immediately be discredited if he were to recognize Israel with no guarantee of gaining anything in return. However, he suggested, it might be possible to agree to recognize the Zionist state in return for a simultaneous Israeli withdrawal from the newly occupied territories. The Israelis, however, had long since locked in a depiction of Nasser as an implacable Hitler-like foe and called for his ouster rather than being willing to engage in any form of negotiations with the Egyptian strongman.[47] American and Israeli hopes that the humiliating defeat in the June war might lead to Nasser's "Sukharnoization" – a reference to the blood-drenched military overthrow of Indonesia's longtime ruler in 1965 – failed to materialize.[48]

The Israelis, backed by AIPAC, rejected the opportunity to engage in meaningful negotiations with Jordan, Egypt, or Palestine. While the settler state went about its expansionist course, AIPAC called for the overthrow of Hussein and Nasser. "The Near East would be better served by the abdication and retirement of discredited Arab leaders," the *NER* declared. In the meantime, the newsletter added, invoking its favorite metaphor, Israel must "beware of any Munich-like compromises."[49]

Johnson, who had expected the Israelis to negotiate from a position of strength in the wake of their military victory, confronted a Zionist state committed to a diplomacy of annexation and averse to peacemaking. The Americans realized the Israelis would not negotiate with the hated Nasser, but hoped they might with Hussein. Accordingly, Johnson approved a secret program of US encouragement of Israeli–Jordanian talks but SAND STORM, as the initiative was code-named, also met with summary rejection. Secret planning sessions on SAND STORM were held beginning in mid-July, but within a week US officials found that "The Israelis are now telling us that they are not ready for serious talks."[50] The Israelis "canceled at a late moment" plans for a secret meeting with Hussein. By the end of July, Hussein alluded to a "descending curve" of US support for peace talks after the initial hopeful outlook that accompanied the launch of SAND STORM.[51]

Israel rejected an opportunity to pursue a negotiated settlement with Hussein because of its determination to extend authority over Jerusalem and to expand national boundaries into the West Bank. Biblical literalists and hardliners advocated these positions but, as the moderate Eban explained, the euphoric Israeli public also had become increasingly enamored with Eretz Israel. "Now that Israelis had for the first time the opportunity to visit areas of historic significance to them," he told US officials, "it would be difficult for [Israeli] citizens to understand simply turning the area back."[52]

Israel and the American lobbyists mounted a hasbara campaign against Johnson's belated efforts to forge a peace agreement. Declaring on July 18 that "the clock is ticking" and "the Arabs have no confidence in us," Johnson urged meaningful negotiations, but Israel's domestic supporters inundated the White House with protest notes and requests for meetings. Johnson felt so hounded by the lobby campaign that he directed aides to "channel future requests by Jewish leaders to [special adviser McGeorge]

Bundy and not to the President. The President said he was seeing too many." On July 26, Bundy reported that he met with Ginsburg and Feinberg, directing them to "not bother you for a while" and to support US efforts to bring stability to the region.[53]

Evron maintained a steady drumbeat against the allegedly "strongly pro-Arab" bias of the DOS. He declared it was "clear that Secretary Rusk had an anti-Israel bias," hence "the President was being urged by forces to be easy on the Arabs and tough on Israel." Administration efforts to "pressure the Israelis to be more amenable" on the determining borders and on Jerusalem "had to be resisted." Expressing his concerns to Feldman, Evron pointed to damage being done by "propaganda of Arabs being abused in Israel." In response, Feldman, now a private attorney but still active in the lobby, suggested as a countermove that Evron should publicize "pictures of Israelis in jail in Arab countries – even if he had to fake the pictures. He said he would."[54]

While Rusk and DOS diplomats wanted to nudge the Israelis toward negotiations, Bundy by contrast played a crucial role in enabling postwar Israeli expansion. Brought in to anchor an executive committee on Johnson's policies in response to the June war, Bundy uncritically accepted the Israeli/AIPAC position of no negotiations absent direct talks with the Arab states. Bundy realized that the Zionist position was "hardening" and that the Israelis were proceeding with "great confidence" with plans "to keep not only all of Jerusalem but the Gaza Strip and the West Bank." As Bundy saw it, until the Arabs capitulated to the Israeli demand for direct negotiations, "I doubt if we can or should make the Israeli view of Jerusalem or the West Bank into a federal case. We can't tell the Israelis to give things away to people who won't even bargain with them," he declared, a comment that elided both the Palestinians' and Hussein's demonstrated eagerness to negotiate as well as Nasser's openness to talks. Bundy recommended a "low-key" approach of "quiet, watchful waiting" that combined "encouragement to responsible Arabs" with a decision to "not affront the Israelis." With seeming equanimity, Bundy acknowledged that "We may well be heading toward a de facto settlement on the present cease-fire lines."[55]

Bundy advocated aligning US policy with "the rights and hopes of Israel," not merely as a matter of expediency or to appease "the Abe Feinbergs or even the Arthur Krims," but rather because the special relationship was rooted in the "wider grounds of national sympathy and interest." As he saw it, the DOS since the Truman years "has learned to mistrust this White House attitude" and to resent the "heavy-handed agents of the Jewish community like Mike Feldman." Resentment of the lobby had caused the professional diplomats to "weight their advice ... against any pro-Israel course."[56]

Bundy's acquiescence to annexation and colonization of the OT aligned US policy with Israel and AIPAC. As Israel reinforced the occupation, Eban warned the Americans against "becoming jumpy, nervous, and running around excitedly in Washington." The Arabs were "just now" accepting the "realities" of their predicament, and in "another few weeks or months more progress could be expected from them." Johnson should continue to do as he had done in 1957 and avoid "appeasement," the *NER* advised; "He will have Congressional support for a firm policy insisting on negotiations and a peace settlement."[57]

By mid-summer 1967, it was obvious to US diplomats that Israel had embarked on a course of rejecting a negotiated settlement in deference to establishing a "permanently expanded Israel." Barbour described Israel as sitting "in Olympian grandeur and immobility in the mountains of Jerusalem in the expectation that they could dictate a settlement in the Middle East ... as if its interests were the only factor involved."[58]

Committed to an intransigent negotiating posture intended to safeguard the emerging new settlements in the OT, Israel rejected Arab moderation shown at the Khartoum summit in late August. The Arabs were far from united at the meeting, as Syria boycotted the Sudan summit and together with Algeria advocated a "large-scale and sustained guerrilla campaign" against the Israeli occupation.[59] The Arab states rejected Israel's demand for direct negotiations and signing of peace agreements in advance of an Israeli withdrawal, especially with the Israelis laying claim to Jerusalem and extending authority across the OT. The Khartoum resolution thus concluded with the infamous "three No's": "no peace with Israel, no recognition of Israel, and no negotiations with it" amid the continuing occupation of Arab lands.

The "three No's" belied clear signs of Arab flexibility while providing the Israelis with a useful discourse to claim that the Arabs were the intransigent party out to destroy Israel. The Khartoum summit had actually been "a turning point," as Hussein put it, in which the moderate forces had prevailed by rejecting the past approach of committing the Arab world to military liberation of Palestine. Rejecting the military option thus enabled the Arab states, despite the "three No's," to pursue a settlement through indirect negotiations under international auspices. During the summit, Nasser and Hussein acknowledged their defeat in the war and showed a willingness to come to terms, as both the Americans and the Israelis recognized. Israel, however, as Shlaim, among other scholars, points out, "deliberately misrepresented the conclusions of the summit as the climax of Arab intransigence in order to justify the toughening of their own posture."[60]

Even AIPAC acknowledged the flexibility shown at Khartoum but dismissed it as a propaganda gambit. The Arabs "made conciliatory gestures at the Khartoum summit conference" and "toned down" their propaganda, the *NER* acknowledged, but the actions were merely "calculated to win votes" in the UN.[61]

CREATING NEW FACTS ON THE GROUND

Israel gradually but inexorably created "facts on the ground" in the OT in the wake of the War of 1967. New settlements, which coalesced behind the drives of religious fundamentalists and the acquiescence of policymakers, followed the historic formula of settler colonial states: securing as much land as possible with as few indigenous people as possible living on it.[62] The Johnson administration "failed to respond with a consistent policy," acquiesced to Israeli obfuscation tactics, and thus squandered an early opportunity to rein in settlements in the OT whose proliferation in the ensuing decades would render a "two-state solution" virtually impossible to achieve.[63]

The Israelis authorized the first of many settlements in the West Bank between Hebron and Bethlehem and began referencing "liberated lands" and "administered territories" rather than "occupied" territories. The biblical names Judea and Samaria increasingly displaced the West Bank in popular discourse. Israel authorized, but did not publish, a new map devoid of the 1949 armistice lines. "Jews have lived in *Eretz Israel* since the days of Abraham, about 2000 BC," the *NER* advised. Thus, Israel staked its legitimate claims "going back to the Bible. And no state has such an impressive international birth certificate."[64]

Proposed in July, the Allon Plan entailed Israeli annexation of territory along the Jordan River and the Dead Sea, solidifying control of Jerusalem while converting the remaining portions of the West Bank into a neocolonial autonomous region tied to Israel's economy.[65] In direct violation of international law, the Israeli Cabinet authorized new Jewish settlements in the Syrian Golan Heights and northern Sinai. Fully aware of the plans for the "establishment of Israeli settlements on the West Bank and Syrian border," the Johnson administration demanded an explanation.

Israel and AIPAC followed a propaganda strategy of downplaying the new settlements as strategic outposts with no implications regarding the "future of the areas under its control." Harman explained that the new developments were not actually settlements, but rather "strong points" that were "vital from a security point of view." Did this mean they were temporary and could be removed in the event of a peace agreement? Harman would not say.[66] "Military security" rather than permanent settlement "was the reason for the West Bank settlements," echoed the *NER*.[67]

In mid-October, Saunders charged in a sharply worded memorandum that the administration was "weaseling in the face of Israeli intransigence." Whereas it was "hard to dispute that for 17 years our commitment referred to 1949 Armistice lines," the United States had cast that position aside for a posture that "In essence ... says we'll settle for whatever the parties can negotiate." The problem was that the Israelis rejected third-party negotiations and opposed settlement talks in the UNSC as well as Soviet–American collaboration on a peace agreement. Saunders advised Rostow to urge Johnson to "begin showing Eban a little muscle," even as he acknowledged that DOS diplomats "frankly doubt that the President will be willing in an election year to exert the kind of pressure on Israel that would be necessary to restore armistice lines, even as permanent boundaries. The President himself feeds this view when he tells all his Arab visitors that he *can't* influence Israel to do what it doesn't want to do."[68]

As the UNSC aimed at achieving resolution of the conflict, the Arabs reiterated their support for an accord. In early November, Nasser told Anderson that he continued to reject Syrian and Algerian calls for guerrilla war and could instead support a UN settlement of the conflict. He reiterated, however, that direct negotiations with Israel would be "an act of suicide for me ... or any other Arab leader." As for Hussein, Anderson reported, the "King obviously wants to do business" and remained willing to accept "territorial adjustments."[69]

Both Jordan and Egypt thus "proposed peaceful coexistence with the Jewish state" – offers that met with a swift rejection in Tel Aviv. On November 8, the Israeli Cabinet gave a "formal stamp of approval" to a policy of rejecting any settlement not achieved by "direct negotiations" and formal "peace treaties." The Cabinet resolution was a "prescription for 'instant peace' entirely on Israel's terms," Battle told

Rusk. "It is patently unrealistic" and "a profoundly disturbing development" meant to establish "a legally unassailable rationale for remaining in
the occupied territories indefinitely." Israel was staking its claim to "the
entire city of Jerusalem but also a good slice of the Syrian Golan Heights
(which lie outside Mandated Palestine) and the entire Gaza Strip (whose
Arab Palestinian inhabitants can by no means be assumed to prefer
a future under Israeli rule)." As Saunders had feared, "Israel was defying
the world and trying to make its way by itself."[70]

While cementing authority over the OT, Israel and AIPAC received
backing from Goldberg as they fended off efforts to hold the Zionist state
responsible for initiation of the Six-Day War. After insisting for weeks
that the Arabs had started the war, the propaganda line shifted to the
Israelis having been forced to launch a preemptive war. In the 32-page
special supplement of "myths and facts" of the war published in August,
the *NER* declared that history had repeated the events of 1948, as
"The Egyptians and the Syrians once again forced war on Israel."
The *NER* dismissed the issue of origins, explaining, "The question of
who fired the first shot that morning was irrelevant and insignificant,
because Arabs had fired many first shots on many mornings for some 19
years."[71]

On November 22, after weeks of wrangling, the UNSC adopted
Resolution 242, which decades later remains the official framework for
setting the conflict. As a result of Goldberg's opposition, the UNSC gave
up on assigning responsibility for initiation of the conflict and settled for
reiterating in the preamble of Resolution 242 "the inadmissibility of the
acquisition of territory by war and the need to work for a just and lasting
peace in which every state in the area can live in security." Israel continued
to avoid responsibility for launching the June conflict, which thus served
as a precedent for "constructing expanded versions of self-defense" that
would be cited in justification of future Israeli attacks against Iraq,
Lebanon, and Gaza.[72]

Unanimously approved by the UNSC, Resolution 242 called for "withdrawal of Israel from territories occupied in the recent conflict" and for
"termination of all claims or states of belligerency." The resolution advocated "a just settlement of the refugee problem" and concluded with the
appointment of a UN special representative to carry out negotiations
based on the provisions.[73] Resolution 242 mandated withdrawal from
the OT because the occupation was illegal under international law. Even
under a generous interpretation of Israel's initiation of the war – that it
was a preemptive strike justified by the requirements of self-defense –

international law held that "A state that takes territory while exercising a right of defense may remain only as long as necessary to protect against the attack to which it was responding." Under no circumstances could land taken under a claim of self-defense be settled, incorporated as the newly sovereign territory of the aggressor, and the residents subjected to alien rule. In 2004, the International Court of Justice formally ruled that the Israeli settlements in the OT were illegal.[74]

In the fall of 1967, Goldberg collaborated with the Israelis in rendering the withdrawal resolution feckless through the deliberate omission of the article "the" from the portion of UN Resolution 242 requiring "withdrawal of Israel from territories occupied." The deliberate omission allowed the Israelis to oppose withdrawal from all of "the" OT. The United States backed this position and called for modest territorial adjustments to the new boundary lines, keeping intact the notion that the resolution essentially entailed "land for peace" – an Israeli withdrawal from occupied territories only in response to diplomatic recognition and peace accords with the Arab states. Gunnar Jarring – a distinguished diplomat with an academic background in Turkic studies, who had served as Sweden's ambassador to the both the United States and the Soviet Union – accepted the post as the UN envoy whose mission was to bring the parties together to achieve the final settlement.[75]

The lobby celebrated the failure of Resolution 242 to force Israel into a compromise settlement. "The change in US policy" in which de jure recognition and direct negotiations became a prerequisite for talks still held. In a nod to the effectiveness of AIPAC lobbying, the *NER* noted in January 1968, "Congress did not want Israel to lose the peace." Thus, Resolution 242 "intentionally does not say *all* the territories," meaning that the June war "may have changed the map of the region's ever-shifting boundaries." Asserting there were "no hard and fast plans" for Israel's expansion, one thing was certain: "Israelis have returned to their ancient capital" of Jerusalem, whose holy places would be "protected under Israel rule." Concluding with an Orientalist flourish, the *NER* declared that "It is difficult to believe that many governments would really want to restore the slum and stagnation of the past."[76]

After sidestepping the UN resolution, the Israel lobby threatened a "confrontation" if the United States maintained an embargo on US arms shipments, which had been cut off to all belligerents with the outbreak of the June War. The outcome of the conflict, in which Israel had destroyed massive supplies of military equipment and installations, left the Zionist state militarily far superior to its neighbors, but the Soviet

Union responded with stepped up arms shipments to Egypt and Syria. The *NER* promoted rearmament of the Zionist state in another special supplement, "The Arms Race in the Near East."[77]

The Soviet resupply ignited Israeli anxieties and fueled threats from Israel and AIPAC that US–Israeli relations were on a "collision course" if the Americans refused to lift the embargo or tried to link arms sales with demands for withdrawal from the OT. Evron told Rostow and McPherson that the "Jewish community" in the United States remained resentful of US neutrality in the June War, and many believed that the United States would not have intervened had the war gone badly for Israel. Rostow reassured his friend, "There is no question at any point before or during the war that we would not have let Israel be seriously hurt or destroyed."[78]

The threats to unleash AIPAC alarmed Vice President and longtime lobby backer Humphrey, who "noted the difficulty of explaining to the American Jewish community how much we had done over the past year in support of Israel." The veteran diplomat Averill Harriman, however, resigned in disgust as "ambassador at large," citing "the excess of Jewish chauvinism which existed on the Hill in some of the less responsible Congressmen who were clamoring for a stronger pro-Israel attitude on the part of the United States."[79]

In anticipation of Johnson's impending summit with Eshkol in January, Saunders proposed offering "our political support and the equipment it needs to defend itself provided Israel makes an honest effort to reach a settlement with its neighbors." Bundy, however, again rejected linkage, declaring that arming the Israelis was "not a great cosmic issue," but he also advised that "the whole New York crowd" would come down on the administration if sale of the Skyhawk aircraft were not resumed. Rostow agreed, telling Johnson that the pro-Israel lobby "will be ginned up to put maximum pressure on you." In the public statement marking the end of the Texas summit, "The President agreed to keep Israel's military defense capability under active and sympathetic examination," but by then the embargo had already been lifted.[80]

Rostow hoped in vain that the renewed sale of the Skyhawk would enhance the prospects of "our coming approaches to Eshkol and Eban to get the Jarring exercise off dead center," but Israel once again received US military hardware with no strings attached. Israel took the jets but had no intention of facilitating the UN land for peace negotiations. Renewed sale of the planes and other weapons and spare parts did pave the way for Israeli acquiescence to the quiet renewal of arms sales to Jordan, which the

FIGURE 24 President Lyndon Johnson receives Israeli Prime Minister Levi Eshkol at Randolph Air Force base in Texas on January 7, 1968, prior to meetings at the president's ranch. Johnson subsequently approved the sale of Phantom jets to Israel with no political strings attached amid the cementing of Israeli occupation of Palestinian territories in the wake of the June 1967 War.
Lynn Pelham/Getty Images

United States again pursued in order to bolster Hussein and keep Jordan out of the Soviet supply orbit. After making "discreet inquiries," Rostow reported that "the Jewish community is relaxed" and "Jewish contacts on the [Capitol] Hill" indicated limited arms sales to Jordan would not be a bone of contention.[81]

Relations with Hussein's regime remained violently unstable, however, as Israel carried out "ever increasing large scale retaliatory excursions into Jordan."[82]

On March 21, Israel launched a preplanned major operation, sending an invasion force of some 15,000 troops to destroy a Fatah guerrilla stronghold in the West Bank border town of Karameh. The rebels were driven out but the level of resistance stunned the Israelis, who suffered 28 deaths in the battle. Fatah claimed a victory for the guerrilla movement, which helped solidify its growing support among Palestinians and other Arabs.[83] The United States condemned the Karameh assault, which had been launched despite its objections. Despite Israeli protests the United

States joined in the 15–0 UNSC condemnation of the Israeli attack, as Resolution 248 declared that Israel had violated the ceasefire and the UN Charter. "The Israelis always push very hard. They always weigh in pretty heavily," Goldberg told Johnson. "They would like no resolution, but that's impossible, there's going to be a resolution," but the action, he added, was merely a "slap on the wrist to Israel."[84]

The characteristically disproportionate Israeli assault destabilized Hussein's regime and, moreover, undermined Jarring's efforts to get the peace process moving. Even before the Israeli attack Jarring was "pessimistic" and "discouraged," as well as "physically exhausted from constant shuffling between capitals." In the wake of the assault, Jarring told a US diplomat that the disproportionate "Israeli policy of four eyes for one" was impeding efforts to pursue a negotiated settlement. Moreover, the Israelis "repeatedly warned" the UN envoy "that if he put forward his own plan his mission was finished."[85]

As Israel rejected negotiations and stepped up colonization of the OT, diplomats called on Johnson to act, but "Goldberg felt it was too tough for the President."[86] Although Johnson had heard from his advisers that the situation was deteriorating, he declined to take action. In view of Johnson's "strong personal determination not to let Israel down, we have to exclude any dramatic shift in our position," Saunders concluded. In desperation, the diplomat called for Johnson to appeal to the Israelis that he "may be the best friend Israel will have in the White House for some time" as a tactic to "bring pressure on Israel and begin re-balancing our position toward the Arabs ... If the president wants to make one last effort for peace now is the time," though he suspected "it may already be too late."[87]

By the spring of 1968, the peace effort was clearly failing as a result of Israeli intransigence and Johnson's inaction. Overwhelmed by the escalating Indochina War, particularly in the wake of the Tet Offensive, Johnson had lost public support. He abandoned plans to seek another term in office and settled into the final months of a "lame duck" presidency. As his political career imploded amid the Indochina debacle, Johnson intended to stand by Israel "because they haven't got many friends in the world. They are in about the same shape I am. And the closer I got to face adversity the closer I get to them."[88]

While Hussein continued to plead for a settlement, Bundy bluntly told the king that the Americans were "heavily preoccupied with the war in Vietnam and with elections, and that there was little incentive to expend energy on a no-result exercise in the Arab-Israel contest." Capitalizing on the American morass in Vietnam to bolster Israeli intransigence, Evron declared that the United States "would not trust [UN General Secretary] U Thant to settle the war in Vietnam; we don't trust him to settle our problem."[89]

As the Johnson administration floundered, the Israeli commitment to settler colonization became "firmer and firmer." Hawkish Israeli officials were increasingly transparent about their plans. On April 1, the new Ambassador Yitzhak Rabin told the Americans, "Israel will remain where she is," and, despite advice to the contrary, would continue to lash out beyond its borders to combat "terrorists."[90]

The economic costs to Israel of establishing and maintaining long-term occupation of the Palestinian territories were "remarkably small," a CIA assessment concluded; "They bring little pressure on Israel to settle the Arab-Israeli difficulties."[91] Israel could thus "maintain the status quo – we can do it," Dayan echoed in a public interview; "There will not be a severance between us and the West Bank." Palestinians under occupation could "preserve their way of life" – homes, mosques, schools, travel to and from Arab world – even as they "acquiesced" to Israeli-dominated "political frameworks." Colonization would enable Palestinians to live but not become citizens of a democracy "because I don't want such and such an added number of Arab voters," Dayan explained.[92]

While Dayan asserted that "coexistence between the Jewish people and the Palestinian Arabs" could be achieved within a framework of settler colonization, other observers foresaw a "chilling prospect" of a spiral of violence emanating from the failure of negotiations. "Up to now Palestinians in Arab Jerusalem and the West Bank, though bitterly opposed to the Israeli occupation, have shown little enthusiasm for any direct and violent reaction," reported the US consulate in Jerusalem. The *Israelis* believed that *"Palestinians deplore terrorism"* [emphasis added], hence they "have been much too eager to interpret this reaction as toleration of occupation." A "genuine Palestinian desire for peace with Israel could be exploited" on the basis of Resolution 242, but in the absence of a settlement the "alternative for Israel, it seems to us, is a rising tempo of terrorism, increasingly fanatical and increasingly effective." Saunders forwarded this report to Rostow, adding that "Israeli intransigence" was convincing the Arabs "that they have no alternative but a military solution."[93]

The cementing of the occupation, bolstered by IDF assaults and removal operations, were turning masses of Arabs against Israel and its US backer. "To the Arabs," the *Sunday Times* of London reported on December 1, 1967, "inevitably, every act of violence or intimidation seems part of a Zionist master plan to drive still more of them out of their homeland." The *Times* story quoted one man as saying "I was a very moderate Arab" prior to the war, the occupation, the "sweeping destruction of Arab homes," arrests, beatings, night raids, and other forms of violence and intimidation. He previously thought that Jews "deserved so much sympathy ... Now, I just hate their guts."[94]

"From the Jordan River to the sea, that is *Eretz Israel*," Dayan declared during a closed session in the Knesset a year after the June 1967 War; "I will oppose with all my strength that any kind of border should split that territorial unit."[95] To reinforce the hardline position with the special ally, Rabin summoned Begin from the Israeli Cabinet to Washington to meet with administration officials. Begin championed Eretz Israel, new Zionist settlements, and declared "Jerusalem [i]s the capital of Israel." The meeting left Rostow "more pessimistic for peace in the Middle East (as a result of this conversation) than he had been for some time." Rabin and Begin represented an Israel that felt no obligation to take any steps or make any compromise toward achievement of a peace settlement.[96]

While Jarring believed that Egypt, and certainly Jordan, were "ready to end belligerency," the "main roadblock" to viable negotiations remained "Israel's inability to state its view of where boundaries should be." The Arabs would not "surrender their trump card – symbolizing recognition of Israel – until they believe the Israeli government has committed itself to withdrawal."[97] Jarring's efforts, including a Stephen Douglas-style piecemeal approach attempting to separate out the issues in dispute, all came to grief. Rusk implored Jarring to "intensify his efforts," but by the beginning of October the UN envoy was exhausted and "depressed because the Israelis have not given him anything."[98]

PHANTOMS AND THE NPT

Beginning with the lead-up to the Eshkol summit, Israel and AIPAC set their sights on an arms breakthrough by securing a supply of powerful F-4 Phantom supersonic aircraft. The Israelis made the "strongest possible case" about the extent of Soviet assistance to the Arabs to justify their request for the Phantom, a lethal fighter-bomber being deployed extensively in Vietnam. Doubting "whether the Israelis [we]re telling the truth" in their intelligence reports on the extent of Soviet arms and on-site assistance to the Arabs, Rostow sought confirmation from US sources. Diplomat Parker Hart advised Rusk, "The acquisition of the F-4s will represent a major policy move by this Government in support of Israel," as it would "end our long-standing policy of not being the principal supplier of Israel's military needs." As it was "not feasible" to persuade Israel to negotiate a postwar settlement in the UN, the administration should instead "link the F-4s to Israeli concessions on its nuclear and missile policy" and secure Israel's signature on the Treaty on Non-Proliferation of Nuclear Weapons (NPT) of 1968.[99]

The run-up and then the fighting of the June war had deflected attention away from the effort to contain the Israeli nuclear program, but in the aftermath of the conflict and the ensuing arms race US officials revivified their efforts.[100] While the vast majority of nations in the world – including all the Arab states – embraced the landmark NPT, Israel continued to reject international efforts to contain the spread of nuclear weapons.[101] "We expect Israel to sign the NPT," Saunders declared in December 1967: "Will it?" The Israelis did not sign the NPT, and instead reiterated the pledge not to "introduce" nuclear weapons into the Middle East, meaning that Israel would not conduct a test blast or announce its possession of the bomb. Thus, Israel would continue to possess the bomb while not acknowledging it.[102]

Despite his claim of reluctance to "be a goddamned arms merchant" in the Middle East, Johnson decided in January to sell Israel the Phantom jets without exacting any concessions on arms control or a Middle East settlement. "I never have told anybody I'm going to give them [Phantoms] to [Israel]," the president told Fortas by telephone in June 1968. "But I made up my mind a long time ago I was going to give them to them."[103]

Rejecting Saunders' advice that "no one is prepared to recommend ... releas[ing] the Phantoms to Israel" without securing some diplomatic cooperation in return, Johnson sold the planes with no strings attached:[104]

I made a decision I was gonna sell 'em before I went out of office, [it was] just a question of when I could get the best price for them and I want to work up that price, make it reasonable. And I think we ought to say to Israel "Now you give us your boundary, put something on paper here and then we'll move with the Phantoms+."

As a result of their backchannel ties with Goldberg, Fortas, and many others, however, the Israelis and AIPAC already knew that Johnson had decided to sell the Phantom jets, hence there was no need to make any concessions in return.[105]

Inflexible on postwar boundaries as well as the NPT, Israel and AIPAC lobbied vigorously for the sale of the Phantom. Both political parties quickly fell into line. After Johnson dropped out of the 1968 presidential race at the end of March, both the eventual Republican and Democratic nominees, Nixon and Humphrey, backed Israel and publicly advocated sale of the Phantom jets. During Johnson's last months in office, seemingly "every Jew in the country" was "hepped up" for sale of the jets, Johnson observed. Rostow noted that pressure was "mounting deliberately to press us to separate the Phantoms and NPT."[106] Johnson told Rusk in mid-October, "Now, you can tell them we've got to have this, we've got to have that and I'll tell them the same thing and shove and fight, they can't use nuclear, they can't do this and they got to sign the nonproliferation treaty, I don't care what all we say, I'm not gonna tell them but that decision is already wrapped up." Rusk responded that sale of the jets would satisfy Israel's needs without any concession on its part. "They've already got out of there what they want short of the delivery of the planes themselves," he noted. Johnson affirmed that, adding "I want to be damn sure that I do it and don't wait until after the election and Nixon and Humphrey do it."[107]

On November 1, Rusk informed Clifford, an advocate of linking sale of the jets with the NPT, that Johnson was "strongly opposed to twisting arms on the nuclear thing in connection with the Phantoms. Doesn't want them linked."[108] In the end, the only linkage the White House secured for the shipment of 50 Phantom jets was that Israel would stick with its pledge not to be the first nation to "introduce" nuclear weapons to the Middle East, and specifically not to place nuclear warheads on any aircraft sold to them by the United States.[109] Clifford sought, but the Israelis backed by Johnson rejected as an infringement on their sovereignty, a provision about canceling the sale if Israel violated certain diplomatic accords. Feinberg, Krim, and others later complained about the financial terms Clifford offered for sale of the jets, arguing that the Shah of Iran was receiving more favorable terms for his purchase of a shipment of Phantoms. "Everybody was mad ... may blow the whole deal," Krim told Rostow. Johnson backed the Israelis and advised Clifford on November 23, "Wrap it up ... I'm getting a lot of heat." He reiterated that he did not want president-elect Nixon to take credit for the Phantom sale.[110]

While the Israelis were "overjoyed" by the sale, the Phantom decision was another blow to the Arabs and to Jarring. In October the UN envoy had reported that "The Arabs are upset" about the prospect of sale of the Phantom. A US diplomat reported that Jarring "very much hopes that the negotiations on the subject will be used as leverage on Israel to move them toward a political settlement." When the administration instead rejected linkage, Jarring concluded that nothing would come of his mission during the Johnson presidency.[111]

"Disillusioned" by Johnson's ultimate decision, Hussein declared "The supply of Phantoms to Israel, if it does not increase her belligerent ambitions, then it certainly does not contribute toward curtailing them." His country continued to be slighted in arms sales in comparison with provisions to the Israelis, Hussein declared, adding that "American actions and positions regarding the problems of our area are making it difficult, if not impossible, for me and for your other Arab friends to defend or justify American policy in the Middle East." In addition, US officials expected and received a "heavy reaction, especially in the Arab press" as news of the sale of the Phantom spread.[112]

As Johnson left office in January 1969, the DOS noted that the United States "is presently Israel's principal arms supplier – Hawks, tanks, 100 Skyhawk, 50 Phantoms and many million dollars annually of miscellaneous supplies and equipment." Thanks to the American military assistance, "Israel today is militarily superior to any and all of its immediate neighbors." Although Johnson claimed he had not wanted to become Israel's chief arms supplier, and US officials had wanted to exact concessions on negotiations and the NPT, Israel and the lobby instead received both weapons and political backing with no strings attached.[113]

After assuming office in January 1969, Nixon and Henry A. Kissinger, his national security adviser, acquiesced to the fait accompli of Israel's refusal to sign the NPT and to its status as a nuclear power. Opting to "avoid direct confrontation" with Israel, Kissinger centralized command over the issue to rein in the State and Defense department advocates of taking a hardline with the Israelis.[114] On April 3, diplomat Joseph Sisco advised that only a "fundamental change in the US-Israel relationship" could force the Israelis to submit to supervision by the IAEA.[115] Nixon and Kissinger rejected this option, as well as advice to hold up delivery of the Phantom until Israel renounced the bomb. Years later Nixon and Israeli Prime Minister Meir hinted that she told him directly in an Oval Office meeting in September 1969 that Israel possessed the bomb but would not test or announce it in an effort to keep the international political fallout to a minimum.[116] Israel, along with India and Pakistan, are the only states never to have ratified the NPT, but unlike the two South Asian nations Israel has also never admitted to its de facto possession of nuclear weapons.

JOHNSON'S LEGACY

The political clout of the Israel lobby combined with Johnson's deeply rooted sympathy precluded the president from confronting the Zionist state over its aggressive expansion, thus stalemating the peace process in the wake of the June 1967 War. Locked into perceptions of "little Israel" as invariably besieged and victimized – a view repeatedly reinforced by Goldberg, Evron, Feinberg, and the Krims, among other lobby stalwarts – Johnson failed to grasp that Israel was a messianic and aggressive settler state.

Much like Truman, Johnson came to view himself as something of a savior presiding over the security of the Jews in their return to the Promised Land. While he "knew the Israeli people were superior in ability to their neighbors," the president had "deep concern over the odds working against Israel." In fact, he worried "as deeply" about the security of Israel as did Eshkol.[117] "The only people in the world they got faith in I think is me and you," Johnson confided to Goldberg; "They don't know when they're going to be run over, they don't know when they're going to die, they don't know when the goddamned Russians are going to come in there . . . The only thing they got is a little hope and a prayer and a wing for me if my heart keeps beating."[118]

Ever mindful of his aunt's admonition never to "forget the Jews, God's chosen people," Johnson's gut instinct was to uphold the vow he made in 1958: "I have always been pro-Israel and will continue to be so."[119]

The Israel lobby freely tapped into Johnson's pro-Israel sympathies, but also did not hesitate to play a heavy head whenever any threat to Israeli interests appeared on the horizon. By the time of June 1967 War, AIPAC had command of the US Congress, a command that has grown even stronger in subsequent years. The Israel lobby thus played a central role in forging an American foreign policy that enabled Israeli aggression and colonization of territory in defiance of international law and in rejection of Palestinian, Jordanian, Egyptian, and UN efforts to forge a Middle East peace.

Conclusions

"The US position is all that can be desired," I. L. Kenen declared in the immediate aftermath of the June 1967 War; "The US is working like never before."[1] The lobbyist had reason for sanguinity, as a quarter-century of dedicated effort had paid off in lopsided US support for Israel during and after the pivotal conflict. Moreover, Kenen and his colleagues had established AIPAC at the forefront of the most powerful lobby advancing the national interests of a foreign nation in all of American history.

The Israel lobby achieved its success by circumventing the foreign policy bureaucracy and applying pressure directly on the president and the Congress to secure financial assistance, armaments, and diplomatic backing for Israel. By 1968, the long-term lobbying effort had cemented the support of both political parties firmly behind Israel. "Once again the Republican and Democratic parties are in agreement on US policy in the Near East," the *NER* proudly observed a month before the 1968 election, thus the Middle East conflict was "not an issue in the current campaign."[2] Neither party pressed Israel on the postwar occupation, and both approved arms supplies, culminating in the sale of the Phantom jets. With the crucial support of the lobby, Israel was on its way to becoming the largest recipient of US foreign assistance for decades to come.[3]

As the political influence of the lobby continued to grow in the years after the 1967 war, Kenen began to be publicly identified and was sometimes asked how AIPAC worked and what it sought to achieve. "I put it very succinctly in one sentence," he responded in 1973: "'We appeal to local leadership to write or telegraph or telephone their Congressmen and urge them to call upon the President to overrule the Department of State,' and this has been going on, now for some 20 years."[4]

As Kenen freely acknowledged, and as this book has shown, throughout the first generation of its existence Israel and the domestic lobby
worked in tandem to circumvent the federal bureaucracy whose mission
was to conduct US foreign policy in the national interest. From the late-
Roosevelt through the Johnson years, from AZEC to AIPAC, the Zionist
lobby successfully opposed DOS efforts to forge an "impartial" or
"balanced" diplomacy in the Middle East. Beginning with the 1944 elections, the Zionist lobby discovered it could exert substantial influence on
Congress as well as the major party platforms. By 1968, as Kenen noted,
both parties had become committed to arming and providing virtually
unquestioned political support to Israel.

   After its victory in the 1967 war, Avi Raz argues, "Israel desperately
needed to be saved from itself in those heady days, and only the United
States possessed the necessary levers of influence. However, Washington
did not use these levers."[5] Focusing primarily on Israeli policy, Raz
acknowledges that American diplomacy was beyond the scope of his
research, and thus he suggests too easily that the United States could
have reined in the ebullient Israelis. Because of the broad-based support
for Israel – and not least the efforts of Kenen, Eban, Feinberg, Goldberg,
the Krims, and many others within the lobby – it is doubtful that Johnson
could have secured the political backing to force an Israeli withdrawal, as
Eisenhower had done a decade earlier, even had he desired to do so.
Johnson had no such desire, however, because he, like millions of
Americans, identified with "poor little Israel" (in reality, as Avi Shlaim
notes, "poor little Samson").[6]

   In the wake of the June 1967 War, American Jews rallied behind Israel.
Contributions poured into the United Jewish Appeal, the chief
US fundraising arm, with the overwhelming majority of the money earmarked for Israel, thus helping to finance new settlements in the OT.[7]
The renegade American Council for Judaism denounced the 1967 war as
an act of Israeli "aggression," and in response suffered the resignation of
several leading members. The ACJ thus lost what little influence it still had
over American Jewry and went into decline.[8]

   Precisely what the ACJ had fought for years to avoid – the conflation of
American Jewish identity with unquestioned support for Israel – largely had
come to pass in the aftermath of Israel's triumph. As scholars note in a recent
study, "Periodic discontent notwithstanding, Israel is now the most important element of liberal Jewish identity and mobilization in the United
States." If American Jews today wanted to "check their Zionism at the
door," they would risk "checking their Judaism as well." The support for

an imperial and increasingly intolerant Israel on the part of American Jews – who otherwise have long been associated with championing progressive causes – has created, as Peter Beinart has argued, "a crisis of Zionism."[9]

Jews are a distinct minority in American life, thus the broad-based support of majority Protestants has from the outset been essential to the success of the Israel lobby. By the time of the June 1967 War, the ACPC – the most powerful pro-Israel Christian organization in the United States – had formally disbanded, but unlike the ACJ had done so in triumph. The ACPC had "succeeded in its mission to develop a solid grassroots basis for Protestant support for Israel." In 1966, in a speech at Hebrew University in Jerusalem, the ACPC's Carl Herman Voss, who worked closely with Israel and its supporters and later wrote the introduction to Kenen's memoirs, took pride in the effectiveness of ACPC lobbying, declaring that he could "go on at great lengths about the kind of influence we had on Congressmen." When Jews and Christians lobbied them, "they reacted positively."[10]

In the post-World war II era, Zionism found growing support among Christian fundamentalists as well as modernists. "Whereas Jews had once been vilified as Christ-killers and money manipulators," the growing popularity of premillennial prophecy broadened their acceptance within "mainstream culture." Thus, as Andrew Preston notes, "In order to protect Israel, and thus help ensure the unfolding of prophecy, Bible-believing Christians became arch-Zionists."[11]

As with the mythic history of their own country, many Americans appeared to perceive the Israelis as a people chosen by God to redeem a promised land through conquest. Having internalized their own national triumph over putatively uncivilized foes on the "frontier," Americans could intuitively embrace Israel and elide its history of dispossession and repression of indigenous Palestinians. As in the United States, Australia, and other settler states, aggression and removal of indigenous people inhered in the logic of Zionism, which aimed to carve out an ethnically exclusive "Jewish state."

While Israel is part of a long global history of settler colonialism, it is distinguished by the belated nature of the Zionist project. Culminating as it did in the second half of the twentieth century, and going against the grain of history in an age otherwise characterized by self-determination, decolonization, and human rights discourse, Israeli settler colonialism has been especially consequential.

Over the years, DOS diplomats argued that the United States had allowed its idealistic identification with Israel to undermine more realistic

Middle East diplomacy that would take into consideration the interests of the geographically much broader and oil-producing Arab world. The supposedly "pro-Arab" diplomats were proven correct in their assessment that there would be a price to pay for US enabling of Israeli expansion, repression of Palestinians, and repeated military humiliations of the Arabs. To its credit, the DOS as well as Presidents Truman, Eisenhower, and Kennedy labored sincerely to get the Israelis to take to heart the open wound of the Nakba, the plight of the Palestinian refugees. To its discredit, Israel routinely dismissed such pleas with contempt and obloquy. The open wound festered and metastasized.

Following the June 1967 War, Arab moderates backed by DOS diplomats warned, "It will be impossible to continue to hold the line against the 'extremists' if the US does not come out unequivocally for withdrawal of Israeli forces."[12] They were right: Guy Laron recounts 125 Fatah attacks killing 11 Israelis from 1965 to 1967; however, "In the three years following the Six-Day War there were 5,840 Fatah operations against Israel killing 141 civilians and military personnel." In subsequent years, as Paul Chamberlin notes, "The State Department's fears about the future of the Arab world and the danger of global radicalism were validated by the phenomena occurring in the global system." Adds Shlaim, "The long-term consequences of 1967 led to the revival of the pan-Islamist movement."[13] Although it is frequently denied, the lopsidedly pro-Israeli US policy and the seemingly endless "global war on terror" are thus inextricably linked.

The special relationship has not been the sole cause – oil extraction, support for reactionary regimes throughout the Arab world and in Iran under the Shah, and the blundering but no less devastating American wars in Iraq, Afghanistan, and other venues have also weighed in, to be sure – but there is little doubt that the "homeland" became a target for Muslim radicals in part because of the US polices of enabling Israeli aggression, expansion, and, above all, efforts to exert unilateral authority over the holy city of Jerusalem. For decades, an otherwise nearly universally pro-Israeli American diplomacy stopped short of recognizing Israel's unceasing claims to unilateral authority over Jerusalem, but the last domino fell with the arrival of Donald J. Trump in the White House. Naming his son-in-law, an Orthodox Jew and longtime proponent of Israeli settlement of the OT, as the chief adviser on the Arab–Israeli conflict, it was only a matter of time – less than a year, as it turned out – until the new administration recognized Jerusalem as Israel's "eternal capital."

The Trump administration also decertified the Iran nuclear treaty of 2015, promoting a demonizing discourse emphasizing Iranian efforts to destabilize the Middle East through nuclear proliferation in violation of international norms. Unmentioned was the long history of Israeli dissimulation and actual responsibility for undermining US and international efforts to keep the Middle East a nuclear-free zone. In contrast to the history of Israeli duplicity, the Iran nuclear treaty was a model of transparency and global cooperation on nuclear nonproliferation.

While this study has homed in on US–Israeli relations, the policies and actions of the Arab states frequently come into sharp relief. Beyond question, these policies were often ill conceived and self-destructive. Nonetheless, as this book has demonstrated, Israel was more often than not the aggressor, one that when given a choice typically chose force over diplomacy. The Israelis crushed their foes militarily and, with the lobby at the forefront, also dominated the propaganda battle in the United States, framing a peaceful Zionist state forced to live under a persistent existential threat. Arab propaganda mills could be counted on to provide a steady supply of reckless statements promising to drive the Jews from Palestine. As Egyptian Foreign Minister Mahmoud Riad belatedly acknowledged after the 1967 war, "It has been a mistake for the Arabs to talk of Israel's destruction." The issue was a matter of borders, refugees, and justice, rather than being a "quarrel about the existence of Israel."[14]

Despite the standard propaganda line about the refusal to recognize Israel, the Arabs had consented to de facto recognition through the armistice agreements after the 1948 war and following the Sinai War. Both Jordan and Palestinian entities were eager for land for peace agreements after their humiliating defeat in the 1967 war, and Egypt offered coexistence as well. Israel summarily rejected all of them and chose an illegal occupation over the prospect of peace.

Whatever else one might say about the "Middle East conflict," it has entailed an absence of justice for the Palestinians. The second-class treatment of Palestinians within Israel as well as in the OT undermines Israel's much-vaunted claim to be the "sole democracy in the Middle East." Israel can be described more accurately as an imperial settler state, one that came to rely – with a big assist from the lobby – on the backing of its large, powerful, and similarly constituted special ally.

While the prospects appear dim, especially in the wake of the annexation of Jerusalem, democracy may yet represent hope of salvation for Israel and the Palestinians. Genuine pluralism and inclusion could, conceivably, establish a framework to bring peace to the region. Israeli settlements have proliferated to such an extent that the long-sought two-state solution has become a virtual impossibility. Because of the proliferation of settlements there is no longer enough of Palestine left for the Palestinians to construct a viable homeland free of checkpoints, bypass roads, violence, and humiliation. A one-state solution – a free and democratic polity, with Jerusalem shared by people of all faiths – may offer the last remaining hope for Israel, for the Palestinians, for peace, and for resolution of the crisis of American Zionism as well.

Notes

INTRODUCTION

1. As of December 2016, "The United States has provided Israel $127.4 billion (current, or non-inflation-adjusted, dollars) in bilateral assistance." In September 2016, the United States and Israel signed off on a 10-year, $38 billion program of additional assistance. "Almost all US bilateral aid to Israel is in the form of military assistance, although in the past Israel also received significant economic assistance." Jeremy Sharp, "US Foreign Aid to Israel," Dec. 22, 2016, Congressional Research Service. https://fas.org/sgp/crs/mid east/RL33222.pdf

2. Grant F. Smith, *Big Israel: How Israel's Lobby Moves America*. Washington: Institute for Research: Middle Eastern Policy, 2016; John J. Mearsheimer and Stephen M. Walt, *The Israel Lobby and US Foreign Policy*. New York: Farrar, Srauss, and Giroux, 2007.

3. Josh DeWind and Renata Segura, "Diaspora-Government Relations in Forging US Foreign Policies," in DeWind and Segura, eds., *Diaspora Lobbies and the US Government*. New York: New York University Press, 2014: 7; Smith, *Big Israel*, passim; see also Tony Smith, *Foreign Attachments: The Power of Ethnic Groups in the Making of American Foreign Policy*. Cambridge, MA: Harvard University Press, 2005.

4. "Zionist on Capitol Hill: I. L. Kenen at 75," *The Jewish Week*, Mar. 13–19, 1980, Papers of Isaiah Leo Kenen (KP), Center for Jewish History, New York, Box 14.

5. I. L. Kenen, *Israel's Defense Line: Her Friends and Foes in Washington*. Buffalo: Prometheus Books, 1981; Address by Lipsky, Zionist Organization of America annual convention, June 17, 1951, KP, Box 5.

6. DeWind and Segura, "Diaspora-Government Relations in Forging US Foreign Policies," 6.

7. Peter Novick, *The Holocaust in American Life*. Boston: Houghton Mifflin Co., 1999; Norman G. Finkelstein, *The Holocaust Industry*. London: Verso Books, 2000.

8. This theme is developed throughout the book. In a broader context, American foreign relations have undergone a "religious turn" in recent years, shedding new light on the intersection between religiosity and foreign policy. For a comprehensive history, see Andrew Preston, *Sword of the Spirit, Shield of Faith: Religion in American War and Diplomacy*. New York: Anchor Books, 2012.

9. Historical, archaeological, and anthropological research has largely disproven the biblical narrative of ancient Israel. Israeli scholar Shlomo Sand notes that the saga of the ancient Jews has been "relegated to the status of fiction, with an unbridgeable gulf gaping" between the biblical stories and what is known of the actual history. Sand, *The Invention of the Jewish People*. New York: Verso Books, 2010: 122. British theologian Michael Prior alludes to the "virtually unanimous scholarly skepticism concerning the historicity of the patriarchal narratives." Rather than conquering the "Canaanites," as per biblical mythology, the Israelites *were* the Canaanites – that is, they were among the "multiplicity of ethnic identities" within ancient Canaan. Prior, *The Bible and Colonialism: A Moral Critique*. Sheffield: Sheffield Academic Press, 1997: 251. Thus, as Thomas Romer notes, "The opposition we find in the Bible between 'Israelites' and 'Canaanites,' was in no way based on an existing ethnic difference, but is a much later theoretical construction in the service of a segregationist ideology." Romer, *The Invention of God*. Cambridge, MA: Harvard University Press, 2015: 13. See also Israel Finkelstein and Neil A. Silberman, *The Bible Unearthed: Archaeology's New Vision of Ancient Israel and the Origin of Its Sacred Texts*. New York: Touchstone, 2001; Thomas L. Thompson, *Early History of the Israelite People: From the Written and Archeological Sources*. Leiden: E. J. Brill, 1992; J. W. Rogerson and Judith M. Lieu, *The Oxford Handbook of Biblical Studies*. New York: Oxford University Press, 2006; Nur Masalha, *The Zionist Bible: Biblical Precedent, Colonialism, and the Erasure of Memory*. Berne: Acumen, 2013; Keith W. Whitelam, *The Invention of Ancient Israel: The Silencing of Palestinian History*. London: Routledge, 1996; and Emanuel Pfoh, "From the Search for Ancient Israel to the History of Ancient Palestine," in Ingrid Hjelm and Thomas L. Thompson, eds., *History, Archaeology and the Bible Forty Years after "Historicity."* New York: Routledge, 2016: 143–58.

10. The framework of settler colonialism interprets the United States, Israel, and many other modern nations as distinctive settler societies. As Donald H. Akenson notes, "There is no doubt that from at least 1917 onward, the movement by Zionists to the land of Israel was a self-conscious work of colonization and that its intention was to create a settler society"; Akenson, *God's Peoples: Covenant and Land in South Africa, Israel, and Ulster*. Ithaca: Cornell University Press, 1992: 167. "Today," adds Shira Robinson, "across the ideological perspective, few historians dispute the social, economic, and cultural ties between the early Zionist settlement project in Palestine and the more 'classical' European settler-colonies in North America, South Africa, and Australia"; Robinson, *Citizen Strangers: Palestinians and the Birth of Israel's Liberal Settler State*. Palo Alto: Stanford University Press, 2013: 4; See

also Lorenzo Veracini, *Israel and Settler Society*. London: Pluto Press, 2006 and Gabriel Piterberg, *The Returns of Zionism: Myths, Politics and Scholarship in Israel*. London: Verso Books, 2008. On the United States, see the discussion and myriad references in Walter L. Hixson, *American Settler Colonialism: A History*. New York: Palgrave Macmillan, 2013; for comparative perspectives, see Edward Cavanagh and Lorenzo Veracini, eds., *The Routledge Handbook of the History of Settler Colonialism*. London: Routledge, 2017.

11. For a comprehensive analysis of the evolution of the intimate cultural relationship between the United States and Israel, see Amy Kaplan, *Our American Israel: The Story of an Entangled Alliance*. Cambridge, MA: Harvard University Press, 2018.

12. Janice J. Terry, *US Foreign Policy in the Middle East: The Role of Lobbies and Special Interest Groups*. London: Pluto Press, 2005: 68–81; Lee O'Brien, *American Jewish Organizations and Israel*. Washington: Institute for Palestine Studies, 1986: 158–190.

13. Seth P. Tillman, *The United States in the Middle East: Interests and Obstacles*. Bloomington: Indiana University Press, 1982: ix–xi; 288–89; Paul Findley, *They Dare to Speak Out: People and Institutions Confront Israel's Lobby*. Westport: Lawrence Hill and Co., 1985.

14. Noam Chomsky, *The Fateful Triangle: The United States, Israel and the Palestinians*. Boston: South End Press, 1983: 13–37.

15. Cheryl A. Rubenberg, *Israel and the American National Interest: A Critical Examination*. Urbana and Chicago: University of Illinois Press, 1986: 375; see reviews by Granville Austin in *Journal of Palestine Studies* 16, No. 4 (Summer, 1987): 140–42 [quote from p. 140]; and Aaron David Miller in *Political Science Quarterly* 102, No. 4 (Winter, 1987–1988): 677–678.

16. Edward Tivnan, *The Lobby: Jewish Political Power and American Foreign Policy*. New York: Touchstone, 1987; Lucy Despard, "Capsule Review" of Tivnan in *Foreign Affairs* 65 (Summer 1987); Joshua Muravchik, "Attacking AIPAC," *Commentary*, July 1, 1987. www.commentarymagazine.com/arti cles/the-lobby-by-edward-tivnan/; Spiegel review of Tivnan. *Los Angeles Times*, May 31, 1987: http://articles.latimes.com/1987–05-31/books/bk-912 7_1_israeli-economy; Steven L. Spiegel, *The Other Arab-Israeli Conflict: Making America's Middle East Policy, From Truman to Reagan*. Chicago: University of Chicago Press, 1985.

17. George W. Ball and Douglas B. Ball, *The Passionate Attachment: America's Involvement with Israel, 1947 to the Present*. New York: W. W. Norton and Co., 1992. According to Richard H. Curtiss, "Among major US daily newspapers only *The Washington Post* had deigned to acknowledge the existence" of *The Passionate Attachment*. "To review it, however, the *Post* selected Walter Laqueur, an historian who has made a career of defending Israel and denigrating the Palestinians." Curtiss, "George Ball's Mideast Views Were Muffled by US Media," *Washington Report on Middle East Affairs*, July/ August 1994: 20.

18. Mearsheimer and Walt, *The Israel Lobby*, 77, 111.

19. Abraham H. Foxman, *The Deadliest Lies: The Israel Lobby and the Myth of Jewish Control.* New York: Palgrave Macmillan, 2007; The Wikipedia entry, *"The Israel Lobby and US Foreign Policy,"* while uneven in its treatment of the controversy, contains scores of useful footnote references to reviews of the Mearsheimer–Walt book. https://en.wikipedia.org/wiki/The_Israel_Lobby_a nd_U.S._Foreign_Policy#Criticism

20. Andrew Preston, "H-Diplo Roundtable Review of *The Israel Lobby and US Foreign Policy,"* *H-Diplo Roundtables VIII*, No. 18, 2007. www.h-net.org/~diplo/roundtables/PDF/IsraelLobby-Roundtable.pdf

21. Tony Smith, "Convergence and Divergence Yesterday and Today in Diaspora-National Government Relations," in DeWind and Segura, eds., *Diaspora Lobbies and the US Government*, 260.

22. Natan Aridan. *Advocating for Israel: Diplomats and Lobbyists from Truman to Nixon.* Lanham: Lexington Books, 2017.

23. See Laurence J. Silberstein, *Post-Zionism: A Reader.* New Brunswick: Rutgers University Press, 2008.

24. Smith, Big Israel; see also Smith, *Spy Trade: How Israel's Lobby Undermines America's Economy.* Washington: IRMEP, 2009; Smith, *Foreign Agents: The American Israel Public Affairs Committee from the 1963 Fulbright Hearings to the 2005 Espionage Scandal.* Washington: IRMEP, 2007.

PROLOGUE

1. Although Jews were a tiny minority in France, the famous Dreyfus Affair underscored deeply entrenched anti-Semitism. In 1894, French authorities accused Captain Alfred Dreyfus, the first Jew to become an officer on the French general staff, of selling military secrets to Germany. Dreyfus, whose father had been a wealthy industrialist, was found guilty of treason and exiled to Devil's Island off the coast of South America. Public outcry over charges of anti-Semitism forced a retrial in which Dreyfus was again convicted, but in 1906 he received a full pardon and was declared innocent. See Marsha L. Rozenblit, "European Jewry, 1800–1933," in Judith R. Baskin and Kenneth Seeskin, eds., *Jewish History, Religion, and Culture.* New York: Cambridge University Press, 2010: 192–94.

2. Gudrun Kramer, *A History of Palestine: From the Ottoman Conquest to the Founding of the State of Israel.* Princeton: Princeton University Press, 2008: 114–15.

3. Akenson, *God's Peoples*, 156–57; Masalha, *Zionist Bible*, 28–29; Theodor Herzl, *The Jewish State.* New York: Dover Publications, 1988: 43.

4. Rozenblit, "European Jewry, 1800–1933," 195.

5. Kramer, *History of Palestine*, 183; Eugene Rogan, *The Arabs.* London: Penguin Books, 2012, 2nd edn.: 246.

6. Mark A. Raider, *The Emergence of American Zionism.* New York: New York University Press, 1998: 1; see also Zeev Sternhell: *Nationalism, Socialism, and the Making of the Jewish State.* Princeton: Princeton University Press, 1998.

7. Samih Farsoun and Christina Zacharia, *Palestine and the Palestinians.* Boulder: Westview Press, 1997: 21–65.

8. Rogan, *The Arabs*, 104–33; Tamim Ansary, *Destiny Disrupted: A History of the World through Islamic Eyes*. New York: Public Affairs, 2009: 286–87.

9. Farid Al-Salim, *Palestine and the Decline of the Ottoman Empire*. London: I. B. Taurus, 2015: 195, 198.

10. Ronald Robinson and John Gallagher, *Africa and the Victorians: The Official Mind of Imperialism*. 2nd edn. London: Macmillan, 1981; Rogan, *The Arabs*, 134–81.

11. Rogan, *The Arabs*, 182–216.

12. Ira M. Lapidus, *A History of Islamic Societies*. New York: Cambridge University Press, 2014, 3rd edn.: 514, 611–13; Ansary, *Destiny Disrupted*, 252–57.

13. Ansary, *Destiny Disrupted*, 293–99; Rogan, *The Arabs*, 201–16.

14. Kramer, *History of Palestine*, 164.

15. Ibid., 16.

16. Balfour Declaration:
www.jewishvirtuallibrary.org/jsource/History/balfour.html.

17. Lord Balfour, "A Defense of the Mandate," June 21, 1922, reprinted in *The New Palestine*, Sept. 1, 1929, Papers of Felix Frankfurter, Box 87A (microfilm), Library of Congress, Washington, DC; Rogan, *The Arabs*, 245.

18. Avi Shlaim, *The Iron Wall: Israel and the Arab World*. New York: W. W. Norton, 2014: 7.

19. Kramer, *History of Palestine*, 112, 167.

20. Shlaim, *The Iron Wall*, 11–17.

21. Rogan, *The Arabs*, 194.

22. Rashid Khalidi, *Palestinian Identity: The Construction of Modern National Consciousness*. New York: Columbia University Press, 1997: 30 and passim; see also Kramer, *History of Palestine*, 123.

23. Khalidi, *Palestinian Identity*, 149, 172; see also Kramer, *History of Palestine*, 123–27.

24. Rogan, *The Arabs*, 201.

25. Shlaim, *The Iron Wall*, 17.

26. Sternhell, *Founding Myths of Israel*, 4.

27. Rogan, *The Arabs*, 247.

28. Kramer, *History of Palestine*, 116; Shlaim, *The Iron Wall*, 15.

29. Kramer, *History of Palestine*, 232–36.

30. Rozenblit, "European Jewry, 1800–1933," 198.

31. Phyllis Goldstein, *A Convenient Hatred: The History of Antisemitism*. Brookline: Facing History and Ourselves, 2012: 243–45.

32. Rozenblit, "European Jewry, 1800–1933," 205.

33. Goldstein, *Convenient Hatred*, 260–73.

34. Ibid., 240–41.

35. Charles D. Smith, *Palestine and the Arab-Israeli Conflict: A History with Documents*. Boston: Bedford St. Martin's, 2010: 131–33.

36. Peel Commission Report:
http://unispal.un.org/UNISPAL.NSF/0/88A6BF6F1BD82405852574CD006
C457F

37. Rogan, *The Arabs*, 256

38. Ibid.
39. Smith, *Palestine and Arab-Israeli Conflict*, 140; Shlaim, *Iron Wall*, 23; Akenson, *God's Peoples*, 177.
40. Rogan, *The Arabs*, 256.
41. Kramer, *History of Palestine*, 264–95.
42. Rogan, *The Arabs*, 256–58; Smith, *Palestine and Arab-Israeli Conflict*, 141.
43. Rashid Khaladi, *The Iron Cage: The Story of the Palestinian Struggle for Statehood*. Boston: Beacon Press, 2006: 105.
44. MacDonald White Paper: http://unspal.un.org/UNISPAL.NSF/0/EB5B88C94 ABA2AE585256D0B00555536
45. Rogan, *The Arabs*, 312–13.
46. *Struma* Disaster: www.ushmm.org/wlc/en/article.php?ModuleId=10005410
47. Shlaim, *Iron Wall*, 24.
48. Melani McAlister, *Epic Encounters: Culture, Media, and US Interests in the Middle East Since 1945*. Berkeley: University of California Press, 2005; 2001: 1–2.
49. Michael B. Oren, *Power, Faith, and Fantasy: America in the Middle East 1776-Present*. New York: W. W. Norton, 2007: 84; Peter Grose, *Israel in the Mind of America*. New York: Schocken Books, 1983: 3–22; Paul S. Boyer, *When Time Shall Be No More: Prophecy Belief in Modern American Culture*. Cambridge, MA: Harvard University Press, 1992: 74–75.
50. Karine V. Walther, *Sacred Interests: The United States and the Islamic World, 1881-1921*. Chapel Hill: University of North Carolina Press, 2015: 5–6; 33–67; 157–237; see also Malini Johar Schueller, *US Orientalisms: Race, Nation, and Gender in Literature*. Ann Arbor: University of Michigan Press, 1998.
51. Brandeis to James Arthur Balfour, Feb. 3, 1920; Brandeis to Lord Curzon, Feb. 3, 1920, both in Benjamin V. Cohen Papers, Jacob Rader Marcus Center of the American Jewish Archives (AJA), Cincinnati, Box 1; Irvine H. Anderson, *Biblical Interpretation and Middle East Policy*. Gainesville: University Press of Florida, 2005: 61; Matthew F. Jacobs, *Imagining the Middle East: The Building of an American Foreign Policy, 1918-1967*. Chapel Hill: University of North Carolina Press, 2011: 190–92; John B. Judis. *Genesis: Truman, American Jews, and the Origins of the Arab/Israeli Conflict*. New York: Farrar, Straus and Giroux, 2014: 144–63.
52. Walther, *Sacred Interests*, 274–75.
53. David A. Gerber, ed., *Anti-Semitism in American History*. Champaign-Urbana: University of Illinois Press, 1986.
54. Pamela S. Nadell, "Jews and Judaism in the United States," in Baskin and Seeskin, eds., *Jewish History, Religion, and Culture*, 223; Leonard Dinnerstein, *The Leo Frank Case*. Athens: University of Georgia Press, rev. edn., 2008; "Frank, Leo, 1914-1919, 1982-1987," Anti-Defamation League, 1913-1995, B'nai B'rith International Archives, AJA, Box C1–3.
55. Goldstein, *Convenient Hatred*, 251–53; Anti-Defamation League, 1913–1995, B'nai B'rith International Archives, Boxes C1–1 to C1–6.

56. Frankfurter amassed a substantive file on Zionism. "Zionist File," Frankfurter Papers, LOC, Boxes 85–88 (microfilm); Jacobs, *Imagining the Middle East,* 197.

57. Elizabeth P. MacCallum, "The Palestine Conflict," Foreign Policy Association, Oct. 16, 1929, Frankfurter Papers, Box 87A.

58. Richard Breitman and Allan J. Lichtman, *FDR and the Jews.* Cambridge: Harvard University Press, 2013: 141, 316.

59. Mark A. Raider, *The Emergence of American Zionism.* New York: New York University Press, 1998: 3, 29, 124, 201; Naomi W. Cohen, *The Americanization of Zionism, 1897-1948.* Hanover and London: Brandeis University Press, 2003: 2

60. Raider, *The Emergence of American Zionism,* 209.

61. Mark A. Raider et al., ed., *Abba Hillel Silver and American Zionism.* London: Frank Cass, 1997: 102; Judis, *Genesis,* 150.

62. Caitlin Carenen, *The Fervent Embrace: Liberal Protestants, Evangelicals, and Israel.* New York: New York University Press, 2012: 21–22; Breitman and Lichtman, *FDR and the Jews,* 294.

63. *New York Times,* March 28, 1939; Smith, *Foreign Agents:* 15.

"FRIENDSHIP OF THE AMERICAN PEOPLE FOR THE ZIONIST IDEAL"

1. Declaration Adopted by the Biltmore Conference," May 11, 1942. www.jewishvirtuallibrary.org/the-biltmore-conference-1942

2. Timothy Snyder, *Bloodlands: Europe between Hitler and Stalin.* New York: Basic Books, 2010.

3. Raider et al., eds., *Silver and American Zionism,* 110.

4. Christopher R. Browning, "The Nazi Genocide," in Donald Bloxham and A. Dirk Moses, eds., *The Oxford Handbook of Genocide Studies.* Oxford: Oxford University Press, 2001: 407–25.

5. Breitman and Lichtman, *FDR and the Jews,* 245–57; Judis, *Genesis,* 180.

6. Breitman and Lichtman, *FDR and the Jews,* 325.

7. Frank W. Brecher, *Reluctant Ally: United States Foreign Policy toward the Jews from Wilson to Roosevelt.* New York: Greenwood Press, 1991: 88, 113–17; Breitman and Lichtman, *FDR and the Jews,* 258–59; 321–23.

8. "American Jewish Conference. 1943-1944," AJA, Box 1; "The Zionist Position: A Statement Submitted to the Delegates to the American Jewish Conference," Aug. 29, 1943, Abba Hillel Silver Papers, Western Reserve Historical Society (WRHS), Cleveland, Series III, 1916–1945, Box 2; Marc Lee Raphael. *Abba Hillel Silver: A Profile in American Judaism.* New York: Holmes and Meier, 1989: 85–89.

9. Raider et al., ed., *Silver and American Zionism,* 116; AZEC documents, Silver Papers, WRHS, Box 8.

10. Doreen Bierbrier, "The American Zionist Emergency Council: An Analysis of a Pressure Group," *American Jewish Historical Quarterly* LX (September 1970): 87–93.

11. Lessing J. Rosenwald (ACJ) to Harry Truman, Oct. 1, 1946, Official File 204, Papers of Harry S. Truman, Harry S. Truman Library Institute, Independence, Mo., (HSTL), Box 914. See also Thomas A. Kolsky, *Jews against Zionism: The American Council for Judaism, 1942–1948.* Philadelphia: Temple University Press, 1990.

12. "Statement of the American Jewish Conference on the Withdrawal of the American Jewish Committee," Nov. 7, 1943, Series III, 1916–1945, Silver Papers, Box 1.

13. I. L. Kenen to Meir Grossman, Oct. 28, 1945, KP, Box 4.

14. Judis, *Genesis,* 164–65; David K. Niles to Matt Connelly, May 1, 1946, President's Secretary's Files, Papers of Harry S. Truman, HSTL, Box 161.

15. "Hearings Reveal Strong Desire for Permanent Body," undated, KP, Box 3.

16. Maurice Bisgyer to Kenen, Nov. 1, 1943, KP, Box 3; for Kenen's early work promoting Zionism in Cleveland, see Box 8; Kenen, *Israel's Defense Line,* 14.

17. Kenen to Henry Montor, Nov. 25, 1943, KP, Box 3; "Rally for Palestine" March 21, 1944, KP, Box 6.

18. Kenen to Delegates of the American Jewish Conference, Feb. 24, 1944, Silver Papers, Series III, 1916–1945, Box 1.

19. Carenen, *The Fervent Embrace,* 27.

20. Kenen, *Israel's Defense Line,* 18.

21. Netanyahu to Silver, July 6, 1944, Silver Papers, Series I, Box 6.

22. Text of Address by I. L. Kenen, National Convention of Hadassah, Aug. 19, 1964, KP, Box 19; Kenen, *Israel's Defense Line,* 18.

23. Kramer, *History of Palestine,* 307–9; Judis, *Genesis,* 216.

24. *Foreign Relations Series of the United States (FRUS) 1945, VIII, The Near East and Africa.* Washington: USGPO, 1969: 694–95. Doc. 867N.01/3-1845; Irvine H. Anderson, *Aramco, the United States, and Saudi Arabia: A Study of the Dynamics of Foreign Oil Policy, 1933–1950.* Princeton: Princeton University Press, 1981.

25. Warren F. Kimball, *The Juggler: Franklin D. Roosevelt as Wartime Statesman.* Princeton: Princeton University Press, 1991.

26. Breitman and Lichtman, *FDR and the Jews,* 251; *FRUS 1945, VIII, The Near East and Africa.* Washington: USGPO: 1969, 698, 703–4; Doc. 867N.01/4-545.

27. Judis, *Genesis,* 193.

28. "At War with the Experts," Episode Six of "Decision: The Conflicts of Harry S. Truman" (Television series), 1964, HSTL.

29. Stettinius to Truman, April 18, 1945, President's Secretary's Files, HSTL, Box 161.

30. DOS Memorandum for the President, May 28, 1945; Joseph Grew to Truman, May 1, 1945; Loy Henderson to Secretary, Aug. 31, 1945, all in President's Secretary's Files, Box 161.

31. Loy Henderson to Dean Rusk, Nov. 20, 1977, The Papers of Loy Henderson, LOC, Box 11

32. *FRUS 1945, VIII,* 770–71, Docs. 867N.01/8-1845 and 867N.01/10-1845, 722; Truman to Ibn Saud, Oct. 28, 1946, President's Secretary's Files, Box 162, HSTL.

33. Statement by the President, Nov. 13, 1945, President's Secretary's Files, Box 162.

34. "Report of the Anglo–American Committee of Inquiry," April 20, 1946, President's Secretary's Files, Box 162; Report of Anglo–American Committee of Inquiry is in Official File 204, Box 916; "Cabinet Committee on Palestine," Official File 204, Box 915, all HSTL.

35. *FRUS 1946, The Near East and Africa, VII.* Washington: USGPO, 1969, 604–5, Doc. 867N.01/5-1046, 714–17, Doc. 867N.01/10-1546; see also Department of State *Bulletin*, May 26, 1946, 917.

36. *FRUS 1946, VII*, 601, Doc.740.00119 Council/5-945; Atlee to Truman, June 10, 1946; Truman to Atlee, June 14, 1946, both in President's Secretary's Files, Box 161, HSTL.

37. "Telephone Conversation with Henry Monsky," Feb. 10, 1947, KP, Box 3.

38. *FRUS 1946, VII*, 642–43, Doc. 867N.01/7-346; White House Press Release, July 2, 1946, Official File 204, Box 915.

39. Rogan, *The Arabs*, 311–15.

40. The Official File 204 (HSTL) contains files of letters in myriad boxes supporting Jewish immigration to Palestine.

41. Harry Louis-Selden to Charles G. Ross, July 9, 1946, Official File 204, Box 914; Wagner to Truman, June 20, 1946, President's Secretary's Files, Box 161.

42. Celler to Connelly, June 25, 1946; Celler to Truman, July 31, 1946; "Memorandum for Mr. Connelly," June 19, 1946; A. J. Sabath to Truman, Feb. 18, 1947, all in Official File 204, Box 914.

43. Loy Henderson interview by Richard D. McKinzie, Washington, DC, June 14, 1973: 110–11, HSTL.

44. Niles to Lehman, July 8, 1946, Official File 204, Box 914; Niles to Truman, May 27, 1946, Papers of David K. Niles, Box 29, HSTL.

45. Clayton to Truman, Sept. 12, 1946, President's Secretary's Files, Box 161.

46. Abraham Feinberg interview by Richard D. McKinzie, New York, Aug. 23, 1973: 33, HSTL. Stephen D. Isaacs described Feinberg as "the first Jewish fund raiser for national politics"; Isaacs, *Jews and American Politics.* New York: Doubleday, 1974: 121.

47. Statement by the President, Oct. 4, 1946, Official File 204, Box 915.

48. Matthew J. Connelly interview by Jerry N. Hess, New York, Nov. 30, 1967: 383–88, HSTL; Judis, *Genesis*, 209.

49. Jacobson to Truman, Oct. 3, 1947, President's Secretary's Files, Box 161.

50. *FRUS 1947, V, The Near East and Africa.* USGPO, 1971, 1056–57, Doc. 867N.01/2-2547; 1074–77, Doc. 867N.01/4-2347; 1094–96, Doc. 867N.01/5-2947; *FRUS 1946, VII*, 618, Doc. 867N.01/6-546; for a magisterial analysis of British policy during this period in Palestine, see William Roger Louis, *The British Empire in the Middle East, 1945-1951: Arab Nationalism, the United States, and Postwar Imperialism.* London: Oxford University Press, 1984: 381–572.

51. Wise to Truman, Oct. 7, 1946, President's Secretary's Files, Box 161; Jewish Agency to Truman, May 2, 1946, Official File 204, Box 914.

52. *FRUS 1946*, VII, 604–5, Doc. 867N.01/5-1046, 714–17, Doc. 867N.01/10-1546; see also Department of State *Bulletin*, May 26, 1946, 917; *FRUS 1947*, V, 1971, Doc. 867N.01/1-1747, 1011–14.

53. Niles to Truman, July 29, 1947; Truman to Undersecretary of State, Aug. 6, 1947, both in President's Secretary's Files, Box 161.

54. Harry S. Truman, *Memoirs: Years of Trial and Hope*. Garden City: Doubleday, 1955–56: 158.

55. Oren, *Power, Faith, and Fantasy*, 492.

56. AZEC Executive Committee minutes, Feb. 24, 1947, Silver Papers, Series I, Roll 4; American Jewish Conference, Minutes of Meeting of the Interim Committee, Sept. 18, 1947, KP, Box 3; Report of the Interim Committee to the Fourth Session American Jewish Conference, Nov. 20, 1947, KP, Box 4.

57. Carenen, *Fervent Embrace*, 25.

58. *FRUS 1947*, V, 1143–44, Doc. 501.BB Palestine/9-247.

59. *FRUS 1947*, V, 1152-53, Doc. 501.BB Palestine/9-1847; "Transcript of the Secretary's Remarks on the Palestine Problem," President's Secretary's Files, Box 161.

60. Ibid., 1170, Doc. 501.BB Palestine/10-1646; 1171–74, Doc. 501.BB Palestine/10-347; 1176–77, Doc. 501.BB Summaries/10-747; 1212–13, Doc. 867N.01/10-3047.

61. The Declaration of the Arab Higher Committee for Palestine," Feb. 6, 1948, Clark M. Clifford Papers, Box 13, HSTL; Peter L. Hahn, *Caught in the Middle East: The US Policy toward the Arab-Israeli Conflict, 1945-1961*. Chapel Hill: University of North Carolina Press: 204: 41; Oren, *Power, Faith, and Fantasy*, 492.

62. Shlaim, *Iron Wall*, 28.

63. Ilan Pappé, *The Ethnic Cleansing of Palestine*. Oxford: Oneworld Publications, 2006: 35.

64. Frank Goldman, "Behind the Scenes of the UN Decision," *The National Jewish Monthly* (January 1948): 163, Official File 204, Box 916; Weizmann to Truman, Dec. 9, 1947, Official File 204, Box 915.

65. George Wadsworth to Herschel Johnson, Sept. 18, 1947, President's Secretary's Files, Box 161.

66. *FRUS 1947*, V, 1153–58, Doc. 501.BB Palestine/9-2247.

67. Ibid., 1281–83, Doc. 867N.01/11-2447.

68. Kramer, *A History of Palestine*, 317; Rogan, *The Arabs*, 333.

69. Eugene L. Rogan and Avi Shlaim, eds., *The War for Palestine: Rewriting the History of 1948*. Cambridge: Cambridge University Press, 2001/2007.

70. Ibid.; Shlaim, *Iron Wall*, 35–40.

71. Pappé, *Ethnic Cleansing of Palestine*, 131.

72. Morris, "Revisiting the Palestine Exodus of 1948," in Rogan and Shlaim, eds., *War for Palestine*, 56.

73. Pappé, *Ethnic Cleansing of Palestine*, 42, xiii.

74. Nur Masalha, *The Politics of Denial: Israel and the Palestinian Refugee Problem*. London: Pluto Press, 2003: 18–20.

75. Pappé, *Ethnic Cleansing of Palestine*. 188; Rogan, *The Arabs*, 330.

76. Shlaim, *Iron Wall*, 35–43.

77. *FRUS 1948, V, Part 2, The Near East, South Asia, and Africa.* Washington: GPO, 1976, 545–54, Doc. PPS Files, Lot 64 D 563, Near and Middle East, 1947-1948; 619–25, Doc. PPS Files, Lot 64 D 563; 637–40, Doc. PPS/21, Document 501.BB Palestine/2-2148; PPS, "The Problem of Palestine," Feb. 11, 1948, National Security Council File, Box 13.
78. NSC, "The Position of the United States with Respect to Palestine," Feb. 17, 1948, President's Secretary's Files, Box 162.
79. *FRUS 1948, V, Part 2,* 666–75, Doc. ORE 7-48; 645, Doc. Elsey Papers.
80. Ibid., 742–51, Doc. 501.BB Palestine/3-2248; 778-96, Doc. 501.BB Palestine/4-848; Truman Public Statement, March 25, 1948, "Official File 204, Box 916.
81. *FRUS 1948, V, Part 2,* 739, Doc. 501.BB Palestine/3-1848, 840–41, Doc. 867N.01/4-2248; 877–79, Doc. 501.BB Palestine/4-3048; Truman cut off communication with Silver, whose attorney demanded an interview claiming that his client was the leader of the "Jews of the world"; Joseph P. Parris to Matthew Connelly, Nov. 14, 1946, Official File 204, Box 914.
82. St. Louis Council, American Jewish Congress to Truman, Feb. 26, 1948, Official File 204, Box 916; Weizmann to Truman, Apr. 9, 1948, Official File 204, Box 916.
83. Press Analysis, American Christian Palestine Committee, 1948, KP, Box 2.
84. "Memorandum of Conference on Palestine," March 24, 1948, Clark M. Clifford Papers, Box 13, HSTL.
85. Kirchwey to Truman, June 19, 1948, Weizmann Archives Records, Box 1, HSTL; Hahn, *Caught in the Middle East,* 30–31, 48.
86. Truman to Niles, May 13, 1947, Confidential File, Box 43; Truman to Dean Alfange, May 18, 1948, President's Secretary's Files, Box 161.
87. Tivnan, *The Lobby,* 18; Jacobson to Truman, Feb. 21, 1948; Truman to Jacobson, Feb. 27, 1948, both in Official File 204, Box 916; Film, "Decision: The Conflicts of Harry S. Truman," Episode Six, "At War with the Experts," HST Associates, 1964, HSTL.
88. *FRUS 1948, V, Part 2,* 687–96, Doc. Clifford Papers; Anderson, *Biblical Interpretation and Middle East Policy:* 97.
89. *FRUS 1948, V,* 972–75, Doc. 501.BB Palestine/5-1248.
90. Austin to Marshall, May 19, 1948, President's Secretary's Files, Box 161; Hahn, *Caught in the Middle East,* 69.
91. Truman de facto recognition statement, May 14, 1948, Official File 204, Box 917; *FRUS 1948, Part 2* 1005, Doc. 867N.01/5-1748; Hahn, *Caught in the Middle East,* 50.
92. Frank W. Brecher, *American Diplomacy and the Israeli War of Independence.* Jefferson: McFarland Publishing, 2013: 32–36; Kenen to James McDonald, undated [1949], KP, Box 8.
93. Allis Radosh and Ronald Radosh, *A Safe Haven: Harry S, Truman and the Founding of Israel.* New York: Harper, 2009: 47.
94. Anderson, *Biblical Interpretation and Middle East Policy,* 75.
95. Ibid., 108, 32–50, 29, 19.
96. Truman to Emanuel Neumann, June 29, 1948, Niles Papers, Box 30.

"NEW FORMS OF PROPAGANDA HAD TO BE FOUND"

1. Jewish Agency for Palestine, "Memorandum on Acts of Arab Aggression," Feb. 2, 1948, President's Secretary's Files, Box 161.
2. *FRUS 1948, V, Part 2*, 1265, Doc. 501.BB Palestine/8-148: Telegram.
3. Ibid., 1240–48, Doc. CIA Files ORE 38–48; 1263, Doc. 501.BB Palestine/7-3148.
4. Ibid., Document 501.BB Palestine/8-748, 1295, Document "Progress Report of the United Nations Mediator in Palestine," Document 501.BB Palestine/9-1648, 1401–8, Document 501.MA Palestine/8-1948, 1324–25, Document 501.BB Palestine/9-948, 1384–86.
5. Kenen, *Israel's Defense Line*, 61; Judis, *Genesis*, 332; "Republican Party Platform of 1948," June 21, 1948, UCSB, The American Presidency Project. Online: www.presidency.ucsb.edu/ws/index.php?pid=25836.
6. *FRUS 1948, V, Part 2*, 1295–96 Doc. 501.BB Palestine/8-748; Bernadotte to Secretary General, Aug. 19, 1948, Clifford Papers, Box 13; Hahn, *Caught in Middle East*, 54.
7. *FRUS 1948, V, Part 2*, 1328, Doc. 501.BB Palestine/8-1948; 1541, Doc. 501.BB Palestine/11-148; 1298–1301, Doc. 501.BB Palestine/8-948: Telegram; 1313–15, Doc. 501.BB Palestine/8-1648.
8. Marshall to Truman, Aug. 16, 1948; Marshall to Lovett, undated, both in President's Secretary's Files, Box 161.
9. *FRUS 1948, V, Part 2*, 1401–6, Doc. "Progress Report of the United Nations Mediator in Palestine."
10. Ibid., 1384–86, Doc. 501.BB Palestine/9-948.
11. Ibid., 1412–13, Doc. 501.BB Palestine/9-1748.
12. Ibid., 1113, Doc. 501.BB Palestine/6-1448; 1141, Doc. 867N.01/6-2448; Kramer, *History of Palestine*, 319; Shlaim, *The Iron Wall*, 39; *FRUS 1948, V, Part 2*, 1296, Doc. 501.BB Palestine/8-748.
13. Crum to Clifford, Sept. 28, 1948, Clifford Papers, Box 13; Truman to Marshall, Sept. 29, 1948, Clifford Papers, Box 14.
14. *FRUS 1948, V, Part 2*, 1390–91 Doc. 501.BB Palestine/9-1048; 1430–31, Doc. 501.BB Palestine/9-2948; Hahn, *Caught in Middle East*, 56–58.
15. Jacobson to Weizmann, Nov. 29, 1948; Weizmann to Jacobson, Dec. 14, 1948, both in Jacobson Papers, Box 1; Weizmann telegram to Jacobson, undated; Truman to Weizmann, Nov. 29, 1948, both in Clifford Papers, Box 13; Hahn, *Caught in Middle East*, 87–89.
16. Hahn, *Caught in the Middle East*, 60.
17. Kramer, *History of Palestine*, 320.
18. Nur Masalha, *The Palestine Nakba: Decolonizing History, Narrating the Subaltern, Reclaiming Memory*. London: Zed Books, 2012.
19. "The American Public and Israel," Roper Center, Cornell University. https://ropercenter.cornell.edu/american-public-israel/
20. Akenson, *God's Peoples*, 241; Ilan Pappé, *The Forgotten Palestinians: A History of the Palestinians in Israel*. New Haven: Yale University Press, 2011.
21. Chester Bowles to Clifford, Sept. 23, 1948; Crum to Clifford, Oct. 3, 1948, both in Clifford Papers, Box 13.

22. "The Admission of the State of Israel to the United Nations" attached to Hyman Schulson to David Niles, Aug. 5, 1948; Feinberg to Truman, Feb. 4, 1949, both in Niles Papers, Box 30; Announcement of de jure recognition, Jan. 31, 1949, Official File 204, Box 917.

23. "Abraham Feinberg's FBI File," The Israel Lobby Archive. www.israel lobby.org/feinberg/.

24. Jewish War Veterans press release, July 26, 1948, Niles Papers, Box 30; Weizmann to Truman, Jan. 21, 1949, Official File 204, Box 917; Robert Lovett to Truman, Aug. 11, 1948; Truman to Lovett, Aug. 16, 1948, both in President's Secretary's Files, Box 158.

25. Epstein to Clifford, Aug. 3, 1948, Clifford Papers, Box 13; Jacobson to Weizmann, Aug. 6, 1948, Jacobson Papers, Box 1.

26. Shlaim, *Iron Wall*, 53.

27. Benny Morris, *Israel's Border Wars, 1949-1956: Arab Infiltration, Israeli Retaliation, and the Countdown to the Suez War*. New York: Oxford University Press, 1993, 410.

28. Burdett Memorandum, April 13, 1949, President's Secretary's Files, Box 158.

29. Hahn, *Caught in Middle East*, 100; Akenson, *God's Peoples*, 234.

30. UN Reso. 194 (Dec. 11, 1948) in Walter Laquer and Barry Rubin, eds., *The Israel-Arab Reader: A Documentary History of the Middle East Conflict*. New York: Penguin Books, 2008, 85.

31. *Foreign Relations Series of the United States (FRUS) 1949, The Near East, South Asia, and Africa*, VI. Washington: USGPO, 1977: 828, Doc. 501.MA Palestine/3-1749; 880–81, Doc. 501.BB Palestine/3-2949; on the persistent US inability to comprehend Palestinian nationalism, see Kathleen Christison, *Perceptions of Palestine: Their Influence on US Middle East Policy*. Berkeley: University of California Press, 1999.

32. *FRUS 1949: Near, East, South Asia, Africa*, 880, Doc. 501.BB Palestine/3-2949.

33. On this point see Ofer Shiff, *The Downfall of Abba Hillel Silver and the Foundation of Israel*. New York: Syracuse University Press, 2014.

34. Asaf Siniver, Eban's sympathetic biographer, may exaggerate the diplomat's influence, arguing, "The development of a US–Israeli special relationship cannot be attributed to Eban alone, but there is little doubt had it not been for his decade-long successful tenure as the voice and face of Israel in the United States the natural affinity between the two peoples would not have bloomed into one of the most enduring alliances of modern times." Siniver, *Abba Eban: A Biography*. New York; Overlook Duckworth, 2015: 174–75.

35. Aridan, *Advocating for Israel*, 29.

36. Address by Lipsky, ZOA annual convention, June 17, 1951, Kenen Papers, Box 5.

37. Kenen, *Israel's Defense Line*, 69.

38. American Jewish Conference, Final Report of the Executive Committee, Jan. 31, 1949, Kenen Papers, Box 4.

Notes to pages 66–71

54

. "American Zionist Council Elects Presidium to Succeed Dr. Silver as Chairman," Jewish Telegraph Agency, June 17, 1949; accessed online: www.jta.org/1949/06/19/archive/american-zionist-council-elects-praesidium-to-succeed-dr-silver-as-chairman.

40. American Jewish Conference, Final Report of the Executive Committee, Jan. 31, 1949, Kenen Papers, Box 4; Aridan, *Advocating for Israel*, 23.

41. Aridan, *Advocating for Israel*, 19, 35–36.

42. Ibid., 831.

43. Masalha, *The Politics of Denial*.

44. *FRUS 1949: Near, East, South Asia, Africa*, 828–42, Doc. 501.MA Palestine/3-1749; 855, Doc. 501.BB Palestine/3-2249.

45. Acheson, "Memorandum of Conversation with Israeli Ambassador," Feb. 5, 1949. Papers of Dean G. Acheson–Secretary of State File, HSTL; Acheson, "Memorandum of Conversation with Moshe Sharett," April 5, 1949; Weizmann to Truman, June 24, 1949, both in President's Secretary's Files, Box 158.

46. Acheson, "Memorandum of Conversation with Sharett"; Weizmann to Truman, June 24, 1949.

47. Ethridge to Truman, April 11, 1949, President's Secretary's Files, Box 158; *FRUS 1949: Near East, South Asia, Africa*, 905–6, Doc. 501.BB Palestine/4-1149; *New York Times*, April 28, 1949.

48. Truman to Weizmann, Aug. 13, 1949, Confidential File, Box 43.

49. "Note Delivered by the United States Ambassador in Tel Aviv to the Prime Minister of the Government of Israel on May 29, 1949"; "Note Delivered by FM of Israel to the United States ambassador at Tel Aviv on June 8, 1949," both in President's Secretary's Files, Box 161.

50. *FRUS 1949: Near East, South Asia, Africa*, 1020, Doc. 501.BB Palestine/5-1749: Telegram.

51. "Aide-Memoire," June 21, 1949, President's Secretary's Files, Box 161.

52. James E. Webb to Truman, undated, President's Secretary's Files, Box 158.

53. Memorandum from American Zionist Emergency Council; Hyman Schulson to Niles, June 10, 1949, Niles Papers, Box 30; Epstein to Clifford, Aug. 15, 1949, Clifford Papers, Box 13; Hahn, *Caught in Middle East*, 104; Feinberg to Niles, Mar. 7, 1950, Niles Papers, Box 30.

54. Hahn, *Caught in Middle East*, 104–11; Weimann to Jacobson, July 18, 1949, Jacobson Papers, Box 1.

55. *FRUS 1949: Near, East, South Asia, Africa*, 1124–25, Doc. 501.BB Palestine/6-1249; 1317, Doc. 501.BB Palestine/8-1649L Circular Telegram; 1321, Doc. 501.BB Palestine/8-849: Telegram; 1376–77, Doc. 867N.01/9-1349.

56. Shlaim, *Iron Wall*, 62; Hahn, *Caught in Middle East*, 113, 120; "Memorandum on Jerusalem," October 1949, Niles Papers, Box 30. On the biblical narrative, see the Introduction, note 9.

57. Spellman to Truman, June 10, 1949; Spellman to HST, April 29, 1949, both in Confidential File, Box 43; *FRUS 1949: Near, East, South Asia, Africa*, 1015–18, 1383–87, 1498–99.

58. Aridan, *Advocating for Israel*, 29.

59. *FRUS 1949: Near, East, South Asia, Africa*, 1521; "UN Votes International Regime for Jerusalem but Talk of Reconsideration Begins," Dec. 12, 1949; "Public Opinion Opposes UN Jerusalem Resolution," Dec. 23, 1949, both in Kenen Papers, Box 11.

60. *FRUS 1949: Near, East, South Asia, Africa*, 1322–23, Doc. 867N.01/5-449; 1530–31, Resolution 303; 1551–56, Doc. 501.BB Palestine/12-2049.

61. Ibid., 1537.

62. Hahn, *Caught in Middle East*, 73–79.

63. *FRUS 1950, The Near East, South Asia, and Africa*, V. Washington: GPO, 1978: 661, Doc. 784.02/1-350; 671–74, Doc. 784A.00/1-950, 742–45, Doc. 884A.00/2-1550.

64. *FRUS 1951, V, The Near East and Africa*. Washington: USGPO, 1982: 734, Doc. 780.5/6-2651; 738, London Embassy Files: Lot 54 F 59: 500 Israel.

65. Acheson to Lipsky, June 7, 1950, Jacobson Papers, Box 1; "Memorandum of Conversation with Eliahu Elath," Jan. 31, 1950; "Memorandum of Conversation with Nahum Goldman," Mar. 28, 1950, both in Acheson Papers – Secretary of State File.

66. "Memorandum Presented to the President of the United States," Nov. 15, 1950, KP, Box 1.

67. Ibid.; see also a massive report from the Israel Embassy on "Proposed Utilization of Dollar Aid in Connection with Israel's Program of Refugee Relief and Resettlement," KP, Box 1.

68. Jerome Unger to the Local Committees of the American Zionist Council, Oct. 2, 1950; Unger to the Local Committees of the AZC, Oct. 10, 1950, both in KP, Box 5.

69. Lipsky to Local Committees of the AZC, Jan. 8, 1951, KP, Box 5.

70. Lipsky to Kenen, Feb. 12, 1951, KP, Box 4; Eban to Kenen, Feb. 22, 1951, both in KP, Box 9.

71. Eban, "The Mysterious Texture of US-Israeli Relations," AIPAC Address, April 14, 1975, McGeorge Bundy Personal Papers, Ford Foundation, Subject Files, Box 48, JFK Library.

72. Lipsky to Kenen, Feb. 12, 1951, KP, Box 4.

73. Aridan, *Advocating for Israel*, 24–26; "1951–1964 Lobby Disclosures," The Israel Lobby Archive: The Institute for Research: Middle Eastern Policy (IRMEP), Washington, DC: www.israellobby.org/AZCPA/

74. Wagner, KP, Box 2; Kenen to Philip Lown, Feb. 28, 1951, KP, Box 1; Kenen to Lipsky, Mar. 28, 1951, KP, Box 5.

75. AZC, Minutes of Meeting of the Executive Committee, Mar. 19, 1951; Kenen to Lipsky, Mar. 12, 1951, both in KP, Box 5.

76. "1951–1964 Lobby Disclosures," The Israel Lobby Archive.

77. Kenen to Lipsky, June 22, 1951; Address by Lipsky to ZOA, June 17, 1951, both in KP, Box 5.

78. *FRUS 1950, V*, 895–96, Doc. 784.02/5-1150; *FRUS 1951, V*, 595–96, Doc. 884A.00/3-1551; Hahn, *Caught in Middle East*, 135;

79. Document State-JCS Meeting: Lot 61 D 417, 655.

80. Maurice Labelle, "'The Only Thorn': Early Saudi-American Relations and the Question of Palestine," *Diplomatic History* 35, April 2011: 280.

81. Irene L. Gendzier, *Dying to Forget: Oil, Power, Palestine, and the Foundations of US Policy in the Middle East*. New York: Columbia University Press, 2015: xx, 110–11, 243–305.
82. *FRUS 1951*, V, 1006–9, Doc. 611.84A/9-1450, 1006–9.
83. Ibid., 819, Doc. 800.413/8-351, 819.
84. Ibid., 599, Doc. 784A.5 MSA/3-1751; 610, Doc. 884A.00/3-1551; 615, Doc. 884A.00/3-1551; 775–76, Doc. McGee Files: Lot 53 D 468.
85. Ibid., 564, Doc. McGee Files: Lot 53 D 468; 619–20, Doc. 884A.00 R/4-551; 657, Doc. Secretary's Memoranda of Conversation: Lot 65 D 238; 707–12, Docs. 784A.00/6-1151, 784A.00/6-1251.
86. Hahn, *Caught in Middle East*, 80.
87. Kenen to Rabbi Martin Douglas, Oct. 24, 1951, KP, Box 1.
88. Acheson, Memorandum of Conversation with Ben-Gurion and Eban, May 8, 1951; Acheson, Memorandum of Conversation with Feinberg and John Waldo, July 17, 1951, both in Acheson Papers – Secretary of State File; Kenen, *Israel's Defense Line*, 80–86.
89. Kenen to Lipsky, Oct. 24, 1951, KP, Box 5; Kenen, *Israel's Defense Line*, 79.
90. Blaustein to Ben-Gurion, Aug. 15, 1951, Niles Papers, Box 30; see also Blaustein, Statement by President AJC, Oct. 27, 1949, AJC Records, Box A24.
91. "Resolution on Israel," AJC, Oct. 14, 1951; Josef Cohn to Niles, Oct. 5, 1951, both in Niles Papers, Box 30; "Cable Addressed by the Prime Minister of Israel [Ben-Gurion], Sept. 30, 1951, "Israel-Diaspora Relations, 1951-1993," B'nai B'rith International Archives, Box D2–3; the AJC has archived the "1951 Blaustein-Ben-Gurion Agreement": www.ajcarchives.org/main.php?GroupingId=1320.
92. Lessing J. Rosenwald to Niles, Aug. 1, 1950, Niles Papers, Box 27.
93. Jerome Unger to Local Committees, AZC, Dec. 22, 1953, KP, Box 5.
94. Carenen, *Fervent Embrace*, 63–81.
95. Rev. Karl Behr to Members of the Clergy in ACPC, Apr. 28, 1952, KP, Box 2; Acheson, Memorandum of Conversation with Blaustein et al., May 5, 1952; Acheson, Memorandum of Conversation with Eban, Sept. 22, 1952, both in Acheson Papers – Secretary of State File; Rudolf G. Sonneborn to Niles, April 4, 1951, Niles Papers, Box 30.
96. Blaustein to members, AJC, Nov. 18, 1952, AJC Records, Box A24.
97. Acheson to Truman, April 22, 1952, President's Secretary's Files, Box 158; Hahn, *Caught in Middle East*, 130–31.
98. *FRUS 1951*, V, 862–69, Docs. 357.AC/9-1251, 357.AC/9-1451, 320.2 AA/9-1451, 357.AC/9-1851; 878, Doc. 357.AC/9-2651; 894, Doc. SD/A/C.1/373; 916, Doc. McGhee Files: Lot 53 D 468; 959, Doc. 320/12-851.
99. Ibid., 564, Doc. McGhee Files: Lot 53 D 468; 878, Doc. 357.AC/9-2651; 894, Doc. SD/A/C.1/373; 904–5, Doc. SD/A/C.1/372; 916, Doc. McGhee Files: Lot 53 D 468.
100. "Israel's Frontiers"; Kenen to Rep. Albert Gore, Oct. 11, 1951; Kirchwey to Virginia Gildersleeve, Mar. 19, 1952, all three in Kenen Papers, Box 2; "Refugees, 1948-1966," Kenen Papers, Box 13.
101. *FRUS 1952–1954, IX, The Near and Middle East, Part I*. Washington: USGPO, 1986, Document 523, 1068–69.

102. Kenen to Lipsky, July 14, 1952, KP, Box 8.
103. AZC, "Memorandum on Aid to the Near East," April 7, 1952, KP, Box 2.
104. "Arab Threats against Israel," undated [early 1950s], KP, Box 9.
105. *FRUS 1951*, V, 971–72. Doc. Secretary's Memoranda: Lot 53 D 444.
106. Shlaim, *Iron Wall*, 72.
107. Ibid., 74–77; See also Hahn, *Caught in Middle East*, 93–97.
108. *FRUS 1951*, V, 676–77, Doc. 683.84A/5-1051.
109. Lipsky ZOA address, June 17, 1951, KP, Box 5; Hahn, *Caught in Middle East*, 94.
110. *FRUS 1952–1954*, IX, *The Near and Middle East*. Washington: USGPO, 1986: 1128–29, Doc. 684A.86/2-1153; Shlaim, *Iron Wall*, 80.
111. Lipsky to Kenen, Mar. 5, 1952, KP, Box 4.
112. Kenen to Feinberg, June 16, 1952, Niles Papers, Box 30; AZC press release, July 22, 1952, KP, Box 5; Kenen to Lipsky, Nov. 3, 1952, KP, Box 5; see also Kenen, *Israel's Defense Line*, 87–91.
113. AZC, "The Attitude of the Major Candidates and Political Parties on Israel and the Near East," Aug. 7, 1952, quoted in Kenen, *Israel's Defense Line*, 82; Kenen to Lipsky, Nov. 3, 1952, KP, Box 5.
114. Kenen to Lipsky, Nov. 10, 1952; Kenen to Lipsky, Nov. 18, 1952, both in KP, Box 5.
115. Josef Cohn to A. J. Granoff, Mar. 20, 1952, Papers of A. J. Granoff, Box 2, HSTL.
116. Harris J. Levine to Truman, May 31, 1950, Niles Papers, Box 30; Eric R. Crouse, *American Christians Support for Israel: Standing with the Chosen People, 1948 to 1975*. Lanham, Md., Lexington Books 2015: 55; Radosh and Radosh, *A Safe Haven*, 344–46; Preston, *Sword of the Spirit*, 437.

"WE SHOULD NOT BE DETERRED BY POLITICAL PRESSURES"

1. Hahn, *Caught in Middle East*, 142.
2. Lipsky to Dulles, Feb. 27, 1953, Box 8; Memorandum of Conversation with Jacob K. Javits, Jan. 27, 1953, JFD Chronological Series, Dulles Papers, Dwight D. Eisenhower Presidential Library (DDE), Box 1.
3. Salim Yaqub, *Containing Arab Nationalism: The Eisenhower Doctrine and the Middle East*. New York: University of North Carolina Press, 2004: 66.
4. *FRUS 1955–1957*, XVII, *Arab-Israeli Dispute, January 1–July 26, 1956*. Washington: USGPO, 1989: 327, Doc. 177.
5. Dulles, "Memorandum of Conversation with Nixon," Oct. 18, 1955, Dulles Papers, Subject Series, Box 11; Dulles, "Memorandum of Conversation with Jacob K. Javits," Jan. 27, 1953, Dulles Papers, Chronological Series, Box 1.
6. Kenen to Lipsky, Feb. 12, 1953; Kenen to Lipsky, Mar. 16, 1953, both in Kenen Papers, Box 5.
7. Michelle Mart, *Eye on Israel: How America Came to View the Jewish State as an Ally*. Albany: State University of New York Press, 2006: 127–28.
8. Bernard Katzen to Rabb, Mar. 26, 1953, Maxwell M. Rabb Papers, DDE, Box 26; on liaison with various Jewish and Zionist organizations, see Rabb

Papers, Box 59. Rabb, chairman the Government Division of United Jewish Appeal, used his position to solicit funds "from government employees of the Jewish faith": Rabb to Sinclair Weeks, Feb. 25, 1955, Rabb Papers, Box 58.

9. Kenen to Lipsky, Mar. 24, 1953, KP, Box 5; Dean Alfange et al. to Dear Friend, Apr. 2, 1953, KP, Box 2.

10. Eleanor Roosevelt to Dwight Eisenhower, April 4, 1953, KP, Box 2; Eisenhower to Roosevelt, Apr. 16, 1953, Dwight D. Eisenhower Papers, Ann Whitman File (AWF), Name Series, DDE, Box 30.

11. Hugh Wilford, *America's Great Game: The CIA's Secret Arabists and the Shaping of the Modern Middle East.* New York: Basic Books, 2013: 147, 178.

12. Excerpts from Address by I. L. Kenen, Jewish Community Federation of Cleveland, Dec. 9, 1953, KP, Box 8; Kenen to Lipsky, June 8, 1953, KP, Box 5.

13. Aridan, *Advocating for Israel*, 81.

14. *FRUS 1952–1954, IX*, 1275–90, NIE-92.

15. Morris, *Israel's Border Wars*, 412. Morris found that "the vast bulk of the infiltrations, 90 percent and more, through 1949–56, were economically or socially motivated." Rather than attacking Israel, these nonpolitical refugees sought to return to their homes, retrieve property, or renew cultivation of fields that now lay behind the expanded border. See also David Tal, "Israel's Road to the 1956 War," *International Journal of Middle East Studies* 28 (February 1996): 59–81.

16. Morris, *Israel's Border Wars*, 416.

17. Ibid., 414.

18. Shlaim, *Iron Wall*, 89–91.

19. President's Secretary's Files, undated, HSTL, Box 161.

20. *FRUS 1952–1954, IX*, 1175, Doc. 674.853/4-2253; 879–96, Docs. 683.84A/1-1652, 683.84A/1-1852, 784A.00/1-2152, 683.84A/1-2152, 683.84A/1-2252, 320/1-2252, 785.00/1-2352, 684A.85/1-2852, 320/1-2252, 684A.85/1-3152, 684A.85/2-452, 683.84A/2-652, 884A.00/2-852, 974.5301/2-852, 320.2AA/2-852, 784A.5 MSP/2-1152.

21. Shlaim, *Iron Wall*, 103; Robert Slater, *Warrior Statesman: The Life of Moshe Dayan.* New York: St. Martin's Press, 1991: viii.

22. N. C. Debevoise to Dr. H. S. Craig, Oct. 16, 1953, Operations Control Board report, Records of the President, White House Central Files, Subject Series, DDE, Box 49.

23. "Statement by the Prime Minister of Israel in a Broadcast over the Israel Radio," Oct. 19, 1953, KP, Box 9.

24. Shlaim, *Iron Wall*, 97.

25. *FRUS 1952–1954, IX*, 1367, Doc. S/PRS Files, Lot 77 D 9; see also Shlaim, *Iron Wall*, 95–98.

26. AZC Press Release, Oct. 19, 1953, KP, Box 9; Kenen to Dear Friend, Oct. 30, 1953, KP, Box 5.

27. *FRUS,1952–1954, IX*, 1372, Doc. 699.

28. Shlaim, *Iron Wall*, 94.

29. *FRUS 1952–1954, IX*, 1418–23, S/PRS Files, Lot 77 D 22, 1370, Doc. 120.1580/11-1753; Shlaim, *Iron Wall*, 94–95.

30. *FRUS 1952–1954, IX*, 1189, Doc. 611.80/5–953.
31. AZC Press Release Oct. 19, 1953; AZC Emergency Bulletin No. 1, Oct. 23, 1953, both in KP, Box 9; ACPC press release, Oct. 22, 1953, KP, Box 2; Excerpts from Address by Kenen, Jewish Community Federation of Cleveland, Dec. 9, 1953, KP, Box 8.
32. ACPC letter, Karl Behr to Dear Friends, Oct. 27, 1953; Abstract of Meeting of Jewish Representatives with Secretary of State Dulles," Oct. 26, 1953, both in KP, Box 9; *FRUS 1952–1954, IX*, 1386. Doc. 784A.5 MSP/10/2653.
33. DOS Press Release, Oct. 28, 1953, JFD Papers, Subject Series, Box 11; Shlaim, *Iron Wall*, 94–95.
34. UN Security Council Resolution on Qibya, Nov. 24, 1953. http://avalon.law .yale.edu/20th_century/mid009.asp
35. Lipsky to Local Committees of AZC, Nov. 25, 1953, KP, Box 5.
36. Kenen to Lipsky, Nov. 23, 1953, KP, Box 5; Doug Rossinow, "The Edge of the Abyss: The Origins of the Israel Lobby, 1949–1954," *Modern American History* 1 (March 2018): 23–43.
37. Memorandum to John Foster Dulles by Presidents of 16 American Jewish organizations, Oct. 25, 1954, KP, Box 9; Siniver, *Abba Eban*: 174–77; O'Brien, American Jewish Organizations, 191–202; Tivnan, *The Lobby*, 41, 60.
38. Kenen, *Israel's Defense Line*, 106–7.
39. "1951–1964 Lobbying Disclosures," IRmep. www.israellobby.org/ AZCPA/
40. Wilford, *America's Great Game*, 118–31.
41. Ibid., 125.
42. "Fifteen Questions and Answers about the American Council for Judaism," undated, Box 2; Elmer Berger, "Some Simple Facts," Twelfth Annual Conference, ACJ, Apr. 28, 1956, Chicago, Box 1, both in American Council for Judaism Collection (ACJC), Center for Jewish History, New York.
43. AZC, "False Witness: The Record of the American Council for Judaism," 1955, Box 2, ACJC.
44. Dulles, "Memorandum for the President," Oct. 26, 1954, AWF, Dulles-Herter Series, Box 4.
45. *FRUS 1952–1954, IX*, 1406–9, Doc. 684A.86/11–1053.
46. Ibid., 1542–45, Doc. 684A.86/5–554; 1555–57, Docs. 684A.86/5–1254, 611.84A/5–1354; *Department of State Bulletin*, April 26, 1954, 628; *Department of State Bulletin*, May 10, 1954, 708.
47. Meeting with Henry A. Byroade, Apr. 30, 1954, KP, Box 8; Report from Washington, May 25, 1954, KP, Box 4.
48. Wilford, *America's Great Game*, 186.
49. Dulles to Lipsky, Aug. 2, 1954, JFD Chronological Series, Box 9.
50. Dulles to Herbert Hoover, Jr, Nov. 1, 1955; Dulles, "Telephone Call to Mr. Nixon," Aug. 13, 1954, both in JFD Personnel Series, Box 1.
51. Wilford, *America's Great Game*, 239; Carenen, *Fervent Embrace*, 90–92; see also Stephen Spector, *Evangelicals and Israel: The Story of American Christian Zionism*. New York: Oxford University Press, 2009.

52. The first 400 pages of *FRUS 1955–1957, XVI, Arab-Israeli Dispute 1955.* Washington: USGPO, 1989, focus on Project Alpha.

53. C. D. Jackson to Dulles, Nov. 10, 1953, Dulles Papers, Subject Series, Box 11; Roderic O'Connor to C. D. Jackson, Nov. 16, 1953; Maxwell Abbell to Sherman Adams, Oct. 30, 1953, Records of the President, White House Central Files, General File, Box 817; Telephone Conversation with Governor Dewey, Mar. 30, 1954, Dulles Chronological Series, Box 7.

54. Kenen Memorandum to Lipsky, undated, KP, Box 8.

55. "Dulles Reply to 40 members of Congress," Dulles Papers, Chronological Series, Box 13.

56. *FRUS 1955–1957, XVII, Arab-Israeli Dispute, 1957.* Washington: USGPO, 1990: 655, Doc. 345.

57. *FRUS 1952–1954, IX,* 1528–29, Doc. 806.

58. "Telephone call from Mr. Dean," Oct. 18, 1954, Dulles Papers, Telephone Conversation Series, Box 3.

59. "Memorandum of Conversation with Ambassador Eban of Israel," Oct. 26, 1954, Dulles Papers, Subject Series, Box 11; AZCPA press release, Oct. 30, 1954, KP, Box 2.

60. Morris, *Israel's Border Wars,* 419; *FRUS 1952–1954, IX,* 1503, Doc. 684A.86/4–754; 1533, Doc. 684A.86/4–2854.

61. Hahn, *Caught in Middle East,* 126–28, 180.

62. Motti Golani, *Israel in Search of a War: the Sinai Campaign, 1955–1956.* Brighton: Sussex Academic Press, 1998, 182; Shlaim, *Iron Wall,* 147–48.

63. CIA Memorandum, "Prime Minister Ben-Gurion's Resignation," Feb. 7, 1961, Papers of President Kennedy, National Security Files, Countries, Israel, JFK Library, Box 118.

64. The plot failed resulting in the arrest of 13 conspirators, mostly Egyptian Jews, who were tried; two of them were executed, and others imprisoned, including one who committed suicide. The failed operation further embittered Israeli–Egyptian relations while the US reaction to the Israeli terror scheme was muted. CIA, "Prime Minister Ben-Gurion's Resignation"; Shlaim, *Iron Wall,* 104–6; 117–30.

65. Shlaim, *Iron Wall,* 112.

66. Golani, *Israel in Search of a War,* 18, ix; Despite the Israeli provocation Nasser was willing to discuss an overall settlement, but "this offer was spurned," calling into question, as Shlaim notes, "the official version that says Israel always strove for direct contact and always met with Arab refusal." Rejecting diplomacy, the Israeli militarists sought "to foment an atmosphere of public alarm to serve the policy of a deliberately provoked war." Dayan was regularly "bombarding Ben-Gurion with proposals for direct military action"; Shlaim, *Iron Wall,* 129, 157–59.

67. "Report by the Chief of Staff of the Truce Supervision Organization Concerning the Incident of 28 February 1955 Near Gaza," Mar. 17, 1955, KP, Box 10; Shlaim, *Iron Wall,* 132–33.

68. *FRUS 1955–1957,* XIV, 76–78.

69. The unprovoked Gaza assault was a "turning point" that convinced Nasser there could be no accommodation with the Israelis. Prior to the Gaza attack,

Nasser exercised restraint, pursued a "firm policy of curbing infiltration by Palestinians from the Gaza Strip into Israel," and had been willing to conduct talks, which Israel had rejected. In the wake of the Israeli raid, Nasser lifted the restraints, fomented irregular warfare, and sought new sources of armaments to defend his regime. Anguishing in "personal guilt at the deaths of his soldiers in Gaza," Nasser "had been led by Israeli contacts and to some extent by the US into complacency that Israel really wanted a settlement."; "cradle" quotation from Wilford, *America's Great Game*, 187; see also Shlaim, *Iron Wall*, 128–36; *FRUS 1955–1957*, XIV, 238; Hahn, *Caught in Middle East*, 193.

70. Dulles to Eisenhower, Sept. 1, 1955, AWF, Dulles-Herter Series, Box 6.
71. Hahn, *Caught in Middle East*, 164–66; Shlaim, *Iron Wall*, 154–55.
72. "Reaction to Secretary Dulles' August 26 Statement on Israel-Arab Settlement," Aug. 29, 1955, Dulles Papers, Subject Series, Box 1; Dulles to Eisenhower, Sept. 1, 1955, AWF, Dulles-Herter Series, Box 6; Hahn, *Caught in Middle East*, 186.
73. *FRUS 1955–1957*, XV, 305, Doc. 164.
74. The Aswan Dam issue is covered in ibid., 346–906.
75. *New York Times*, May 23, 1956.
76. *FRUS 1955–1957*, XV, 682–83, Doc. 371.
77. Golani, *Israel in Search of a War*, ix, 46.
78. Ibid., 187.
79. *FRUS 1955–1957, Suez Crisis, July 26-December 31, 1956*, XVI. Washington: USGPO, 1990: 106, Doc. 45; 126–27, Doc. 53; 184, Doc. 77.
80. Ibid., 98, Doc. 42; 22, Doc. 12; 182, Doc.76.
81. Kenen, "Memorandum on the Secretary of State's letter of February 6, 1956 on American Policy in the Near East"; AZCPA press release, Feb. 7, 1956, both in KP, Box 2.
82. AZCPA "Dear Friend" letter, Feb. 6, 1956, KP, Box 2; AZCPA "Dear Friend" letter, Aug. 21, 1956, KP, Box 8; KP, Box 2; "The American Israel Public Affairs Committee from 1955 Until 1968," KP, Box 20; Hahn, *Caught in Middle East*, 197–99.
83. Kenen, *Israel's Defense Line*, 130; "Excerpt from Address by Adlai E. Stevenson," May 11, 1956, West Side Jewish Community Center, Los Angeles, KP, Box 2.
84. *FRUS 1955–1957*, XVI, 786–822, Docs. 381–406; 855, Doc. 420; Golani, *Israel in Search of a War*, 138, 146.
85. Yaqub, *Containing Arab Nationalism*, 175–78.
86. *FRUS 1955–1957*, XVI, 844–50, Docs. 415–18; 902–16, Doc.455; 1018–20, Doc. 521.
87. *FRUS 1955–1957*, XVI, 834–36, Doc. 411.
88. Golani, *Israel in Search of a War*, 146.
89. *FRUS 1955–1957*, XVI, 1025–27, Doc. 525.
90. Ben-Gurion, "Speech to Knesset Reviewing Sinai Campaign," Nov. 7, 1956, Jewish Virtual Library (online): www.jewishvirtuallibrary.org/ben-gurion-spe ech-to-knesset-reviewing-the-sinai-campaign-november-1956; Hahn, *Caught in the Middle East*, 211–12.

91. *FRUS 1955–1957*, XVI, 1038, Doc. 534, 1063–64, Doc. 550.
92. Ibid., 1095, Doc. 560; 1107–10, Doc. 567; Yaqub, *Containing Arab Nationalism*, 109.
93. *FRUS 1955–1957*, XVI, 1158–59, Doc. 591.
94. Ibid., 1338–44, Doc. 669.
95. Aridan, *Advocating for Israel*, 140–41.
96. Hahn, *Caught in Middle East*, 211; Rabbi Jerome Unger to Local Committees of AZC, Feb. 8, 1957; "Congressional Reaction to Sanctions and Withdrawal from Gaza and Gulf of Aqaba," undated, both in KP, Box 15.
97. Olivia Sohns, "The Future Foretold: Lyndon Baines Johnson's Congressional Support for Israel," *Diplomacy & Statecraft* 28 (2017): 60.
98. Johnson to Dulles, Feb. 11, 1957, AWF, Dulles-Herter Series, Box 8; Sohns, "The Future Foretold," 57–84.
99. "The American Israel Public Affairs Committee from 1955 Until 1968," Kenen Papers, Box 20.
100. *FRUS 1955–1957*, XVI, 1230–31, Doc. 627; 1341–44, Doc. 671; 107, Doc.45; Hahn, Caught in Middle East, 215; Kenen, *Israel's Defense Line*, 136.
101. Ibid., Document 636, 1244–48.
102. *FRUS 1955–1957, Arab-Israeli Dispute, 1957, XVII*. Washington: GPO, 1990: 625, Doc. 332; 681–94, Docs. 352–57; Doc. 78; "Memorandum of Conversation with the Counselors to King Saud," Feb. 1, 1957, Dulles Chronological Series, Box 14.
103. Jacob Katzman, "Why Israel Withdrew," Mar. 11, 1957, Kenen Papers, Box 15.
104. *FRUS 1958–1960, XII, Near East Region; Iraq; Iran; Arabian Peninsula*. Washington: GPO, 1993: 98, Doc. 30.
105. Yaqub, *Containing Arab Nationalism*, 269–71.
106. *FRUS 1955–1957*, XVII, 837–38, Doc. 417.
107. Ibid.
108. Hahn, *Caught in Middle East*, 232.
109. Rogan, *The Arabs*, 246, 392; Wilford, *America's Great Game*, 268–69, 288.
110. Maurice Labelle, "A New Age of Empire? Arab 'Anti-Americanism,' US Intervention, and the Lebanese Civil War of 1958," *International History Review* 35, 1 (March 2013): 42–69.
111. Shlaim, *Iron Wall*, 203; *FRUS 1955–1957, Arab-Israeli Dispute, 1957, XVII*, 728, Doc. 371; 828–30, Doc. 414.
112. *FRUS 1958–1960, Arab-Israeli Dispute; United Arab Republic; North Africa, XIII*. Washington: GPO, 1992: 95–96, Doc. 39.
113. Kenen to Larry Laskey, Feb. 6, 1957; Kenen to Laskey, Jan. 9, 1958, both in KP, Box 13.
114. Kenen to Laskey, Jan. 9, 1958.
115. Kenen to Larry Laskey, May 31, 1957; Kenen to Laskey, Dec. 6, 1957, both in KP, Box 13; Kenen, "ACZPA letter, Confidential – Not for Publication," May 7, 1959, KP, Box 2.
116. Kenen to Laskey, Dec. 6, 1957; Kenen to Laskey, Jan. 2, 1958, both in KP, Box 13; Kenen, "ACZPA letter, Confidential – Not for Publication," May 7, 1959, KP, Box 2.

117. Kenen to Laskey, Dec. 6, 1957; Kenen to Laskey, Jan. 9, 1958.
118. "Arab Blacklist," *NER VI* (June 19, 192): 49; "Nasser Rebuffed US Peace Bid," *NER VI* (Sept. 25, 1962): 77; "Wheat, Cotton and MIGS," *NER VI* (Nov. 20, 1962): 94.
119. Ibid.; Kenen to Larry Laskey, Dec. 6 1957, KP, Box 13.
120. Ibid., 8–15, Doc. 4; 168–69, Doc. 75.
121. Kenen, "Memorandum for Rabbi Philip S. Bernstein," Aug. 29, 1957, KP, Box 7.
122. "Dear Friends," Mar. 27, 1959, Box 2; Kenen to Rep. Laurence Curtis, May 7, 1959, Box 2; Kenen, "ACZPA letter, Confidential – Not for Publication," May 7, 1959, all in KP, Box 2.
123. Kenen to Eban, Aug. 1, 1960; Kenen, *Israel's Defense Line*, 148–53.
124. *FRUS 1958–1960, XII*, 98, Doc. 30; *FRUS 1955–1957, XVII*, 832, Doc. 415.
125. *FRUS 1955–1957, XVII*, 832, Doc. 415.

"WHAT KIND OF RELATIONSHIP WAS THIS?"

1. "The American Israel Public Affairs Committee from 1955 Until 1968," KP, Box 20.
2. "The American Israel Public Affairs Committee from 1955 Until 1968," Box 20; Kenen to Marver Bernstein, Nov. 8, 1960, Box 11, both in KP.
3. Kenen to Philip Bernstein, January 1961, KP, Box 7.
4. Hirsh Freed, recorded interview by Ed Martin, June 5, 1964, 1–20, John F. Kennedy Library Oral History Program (JFK OHP); Lewis H. Weinstein, recorded interview by Sheldon Stern, June 3, 1982, 10, JFK OHP; See also Weinstein, "John F. Kennedy: A Personal Memoir, 1946–1963," *American Jewish History* 75 (September 1985): 5–30.
5. Kenen to Lipsky, Nov. 10, 1952, KP, Box 5.
6. Weinstein to Kenen, Apr. 6, 1959, KP, Box 2; "Speech of February 24, 1952," Congressman John F. Kennedy, Hirsh Freed Papers, 1952, Box 1, JFK Library, Boston.
7. Kenen to Philip Bernstein, January 1961, KP, Box 7; JFK to Dulles, Feb. 11, 1957, KP, Box 13.
8. John F. Kennedy, "Israel – A Miracle of Promise, "Sept. 28, 1958, before Golden Jubilee Banquet of B'nai Zion, New York City"; JFK, "Israel – A Land of Paradoxes," Oct. 1, 1959, Temple B'rith Kodesh Temple Club, Rochester, N.Y; JFK speech before Zionist Organization of America, New York, "American Leadership for Peace in the Middle East," Aug. 26, 1960, all in The Papers of President Kennedy, Pre-Presidential Papers, Box 1030, JFK Library.
9. Kenen to Bernstein, January 1961, KP, Box 7.
10. Myer Feldman, recorded interview by John Stewart, August 26, 1967, 560, JFK OHP.
11. "Remarks by Myer Feldman at meeting of the American Israel Public Affairs Committee and the Jewish Community Council of Greater Washington,"

May 5, 1963, Myer Feldman Personal Papers, Box 29, JFK Library; Feldman interview by John F. Stewart, Dec. 11, 1966, 474–75, JFK OHP.

12. *FRUS 1961–1963, XVIII, Near East*. Washington: USGPO, 1995: 59–61, Docs. 20–21; 526–27, Doc. 244.

13. Memorandum for President, "Your Meeting with Israel Prime Minister Ben-Gurion," May 25, 1961; State Department, "Talking Outline for Subjects to be Raised by the President," both in President's Office Files; Israel, General, 1961–1963, Papers of President Kennedy, Box 119A, JFK Library.

14. "Background: David Ben-Gurion," January 1961 to May 1961, President's Office Files; Israel, Security 1961–1963, Kennedy Papers, Box 119A; CIA Memorandum, "Prime Minister Ben-Gurion's Resignation," Feb. 7, 1961, Kennedy Papers, National Security Files, Countries, Israel, Box 118, JFK Library.

15. News accounts of Ben-Gurion speech, Dec. 28, 1960, in "Israel; Ben-Gurion," Box 501, The Papers of Emanuel Celler, Library of Congress (LOC).

16. Elmer Berger to President of United States, May 23, 1961, Papers of John F. Kennedy, White House Central Files, Subject File, Israel, Box 60, JFK Library; Feldman, "Issues Affecting Jewish Community in New York State," undated, Feldman Papers, Box 56.

17. Kenen to Bernstein, January 1961, KP, Box 7.

18. David Ben-Gurion, recorded interview by E. A. Bayne, July 16, 1965, 1–3, JFK OHP.

19. *FRUS 1961–1963, XVII, Near East*. Washington: USGPO, 1994: 712–15, Doc. 290.

20. William Brubeck to McGeorge Bundy, May 29, 1962, Kennedy Papers, Box 118.

21. *FRUS 1961–1963, XVII*, 715–18, Doc. 290.

22. *FRUS 1958–1960, XIII, Arab-Israeli Dispute; United Arab Republic; North Africa*. Washington: USGPO, 1992: 65–66, Doc. 27; 151, Doc. 67; Department of State Circular, July 12, 1962, Kennedy Papers, Box 118 A.

23. *FRUS 1958–1960, XIII*, 148, Doc. 65; 20–23, Doc. 8; *FRUS 1951, V*, 575–76, Doc. 611.84A/2–651; William Brubeck to McGeorge Bundy, May 31, 1962, Kennedy Papers, Box 118; *FRUS 1961–1963, XVII*, 688–91, Doc. 281; 738, Doc. 301; *FRUS 1964–1968, XVIII, Arab-Israeli Dispute, 1964–1967*. Washington: US GPO, 2000, 231, Doc. 102; Robert Komer, "Memorandum for the Record" Aug. 28, 1963, Kennedy Papers, Box 119A.

24. *FRUS 1955–1957, XVII*, 772, Doc. 388; 779 Doc. 391; 831–32, Doc. 415.

25. Feldman, "Issues Affecting the Jewish Community in New York State," undated, Feldman Papers, Box 56; Damascus to Rusk, Aug. 20, 1963, Kennedy Papers, Box 119A.

26. *FRUS 1961–1963, XVII*, 534–64, Doc. 216–229; 676–77, Doc. 275; *FRUS 1961–1963, XVIII*, 769, Doc. 353; 374, Doc. 168; Zeev Maoz, *Defending the Holy Land: A Critical Analysis of Israel's Security and Foreign Policy*. Ann Arbor: University of Michigan Press, 2009: 240.

27. UN Security Council Resolution 171 (April 9, 1962). http://unscr.com/en/r esolutions/171
28. "Was This Vote Necessary?" *NER, VI* (April 24, 1962): 33.
29. *FRUS 1961–1963, XVII,* 150, Doc. 60; Myer Feldman recorded interview by John F. Stewart, Dec. 11, 1966, 470–71, JFK OHP.
30. *FRUS 1961–1963, XVII,* 737, Doc. 300.
31. "Statement by Ambassador Adlai Stevenson on the Lake Tiberius Incident," undated, Feldman Papers, Box 55; Stevenson to Department of State, June 1, 1962, Kennedy Papers, Box 118 A.
32. Jacob K. Javits, "What Is the US Policy in the Near East?" *Congress Bi-Weekly: A Review of Jewish Interests,"* May 14, 1962, Feldman Papers, Box 55; Javits speech Monitcello, New York, June 3, 1962, "Subject File-Israel," Box 502, Celler Papers.
33. Hubert Humphrey to Dean Rusk, undated, Feldman Papers, Box 55; "News Release, Celler calls for Strong Stand Against Syrian War," "Subject File-Israel," Box 502, Celler Papers.
34. Javits speech Monticello, NY; Seymour Halpern to Dean Rusk, June 29, 1961; Seymour Halpern to John F. Kennedy, Feb. 9, 1962, in "Israel, 1963," Feldman Papers, Box 56.
35. Feldman to Emanuel Celler, June 12, 1962, in "Israel, 1963," Box 56, Feldman Papers.
36. *NER V* ("Has There Been a Change?" Sept. 1, 1961): 30–31.
37. Feldman to Celler, June 12, 1962; Louis Caplan to Feldman, May 1, 1962; and Abba Schwartz to Feldman, April 26, 1962, all in "Israel, 1963," Box 56, Feldman Papers; Feldman OHP (Dec. 11, 1966): 472–73.
38. Robert W. Komer recorded interview by Dennis J. O'Brien, Dec. 22, 1969, 77, JFK OHP.
39. Feldman to McGeorge Bundy, May 18, 1962; Brubeck to McGeorge Bundy, May 14, 1962; William Bundy memorandum for Phillips Talbot, May 23, 1962, all in Kennedy Papers, Box 118.
40. Robert Komer, Memorandum for President, Aug. 14, 1962, Box 119A, Kennedy Papers.
41. JFK to Ben-Gurion, Aug. 15, 1962, Kennedy Papers, Box 118A.
42. Walworth Barbour to Dean Rusk, Dec. 13, 1962; Barbour to Rusk, Dec. 14, 1962, both in Kennedy Papers, Box 119.
43. Phillips Talbot to Dean Rusk, Dec. 4, 1962, Kennedy Papers, Box 119A.
44. *FRUS 1958–1960, XIII,* 141, Doc. 61.
45. Ibid., 292, Doc. 133.
46. *FRUS 1961–1963, XVII,* 95, Doc. 39; 145–47, Doc. 59; 670, Doc. 272.
47. *FRUS 1961–1963, XVII,* 763, Doc. 314; *FRUS 1961–1963, XVIII,* 34, Doc. 15.
48. *FRUS 1958–1960, XIII,* 300–2, Doc.138; 335, Doc. 152.
49. *FRUS 1961–1963, XVIII,* 35, Doc. 15; Adlai Stevenson to Dean Rusk, Sept. 21, 1962, Kennedy Papers, Box 118A.
50. *FRUS 1961–1963, XVIII,* 27–47, Docs. 14–15; *FRUS 1961–1963, XVII,* 763, Doc. 314.
51. *FRUS 1961–1963, XVIII,* 33, Doc. 14.

52. Ibid., 56–57, Doc. 19.
53. *FRUS 1961–1963, XVII*, 193–94, Doc. 387.
54. *FRUS 1958–1960, XIII*, 337–49, Docs. 153–56.
55. *FRUS 1961–1963, XVII*, 747, Doc. 306; 716, Doc. 290.
56. Feldman interview by John F. Stewart, July 29, 1967, 540–46, JFK OHP.
57. Ibid., 537; Feldman Memorandum to President, Aug. 10, 1962, Kennedy Papers, Box 118A; William Brubeck to Robert Komer and Myer Feldman, Sept. 22, 1962, Kennedy Papers, Box 119.
58. *FRUS 1961–1963, XVIII*, 67, Doc. 25.
59. Feldman, OHI (July 29, 1967); 415–17 (Dec. 11, 1966), both in JFK OHP; Feldman to Rusk, Aug. 19, 1962; Feldman Memorandum to President, Aug. 10, 1962, both in Kennedy Papers, Box 118A.
60. Ben-Gurion to JFK, Aug. 20, 1962, President's Office Files, Israel, Security, 1961–1963; Ben-Gurion to Avraham Harman, Sept. 17, 1962, both in Kennedy Papers, Box 119A.
61. Myer Feldman to Secretary of State, Sept. 20, 1962; Feldman to Dean Rusk, Aug. 21, 1962, both in Kennedy Papers, Box 118A; Feldman OHI, 421–22.
62. *FRUS 1961–1963, XVIII*, 73, Doc. 30; 112–16, Doc. 48; 146, Doc. 62.
63. *FRUS 1961–1963, XVIII*, 122–23, Doc. 52; 76, Doc. 31; 89, Doc. 36.
64. Ibid., 148, Doc. 62; 119, Doc. 50.
65. Ibid., 96, Doc. 41; 151–52, Doc. 64; Feldman, "Memorandum for the President," Nov. 27, 1962; Feldman, "The Johnson Plan," Sept. 25, 1962, both in Feldman Papers, Box 55; Talbot OHI, 26–27.
66. *FRUS 1961–1963, XVIII*, 336, Doc. 150; 255, Doc. 99.
67. Ibid., 97, Doc. 41; 126, Doc. 54; 256, Doc. 109.
68. Ibid., 123, Doc. 52; 272, Doc. 118; 318, Doc. 139; 336–37, Doc. 150.
69. William Brubeck to McGeorge Bundy, "President's Meeting with Israel Foreign Minister: Briefing Materials," Dec. 21, 1962, Kennedy Papers, Box 119.
70. *FRUS 1961–1963, XVIII*, 280–82, Doc. 121; "Conversation with Israel Foreign Minister Meir," Dec. 27, 1962, Kennedy Papers, Box 119.
71. Walworth Barbour to Dean Rusk, Oct. 16, 1962, Kennedy Papers, Box 119; "Foreign Radio and Press Reaction to US Decision to Sell Missiles to Israel," Oct. 1, 1962; John Badeau to Dean Rusk, Sept. 29, 1962, both in Kennedy Papers, Box 118 A.
72. *FRUS 1961–1963, XVII*, Document 42, 100; Feldman JFK OHI, 421.
73. John S. Badeau interview by Dennis J. O'Brien, February 25, 1969, 11, JFK OHP.
74. Roger Seely, Foreign Broadcast Information Service, "FBIS Impressions of Egyptian Anti-Israeli Propaganda During 1962," Jan. 3, 1963, "Israel, 1963," Feldman Papers, Box 55.
75. *FRUS 1961–1963, XVIII*, 267–68, Doc. 115; 311, Doc. 136; 367, Doc. 166.
76. *FRUS 1961–1963, XVII*, 658, Doc. 264.
77. Ibid., 93, Doc. 39; Ben-Gurion to Kennedy, May 12, 1963, Kennedy Papers, Box 119A.
78. Komer, JFK OHI, 75; Badeau JFK OHI, 14–15.

79. "US Security Guarantee to Israel," May 8, 1963, Kennedy Papers, Box 119; Memorandum for the President," April 26, 1963, Feldman Papers, Box 55.
80. *FRUS 1961–1963, XVII*, 668, Doc. 271.
81. Rogan, *The Arabs*, 416–18; Warren Bass, *Support Any Friend: Kennedy's Middle East and the Making of the US-Israel Alliance*. New York: Oxford University Press, 2003: 98–143.
82. Kenen, "Analysis of American Policy in the Middle East Since 1960," undated, KP, Box 8; "The American Israel Public Affairs Committee from 1955 Until 1968," KP, Box 20.
83. "The Implications for Israel of the Arab Unity Proclamation of April 17" [1963], Kennedy Papers, Box 119.
84. Robert Strong, "Objectives of Israel and American Zionists in 1963-64," May 7, 1963, Kennedy Papers, Box 119; Myer Feldman to Emanuel Celler, July 12, 1963, Celler Papers, Box 502.
85. Gruening, *Congressional Record, Senate*, May 12, 1963, Feldman Papers, Box 56; Kenen to Executive, National and Local Committees, Nov. 8, 1963, KP, Box 10.
86. Leonard Farbstein press release, "Israel, 1963," Feldman Papers, Box 55; *FRUS 1961–1963, XVIII*, 2–5, Doc. 2.
87. "Memorandum for the President," April 26, 1963, "Israel, 1963," Feldman Papers, Box 55.
88. *FRUS 1961–1963, XVIII*, 505–6, Doc. 231.
89 *FRUS Vol XVIII*, Doc. 244.
90. *FRUS 1961–1963, XVIII*, 536–37, Doc. 248; 798–99, Doc. 368.
91. Kenen to Bernstein, June 19, 1961, KP, Box 7.
92. J. W. Fulbright to The President, Sept. 29, 1962, Kennedy Papers, White House Central Files, "Subject File-Israel," Box 60.
93. See analysis and transcripts of the Fulbright hearings in Smith, *Foreign Agents*, 19–65; www.israellobby.org/JA-AZC/default.asp
94. "1951-1964 Lobbying Disclosures, AZC, AZCPA, AIPAC," Israel Lobby Archive: www.israellobby.org/AZCPA/
95. Ibid.
96. Feldman, "Memorandum for the President," April 26, 1963, "Israel, 1963," Feldman Papers, Box 55.
97. Berger, "Zionist 'Agents' in the United States," speech to ACJ New York chapter, June 1963, ACJ Papers, Box 1.
98. Randall Bennett Woods, *Fulbright: A Biography*. New York: Cambridge University Press, 1995: 309–11.
99. "No Sensations," *NER, VII* (August 13, 1963): 70–71.
100. Bernstein to Kenen, May 28, 1965, KP, Box 7.
101. Woods, *Fulbright*, 670–72.
102. *FRUS 1958–1960, XIII*, 393, Doc. 178.
103. Ibid., 398, Doc. 180
104. Ibid., 391–93, Docs. 177–78; 400, Doc. 181
105. *FRUS 1961–1963, XVII*, 4–5, Doc. 3; 36, Doc. 15.
106. Recently declassified documents have illuminated the previously secreted history of Israel's drive to obtain the bomb. See Avner Cohen and William Burr,

"How Israel Hid Its Secret Nuclear Weapons Program," *Politico*, April 15, 2015, www.politico.com/magazine/story/2015/04/israel-nuclear-wea pons-117014?o=1. See also "Concerned About Nuclear Weapons Potential, John F. Kennedy Pushed for Inspection of Israel Nuclear Facilities," The National Security Archive, George Washington University. http://nsarchive.gwu.edu/nukevault/ebb547-Kennedy-Dimon a-and-the-Nuclear-Proliferation-Problem-1961-1962/. See also two books by Cohen, *Israel and the Bomb*. New York: Columbia University Press, 1998; and *The Worst-Kept Secret: Israel's Bargain with the Bomb*. New York: Columbia University Press, 2010.

107. Memorandum for the President, Jan. 30, 1961; Dean Rusk Memorandum for President, "Israel Reactor," Feb. 8, 1961; G. Lewis, Memorandum of Conversation with Avraham Harman, Feb. 3, 1961, all in Kennedy Papers, Box 119A.

108. *FRUS 1961–1963*, XVII, 9, Doc. 5; 14, Doc. 7; 29, Doc. 12; 134–41, Doc. 57; Walworth Barbour, interview by Sheldon M. Stern, May 22, 1981, 1–3, JFK OHP.

109. William Brubeck to McGeorge Bundy, undated; Tel Aviv to Department of State, June 4, 1961, both in Kennedy Papers, Box 118.

110. Phillips Talbot, "Telephone Conversations with Mr. Feldman of the White House," April 5, 1963, Kennedy Papers, Box 119A.

111. *FRUS 1961–1963*, XVII, 283, Doc. 120.

112. *FRUS 1961–1963*, XVIII, 398–99, Doc. 179.

113. Phillips Talbot to Dean Rusk, May 14, 1963, Kennedy Papers, Box 119; "The Advanced Weapons Programs of the UAR and Israel," May 8, 1963, Feldman Papers, Box 55.

114. *FRUS 1961–63 XVII*, 435, Doc. 199.

115. "President's Office Files; Israel, Security, Arms Control, 1961-1963," Kennedy Papers, Box 119A.

116. Walworth Barbour to Dean Rusk, May 16, 1963, Kennedy Papers, Box 119A.

117. *FRUS 1961–1963*, XVIII, 659–60, Doc. 303; 127, Doc. 55; 612–14, Doc. 283.

118. *FRUS 1961–1963*, XVIII, 543, Doc. 252; 558, Doc. 258; 576, Doc. 267; 592–93, Doc. 274; Kennedy to Ben-Gurion, June 15, 63, Kennedy Papers, Box 119A.

119. Barbour to Rusk, Aug. 19, 1963, Kennedy Papers; Kennedy to Eshkol, Aug. 26, 1963, both in Box 119A.

120. *FRUS 1961–1963*, XVIII, 525, Doc. 243; 1–2, Docs. 1–2; 651, Doc. 300.

121. Ibid., 590, Doc. 273; 720–22, Doc. 332; 536, Doc. 248; 780–81, Doc. 360; 667, Doc. 308; JFK to Levi Eshkol, Oct. 2, 1963, Kennedy Papers, Box 119A; JFK to Emanuel Celler, Jan. 15, 1963, Feldman Papers, Box 56.

122. Memorandum of Conversation, Israel's Security, Oct. 31, 1963, Kennedy Papers, Box 119A.

123. Shlaim, *The Iron Wall*, 224.

"THE BEST FRIEND THAT ISRAEL COULD HAVE"

1. "To the Executive and National Committee from I. L. Kenen, Not for Publication or Circulation," Nov. 26, 1963, Feldman Papers, Box 93; Sohns, "The Future Foretold," 60.
2. Ibid.
3. Johnson, April 23, 1958, *Congressional Record* 8th Cong., 2nd session, 3; Kenen, *Israel's Defense Line*, 134–37; Woods, *Fulbright*, 311.
4. George R. Davis to Jackie Lee Pruett, April 30, 1974, "Religion of President Johnson," Papers of LBJ, President, 1963–69 (Johnson Papers), Lyndon Baines Johnson Presidential Library, Austin, TX. (LBJL), Box 6; Oren, *Power, Faith, and Fantasy*, 523.
5. Billy Graham Oral History Interview (telephone) by Monroe Billington, Oct. 12, 1983, 2, LBJL.
6. Johnson to King Hussein Jan. 2, 1964 *Foreign Relations of the United States (FRUS) 1964 to 1968, XVII, Arab-Israeli Dispute 1964 to 1967.* Washington: USGPO, 2000: Doc. 2.
7. Horace Busby to John Bird, May 19, 1964, "Religion of President Johnson"; George R. Davis Oral History Interview, Feb. 13, 1969 by Dorothy Price, 10, LBJL.
8. LBJ to Rev. Canon Bayard Clark, July 10, 1964, "Religion of President Johnson."
9. Jessie Hatcher Oral History Interview, Mar. 28, 1968 by Paul Bolton, San Saba, TX, 38–39, LBJL; Graham interview, 6.
10. National Security File (NSF), Country File, Israel, Johnson Papers, Box 144.
11. Lyndon B. Johnson, *The Vantage Point: Perspectives on the Presidency, 1963–1969.* New York: Holt, Rinehart, and Winston, 1971: 297; Johnson, "Weizmann Institute Dinner speech," Feb. 6, 1964, Feldman, Papers, Box 90.
12. Harry McPherson, Interview III, by T. H. Baker, Jan. 16, 1969, Washington DC, 24–25, LBJL.
13. President Johnson Retains Mike Feldman," *Steel and Garnet* (January 1964), "Girard College," Feldman Papers, Box 34; *FRUS 1964–1968, XVIII, Arab-Israeli Dispute, 1964–1967,* Doc. 65; Feldman, "Issues Affecting Jewish Community in New York State," undated; Feldman, "Memorandum for the President, Meeting with Secretary McNamara," Dec. 6, 1963, both in Feldman Papers, Box 56.
14. Feldman, Memorandum for the President, "Tanks for Israel," May 11, 1964, Feldman Papers, Box 55; "Memorandum of Conversation," May 17, 1964; "Mission to Israel, May 1964," both in Feldman Papers, Box 64.
15. *FRUS 1964–1968, XVIII,* 152–59, Doc. 65; *NER,* X (Aug. 9, 1966): 61.
16. "Arab Propaganda ... Line and Apparatus," *NER Special Supplement* (October 1964): B1–30; see also "The Arab Boycott Involves Americans," *NER Special Supplement* (May 1965): B 1–28.
17. *FRUS 1964–1968, XVIII,* 152–59, Doc. 65; "Comments on Memorandum of Conversation on June 1 between President Johnson and Prime Minister Eshkol," June 1964, Feldman Papers, Box 58.

18. "Democratic Plank on Near East," *NER VIII* (Aug. 25, 1964): 69–71; "Disappointing GOP Plank," *NER VIII* (July 14, 1964): 57)

19. *FRUS 1964–1968*, *XVIII*, 17–23, Doc. 9; 43, Doc. 18; 100, Doc. 41; Benjamin Read to McGeorge Bundy, Nov. 5, 1963, Kennedy Papers, Box 119A.

20. *FRUS 1964–1968*, *XVIII*, 100, Doc. 41; 45–46, Doc. 20; 59, Doc. 25.

21. William J. Burns, *Economic Aid and American Policy toward Egypt, 1955–1981*. Albany: State University of New York Press, 1985: 150.

22. *FRUS 1961–1963*, *XVII*, 669, Doc. 272; *FRUS 1964–1968*, *XVIII*, 89, Doc. 38; Shlaim, *Iron Wall*, 241.

23. Paul Thomas Chamberlin, *The Global Offensive: The United States, the Palestine Liberation Organization, and the Making of the Post-Cold War Order*. New York: Oxford University Press, 2012: 1–13.

24. Rogan, *The Arabs*, 432–43; Shlaim, *The Iron Wall*, 242–48; Farsoun and Zacharia, *Palestine and the Palestinians*, 123–212;

25. *FRUS 1961–1963*, *XVIII*, 277, Doc. 121; 128, Doc. 55.

26. Walworth Barbour, "Israel's Security: The Concept of Preventative War and Definitive Victory," Oct. 5, 1962, Kennedy Papers, Box 119.

27. Charles D. Smith, *Palestine and the Arab-Israeli Conflict: A History with Documents*. Boston: Bedford/St. Martin's, 2013: 275.

28. *FRUS 1961–1963*, *XVIII*, 496, Doc. 228

29. *FRUS 1961–1963*, *XVIII*, 504–5, Doc. 230.

30. *FRUS 1964–1968*, *XVIII*, 274, Doc. 124; 284–86, Doc. 129.

31. Ibid., 313, Doc. 140; 343–46, Doc. 157.

32. Tom Segev, *1967: Israel, the War, and the Year That Transformed the Middle East*. New York: Henry Holt and Co., 2005: 302.

33. Feinberg-Johnson Telephone Conversation, Feb. 20, 1965, Tape 6861, 6502.04, PNO 10, The Miller Center (University of Virginia).

34. Ibid.

35. *FRUS 1964–1968*, *XVIII*, 232–34, Doc. 102.

36. Ibid., 407, Doc. 190.

37. *FRUS 1961–1963*, *XVIII*, 497, Doc. 228.

38. ACJ *Information Bulletin* 7 (October 1966), AJHC, Box 2.

39. *FRUS 1964–1968*, *XVIII*, 393, Doc. 182; 548, Doc. 268.

40. Ibid., 334, Doc. 152; 459–60, Doc. 216.

41. "Text of Address by I. L. Kenen," National Convention of Hadassah, Aug. 15, 1966, KP, Box 19.

42. Rusk-Johnson Telephone Conversation, Feb. 28, 1965, Tape 6898, WH6502.06, PNO 17, Miller Center.

43. Feinberg–Johnson, Feb. 20, 1965.

44. "Far Beyond the Call of Appeasement," *NER IX* (Feb. 23, 1965): 14.

45. David Rodman, "Armored Breakthrough: The 1965 American Sale of Tanks to Israel," *Middle East Review of International Affairs* 8 (2004). Rubin Center research in International Affairs: www.rubincenter.org/2004/06/rodman-2004-06-01/

46. Kenen to Celler, Feb. 11, 1966, "Subject File-Israel," Celler Papers, Box 504.

47. Celler to Rusk, Jan. 26, 1966, "Subject File-Israel," Celler Papers, Box 504; "Capitol Hill Asks About Arms," *NER X* (Feb. 8, 1966): 10.

48. *FRUS 1964–1968, XVIII*, 21, Doc. 9; Charles D. Smith, "The United States and the 1967 War," in Shlaim and Louis, *The 1967 Arab-Israeli War: Origins and Consequences*. New York: Cambridge University Press, 2012: 167.

49. Aridan, *Advocating for Israel*, 231; "To Deter Attack," *NER X* (May 17, 1966): 41.

50. Rostow to President, May 21, 1966, Confidential File Name File DEL, Folder FE, Johnson Papers, Box 145.

51. April 1, 66. "Memorandum for Bill Moyers," Saunders Memorandums, NSF Name File, LBJL, Box 7.

52. Tarlov-Johnson Telephone Conversation, Sept. 10, 1966, Tape 10741 WH6609.05 PNO 3, Miller Center; McPherson interview, 27.

53. "Memorandum to the President," May 31, 1967, "The President's Appointment File [Diary backup]," LBJL, Box 67.

54. "Jewish War Veteran Leader Issues Statement on Talk with Johnson," Sept. 12, 1966, *J. A. Daily News Bulletin*, Johnson Papers, Box 6.

55. Tarlov–Johnson Telephone Conversation, Sept. 10, 1966, Tape 10741, The Miller Center (University of Virgina).

56. "Regrettable and Unnecessary," *NER X* (Sept. 20, 1966): 74–75.

57. Feinberg to Philip Klutznick, Sept. 21, 1966, Johnson Papers, Box 6.

58. Marvin Watson to LBJ, Sept. 28, 1966, Johnson Papers, Box 6.

59. Both letter and report "US Help for Israel, 1964–1966," in NSF, Country File, Israel, Johnson Papers, Box 139; Marvin Watson to Feinberg, June 27, 1966, White House Central File, Name File, Feinberg, Abraham, LBJL, Box 47.

60. "US Help for Israel, 1964–1966"; Rostow to Johnson, Dec. 19, 1966, NSF, Country File, Israel, Johnson Papers, Box 140; "Perceptive Understanding," *NER X* (July 12, 1966): 53.

61. *FRUS 1964–1968, XVIII*, 774, Doc. 395; 736–37, Doc. 377.

62. Ibid., 766, Doc. 391; "Israel's Quest for Yellowcake: The Secret Argentine-Israeli Connection, 1963–1966," National Security Archive, June 25, 2013: https://nsarchive2.gwu.edu/nukevault/ebb432/

63. *FRUS 1964–1968, XVIII*, 369, Doc. 170.

64. Ibid., 398–99, Doc. 185; 565, Doc. 279; 454–64, Docs. 214–18; 550, Doc. 269.

65. Ibid., 549–53, Docs. 269–71.

66. Ibid., 589, Doc. 294; 616, Doc. 308.

67. Ibid., 622–23, Doc. 312.

68. *FRUS 1964–1968, XVIII*, 583, Doc. 289; 796–97, Doc. 407; 815, Doc. 415.

69. Rostow to Johnson, undated, Central Foreign Policy Files, 1967–1969 Political and Defense, Record Group 59, General Records of the Department of State (RG 59), Box 1557.

70. RAND, "Proposal to Office of Saline Water," April 30, 1964, Oct. 26, 1964 news release, Feldman Papers, Box 56; Zach Levey, "The United States, Israel, and Nuclear Desalination: 1944–1968," *Diplomatic History* 39 (November 2015): 924.

71. *FRUS 1964–1968, XVIII*, 402, Doc. 187; 285, Doc. 129.

72. Ibid., 325, Doc. 147; Shlaim, *The Iron Wall*, 244–51.

73. Shlaim, *The Iron Wall*, 252.
74. *FRUS 1964–1968, XVIII*, 465, Doc. 219.
75. Smith, *Palestine and the Arab-Israeli Conflict*, 273.
76. *FRUS 1964–1968, XVIII*, 465, Doc. 219; 477–78, Doc. 227.
77. Smith, *Palestine and Arab-Israeli Conflict*, 273–74.
78. *FRUS 1964–1968, XVIII*, 658–700, Docs. 333–56; Smith, *Palestine and Arab-Israeli Conflict*, 274; Shlaim, *Iron Wall*, 248–49.
79. *FRUS 1964–1968, XVIII*, 713, Doc. 364; 666–68, Doc. 338.
80. Clea Lutz Bunch, "Strike at Samu: Jordan, Israel, the United States, and the Origins of the Six-Day War," *Diplomatic History* 32 (January 2008): 75.
81. *FRUS 1964–1968, XVIII*, 667, Doc. 338, 658–60, Doc. 333; Rostow to Johnson, Dec. 13, 1966, NSF, Country File, Israel, Johnson Papers, Box 140.
82. Rostow Memorandum to President, Nov. 15, 1966, NSF, Country File, Israel, Johnson Papers, Box 140.
83. Department of State Airgram Embassy Tel Aviv to State, "Yigal Allon on Security," Feb. 10, 1967, Central Foreign Policy Files, Political and Defense, RG 59, Box 2228.
84. Rostow to Johnson, May 17, 1967, NSF Name File, Box 7; Saunders to Rostow, Nov. 19, 1966, NSF, Country File, Israel, Box 140, both in Johnson Papers.
85. *FRUS 1964–1968, XVIII*, 693–94, Doc. 353.
86. Ibid., 659, Doc. 333
87. Ibid., 663–64, Docs. 336.
88. "Unjust and Unwise," *NER X* (Nov. 19, 1966): 93–94.
89. *FRUS 1964–1968, XVIII*, 707–9, Doc. 362.
90. Ibid., 696–97, Doc. 355; 705–7, Docs. 360–61.
91. Rostow to LBJ. Dec. 8, 1966, NSF, Country File, Israel, Johnson Papers, Box 139.
92. Robert Komer to LBJ, Dec. 9, 1966, NSF, Country File, Israel, Johnson Papers, Box 140.
93. *FRUS 1964–1968, XVIII*, 717, Doc. 366; 705, Doc. 360.
94. Ibid., 723, Doc. 369.
95. Ibid., 748–49, Doc. 383; 761–62, Doc. 389; 810–11, Doc. 413.
96. Ibid., 756–57, Doc. 387; 793, Doc. 405.
97. Ibid., 774–78, Docs. 395–97; 812–19, Docs. 414–16.
98. Ibid., 695–96, Doc. 354; see also Burns, *Economic Aid and American Policy toward Egypt*, 149–73.
99. *FRUS 1964–1968, XVIII*, 738–45, Docs. 378–81; 763–65, Doc. 390; "Food … For Peace or War," *NER X* (April 19, 1966): 31.
100. *FRUS 1964–1968, XVIII*, 739, Doc. 378.
101. Ibid., 763–65, Doc. 390.
102. *FRUS 1964–1968, XVIII*, 755, Doc. 386; 767, Doc. 392.
103. Ibid., 771–73, Doc. 394.
104. "Israel at 18: Partner in Progress: *A Supplement to the NER*," (May 1966), B-4.
105. *FRUS 1964–1968, XVIII*, 563, Doc. 277.
106. Ibid., 16–18, Doc. 12.

107. Shlaim, *The Iron Wall,* 235.
108. Ibid., 248–50.
109. *FRUS 1964–1968, XVIII,* 699, Doc. 356; 743, Docs. 380.
110. Ibid., 758–59, Doc. 388.
111. Shlaim, *The Iron Wall,* 249–51; *FRUS 1964–1968, XVIII,* 789–90, Doc. 402.
112. "A Decisive Air Battle," *NER XI* (April 18, 1967): 29.
113. *FRUS 1964–1968, XVII,* 792, Doc. 405.
114. Ibid., 4–5, Doc. 4; 10, Doc. 8; 19–21, Doc. 13; Segev, *1967,* 253.
115. *FRUS 1964–1968, XIX, Arab–Israeli Crisis and War, 1967.* Washington: USGPO, 2004: 6–7, Doc. 5.
116. Ibid., 64–68, Docs. 37–41; 75, Doc. 45; Smith, "United States and 1967 War," 170.
117. Rogan, *The Arabs,* 421.
118. "The Six-Day War: Statement by President Nasser to Arab Trade Unionists," May 26, 1967, Jewish Virtual Library: www.jewishvirtualli brary.org/statement-by-president-nasser-to-arab-trade-unionists-may-1967.
119. "Report by the Secretary-General," May 27, 1967, NSF, NSC Histories, May 12–June 19, 1967, LBJL, Box 17; Department of State "Memorandum for the White House," undated, NSF, Files of the Special Committee of the NSC, LBJL, Box 7.
120. Tommy Thompson to Walt Rostow, Middle East Crisis Files, June 16, 1967, "Memorandums to the President," NSF, LBJL, Box 17.
121. *FRUS 1964–1968, XIX,* 255, Doc. 134.
122. John Quigley, *The Six-Day War and Israeli Self-Defense: Questioning the Legal Basis for Preventative War.* New York: Cambridge University Press, 2013: 51.
123. Rostow to LBJ, May 30, 1967, "Memos to the President Walt Rostow," NSF, LBJL, Box 16, 2 of 2.
124. Segev, *1967,* 253–54.
125. Kenen, "War Notes," May 21, 1967, KP, Box 11; "AIPAC from 1955 Until 1968," KP, Box 20; Louis Grossberg to Rabbis, Presidents, Delegates, Committee members, Jewish Community Council of Greater Washington, May 23, 1967, Israel-Arab War [Six Day War], 1967, BBIA, Box D2–3.
126. National Security – Defense (Ex ND 19/CO 1-6), June 22, 1967, Johnson Papers, Box 194.
127. "Statement by the President on Rising Tensions in the Near East," May 23, 1967, The President's Appointment File [Diary backup], Johnson Papers, Box 67.
128. Rostow to LBJ, May 24, 1967, NSF "Memos to the President Walt Rostow," Box 16, 2 of 2; Children's letters from Hebrew schools, petitions, statements from synagogues, rabbis, and Jewish Community Centers nation-wide in National Security – Defense (Ex ND 19/CO 1-6) June 22, 1967, Johnson Papers, Box 194.
129. Embassy Amman to Secretary of State and White House, May 26, 1967, NSF, NSC Histories, May 12–June 19, 1967, LBJL Box 17.

130. "Statement by President Nasser to Arab Trade Unionists." www.sixdaywar
.co.uk/historical_documents.htm
131. *FRUS 1964–1968, XIX*, 80–81, Doc. 49; Rusk to Johnson, May 22, 1967,
NSF, NSC Histories, May 12–June 19, 1967, Box 17; "Statement by the
President on Rising Tensions in the Near East," May 23, 1967.
132. *FRUS 1964–1968, XIX*, 200–8, Docs. 108–13.
133. Barbour, Embassy Tel Aviv to Secretary of State, May 23, 1967, NSF, NSC
Histories, May 12–June 19, 67, LBJL, Box 17.
134. Rostow to LBJ, May 26, 1967, NSF "Memos to the President Walt
Rostow," Box 16, 2 of 2; Segev, *1967*, 265.
135. Memo for President May 26, 1967, NSF, NSC Histories, May 12–June 19,
1967; "Israeli-US Working Dinner," May 25, 1967, NSF, NSC Histories,
May 12–June 19, 1967, both in LBJL Box 17.
136. *FRUS 1964–1968, XIX*, 142–43, Doc. 77; see also Siniver, *Abba Eban*, 228–
33.
137. *FRUS 1964–1968, XIX*, 143, Doc. 77.
138. Ibid., 159–63, Docs. 84–86; Quigley, *The Six-Day War and Israeli Self-
Defense*, 35.
139. Shlaim, "Israel: Poor Little Samson," in Shlaim and Louis, eds., *The 1967
Arab-Israeli*, 32–36; Guy Laron, *The Six-Day War: The Breaking of the
Middle East.* New Haven and London: Yale University Press, 2017: 313; see
also Patrick Tyler, *Fortress Israel: The Inside Story of the Military Elite Who
Run the Country – And Why They Can't Make Peace.* New York: Farrar,
Strauss, and Giroux, 2012.
140. Shlaim, *The Iron Wall*, 254.
141. *FRUS 1964–1968, XIX*, 270, Doc. 143.

"LET THE ISRAELIS DO THIS JOB THEMSELVES"

1. "The Fruit of Appeasement," *NER XI* (May 29, 1967): 41–43.
2. *FRUS 1964–1968, XIX*, 219, Doc. 121.
3. Philip Bernstein to All US Senators, May 26, 1967; Javits statement, May 29,
1967, both in KP, Box 11.
4. William Macomber to Benjamin Read, May 26, 1967, Middle East Crisis
Files, 1967, Box 15; Javits to Lyndon Johnson, May 27, 1967, NSF "Memos
to the President," Walt Rostow, Box 16, 1 of 2.
5. Gruening statement, May 31, 1967, The President's Appointment File
[Diary backup], Box 67.
6. Secretary's Appearance before the SFRC, May 23, 1967, NSF, NSC
Histories, May 12–June 19, 1967, LBJL, Box 17.
7. *FRUS 1964–1968, XIX*, 249–50, Doc. 132.
8. Quigley, *Six-Day War and Israeli Self-Defense*, 35; "Memorandum from the
CIA's Board of National Estimates to Director of Central Intelligence
Helms," May 26, 1967, Country File Middle East Crisis Files, LBJL, Box
104; David S. Robarge, "CIA Analysis of the 1967 Arab-Israeli War," CIA
Library (online). https://www.cia.gov/library/center-for-the-study-of-intelli

gence/csi-publications/csi-studies/studies/vol49no1/html_files/arab_israeli_
war_1.html
9. *FRUS 1964–1968, XIX*, 215, Doc. 117.
10. Ibid., 210–11, Doc. 114.
11. Ibid., 266–69, Docs. 141–42; 238, Doc. 130; "Israel-Arab War" [Six Day
War], 1967, B'nai B'rith International Archives (BBIA), AJA, Box D2–3.
12. *FRUS 1964–1968, XIX*, 143.
13. Transcript, Arthur J. Goldberg Oral History Interview I, Washington, DC,
Mar. 23, 1983, by Ted Gittinger, LBJL, 13.
14. Segev, *1967*, 302, 382; Laura Kalman, *Abe Fortas: A Biography*. New
Haven: Yale University Press, 1990: 300–2.
15. NSC meeting May 24, 1967, NSF, NSC Meetings File, LBJL, Box 2.
16. *FRUS 1964–1968, XIX*, 224, Doc. 124; 262–64, Doc. 139.
17. Rostow to LBJ, June 2, 1967, NSF, NSC Histories, May 12–June 19, 1967,
LBJL, Box 18.
18. *FRUS 1964–1968, XIX*, 272, Doc. 144; 286, Doc. 148; Rostow to LBJ, June
2, 1967, Central Files, Political and Defense, RG 59, Box 2230.
19. Smith, "United States and 1967 War," 178.
20. *FRUS 1964–1968, XIX*, 317, Doc. 168n.
21. *FRUS 1964–1968, XIX*, 146–58, Docs. 78–83; 206–7, Doc. 112.
22. *FRUS 1964–1968, XIX*, 236, Doc. 129; 254–57, Doc. 134.
23. Ibid., 278, Doc. 145.
24. Ibid., 272, Doc. 143.
25. Ibid., 283, Doc. 147.
26. Ibid., 224, Doc. 124; Quigley, *Six-Day War and Israeli Self-Defense*, 128–
31.
27. Burns to Secretary, June 4, 1967, Middle East Crisis Files, 1967, Box 11.
28. As Charles D. Smith notes, "There were several flashing lights from persons
close to Johnson, none of them red." Smith, *Palestine and the Arab-Israeli
Conflict*, 176; see also Peter L. Hahn, "The Cold War and the Six Day War:
US Policy towards the Arab-Israel Crisis of June 1967," in Nigel J. Ashton,
ed., *The Cold War in the Middle East: Regional Conflict and the
Superpowers, 1967–1973*. New York: Routledge, 2007: 16–34; and
Patrick Tyler, *A World of Trouble: The White House and the Middle East
– from the Cold War to the War on Terror*. New York: Farrar, Strauss, and
Giroux, 2009: 64–106.
29. Memorandum to the President, May 31, 1967, The President's Appointment
File [Diary backup], LBJL, Box 67.
30. LBJ to Eshkol, May 31, 1967, NSF "Memos to the President Walt Rostow,"
LBJL, Box 16, 2 of 2.
31. May 31 Rostow to Johnson, NSF, NSC Council Histories, May 12–June 19,
1967, LBJL, Box 18.
32. Shlaim, "Israel: Poor Little Samson," 38. Smith's essay, "The United States
and the 1967 War" (165–91), offers a concise analysis of US policy. See also
Richard B. Parker, ed., *The Six-Day War: A Retrospective*. Gainesville:
University of Florida Press, 1996; Laron offers a well-researched international military history of the conflict in *The Six Day War: Breaking of the*

Middle East. The best legal analysis is Quigley, *Six-Day War and Israeli Self-Defense*; the classic work is Segev, 1967.

33. Shlaim, "Israel: Poor Little Samson," 41; Rogan, *The Arabs*, 419.
34. "Interview with Yitzhak Ya'akov" by Avner Cohen, 1999, History and Public Policy Program Digital archive, Cold War International History project, Woodrow Wilson Center, Washington. http://digitalarchive.wilsoncenter.or g/document/145093.pdf?v=9dda72621fa59085333af49cdadda1e7
35. Laron, *Six-Day War*, 293.
36. Ibid., 285.
37. Shlaim, *The Iron Wall*, 262; Avi Raz, *The Bride and the Dowry: Israel, Jordan, and the Palestinians in the Aftermath of the June 1967 War*. New Haven: Yale University Press, 2012: 1.
38. Johnson to Saunders, June 5, 1967 NSF, NSC Histories, May 12–June 19, 1967, LBJL, Box 18.
39. *FRUS 1964–1968, XIX*, 307.
40. Nigel J. Ashton, "For King and Country: Jack O'Connell, the CIA, and the Arab-Israeli Conflict, 1963–1971," *Diplomatic History* 36 (November 2012): 881–910.
41. Johnson–Rusk Telephone Conversation, June 5, 1967, Tape F67.11, Side B PNO 1, Miller Center; *FRUS 1964–1968, XIX*, 293, Doc. 150.
42. *FRUS 1964–1968, XIX*, 295, Doc. 152.
43. Ibid., 300–1, Docs. 156–57.
44. Ibid., Doc. 308.
45. Raz, *Bride and Dowry*, 21–22; Quigley, *Six-Day War and Israeli Self-Defense*, 108; "Let There Be Peace," *NER* XI (June 13, 1967): 45.
46. *FRUS 1964–1968, XIX*, 288, Doc. 149; McPherson, Interview III, Jan. 16, 1969, Washington DC, by T. H. Baker, 18–20, LBJL; CIA Memorandum, "The Arab-Israeli War: Who Fired the First Shot," June 5, 1967, NSF, NSC Histories, May 12–June 19, 1967, LBJL, Box 18.
47. *FRUS 1964–1968, XIX*, 302–6, Docs. 158–60.
48. Barbour to State, "'By Post,' Tel Aviv," June 5, 1967, Middle East Crisis Files, RG 59, Box 10.
49. *FRUS 1964–1968, XIX*, 310n, Doc. 163.
50. Ibid., 290–91, Doc. 149.
51. Walt Rostow to LBJ, June 6, 1967, NSF, NSC Histories, May 12–June 19, 1967, LBJL, Box 18; *FRUS 1964–1968, XIX*, 326–27, Doc. 176; 316, Doc. 167.
52. Arthur Goldberg Interview I, by Ted Gittinger, 10, March 23, 1983, LBJL.
53. Ibid.; "Justice Goldberg on Zionism," *NER* IX (May 5, 1965), 35; Goldberg speech to B'nai B'rith in Tel Aviv, May 27, 1965; *The Jerusalem Post*, May 28, 1965, both in "Subject File, Travel Files, 1965, Israel," The Papers of Arthur Goldberg, the Library of Congress, Washington, DC, Box 196.
54. Goldberg speech to B'nai B'rith, May 27, 1965; "Subject File, Jews; Soviet Jewry," Goldberg Papers, Box 184.
55. Dorothy Goldberg speech, Miami Jewish National Fund, Nov. 9, 1969, "Subject File, Jews; Israel," Goldberg Papers, Box 184.
56. "Subject File, Jews; *Neot Kedumim*," Goldberg Papers, Box 184.

57. Quigley, *Six-Day War and Israeli Self-Defense*, 83–86, 112; *FRUS 1964–1968, XIX*, 334, Doc 183; Goldberg and UN ceasefire resolutions, NSF, NSC Histories, May 12–June 19, 1967, LBJL, Box 20; Resolution 233 reprinted DOS *Bulletin*, June 26, 1967: 947–48. https://unispal.un.org/DP A/DPR/unispal.nsf/o/CEE5B4E9F80ED573852560C3004B16FB

58. Benny Morris, *Righteous Victims: A History of the Zionist-Arab Conflict, 1881–1999*. New York: Knopf, 1999: 313.

59. *FRUS 1964–1968, XIX*, 330, Doc. 179; Quigley, *Six-Day War and Israeli Self-Defense*, 90.

60. *FRUS 1964–1968, XIX*, 311, Doc. 164.

61. McGeorge Bundy Oral History Interview III (Bundy OHI III), New York, March 19, 1969, by Paige E. Mulhollan, LBJL.

62. Joseph A. Califano, Jr. *The Triumph and Tragedy of Lyndon Johnson: The White House Years*. New York: Simon and Schuster, 1991: 205; Segev, *1967*, 302, 572.

63. *FRUS 1964–1968, XIX*, 311, Doc. 164.

64. DOS *Bulletin* 56, June 26, 1967: 949–50.

65. Dixon Donnelley to Rusk, June 14, 1967, Middle East Crisis Files, RG 59, Box 15.

66. Irving Moskovitz to Walt Rostow, June 5, 1967, National Security – Defense (Ex ND 19/CO 1–6 6/22/67), Johnson Papers, Box 194.

67. Edythe M. Lobb to Edward P. Boland, June 5, 1967, National Security – Defense (Ex ND 19/CO 1–6 6/22/67), Johnson Papers, Box 194.

68. Larry Levinson and Ben Wattenberg to Johnson, June 7, 1967, The President's Appointment File [Diary backup], Box 67; *FRUS 1964–1968, XIX*, 354–55, Doc. 198.

69. *FRUS 1964–1968, XIX*, 354–55, Doc. 198.

70. Ibid.

71. Ibid.; Califano, *Triumph and Tragedy of Lyndon Johnson*, 205; Robert Dallek, *Flawed Giant: Lyndon Johnson and His Times, 1961–1973*. New York: Oxford University Press, 1998: 429.

72. "Krim, Matthilde." Office Files of John Macy," LBJ, Box 320; Tyler, *A World of Trouble*, 65–71.

73. Mathilde Krim to President and Mrs. Johnson, Oct. 27, 1965; Mathilde Krim to President and Mrs. Johnson, Dec. 5, 1965; "Krim, Mr. and Mrs. Arthur (Mathilde)," Social Files, Alpha File, Box 1322; Papers of Arthur Krim, Box 1; letters and correspondence in "Arthur B. and Mathilde Krim," Post-Presidential Name File, Box 91, all LBJL.

74. Fortas-Johnson Telephone Conversation, June 21, 1968, Tape 13129, wh6806 PNO 10, Miller Center.

75. Recollections of Lynda Johnson Robb, Dec. 6, 1994. "Remembrance of his Life," (Krim, Arthur and Mathilde), LBJL Reference File.

76. "Mrs. Johnson's Spontaneous Reminiscences about Arthur Krim": "Arthur B. and Mathilde Krim," Post-Presidential Subject and Name Files, LBJL, Box 91.

77. Johnson to Mathilde Krim, Dec. 8, 1971, "Arthur B. and Mathilde Krim," Name File, Box 91.

78. Tyler, *World of Trouble*, 65.
79. *FRUS 1964–1968, XIX*, 349n, Doc. 195.
80. Ibid., 341–42, Doc. 190.
81. "Memorandum for the President from Joseph Califano, June 7, 1967. "The President's Appointment File [Diary backup], LBJL, Box 67.
82. *FRUS 1964–1968, XIX*, 320–22, Docs. 170–72; 328, Doc. 177; 359, Doc. 202; "Basic Issues Concerning the Middle East Crisis, May 18-June 13, 1967," NSF, NSC Histories, May 12–June 19, 1967, LBJL, Box 20.
83. *FRUS 1964–1968, XIX*, 347, Doc. 194; NSC meeting notes, June 6, 1967, NSF, NSC Meetings File, LBJL, Box 2.
84. *FRUS 1964–1968, XIX*, 299, Doc. 155: NSF, NSC Histories, May 12–June 19, 1967, LBJL, Box 19.
85. *FRUS 1964–1968, XIX*, 320, Doc. 170; 336, Doc. 186.
86. Embassy Tel Aviv to DOS, June 8, 1967, Middle East Crisis Files, 1967, RG 59, Box 10.
87. *FRUS 1964–1968, XIX*, 342, Doc. 191; 358, Doc. 202.
88. Ibid., 350n, Doc. 196.
89. Ibid., 346, Doc. 194; NSC meeting June 6, 1967, NSF, NSC Meetings File, LBJL, Box 2.
90. *FRUS 1964–1968, XIX*, 339, Doc. 189; 384, Doc. 226.
91. Ibid., 346, Doc. 194.
92. Bundy OHI III, 21.
93. "Rostow Memorandums," NSF Name File, LBJL, LBJL, Box 7.
94. Memorandum for the President form George Christian, June 7, 1967, NSF, NSC Histories, May 12–June 19, 1967, LBJL, Box 18.
95. "Middle East Settlement," June 7, 1967, NSF, NSC Histories, May 12–June 19, 1967, LBJL, Box 18.
96. *FRUS 1964–1968, XIX*, 339–40, Doc. 189.
97. Joseph Sisco to Dean Rusk, June 7, 1967, Middle East Crisis Files, 1967, RG 59, Box 15.
98. *FRUS 1964–1968, XIX*, 357–59, Docs. 201–2; Shlaim, "Israel: Poor Little Samson," 45.
99. Laron, *Six-Day War*, 297
100. Shlaim, "Israel: Poor Little Samson," 48.
101. *FRUS 1964–1968, XIX*, 77, Doc. 46.
102. Ibid., 360–61, Doc. 204.
103. From Embassy Tel Aviv, June 8, 1967, Middle East Crisis Files, 1967; Chronology, Benjamin Read to Rostow, June 15, 1967, Middle East Crisis Files, 1967, both in RG 59, Box 15.
104. *FRUS XIX*, 388–89, Doc. 229.
105. Ibid., 393, Doc. 233.
106. Ibid., 398, Doc. 236.
107. *FRUS XIX*, 419–20, Docs. 250–51.
108. Ibid., 424–25, Doc. 256.
109. For Ambassador from Secretary, June 9, 1967, Middle East Crisis Files, 1967, RG 59, Box 1. See also Chronology, Benjamin Read to Walt W. Rostow, June 15, 1967, Middle East Crisis Files, 1967, RG 59, Box 15;

110. *FRUS 1964–1968, XIX*, 440–44, Docs. 267–69.
111. *FRUS 1964–1968, XIX*, 444–48, Docs. 269–70. See also Minutes of NSC Special Committee, June 12, 1967, NSF, NSC Histories, May 12–June 19, 1967, LBJL, Box 18;.
112. *FRUS 1964–1968, XIX*, 439–40, Docs. 266–67; *Newsweek* June 19, 1967, 21; *NER XI* (May 29, 1967): 48; Walt Rostow to Lyndon Johnson, June 13, 1967, 1967, "Memos to the President Walt Rostow," NSF, NSC Histories, May 12–June 19, 1967, LBJL, Box 17.
113. *FRUS 1964–1968, XIX*, 517–20, Doc. 307.
114. Ibid., 469–76, Docs. 284–85.
115. Ibid., 537–56, Docs. 317–19; 564n, Doc. 324.
116. Ibid., 678–82, Doc. 373; 796–99, Doc. 424; 1016–17, Doc. 516.
117. See documents posted at the *USS Liberty* Document Center of the USS *Liberty* Alliance, including CIA documents and results of investigations: www.usslibertydocumentcenter.org; the incident has also been the subject of myriad memoirs, books, and documentary films, which include sound recordings and original film. Among published accounts, see James Bamford, who makes an extensive case for a deliberate attack to cover up Israeli summary executions of Egyptian prisoners, in *Body of Secrets: Anatomy of the Ultra-Secret National Security Agency*. New York: Doubleday, 2001: 185–239. Jay Cristol echoes Israeli arguments of an exhaustive investigation revealing the attack was a case of mistaken identity. Contrast his *The Liberty Incident Revealed: The Definitive Account*. Annapolis, MD: Naval Institute Press, 2013, with James Scott, *The Attack on the Liberty: The Untold Story of Israel's Deadly 1967 Assault on a US Spy Ship*. New York: Simon and Schuster, 2009. Journalist Rowland Evans investigated the *Liberty* attack and amassed files on the subject. See "Middle East File," The Papers of Rowland Evans, Box I: 25, LOC.
118. Rogan, *The Arabs*, 429.
119. *FRUS 1964–1968, XIX*, 392–93, Doc. 233.
120. *FRUS XIX*, 409, Doc. 243.
121. Ibid., 410–15, Docs. 244–47.
122. Ibid., 430, Doc. 260.
123. Ibid., 386–87, Doc. 227.
124. Press briefing, June 9, 1967, "The President's Appointment File" [Diary backup], LBJ Library, LBJL, Box 67.
125. *FRUS 1964–1968, XIX*, 457–59, Doc. 277.
126. Walt Rostow to Lyndon Johnson, June 13, 1967, 1967, NSF "Memos to the President Walt Rostow," LBJL, Box 17.
127. Tel Aviv Embassy to Department of State, June 13, 1967, NSF "Memos to the President," Walt Rostow, LBJL, Box 17.
128. *FRUS 1964–1968, XIX*, 450, Doc. 272.
129. CIA Memorandum, "Special Assessments on the Middle East Situation," June 13, 1967, "Intelligence Reports," June 1–13, 1967, NSF, Files of the Special Committee of the NSC, LBJL, Box 13.
130. Robert C. Strong to Lucius Battle, "Political Settlement Proposals," June 13, 1967, Middle East Crisis Files, 1967, LBJL Box 18.

131. *FRUS 1964–1968, XIX*, 443, Doc. 268.
132. Ibid., 504, 443, 439, Docs. 301, 268, 266.
133. Ibid., 436, 566–68, Docs. 264, 325.

"ISRAEL WILL REMAIN WHERE SHE IS"

1. Kenen, "War Notes," 1967, KP, Box 11.
2. Johnson-Everett Dirksen Telephone Conversation, June 12, 1967, Tape WH6706.02 PNO 2, Miller Center.
3. Press conference, June 13, 1967, "The President's Appointment File [Diary backup]," Box 67.
4. "For Rights and Security," *NER XI* (June 13, 1967): 45–46.
5. Ibid.
6. Kenen, "War Notes," 1967, KP, Box 11; Kenen, *Israel's Defense Line*, 207; Jerome Bakst to Arnold Foster, June 26, 1967, "Israel 1967–1973," Anti-Defamation league 1913–1995, BBIA, Box 1a-8.
7. Rabbi Jay Kaufman, "Reports to the B'nai B'rith Triennial Convention," Sept. 7–11, 1968, Washington, DC, BBIA, Box 1a-8.
8. *FRUS 1964–1968, XIX*, 520–21, Doc. 308.
9. McGeorge Bundy, "Memorandum for the President," June 9, 1967, The President's Appointment File [Diary backup], June 8, 1967 to June 18, 1967, Box 18.
10. Marvin Watson to Lyndon Johnson, June 19, 1967, White House Central File, Name File, "Feinberg, Abraham," Box 47, LBJL.
11. "Let the UN Vote for Negotiations," *NER XI* 13 (June 27): 49.
12. Issa Nakhleh and Omar Azouni to Lyndon Johnson, June 20, 1967, National Security – Defense, Johnson Papers, Box 19.
13. Kenen, "War Notes."
14. *FRUS XIX*, 556, Doc. 320.
15. Ibid., 563–64, Doc. 323; see also "Let the UN Vote for Negotiations," *NER*, 49.
16. *FRUS 1964–1968, XIX*, 664–65, Doc. 367; 707, Doc. 385; 775–80, Docs. 415–17.
17. CIA "Arab-Israeli Situation Report," June 22, 1967, "Intelligence Reports," June 22–26, 1967, NSF, Files of the Special Committee of the NSC, Johnson Papers, Box 14.
18. *FRUS 1964–1968, XIX*, 533–37, Docs. 314–16.
19. US Mission UN to New Delhi, June 26, 1967, Middle East Crisis Files, 1967, RG 59, Box 8.
20. *FRUS 1964–1968, XX, Arab-Israeli Dispute, 1967–1968*. Washington: USGPO, 2001: 294–95, Doc. 149.
21. Raz, *Bride and Dowry*, 6; *FRUS 1964–1968, XIX*, 687, Doc. 376.
22. Embassy Tel Aviv to Department of State, "Occupied Territories: Short Items," Nov. 8, 1967, Central Foreign Policy Files, Political and Defense, RG 59, Box 2224.

23. NSF, Files of the Special Committee of the NSC, June 25, 1967, LBJL, Box 9; *FRUS 1964–1968, XIX*, 509, Doc. 303; 588, Doc. 333; 598, Doc. 338; 605–7, Doc. 340.
24. *FRUS 1964–1968, XIX*, 766, Doc. 411; 778, Doc. 416.
25. Ginsburg, "Memorandum for the Vice President," June 17, 1967, NSF NSC Histories, May 12-June 19, 1967, LBJL, Box 18. "Comment," *NER XI* (June 27, 1967): 50, 52.
26. Raz, *Bride and Dowry*, 53–55, 77.
27. "Jerusalem – A Proposal for Partial Internationalization," July 1967, Middle East Crisis Files, 1967, RG 59, Box 18.
28. *FRUS 1964–1968, XIX*, 616–18, Doc. 344.
29. Goldberg–Johnson Telephone Conversation, July 15, 1967, Tape 12003 WH6707.01 PNO 2, Miller Center.
30. Raz, *Bride and Dowry*, 136.
31. *FRUS 1964–1968, XIX*, 642–43, Doc. 454.
32. Ibid., 619, Doc. 346.
33. Raz, *Bride and Dowry*, 39, 125.
34. *FRUS 1964–1968, XIX*, 835, Doc. 442.
35. Raz, *Bride and Dowry*, 103–25.
36. Ibid., 579, 614, 738.
37. Ibid., 134.
38. Ibid., 122–23.
39. Ibid., 84.
40. Ibid., 96.
41. *FRUS 1964–1968, XIX*, 650–52, Doc. 361; CIA Memorandum, "Special Assessments on the Middle East Situation, July 13, 1967 ("Intelligence Reports," July 13–18, 1967, NSF, Files of the Special Committee of the NSC, LBJL, Box 14; Robert Slater, *Warrior Statesman: The Life of Moshe Dayan.* New York: St. Martin's Press, 1991: 285.
42. Raz, *Bride and Dowry*, 4.
43. Ibid., 55, 77, 273, 19.
44. Ibid., 273.
45. *FRUS 1964–1968, XIX*, 583–84, Doc. 331.
46. *FRUS 1964–1968, XIX*, 648–49, Doc. 360; 694n, Doc. 378; 671, Doc. 370.
47. Ibid., 753–54, Doc. 408.
48. NSF, Files of the Special Committee of the NSC, LBJL, Box 7; *FRUS 1964–1968, XIX*, 791–94, Doc. 422
49. "Arms to Jordan?" *NER XI* (July 25, 1967): 57–58.
50. *FRUS 1964–1968, XIX*, 707, Doc. 385; see also ibid., 668–70, Docs. 368–70.
51. *FRUS 1964–1968, Arab-Israeli Dispute, 1967–1968, XX.* Washington: USGPO, 2001: 579, Doc. 294; NSF, Files of Walt W. Rostow, "Arab-Israeli private talks," LBJL, Box 12.
52. *FRUS 1964–1968, XIX*, 836, Doc. 442.
53. Ibid., 685, Doc. 375; 719, Doc. 391.
54. "Meeting on August 27 [1967] between Minister Evron and Myer Feldman," Feldman Papers, Box 56.

55. *FRUS 1964–1968, XIX,* 739–40, Doc. 399.
56. Ibid., 566–68, Doc. 325.
57. Ibid., 757–58, Doc. 409; "Stand Pat for Peace – Nothing Less," *NER* XI (August 8, 1967) 61.
58. *FRUS 1964–1968, XIX,* 782, Doc. 418; 789, Doc. 420.
59. Ibid., 773, Doc. 414.
60. Shlaim, *Iron Wall,* 277; *FRUS 1964–1968, XIX,* 984–85, Doc. 501.
61. "New Arab Diplomatic Offensive," *NER XI* (Sept. 19, 67): 73
62. Idith Zertal and Akiva Eldar, *Lords of the Land: The War Over Israel's Settlements in the Occupied Territories, 1967–2007.* New York: Nation Books, 2007.
63. Shaiel Ben-Ephraim, "Distraction and Deception: Israeli Settlements, Vietnam, and the Johnson Administration," *Diplomatic History* 42 (June 2018): 462.
64. Raz, *Bride and Dowry,* 140, 184; "Myths and Facts – The Background to the Arab–Israel War" *NER Special Supplement* (August 1967): B-4.
65. Avi Shlaim, *Iron Wall,* 273–75.
66. *FRUS 1964–1968, XIX,* 857, Doc. 451; 874–76, Doc. 458.
67. "Settlements," *NER XI* (Oct. 3, 1967): 80.
68. *FRUS 1964–1968, XIX,* 910–13, Doc. 476.
69. *FRUS 1964–1968, XIX,* 973–81, Doc. 500; 984–85, Doc. 501.
70. Raz, *Bride and Dowry,* 154; *FRUS 1964–1968, XIX,* 1043–45, Doc. 530; Eban to Goldberg, Nov. 14, 1967; Saunders, Nov. 2, 1967, both in NSF, Country File, Israel, LBJL, Box 140.
71. "Myths and Facts – The Background to the Arab-Israel War," *NER* (August 1967): B-7, B-4.
72. Quigley, *Six-Day War and Israeli Self-Defense,* 171–72.
73. Resolution 242, *FRUS 1964–1968, XIX,* 1062–63, Doc. 542.
74. Quigley, *Six-Day War and Israeli Self-Defense,* 178.
75. "Statement of Ambassador Arthur J. Goldberg to the United Nations," Sept. 21, 1967, NSF, Agency File, LBJL, Box 69; Goldberg Oral History Interview I, Mar. 23, 1983, by Ted Gittinger, 18, LBJL.
76. "Can There Be Peace?" *A Supplement to the Near East Report* (January 1968): A-14–16.
77. *FRUS 1964–1968, XIX,* 480–81, Doc. 288; 770–74, Doc. 414; 781, Doc. 418; "The Arms Race in the Near East."
78. Ibid., 788–89, Doc. 420; 842, Doc. 445; Walt Rostow to LBJ, Sept. 22, 1967 PLBJ, NSF, Country File, Israel, LBJL, Box 140.
79. *FRUS 1964–1968, XX,* 189–91, Doc. 91; 194–95, Doc. 94; Memo of Conversation Averill Harriman, Feb. 13, 1968, PLBJ, NSF, Country File, Israel, LBJL, Box 141.
80. Saunders to Rostow, Dec. 29, 1967, PLBJ, NSF, Country File, Israel, LBJL, Box 141; Rostow to LBJ, Dec. 17, 1967, NSF, Country File, Israel, LBJL, Box 143; DOS Telegram, Jan. 9, 1968, RG 59 Central F. P. Files, Pol. and Defense, RG 59, Box 2225; *FRUS 1964–1968, XIX,* 894–95, Doc. 468.
81. *FRUS 1964–1968, XX,* 142, Doc. 70; *FRUS 1964–1968, XIX,* 940–41, Doc. 486; Rostow to LBJ, Feb. 2, 1968, NSF, Country File, Israel, LBJL, Box 141; *FRUS 1964–1968, XX,* 248, Doc. 125.

82. Tel Aviv Embassy to State, May 22, 1968, NSF, Country File, Israel, LBJL, Box 141.
83. Shlaim, *Iron Wall*, 437.
84. *FRUS 1964–1968*, XX, 241–42, Docs. 118 and 119; Goldberg–Johnson Telephone, Tape 12843 WH6803.05 PNO 2.
85. Goldberg to Secretary of State, Mar. 8, 1968, NSF, Agency File, LBJL, Box 69; *FRUS 1964–1968*, XX, 690–92, Doc. 350.
86. *FRUS XX*, 251, Doc. 127.
87. Ibid., 255–57, Doc. 129.
88. Goldberg–Johnson Telephone Conversation, Mar. 24, 1968, Tape 12843 (WH6803.05) PNO 2, Miller Center.
89. Ibid., 436, Doc. 220; McPherson to Johnson, NSF, Country File, Israel, LBJL, Box 141.
90. Memo of Conversation, Visit by Israeli Ambassador, April 1, 1968, NSF, Country File, Israel, LBJL, Box 141.
91. CIA Intelligence Memorandum, "Economic Costs to Israel of Retaining Captured Arab Territories." April 1968 NSF, Country File, Israel, LBJL, Box 141.
92. Dayan interview in mass circulation *Maariv* newspaper, May 6, 1968, NSF, Country File, Israel, LBJL, Box 141.
93. Saunders to Rostow, April 16, 1968; Campbell, Report from Jerusalem Consulate, April 31, 1968, both in NSF, Country File, Israel, LBJL, Box 141.
94. David Holden *The Sunday Times* (London), Dec. 1, 1967, PLBJ, NSF, Country File, Israel, LBJL, Box 141.
95. "DOS Telegram," June 19, 1968, Central Foreign Policy Files, Political and Defense, RG 59, Box 2227.
96. Memorandum of Conversation, June 17, 1968, NSF, Country File, Israel, LBJL, Box 142; *FRUS 1964–1968*, XX, 379–80, Doc. 194.
97. *FRUS 1964–1968*, XX, 502–3, Doc. 255.
98. Ibid., 540–42, Doc. 271; UN Mission to Secretary of State, Oct. 1, 1968, NSF, Agency File, LBJL, Box 70.
99. *FRUS 1964–1968*, XX, 194–95., Doc. 94; Parker Hart to Rusk, Oct. 15, 1968, Central Foreign Policy Files, 1967–1969 Political and Defense, RG 59, Box 1558.
100. *FRUS 1964–1968*, XIX, 512–15, Doc. 305; Adrian S. Fisher, "Arms limitations in the Middle East," June 21, 1967, Executive Secretariat, NSC Meeting Files, 1966–68, RG 59, Box 2.
101. Shane J. Maddock, *Nuclear Apartheid: The Quest for American Atomic Supremacy from World War II to the Present*. Chapel Hill: University of North Carolina Press, 2010: 279–84.
102. Saunders to Rostow, Dec. 29, 1967, NSF, Country File, Israel, LBJL, Box 141; *FRUS 1964–1968*, XX, 627–30, Doc. 317.
103. *FRUS 1964–1968*, XX, 563, Doc. 284; Johnson-Fortas Telephone Conversation, June 21, 1968, Tape 13129 wh6806 Program No. 10, Miller Center;
104. *FRUS 1964–1968*, XX, 482–83, Doc. 246.

105. Johnson-Rusk Telephone Conversation, Sept. 23, 1968, Tape 13415 6809.02 PNO 7, Miller Center.
106. Johnson-Rusk Telephone Conversation, Oct. 17, 1968, Tape 13559 WH6810.05 PNO 10, Miller Center; Rostow to Johnson, Oct. 25, 1968, NSF, Country File, Israel, LBJL, Box 142; *FRUS 1964–1968*, XX, 507, Doc. 256; 573, Doc. 290.
107. Johnson-Rusk Telephone Conversation, Oct. 17, 1968.
108. *FRUS 1964–1968*, XX, 585–86, Doc. 299.
109. Ibid., 661–62, Doc. 333.
110. Ibid., 689, Doc. 348; Johnson-Clifford Telephone Conversation, Nov. 23, 1968, Tape 13761 WH6811.08 PNO 1, Miller Center.
111. *FRUS 1964–1968*, XX, 585–86, Doc. 299; Wiggins, US Mission UN to Secretary of State, October 1968, NSF, Agency File, LBJL, Box 70; "Jarring Gloomy on Mideast Peace," *New York Times*, Feb. 15, 1969.
112. Hussein, Dec. 2, 1968, NSF, Country File, Israel, LBJL, Box 143; *FRUS 1964–1968*, XX, 732, Doc. 371; Rodger Davies, "Delivery of F-4 Aircraft to Israel," CFPF 1967–69, Political and Defense, RG 59, Box 1559.
113. Diplomat Alfred Atherton to Parker T. Hart, Jan. 8, 1969, Central Foreign Policy Files, Political and Defense, RG 59, Box 2224; Abraham Ben-Zvi, *Lyndon B. Johnson and the Politics of Arms Sales to Israel*. London: Frank Cass, 2004: 11–23.
114. Avner Cohen and William Burr, "Israel Crosses the Threshold," April 28, 2006, The National Security Archive, George Washington University. http://nsarchive.gwu.edu/NSAEBB/NSAEBB189/
115. Joseph Sisco, "Israel's Nuclear Policy and Implications for the United States," April 3, 1969, Central Foreign Policy Files, 1967–1969, Political and Defense, RG 59, Box 1557.
116. Cohen and Burr, "Israel Crosses the Threshold."
117. *FRUS 1964–1968*, XX, 150–1, Doc. 73.
118. Goldberg–Johnson Telephone Conversation, Mar. 24, 1968, Tape 12843 (WH6803.05) PNO 2, Miller Center.
119. Jessie Hatcher Oral History Interview, 38–39; "To the Executive and National Committee from I. L. Kenen, Not for Publication or Circulation," Nov. 26, 1963, Feldman Papers.

CONCLUSIONS

1. Kenen, "War Notes," June 1967, KP, Box 11.
2. "The Political Party Platforms, 1944–1968: A Supplement to the *Near East Report*," NER (October 1968), 1.
3. Since the 1990s Israel has received more than $3 billion annually in US assistance – "more than the amount for all of sub-Saharan Africa, Latin America and the Caribbean." Terry, *US Foreign Policy in the Middle East*, 80. In September 2016, President Barack Obama – despite being treated contemptuously by Israeli Prime minister Benjamin Netanyahu – signed an unprecedented 10-year, $38 billion military aid package for Israel; "US

Finalizes Deal to Give Israel $38 Billion in Military Aid," *New York Times*, Sept. 13, 2016, 1; see also Introduction, note 1.

4. Kenen Interview by Alvin Goldstein, July 11, 1973, KP, Box 14.
5. Raz, *Bride and Dowry*, 276.
6. Shlaim, "Israel: Poor Little Samson."
7. Tivnan, *The Lobby*, 63; Preston, *Sword of the Spirit*, 561; O'Brien, *American Jewish Organizations*, 114.
8. "A Finding Aid to the American Council for Judaism Records," American Jewish Archives.
9. Yossi Shain and Neil Rogashevsky, "Between JDate and J Street: US Foreign Policy and the Liberal Jewish Dilemma in America," in DeWind and Segura, eds., *Diaspora Lobbies and the US Government*, 66; Peter Beinart, *The Crisis of Zionism*. New York: Henry Holt and Co., 2012.
10. Carenen, *Fervent Embrace*, 124–25.
11. Preston, *Sword of the Spirit*, 561–62.
12. US Mission UN to New Delhi, June 26, 1967, Middle East Crisis Files, Box 8.
13. Laron, *Six-Day War*, 311; Chamberlin, *Global Offensive*, 37; Shlaim, "Israel: Poor Little Samson," 20.
14. *FRUS 1964–1968, XIX*, 862–66, Doc. 454.

Bibliography

PRIMARY SOURCES

American Israel Public Affairs Committee

Near East Report, 1957–1968

Center for Jewish History, New York City

American Council for Judaism Collection
Isaiah Leo Kenen Papers
Louis Lipsky Papers
Records of the American Jewish Committee
Records of the American Jewish Congress

Dwight D. Eisenhower Presidential Library, Abilene, KS

John Foster Dulles Papers
Dwight D. Eisenhower Papers
James C. Hagerty Papers
Christian A. Herter Papers
Maxwell M. Rabb Papers
Records of the President, White House Central Files
Republican National Committee Papers

Foreign Relations of the United States (FRUS), US Department of State Publication:

FRUS 1945, VIII, The Near East and Africa. Washington: United States Government Printing Office (USGPO): 1969.

FRUS 1946, VII, The Near East and Africa. USGPO, 1969.

FRUS 1947, V, The Near East and Africa. USGPO, 1971.

FRUS 1948, V, Part 2, The Near East, South Asia, and Africa. USGPO, 1976.

FRUS 1949, VI, The Near East, South Asia, and Africa. USGPO, 1977.

FRUS 1950, V, The Near East, South Asia, and Africa. USGPO, 1978.

FRUS 1951, V, The Near East, South Asia, and Africa. USGPO, 1982.

FRUS 1952–1954, IX, The Near and Middle East, Part I. USGPO, 1986.

FRUS 1955–1957, XVI, Suez Crisis, July 26–December 31, 1956. USGPO, 1990.

FRUS 1955–1957, XVII, Arab–Israeli Dispute, 1957. USGPO, 1990.

FRUS 1958–1960, XIII, Arab–Israeli Dispute; United Arab Republic; North Africa. USGPO, 1992.

FRUS 1958–1960, XII, Near East Region; Iraq; Iran; Arabian Peninsula. USGPO, 1993.

FRUS 1961–1963, XVII, Near East. USGPO, 1994.

FRUS 1961–1963, XVIII, Near East. USGPO, 1995.

FRUS 1964–1968, XVIII, Arab-Israeli Dispute, 1964–1967. USGPO, 2000.

FRUS 1964–1968, XIX, Arab–Israeli Crisis and War, 1967. US GPO, 2004.

FRUS 1964–1968, XX, Arab–Israeli Dispute, 1967–1968. Washington: USGPO, 2001.

Israel Lobby Archive (Online)

www.israellobby.org/AZCPA/
"1951–1964 Lobbying Disclosures, AZC, AZCPA, AIPAC."

Lyndon Baines Johnson Presidential Library, Austin, TX

Krim, Arthur and Mathilde, Reference File.
National Security File
Lyndon Baines Johnson Papers
The President's Appointment File
Religion File
White House Central Files

LBJL Oral History Interviews

McGeorge Bundy by Paige E. Mulhollan, New York, Mar. 19, 1969
Rev. George R. Davis by Dorothy Price, Washington DC, Feb. 13, 1969
Arthur J. Goldberg by Ted Gittinger, Washington, DC, Mar. 23, 1983

Billy Graham by Monroe Billington, Telephone, Oct. 12, 1983
Jessie Hatcher by Paul Bolton, San Saba, TX, Mar. 28, 1968
Harry McPherson by T. H. Baker, Washington DC, Jan. 16, 1969

John F. Kennedy Presidential Library, Boston, MA

McGeorge Bundy Personal Papers
Myer Feldman Personal Papers
Hirsh Freed Papers
Papers of President Kennedy
National Security Files
Pre-Presidential Papers

JFKL Oral History Interviews

John S. Badeau by Dennis J. O'Brien, New York, Feb. 25, 1969.
Walworth Barbour by Sheldon M. Stern, Gloucester, MA, May 22, 1981.
David Ben-Gurion by E. A. Bayne, Tel Aviv, Israel, July 16, 1965.
Myer Feldman by John Stewart, Washington DC, Aug. 6, 1966, and Aug. 26, 1967.
Hirsh Freed by Ed Martin, Boston, June 5, 1964.
Robert W. Komer by Dennis J. O'Brien, Dec. 22, 1969,
Phillips Talbot by Dennis J. O'Brien, New York, Aug. 13, 1970.
Lewis H. Weinstein by Sheldon Stern, Boston, June 3, 1982.

Library of Congress, Washington, DC

Emanuel Celler Papers
Clark M. Clifford Papers
Benjamin V. Cohen Papers
Rowland Evans Papers
Felix Frankfurter Papers
Arthur J. Goldberg Papers
Loy W. Henderson Papers

Jacob Rader Marcus Center of the American Jewish Archives, Cincinnati, OH

Benjamin V. Cohen Papers
B'nai B'rith International Archives
Records of the American Council for Judaism

Miller Center, University of Virginia

Presidential Telephone Recordings (online):
https://millercenter.org/the-presidency/secret-white-house-tapes
Feinberg-Johnson, Feb. 20, 1965
Rusk-Johnson, Feb. 28, 1965
Tarlov-Johnson, Sept. 10, 1966
Fulbright-Johnson, June 19, 1967
Rostow-Johnson, June 5, 1967
Dirksen-Johnson, June 12, 1967

National Archives and Records Administration, College Park, MD

General Records of the Department of State (Record Group 59)
Middle East Crisis Files, 1967
Political and Defense

National Security Archive, Washington, DC (Online)

http://nsarchive.gwu.edu/NSAEBB/NSAEBB189/
Avner Cohen and William Burr, "Israel Crosses the Threshold," April 28, 2006.
Avner Cohen and William Burr, "Kennedy, Dimona and the Nuclear Proliferation Problem: 1961–1962," April 21, 2016.
"Israel's Quest for Yellowcake: The Secret Argentine-Israeli Connection, 1963–1966," June 25, 2013.

Harry S. Truman Library Institute, Independence, MO

Dean G. Acheson Papers
Clark Clifford Papers
A. J. Granoff Papers
Edward Jacobson Papers
David K. Niles Papers
President's Secretary's Files
Records of the President, White House Central Files
Harry S. Truman Papers

HSTL Oral History Interviews

Matthew J. Connelly by Jerry N. Hess, New York, Nov. 30, 1967.
Mark F. Ethridge by Richard D. McKinzie, Moncure, North Carolina, June 4, 1974.
Abraham Feinberg by Richard D. McKinzie, New York, August 23, 1973.

Loy W. Henderson by Richard D. McKinzie, Washington, DC, June 14
and July 5, 1973.
Henry Byroade by Niel M. Johnson, Potomac, Maryland, Sept. 19 and 21,
1988.
Film.
"Decision: The Conflicts of Harry S. Truman" (1964, HSTL) Episode Six,
"At War with the Experts."

USS *Liberty* Document Center (Online)

www.usslibertydocumentcenter.org

Western Reserve Historical Society, Cleveland, OH

Abba Hillel Silver Papers

BOOKS AND ARTICLES

Akenson, Donald H. *God's Peoples: Covenant and Land in South Africa, Israel,
and Ulster.* Ithaca: Cornell University Press, 1992.
Albright, William F. *From Stone Age to Christianity: Monotheism and the
Historical Process.* Baltimore: Johns Hopkins University Press, 1957.
Al-Salim, Farid. *Palestine and the Decline of the Ottoman Empire.* London:
I. B. Taurus, 2015.
Anderson, Irvine H. *Aramco, the United States, and Saudi Arabia: A Study of the
Dynamics of Foreign Oil Policy, 1933–1950.* Princeton: Princeton University
Press, 1981.
    Biblical Interpretation and Middle East Policy. Gainesville: University Press of
Florida, 2005.
Ansary, Tamim. *Destiny Disrupted: A History of the World through Islamic Eyes.*
New York: Public Affairs, 2009.
Aridan, Natan. *Advocating for Israel: Diplomats and Lobbyists from Truman to
Nixon.* Lanham: Lexington Books, 2017.
Ashton, Nigel J. "For King and Country: Jack O'Connell, the CIA, and the Arab-
Israeli Conflict, 1963–1971," *Diplomatic History* 36 (November 2012):
881–910.
Ball, George W. and Ball, Douglas B. *The Passionate Attachment: America's
Involvement with Israel, 1947 to the Present.* New York: W. W. Norton
and Co., 1992.
Bamford, James. *Body of Secrets: Anatomy of the Ultra-Secret National Security
Agency.* New York: Doubleday, 2001.
Baskin, Judith R. and Seeskin, Kenneth, eds. *Jewish History, Religion, and
Culture.* New York: Cambridge University Press, 2010.
Bass, Warren. *Support Any Friend: Kennedy's Middle East and the Making of the
US-Israel Alliance.* New York: Oxford University Press, 2003.

Beinart, Peter. *The Crisis of Zionism*. New York: Henry Holt and Co., 2012.

Ben-Ephraim, Shaiel. "Distraction and Deception: Israeli Settlements, Vietnam, and the Johnson Administration," *Diplomatic History* 42 (June 2018): 456–86.

Ben-Zvi, Abraham. *Lyndon B. Johnson and the Politics of Arms Sales to Israel*. London: Frank Cass, 2004.

Bierbrier, Doreen. "The American Zionist Emergency Council: An Analysis of a Pressure Group," *American Jewish Historical Quarterly* LX (September 1970): 87–93.

Bloxham, Donald and Moses, A. Dirk, eds. *The Oxford Handbook of Genocide Studies*. Oxford: Oxford University Press, 2001.

Boyer, Paul S. *When Time Shall Be No More: Prophecy Belief in Modern American Culture*. Cambridge, MA: Harvard University Press, 1992.

Brecher, Frank W. *American Diplomacy and the Israeli War of Independence*. Jefferson and London: McFarland Publishing, 2013.

Reluctant Ally: United States Foreign Policy toward the Jews from Wilson to Roosevelt. New York: Greenwood Press, 1991.

Breitman, Richard and Lichtman, Allan J. *FDR and the Jews*. Cambridge: Harvard University Press, 2013.

Brett, Mark G. *Decolonizing God: The Bible and the Tides of Empire*. Sheffield: Sheffield Phoenix Press, 2008.

Bunch, Clea Lutz. "Strike at Samu: Jordan, Israel, the United States, and the Origins of the Six-Day War," *Diplomatic History* 32 (January 2008): 55–76.

Burns, William J. *Economic Aid and American Policy toward Egypt, 1955–1981*. Albany: State University of New York Press, 1985.

Califano, Joseph A. Jr. *The Triumph and Tragedy of Lyndon Johnson: The White House Years*. New York: Simon and Schuster, 1991.

Carenen, Caitlin. *The Fervent Embrace: Liberal Protestants, Evangelicals, and Israel*. New York: New York University Press, 2012.

Cavanagh, Edward and Veracini, Lorenzo, eds. *The Routledge Handbook of the History of Settler Colonialism*. London: Routledge, 2017.

Chamberlin, Paul Thomas. *The Global Offensive: The United States, the Palestine Liberation Organization, and the Making of the Post-Cold War Order*. New York: Oxford University Press, 2012.

Chomsky, Noam. *The Fateful Triangle: The United States, Israel and the Palestinians*. Boston: South End Press, 1983.

Christison, Kathleen. *Perceptions of Palestine: Their Influence on US Middle East Policy*. Berkeley: University of California Press, 1999.

Cohen, Avner. *Israel and the Bomb*. New York: Columbia University Press, 1998.

The Worst-Kept Secret: Israel's Bargain with the Bomb. New York: Columbia University Press, 2010.

Cohen, Naomi W. *The Americanization of Zionism, 1897–1948*. Hanover: Brandeis University Press, 2003.

Collins, John. *Global Palestine*. London: Hurst and Co, 2011.

Cristol, Jay. *The Liberty Incident Revealed: The Definitive Account*. Annapolis: Naval Institute Press, 2013.

Crouse, Eric R. *American Christians Support for Israel: Standing with the Chosen People, 1948 to 1975*. Lanham: Lexington Books, 2015.

Dallek, Robert. *Flawed Giant: Lyndon Johnson and His Times, 1961–1973*. New York: Oxford University Press, 1998.

Davies, Philip R. *In Search of Ancient Israel*. Sheffield: JSOT Press, 1992.

DeWind, Josh and Segura, Renata, eds. *Diaspora Lobbies and the US Government*. New York: New York University Press, 2014.

Dinnerstein, Leonard. *The Leo Frank Case*. Athens: University of Georgia Press, rev. edn., 2008.

Farsoun, Samih and Zacharia, Christina. *Palestine and the Palestinians*. Boulder: Westview Press, 1997.

Findley, Paul. *They Dare to Speak Out: People and Institutions Confront Israel's Lobby*. Westport: Lawrence Hill and Co., 1985.

Finkelstein, Israel and Silberman, Neil A. *The Bible Unearthed: Archaeology's New Vision of Ancient Israel and the Origin of Its Sacred Texts*. New York: Touchstone, 2001.

Finkelstein, Norman G. *The Holocaust Industry*. London: Verso Books, 2000.

Foxman, Abraham H. *The Deadliest Lies: The Israel Lobby and the Myth of Jewish Control*. New York: Palgrave Macmillan, 2007.

Gendzier, Irene L. *Dying to Forget: Oil, Power, Palestine, and the Foundations of US Policy in the Middle East*. New York: Columbia University Press, 2015.

Gerber, David A., ed. *Anti-Semitism in American History*. Champaign-Urbana: University of Illinois Press, 1986.

Golani, Motti. *Israel in Search of a War: The Sinai Campaign, 1955–1956*. Brighton: Sussex Academic Press, 1998.

Goldstein, Phyllis. *A Convenient Hatred: The History of Antisemitism*. Brookline: Facing History and Ourselves, 2012.

Grose, Peter. *Israel in the Mind of America*. New York: Schocken Books, 1983.

Hahn, Peter L. *Caught in the Middle East: The US Policy Toward the Arab-Israeli Conflict, 1945–1961*. Chapel Hill: University of North Carolina Press, 2004.

"The Cold War and the Six Day War: US Policy towards the Arab-Israel Crisis of June 1967," in Ashton, Nigel J. ed., *The Cold War in the Middle East: Regional Conflict and the Superpowers, 1967–1973*. New York: Routledge, 2007.

Herzl, Theodor. *The Jewish State*. New York: Dover Publications, 1988.

Hixson, Walter L. *American Settler Colonialism: A History*. New York: Palgrave Macmillan, 2013.

Hjelm, Ingrid and Thompson, Thomas, eds. *History, Archaeology and the Bible Forty Years after "Historicity."* New York: Routledge, 2016.

Isaacs, Stephen D. *Jews and American Politics*. New York: Doubleday, 1974.

Jacobs, Matthew F. *Imagining the Middle East: The Building of an American Foreign Policy, 1918–1967*. Chapel Hill: University of North Carolina Press, 2011.

Johnson, Lyndon B. *The Vantage Point: Perspectives on the Presidency, 1963–1969*. New York: Holt, Rinehart, and Winston, 1971.

Judis, John B. *Genesis: Truman, American Jews, and the Origins of the Arab/Israeli Conflict*. New York: Farrar, Straus and Giroux, 2014.

Kalman, Laura. *Abe Fortas: A Biography*. New Haven: Yale University Press, 1990.

Kaplan, Amy. *Our American Israel: The Story of an Entangled Alliance*. Cambridge, MA: Harvard University Press, 2018.

Kaplan, Robert D. *The Arabists: The Romance of an American Elite*. New York: The Free Press, 1995.

Kenen, Isaiah Leo. *Israel's Defense Line: Her Friends and Foes in Washington*. Buffalo: Prometheus books, 1981.

Khaladi, Rashid. *The Iron Cage: The Story of the Palestinian Struggle for Statehood*. Boston: Beacon Press, 2006.

Palestinian Identity: The Construction of Modern National Consciousness. New York: Columbia University Press, 1997.

Kimball, Warren F. *The Juggler: Franklin D. Roosevelt as Wartime Statesman*. Princeton: Princeton University Press, 1991.

Kolsky, Thomas A. *Jews against Zionism: The American Council for Judaism, 1942–1948*. Philadelphia: Temple University Press, 1990.

Kramer, Gudrun. *A History of Palestine: From the Ottoman Conquest to the Founding of the State of Israel*. Princeton: Princeton University Press, 2008.

Labelle, Maurice. "A New Age of Empire? Arab 'Anti-Americanism,' US Intervention, and the Lebanese Civil War of 1958," *International History Review* 35, 1 (March 2013): 42–69.

"'The Only Thorn:' Early Saudi-American Relations and the Question of Palestine," *Diplomatic History* 35, April 2011: 257–81.

Lapidus, Ira M. *A History of Islamic Societies*. New York: Cambridge University Press, 2014, 3rd edn.

Laquer, Walter and Rubin, Barry, eds. *The Israel-Arab Reader: A Documentary History of the Middle East Conflict*. New York: Penguin Books, 2008.

Laron, Guy. *The Six-Day War: The Breaking of the Middle East*. New Haven: Yale University Press, 2017.

Levey, Zach. "The United States, Israel, and Nuclear Desalination: 1944–1968," *Diplomatic History* 39 (November 2015): 904–25.

Louis, William Roger. *The British Empire in the Middle East, 1945–1951: Arab Nationalism, the United States, and Postwar Imperialism*. London: Oxford University Press, 1984.

Maddock, Shane J. *Nuclear Apartheid: The Quest for American Atomic Supremacy from World War II to the Present*. Chapel Hill: University of North Carolina Press, 2010.

Makdisi, Saree. *Palestine Inside Out: An Everyday Occupation*. New York: W. W. Norton, 2008.

Maoz, Zeev. *Defending the Holy Land: A Critical Analysis of Israel's Security and Foreign Policy*. Ann Arbor: University of Michigan Press, 2009.

Mart, Michelle. *Eye on Israel: How America Came to View the Jewish State as an Ally*. Albany: State University of New York Press, 2006.

Masalha, Nur. *The Palestine Nakba: Decolonizing History, Narrating the Subaltern, Reclaiming Memory*. London: Zed Books, 2012.

The Politics of Denial: Israel and the Palestinian Refugee Problem. London: Pluto Press, 2003.

The Zionist Bible: Biblical Precedent, Colonialism, and the Erasure of Memory. Berne: Acumen, 2013

McAlister, Melani. *Epic Encounters: Culture, Media, and US Interests in the Middle East Since 1945*. Berkeley: University of California Press.

Mearsheimer, John J. and Walt, Stephen M. *The Israel Lobby and US Foreign Policy*. New York: Farrar, Srauss, and Giroux, 2007.

Morris, Benny. *Israel's Border Wars, 1949–1956: Arab Infiltration, Israeli Retaliation, and the Countdown to the Suez War*. New York: Oxford University Press, 1993.

———. *Righteous Victims: A History of Zionist-Arab Conflict, 1881–1999*. New York: Knopf, 1999.

Niesiolowski-Spano, Lukasz. *Origin Myths and Holy Places in the Old Testament*. London: Equinox Publishing, 2011.

Novick, Peter. *The Holocaust in American Life*. Boston: Houghton Mifflin Co., 1999.

O'Brien, Lee. *American Jewish Organizations and Israel*. Washington: Institute for Palestine Studies, 1986

Oren, Michael B. *Power, Faith, and Fantasy: America in the Middle East 1776-Present*. New York: W. W. Norton, 2007.

Pappé, Ilan. *The Ethnic Cleansing of Palestine*. Oxford: Oneworld Publications, 2006.

———. *The Forgotten Palestinians: A History of the Palestinians in Israel*. New Haven: Yale University Press, 2011.

———. *Ten Myths about Israel*. London: Verso, 2017.

Parker, Richard B. ed. *The Six-Day War: A Retrospective*. Gainesville: University of Florida Press, 1996.

Pfoh, Emanuel. "From the Search for Ancient Israel to the History of Ancient Palestine," in Hjelm, Ingrid and Thompson, Thomas, eds. *History, Archaeology and the Bible Forty Years after "Historicity."* New York: Routledge, 2016.

Piterbeg, Gabriel. *The Returns of Zionism: Myths, Politics and Scholarship in Israel*. London: Verso Books, 2008.

Pitkanen, Pekka "Ancient Israel and Settler Colonialism," *Settler Colonial Studies* 4, (2013): 64–81.

Preston, Andrew. *Sword of the Spirit, Shield of Faith: Religion in American War and Diplomacy*. New York: Anchor Books, 2012.

Prior, Michael *The Bible and Colonialism: A Moral Critique*. Sheffield: Sheffield Academic Press, 1997.

Quigley, John. *The Six-Day War and Israeli Self-Defense: Questioning the Legal Basis for Preventative War*. New York: Cambridge University Press, 2013.

Radosh, Allis and Radosh, Ronald. *A Safe Haven: Harry S, Truman and the Founding of Israel*. New York: Harper, 2009.

Raider, Mark A. *The Emergence of American Zionism*. New York: New York University Press, 1998.

Raider, Mark A., Sarna, Johnathon D., and Zweig, Ronald W., eds. *Abba Hillel Silver and American Zionism*. London: Frank Cass, 1997.

Raphael, Marc Lee. *Abba Hillel Silver: A Profile in American Judaism*. New York: Holmes and Meier, 1989.

Raz, Avi. *The Bride and the Dowry: Israel, Jordan, and the Palestinians in the Aftermath of the June 1967 War*. New Haven: Yale University Press, 2012.

Robinson, Ronald and Gallagher, John. *Africa and the Victorians: The Official Mind of Imperialism*. London: Macmillan, 1981, 2nd edn.

Robinson, Shira. *Citizen Strangers: Palestinians and the Birth of Israel's Liberal Settler State*. Palo Alto: Stanford University Press, 2013.

Rodman, David. "Armored Breakthrough: The 1965 American Sale of Tanks to Israel," *Middle East Review of International Affairs* 8, no. 2 2004: 1–15.

Rogan, Eugene. *The Arabs*. London: Penguin Books, 2012, 2nd edn.

Rogan, Eugene and Shlaim, Avi, eds. *The War for Palestine: Rewriting the History of 1948*. Cambridge: Cambridge University Press, 2007.

Rogerson, J. W. and Lieu, Judith M. *The Oxford Handbook of Biblical Studies*. New York: Oxford University Press, 2006.

Romer, Thomas. *The Invention of God*. Cambridge, MA: Harvard University Press, 2015.

Rossinow, Doug. "The Edge of the Abyss: The Origins of the Israel Lobby, 1949–1954," *Modern American History* 1 (March 2018): 23–43.

Rubenberg, Cheryl. *Israel and the American National Interest: A Critical Examination*. Urbana: University of Illinois Press, 1986.

Sand, Shlomo. *The Invention of the Jewish People*. New York: Verso Books, 2010.

Schueller, Malini Johar. *US Orientalisms: Race, Nation, and Gender in Literature*. Ann Arbor: University of Michigan Press, 1998.

Segev, Tom. *1967: Israel, the War, and the Year That Transformed the Middle East*. New York: Metropolitan Books, 2005.

Shiff, Ofer. *The Downfall of Abba Hillel Silver and the Foundation of Israel*. New York: Syracuse University Press, 2014.

Shlaim, Avi. *The Iron Wall: Israel and the Arab World*. New York: W. W. Norton, 2014.

"Israel: Poor Little Samson," in Louis, William Roger and Shlaim, Avi, eds., *The 1967 Arab-Israeli War: Origins and Consequences*. New York: Cambridge University Press, 2012.

Silberstein, Laurence J. *Post-Zionism: A Reader*. New Brunswick: Rutgers University Press, 2008.

Siniver, Asaf. *Abba Eban: A Biography*. New York; Overlook Duckworth, 2015.

Slater, Robert. *Warrior Statesman: The Life of Moshe Dayan*. New York: St. Martin's Press, 1991.

Smith, Charles D. *Palestine and the Arab-Israeli Conflict: A History with Documents*. Boston: Bedford/St. Martin's, 2013.

"The United States and the 1967 War," in Louis, William Roger and Shlaim, Avi, *The 1967 Arab-Israeli War: Origins and Consequences*. New York: Cambridge University Press, 2012.

Smith, Grant F. *Big Israel: How Israel's Lobby Moves America*. Washington: Institute for Research: Middle Eastern Policy, 2016.

Foreign Agents: The American Israel Public Affairs Committee from the 1963 Fulbright Hearings to the 2005 Espionage Scandal. Washington: Institute for Research: Middle Eastern Policy, 2007.

Spy Trade: How Israel's Lobby Undermines America's Economy. Washington: IRMEP, 2009.

Smith, Tony. *Foreign Attachments: The Power of Ethnic Groups in the Making of American Foreign Policy*. Cambridge, MA: Harvard University Press, 2005.

Snyder, Timothy. *Bloodlands: Europe between Hitler and Stalin*. New York: Basic Books, 2010.

Sohns, Olivia. "The Future Foretold: Lyndon Baines Johnson's Congressional Support for Israel," *Diplomacy and Statecraft* 28 (2017): 57–84.

Spector, Stephen. *Evangelicals and Israel: The Story of American Christian Zionism*. New York: Oxford University Press, 2009.

Spiegel, Steven L. *The Other Arab-Israeli Conflict: Making America's Middle East Policy, From Truman to Reagan*. Chicago: University of Chicago Press, 1985.

Sternhell, Zeev. *The Founding Myths of Israel: Nationalism, Socialism, and the Making of the Jewish State*. Princeton: Princeton University Press, 1998.

Tal, David, "Israel's Road to the 1956 War," *International Journal of Middle East Studies* 28 (February 1996): 59–81.

Terry, Janice J. *US Foreign Policy in the Middle East: The Role of Lobbies and Special Interest Groups*. London: Pluto Press, 2005.

Thompson, Thomas L. *Early History of the Israelite People: From the Written and Archeological Sources*. Leiden: E. J. Brill, 1992.

Tillman, Seth P. *The United States in the Middle East: Interests and Obstacles*. Bloomington: Indiana University Press, 1982.

Tivnan, Edward. *The Lobby: Jewish Political Power and American Foreign Policy*. New York: Touchstone, 1987.

Truman, Harry S. *Memoirs: Years of Trial and Hope*. Garden City: Doubleday, 1955–56.

Tyler, Patrick. *A World of Trouble: The White House and the Middle East – from the Cold War to the War on Terror*. New York: Farrar, Strauss, and Giroux, 2009.

Fortress Israel: The Inside Story of the Military Elite Who Run the Country – And Why They Can't Make Peace. New York: Farrar, Strauss, and Giroux, 2012.

Veracini, Lorenzo. *Israel and Settler Society*. London: Pluto Press, 2006.

Walther, Karine V. *Sacred Interests: The United States and the Islamic World, 1881–1921*. Chapel Hill: University of North Carolina Press, 2015.

Weinstein, Lewis H. "John F. Kennedy: A Personal Memoir, 1946–1963," *American Jewish History* 75 (September 1985): 5–30.

Whitelam, Keith W. *The Invention of Ancient Israel: The Silencing of Palestinian History*. London and New York: Routledge, 1996.

Wilford, Hugh. *America's Great Game: The CIA's Secret Arabists and the Shaping of the Modern Middle East*. New York: Basic Books, 2013.

Woods, Randall Bennett. *Fulbright: A Biography*. New York: Cambridge University Press, 1995.

Yaqub, Salim. *Containing Arab Nationalism: The Eisenhower Doctrine and the Middle East*. New York: University of North Carolina Press, 2004.

Zertal, Idith and Eldar, Akiva. *Lords of the Land: The War Over Israel's Settlements in the Occupied Territories, 1967–2007*. New York: Nation Books, 2007.

Index

ØPLC

6/19-2